SYSTEMS DESIGN
FOR, WITH, AND BY THE USERS

IFIP WG 9.1 Working Conference on
Systems Design For, With, and By the Users
Riva del Sole, Italy, 20-24 September, 1982

NORTH-HOLLAND PUBLISHING COMPANY
AMSTERDAM · NEW YORK · OXFORD

SYSTEMS DESIGN
FOR, WITH, AND BY THE USERS

Proceedings of the IFIP WG 9.1 Working Conference on
Systems Design For, With, and By the Users
Riva del Sole, Italy, 20-24 September, 1982

edited by

U. BRIEFS
WSI/DGB
Düsseldorf
F.R.G.

C. CIBORRA
Politecnico di Milano
Milano
Italy

L. SCHNEIDER
Harvard University
Cambridge MA
U.S.A.

1983

NORTH-HOLLAND PUBLISHING COMPANY
AMSTERDAM • NEW YORK • OXFORD

ISBN: 0 444 86613 2

Published by:
NORTH-HOLLAND PUBLISHING COMPANY – AMSTERDAM • NEW YORK • OXFORD

Sole distributors for the U.S.A. and Canada:
ELSEVIER SCIENCE PUBLISHING COMPANY, INC.
52 Vanderbilt Avenue,
New York, N.Y. 10017

PRINTED IN THE NETHERLANDS

84 006485

PREFACE

The contributions of this book - papers and working group reports - are assembled under the common denominator to reflect participation problems in computer systems design. In this context participation predominantly but not exclusively means the participation of workers and their organizations in the process of computer systems design.

The emphasis thereby is laid on the participation of the most numerous group of the users, the workers, who often are not users but used in systems design.

Nevertheless, in many papers and also in most working group reports issues in users' participation in general are dealt with.

The papers and working group reports are the proceedings of the Working Conference

Systems Design For, With, and By the Users

held in Riva del Sole (Italy) in September 1982.

When Working Group 1 of Technical Committee 9 of IFIP, which deals with the relationship between computers and work, decided to hold this conference, the basic idea was to present a substantive portion of the major materials (textbooks, films, manuals, checklists a.s.o.) developed throughout the different countries - mainly in Europe - and used especially by workers and their trade unions in practical, really existing participation processes in systems design. The idea was simply to promote participatory approaches by exchanging and generating information and knowledge about forms, contents, experiences, results a.s.o. achieved with these materials.

When we tried to go this way into the world of practical participatory approaches, this appeared to be too far off the track of the traditional way of our work at least to be realized on this occasion. In the future, the Working Group will continue these activities along the original lines trying to give additional support to those in the scientific and professional community of computing who are interested in participatory systems design approaches.

The papers presented at the conference comprise a wide range of approaches towards participatory systems design. Not all of them deal with the topic in an exhaustive way examining all essential aspects of the problem. The conference, however, took considerable profit - especially in unusually lively discussions - from the fact that manifold, even if not highly elaborated, approaches to the relevant issues were presented. We decided to conserve this feature of the conference and therefore compiled all the contributions given at the conference - with the exception of a few texts, not handed in in time - in order to give a full impression and expression of the rich discussions at the conference.

In addition to the papers presented at the conference the volume contains the reports of the Working groups. In some of them explicit recommendations are addressed to the IFIP community and to other parties concerned.

We are aware that this assembly of papers and of reports of discussions can only be a first step. Many more and certainly also more substantive steps have to be taken to contribute to promoting participation, especially of the workers affected, in systems design. Such steps appear the more urgent, the more the massive social implications in form of dangers and opportunities in the manifold processes of computerization become visible.

It is our conviction, that very marked steps towards a substantive and large-scale participation of users in general and especially of the workers affected, of those who have to work as the human components of man-machine-systems, have to be taken, quickly, in order to guarantee sensible and sound processes of systems design, good computer systems and human conditions for the workers. The more the general economic and social climate is deteriorating, the more this challenge has to be faced.

We thank the following sponsors of the Working Conference on Systems Design For, With, and By the Users:

    Politecnico di Milano
    CSATA - Bari
    Fondazione Fiorentini Mauro - Politecnico di Milano
    AICA - Associazione Italiana di Calcolo Automatico
    IFAC - Social Effects of Automation Committee
    IEA - International Ergonomics Association
    Norwegian Computing Centre
    CGIL - General Confederation of Italian Workers
    CISL - Italian Confederation of Trade Unions
    UIL - Union of Italian Workers
    FLM - United Federation of Metal Workers - Italy
    TCO - Central Organization of Salaried Employees - Sweden
    TBV - Salaried Employees Educational Association - Sweden

Last but not least, we owe our most sincere thanks to the following friends who contributed to the organization of the Working Conference in Riva Del Sole and to the publication of these proceedings:

        Sebastiano Bagnara (Italy)
        May Briefs-Thevessen (FRG)
        Neggar Dana (Italy)
        Jostein Fjalestad (Norway)
        Sven Jonasson (Sweden)
        Piercarlo Maggiolini (Italy)
        Peter Mambrey (FRG)
        Fred Margulies (Austria)
        Piero Migliarese (Italy)
        Jean-Louis Rigal (France)
        Matteo Rollier (Italy)

We are particularly grateful to them because both events had to
be prepared with an extremely short lead-time.

Ulrich Briefs
Chairman of IFIP's
Working Group 9.1
"Computers and Work"
Chairman of the
editorial board

Claudio Ciborra
Chairman of IFIP's
Working Conference
"System Design
For, With, By
the Users"

Leslie Schneider

CONTENTS

PARTICIPATIVE SYSTEM DESIGN – FROM THE PAST INTO THE FUTURE

SYSTEMS DESIGN FOR, WITH, AND BY THE USERS
U. Briefs, C. Ciborra and L. Schneider (editors)
North-Holland Publishing Company
© IFIP, 1983

USER PARTICIPATION IN SYSTEM DESIGN

SOME QUESTIONS ABOUT STRUCTURE AND CONTENT ARISING FROM RECENT RESEARCH FROM
A TRADE UNION PERSPECTIVE

Herbert Kubicek
Department of Business Administration,
Economics and Sociology
University of Trier
Federal Republic of Germany

User participation in system design means different things to different
people. Adopting a trade union perspective this paper tries to summarize the developments which have preceded the present discussion
and to point out the main themes being discussed today in order to
clarify how user participation should be conceived if it shall offer
a chance for improving the working conditions in the workers' interests. The main thesis is that user participation from this point
of view does not only raise questions about the structure of the participation process but also questions about the content of this process which have been largely neglected in the discussion so far.1)

INTRODUCTION

During the last ten years or so, increasing consent on the fact that user participation should be an integral component of system design has emerged. Note-
worthy agreement on the meaning and implication of user participation, however,
has not been reached. In fact, disagreement on the raison d'être of user participation, its implementation and its results have apparently increased.

The so-called confusion of concepts deplored by some critics of recent research
is, in my opinion, a more fundamental problem than simply one of disagreements
in scientific terminology. I rather find that our scientific attempts concerned
with grasping and structuring the phenomenon inevitably reflect the conflicting
interests in society, socio-economic and technological change, and, finally, the
researcher's personal attitude towards these developments. Because system design
processes imply changes in working conditions and labor relations, they must be
viewed within a context of conflicts of interest between capital and labor. These
conflicts cannot be resolved by a coherent and comprehensive set of concepts. Instead, the observer has to assume the standpoint of one of society's acting
groups which obviously does not yield a clear general conceptual framework.
Although it was the purpose of this conference to approach the question of participation in system design from a trade union perspective much of the initial
disagreement remains. The papers provided for this conference not only reflect
differences in scientific approaches but also the different industrial relations
systems existing in the various countries.

The complexity and dynamics of the problem plus the differences in scientific
approaches and national conditions make it impossible to establish a comprehensive summary of recent research activities which would take the personal views
of all participants into account. The conference itself and the proceedings will
provide the best possible overview of the present state of art. What I will try
to do in this paper is

- to briefly summarize the developments which have preceded the present discussion,

- to point out the main themes being discussed today from a trade union standpoint,

- and finally to raise some questions which I find must be answered in order to better understand what we are doing and where we are going.

Knowing more about some countries than about others, I will concentrate on the developments in the United States, in Great Britain, in the Scandinavian Countries and in West Germany. In my discussion I will be concerned with the structure and process of participation but also pay special attention to its content. I find that the relationship between structure and content of participation is the most important, yet most neglected question in theory and practice.

MAIN LINES OF RESEARCH CONCERNED WITH PARTICIPATION IN SYSTEM DESIGN

In order to provide a general overview of research concerned with participation in system design, a distinction between three research phases seems helpful: 2)

(1) User Involvement and Socio-technical Approaches

During the late sixties and early seventies, a rather intensive debate about user involvement and the behavioral side of management information systems was going on in the USA (cf. the readers by Coleman and Riley (1973), Davis and Everest (1976), and, for example, the work of Henry C. Lucas, f.i. Lucas (1975)). This research stressed the necessity of involving the users should a system be accepted and utilized effectively. It was surely no coincidence, that the user's role and the need of user involvement were stressed in connection with management information systems but not in connection with the application of computer technology in clerical areas. The special type of management related systems (i.e. support systems) and the special status of management as a new user group required special attention if the application of computer technology was to go beyond the clerical level.

At about the same time in Britain, the socio-technical approach which was originally developed by the Tavistock Institute in connection with changes of production technology was applied by Enid Mumford in the design of computer systems (cf. Mumford and Ward (1968), Mumford (1976), Mumford and Weir (1979), Mumford and Henshall (1979)). This approach promised to provide the type of theoretical framework and tool-kit required for installing user involvement into all kinds of system. Job design was seen as an integral part of the design task and job satisfaction was a distinctive goal of the design process. The approach's underlying arguments took into account both humanistic values and economic efficiency. Without exaggeration it can be said that the work of Enid Mumford has greatly influenced the discussion about user participation in the behavioral sciences in the seventies (cf. the First IFIP Conference on Human Choice and Computers in Vienna 1974, Mumford and Sackman (1975)).

(2) Emerging Trade Union Perspective

Trade unions, at least in Germany, have been concerned with problems of computer application since the late sixties. The German Metal Workers Union (IG Metall) organized a conference on Computers and White Collar Employees in 1968 and published the proceedings so as to stimulate discussion (cf. Friedrichs(1971)). These efforts, however, did not bring out any notable trade union research strategy. Instead, a strategy of this type emerged during the seventies in Norway, Sweden and Denmark (cf. Nygaard and Bergo (1975), Sandberg (1979), Fjalestad and Pape (198o)). An initial research project by the Norwegian Metal Workers' Union finally brought about a new form of cooperation between trade unions and researchers. This new approach focussed on entirely different problems, pursued different objectives and also applied different research methods than the Anglo-American research mentioned above. Research in this Scandinavian tradition is mostly concerned with the effects of information technology on workers and with trade union strategies for controlling the system design process and/or the application of computer systems. Such strategies f.i. include data agreements, action programmes, or new curricula and training procedures for union members and shop stewards. The main purpose pursued by this research is the development and distribution of know-how related to information technology specifically about its effects on the worker (cf. Nygaard and Bergo (1975)). By the way, the data agreements received most attention on an international level. During the last three years or so data or technology agreements have become a major theme for union oriented research in several European countries (cf. Williams and Moseley (1982) for Great Britain, Blegvad (1981), and Skonenberg-Rolskov and Vedel (1981) for Denmark, Docherty (198o) for Norway and Sweden, Sedeno-Andres et al. (1981), Trautwein-Kalms (1981), and Kubicek et al. (1981) for West Germany, and the research of the European Trade Union Institute ETUI, Evans (1982)).

(3) Emerging concern for the content of participation

The research on technology or data agreements usually focusses on system design related union control mechanisms concerned with securing jobs and installing health and safety standards. The research in question thus merely investigates traditional trade union issues in connection with the introduction of new technologies. Recently, however, a growing number of researchers have started wondering whether or not this approach can provide an adequate procedure for investigating information technology from a workers' point of view. This train of thought was set in motion by comparing selected characteristics of information technology with former processes of mechanization, by interrogating specific implications for work processes and for products and by defining specific features of system design processes in comparison with other processes of change (cf. Heibey et al. (1977), Briefs (1980a, b, 1981, 1982), Ehn et al. (1982), Göranzon (1982)).

I find that this third phase in participation related research which first focusses on content and only then goes on to investigate the question of adequate structures represents todays biggest research challenge in this area. But before I delve further into this issue let me discuss some questions about the relationship existing between the first two phases.

ON THE RELATIONSHIP BETWEEN USER INVOLVEMENT AND UNION CONTROL

The two approaches mentioned above should not be viewed as consecutive stages of one process, whereby the concept of trade union control has replaced the concept of user involvement. These are much rather distinctly separate but equally topical approaches merely being adopted by different social groups and subgroups within the scientific community.

- The Anglo-American approach of user involvement concentrates on direct user participation, adopts a management perspective and stresses job design, job satisfaction and ergonomic factors.

- The union control approach deals with system design as a matter of industrial relations, concentrates on technology or data agreements, stresses the influence of worker representatives, strives for trade union control of design processes in order to secure workers' interests in such matters as job security, pay, health and safety.

In Germany, perhaps more than in other countries, the approaches are more than just two competing research perspectives. They rather represent two different strategies constantly being played against each other in every-day industrial relations: Employers offer direct user involvement to avoid trade union or shop steward influence and thus evade contractual regulation. Trade unions and shop stewards, on the other hand, distrust direct user involvement. They want agreements stipulating codetermination rights for worker representatives. From a workers' perspective the socio-technical approach is also criticized because it does not take basic conflicts of interests in such issues as employment and pay into account (cf. Fjalestad and Pape 198o).

To put it very simply, the present situation is characterized by the polarization of conflicting interest groups each having a corresponding approach implanted in the scientific community. But does this mean that the continuing management concern for user involvement should be ignored by the union side? At least two arguments definitely speak against such a position. First of all trade unions are historically in a reactive position. The problems they have to deal with are the result of management action and their strategies are reactions to preceding management strategies which in turn induce management counteraction. But management action does not only create union problems, it also creates new opportunities for unions to act successfully in the workers' interest. In our context it is very important to see that management's concern for user involvement is the result of changes in socio-economic and technical conditions which have made user participation a functional necessity despite the risks it implies for the power position of management. Technological development towards decentralized, flexible, dialogue type systems is a management reaction to changing business conditions. And systems of this type cannot be designed successfully by centrally located system designers. This situation does allow some users a certain degree of control over the system and the capital invested. The users' knowledge and their motivation thus become an economic factor for management and in addition open a new base of influence for the workers.

Although the network structure of today's systems exercises a large degree of control over the users, I find it more realistic to view the users in these systems both as object and subject of control. This is the reason why this type of user situation should receive more attention than is the case at present and why it provides an important basis for union strategy building.

This standpoint indicates that a more differentiated judgement of the developments in different industries and occupational groups is necessary. This point of view could furthermore lead to new strategic opportunities (cf. Briefs (1981, 1982)). The trade union discussion in Germany f.i. concentrates almost entirely on the dangers and risks inherent in new technologies and the subsequently required measures for worker protection. In Norway, however, I have actually witnessed that this feeling of fear and resignation can be overcome if the new bases of power which certain users of certain systems have are systematically used for developing new union strategies.

The second argument is based on the fact that the trade union's discussion of information technology induced changes in working conditions concentrates on a limited and, in my opinion classical set of considerations and disregards questions of job content and work organization which are stressed in the socio-technical approach. These limitations become evident if one looks at the contents of technology or data agreements. Most agreements concentrate on two major areas:

- The first area focusses on worker protection by either specifying certain properties or excluding certain effects of systems, i.e. by either specifying ergonomic properties or excluding or compensating effects such as dequalification or displacement. This is absolutely in line with the fundamental union concern in health and safety issues and for wage and job security. These concerns are unquestionably congruent with worker interests and are definitely crucial issues especially in the present economic situation. Exactly these issues, however, result from previous decisions about job design and work organization, i.e. the two features which are not included in the traditional pattern of trade union concern and which are rarely specified in technology or data agreements.

- The second major category of agreements is concerned with codetermination or at least consultation rights. British and German agreements only concentrate

on shop steward rights. Norwegian agreements, however, also include participation rights of effected workers.

It could be argued that content and structure of participation are well matched.
Employment, pay, health and safety, etc. are central issues in the conflict between capital and labor and require a strong power base on the worker side.
Issues of this type can be standardized and formalized and thus negotiated by
worker representatives. This standpoint favors the application of traditional
patterns, which were employed rather successfully during the industrial mechanization process, to the introduction of new technology in the factory and in
the office. But in my opinion this application of traditional patterns has to
fail because the technology, the process of its application and the economic
conditions are different. Compared to the earlier introduction of new machinery
into the factory the application of information technology is not as standardized, software plays an important role as well as the design of work organisation. The flexibility of software and the different alternatives for work organization in one and the same technical system make negotiations on the company or industry level very difficult for the labor side. In addition, questions of job content (variety, challenge, discretion etc.) contain a subjective
element. When compared with the hard facts of job security, pay or ergonomics,
they appear as soft facts which are difficult to standardize and formalize.
But it may be argued that these qualitative changes in work content reflect the
specific features of information technology which will induce future fundamental changes in work processes and personal development requirements for those
still holding a job.

In order to cope with these soft facts or qualitative aspects different structures of participation which should complement not substitute todays dominant
patterns are required. I am convinced that the users should be integrated into
the negotiation structure. From a trade union perspective this is neccesary both
for coping with qualitative issues and for counteracting management strategies
of user involvement. In striving for efficient systems management will have to
involve users and to secure their motivation. Therefore the unions would do well
in accepting the management offer of user involvement and include it in their
negotiations.

This illustrates that technology or data agreements are no final solution. Instead, new forms of agreements will have to be developed and the multitude of
resulting problems will have to be discussed and hopefully solved:

- The idea of combining direct user participation with shop steward and union
  negotiations is easier said than done as it is very difficult to operationa-
  lize the division of functions and their coordination. And if direct user
  participation were to be introduced, differences in interests between employee subgroups, e.g. between skilled and unskilled workers, between men
  and women, between programmers and operators, will appear and have to be
  dealt with. This could be interpreted as a threat to solidarity. On the other
  hand, such differences within the working class may only be hidden today, i.e.
  the now assumed solidarity may only be a myth. In connection with office
  automation for example solidarity between male worker representatives and
  female typists is practically nonexistent. In this case solidarity is not something which has to be preserved, it is something that has to be created.

- Another issue concerns the process of participation and how it is influenced
  by the diversity of computer applications and by the length and uncertainty
  of system design processes. The design process is often a learning process
  for all parties involved. VDU - health hazards posed by different computer
  applications existing within one company, f.i. present entirely different
  problems. If a union strives for one master company-wide agreement, only average solutions can be achieved, as f.i. regarding restrictions in working
  hours. Questions of job content and work organization, in addition, could
  only be regulated in a very general and abstract manner which often does not

lead to concrete results. An alternative strategy, which I have seen in a
Norwegian organization, is based on a general codetermination agreement which
is supplemented by special agreements individually regulating larger systems.
The supplementary agreements are called system contracts and regulate many aspects in detail. On account of the learning process inherent in system design
procedures, the general codetermination agreement requires preceding pilot
projects for which pilot contracts are negotiated. Negotiations for the general implementation and the system contract are then based on the experience
gained in the pilot project. Even if this solution is restricted to certain
situations and by no means the only possible way it is nevertheless some excellent example for an innovative type of agreement taking at least some
specific characteristics of information technology and system design into
account.

- Still another issue is concerned with the concepts and criteria for approaching questions of job content and work organization. Defining these elements as qualitative aspects and soft facts and emphasizing their subjective
  dimension does not necessarily imply that the users concerned should be allowed an entirely subjective decision making basis. Up to date union oriented
  research does not offer much. Here, the socio-technical approach has a few
  concepts and methods. The crucial question, however, is whether or not available concepts can actually cope with the specific characteristics of information technology and whether or not are applicable from the worker perspective, i.e. what exact modifications and/or innovative approaches are actually
  required?

These arguments illustrate that the available form of technology or data agreements is not satisfying, especially regarding the specific characteristics of
information technology and system design. Research on agreements should do more
than just analyze the status-quo situation via surveys. Instead, case studies
about emerging new forms of agreements are urgently needed, in order to stimulate a broad discussion. Union representatives and researchers should get together and develop new approaches for regulating the structure and process of
participation which could then be incorporated into new types of agreements.

BEYOND FORMAL AGREEMENTS

But even agreements which go beyond the present state of the art will only provide necessary but not sufficient conditions for worker protection, improvements
in working conditions and personal development. The experiences gained in Norway, i.e. the country with the oldest tradition in data agreements, are rather
disappointing. The systems and working conditions are not very much different
from those in comparable countries.

This indicates that research is most crucially needed for explaining why codetermination based on formal agreements does not automatically lead to better
systems from a worker point of view. Agreements are only a formal basis for
action. Concrete achievements basing on agreements, however, depend on the
infrastructure or context of participation and on how the objects of participation, i.e. the design process and technology, are conceptualized, dealt with
and evaluated within the participation process.

A multitude of aspects have to be considered when discussing the infrastructure
or context of participation as f.i. overall socio-economic conditions, the
country's individual form of economic crisis and political situation, union
structure and educational policy. In this paper I want to point out three problems related to information technology as an object of participation. They
constitute major challenges to IFIP, but also offer IFIP excellent opportunities for demonstrating its concern for socially acceptable developments.

In selecting these problems I was strongly influenced by the German situation. Some shop stewards here are convinced that the new technology problem is solved when a formal agreement has been reached. Basing on recent Norwegian and Swedish research efforts I find that the following additional conditions are necessary for achieving improvements in the workers' interests:

(1) a changed knowledge base,
(2) changes in the methods and techniques of system design.
(3) changes in the technology itself.

(1) The Knowledge Problem

The idea of emphasizing the need of an autonomous worker sponsored production and distribution of information technology related knowledge is in my opinion the most outstanding contribution of the Scandinavian Trade Union Cooperation Projects and the pioneering work of Kristen Nygaard (cf. Nygaard and Bergo (1975)). This approach is based on the assumption that EDP-knowledge is not impartial to the interests of capital and labor but rather biased by the perspective of capital and management. The unions, therefore, should try to strengthen their influence both through formal agreements and through the production and distribution of knowledge concerning new technologies and their consequences from a workers' perspective. The strategy which is recommended for the production and distribution of interest-specific knowledge involves learning process type activities which should be based on previous experiences of the workers.

In terms of research methodology, this strategy can be called an action research approach. The results of this strategy are not so much research reports, but rather the initiation of learning processes, the creation of new structures for the production and distribution of knowledge, teaching material, and other "practical" things.

At least five projects of this type were carried out in the Scandinavian countries during the seventies. Some of the projects as f.i. the DUE and DEMOS activities, will be presented in these proceedings (cf. also Sandberg (1979)). I am convinced that the projects have diagnosed the knowledge problem correctly. This means that the projects do constitute a fundamental challenge both to IFIP and to traditional social science research. The remedies proposed by the projects, however, raise various practical and theoretical problems.

On the practical side the projects have undoubtedly helped to achieve a higher level of problem awareness and activate members in the respective unions. But even though generous amounts of resources had been devoted to the projects only a relatively small number of workers had the opportunity to participate. This indicates that trade unions now are facing the problem of integrating this approach into existing structures and strategies. Norwegian LO, f.i. is apparently trying to integrate the experience based and action oriented approach of the projects into its educational programme by introducing one week courses where shop stewards from a few companies come together, discuss their experiences and develop "action programmes" similar to the ones developed in the projects over a period of a year or more. At the moment there are only general suggestions for such a strategy, which will demand much additional and intensive reflection and experimentation.

On the theoretical side, the experiential approach has its merits in disclosing worker oriented research areas and in bridging the gap between the production and application of research knowledge. This shift away from traditional surveys on the effects of information technology was absolutely necessary. And yet the approach does have limitations which are discussed in the following.

The most crucial limitation of an experiential approach becomes evident if only limited experience with the subject under investigation is available. And this is the case with information technology. The application of information technology today is hardly comparable with previous technologies employed in the mechanization of production and office work. This means that earlier experiences with mechanization can't be transferred into the modern situation of change. Information technology isn't a question of installing new tools, it is a technology of control mechanisms which change the structure of work processes and the work itself. Visual display units f.i. are connected with computer systems which are combined into network systems. In some areas of application as f.i. the graphics industry past experience was useless for coping with the fundamental change brought by the introduction of information technology (cf. Sandberg (1983)). Another difficulty presented by the experiential approach is that the abstraction of work which is specific to information technology cannot be experienced in advance. And finally, experiential approaches overemphasize the immediate experiences at the work place and somewhat ignore the systems aspects of information technology, i.e. the restructuring of whole areas of work and the changes in control.

These limitations demonstrate that the knowledge problem cannot be solved by an experiential approach alone. Instead a combination of experience and theoretical analysis seems desirable. While theoretical objectives were not explicitly included in the cooperation projects, recent discussions and many papers in these proceedings show strong concern for the development of conceptual frameworks. This development also shows that at present different theoretical approaches are being used for analysing the problems created by the application of information technology and designing adequate problem solving strategies. The spectrum of approaches ranges from Marxist theories to the theory of New Institutional Economics and includes a large variety of organization theories even psychological and linguistic theories. When we analyse previous experiences and draw general conclusions we have to be aware of these differences and be careful in selecting compatible approaches.

I find that researchers should be more explicit in modelling their theoretical frameworks. I also find that such frameworks are necessary for supplementing the experiential approach   used in the cooperation projects. This would help in overcoming the labor side's knowledge problem regarding information technology, its properties and the risks and benefits of its application. By avoiding the traditional forms of research the Scandinavian action research projects have largely neglected the potential of theoretical reflection and have gone too far in reducing the researchers' role to that of a facilitator. I find that this opposition was important both for the union movement and for the scientific community. The insights provided by the project participants enable us to discuss the merits and limitations of this approach and help us draw conclusions for future strategies regarding trade union-research cooperation. When demanding a closer relation between workers' experience and theoretical reflection, we must realize, however, that cooperation will become more difficult as a result. But I hope that it will also make cooperation more rewarding.

(2) Methods and Techniques of System Design

The second condition for improvements in the workers' interest and the second relevant research topic is concerned with methods and techniques of system design. The projects mentioned above were mainly concerned with trade union strategies for gaining control over system design by means of a formal control structure regulating the design process which is still carried out by system specialists. The specialists, however, apply methods, techniques and tools which do not take explicit consideration of changes in working conditions. The methods and tools are furthermore based on implicit assumptions about men and organizations which can be seriously questioned from a social science background.

Again it is the merit of Kristen Nygaard and his scholars, this time at Aarhus University in Denmark, for directing our attention on the special interests

embodied in the methods and techniques of system analysis and design (cf. Kyng
and Mathiassen (1982)). Recently the structure of system development and the
models underlying system design are also critized from a management point of
view. Professional system design and especially software development is critized
because it doesn't take into account the whole and real life situation of system. use. The areas neglected are called informal structures and processes and
the problem is viewed as one of integrating the technical knowledge of designers
and the work experience and "tacit" knowledge of the users. But it might well
be that the problem is more fundamental and indicates basic dilemmas in the
application of information technology due to the underlying models of man and
organization. At present, however, the problem is approached from quite different starting points:

- Ciborra (1981) and Lanzarra in his paper included in these proceedings analyze
  the implicit assumptions about man and organization in system design which in
  the tradition of Herbert A. Simon are based on models of organizations as objective entities having a hierarchical goal structure, rational decision rules
  and hierarchical control of human behavior. The reconstruction of these assumptions provides an understanding of the general tendencies in system analysis
  and design and allows a more general discussion of the tools in question. Such
  a discussion constitutes a fundamental challenge addressing the profession of
  systems people, including IFIP.

- Budde and Züllighoven as well as Floyd and Keil in their papers in these proceedings emphasize the organization of the system development process and
  suggest different, process oriented patterns for matching the models of designers and users.

- Other papers try to analyze methods and techniques of system design from a
  linguistic research viewpoint.

- Still other papers present alternative methods for describing work processes
  in man-machine-systems based on formal network methods such as Petri-nets
  (cf. the papers by De Cindio et.al. in these proceedings).

The DUE and the DEMOS project have developed structural models for negotiations
in the design process (cf. Sandberg (1979), Kyng and Mathiassen (1982)). This
implies a change in the working environment of system specialists but not a
change in the methods and techniques moulding their professional background or
even identity. Taking into account the research mentioned above, I find that
changes in the control structure of the design process should to be supplemented
by changes in the methods and techniques of design if different, and from a workers' point of view better, systems are to be produced. As a social scientist I
couldn't explicitly say how the alternatives should look or whether the network
concepts presented in some of the papers are a more suitable solution from a
worker's standpoint. The proposals are still highly formalized and abstract and
don't seem to cope with the wide range of possible changes in working conditions
implied by the introduction of computer systems. This shortcoming becomes evident when comparing the description of the work processes in computer aided
design based on network methods with the before and after pictures in the book
of photographs by the Swedish TBV and TCO (cf.Gullers(1981)).

One issue in this context requiring special attention is whether or not alternative methods are possible at all as long as they are to be used to design systems for available hardware and the existing logic of microelectronics. This
kind of information technology as such implies a formalization, standardization
and abstraction of cognitive work processes. This could mean that design methods
must be adjusted to the properties of the technology and that the choice for
alternative software development is restricted by the available hardware.

The questions just raised in my opinion are crucial issues for future research.
Improved cooperation between computer science and social science experts seems
necessary in order to provide answers to these questions. The issue of methods

and techniques for system design, however, should not be viewed as an issue for academic research only. It is also a crucial problem for trade union strategy which shall change the results of system design. Union control of design process by codetermination with unchanged methods and techniques of design might only mean an exchange of actors with only minor changes in the actions and their results.

Trade unions also still have to decide whether to treat computer specialists as servants of capital and management, i.e. to put them "on the other side" or whether to integrate the specialists into active union work and provide them with the necessary alternative methods and tools. I have heard about one Danish union which is trying to bring system specialists and shop stewards together in union training courses.

Trade unions obviously cannot develop alternative methods and techniques for design on their own. The enormous capital and military influence which is being exerted on the development of todays methods and techniques, however, indicates that trade union influence is needed as a countervailing power to ensure the resources required for research on alternatives (cf. the recommendations of a working group at the EEC conference on the information society. Bjørn-Andersen et. al. (1982), pp. 312-331).

(3) Alternative Technology

If it is true that todays methods and techniques for system design are influenced by the properties of the technology to be applied, then the technology obviously has to be analysed and re-evaluated. Most unions today do not oppose information technology as such they only oppose specific effects or specific applications. Many different ways of applying information technology are undoubtedly possible, i.e. choices in hardware and software are available. Choices in the design of work organization and choices in regulating personnel matters are also available. Specific constant properties of information technology, however, constrain these choices. If certain negative consequences for workers are the result of constant properties, it is necessary to identify the technology itself as a problem and not just the details of application.

The papers in these proceedings apparently are based on different assumptions in this respect. The summary of th DEMOS project in the paper by Sandberg (1983), however, indicates that trade union control of the design process may result in alternative applications of existing information technology. The alternative would still include some fundamental characteristics of existing technology. Other arguments state that some of the non-replacable characteristics will initiate social changes which are not in the interest of workers or even of mankind.

We all realize that information technology is strongly influenced by activities striving to improve the control of technical military systems. Information technology is accordingly conceptualized for the control of an objective and quantified reality and is based on hierarchical models of control. Military control problems and control models can apparently be applied to situations of hierarchical social control in which the ambiguity of social reality can be deliberately ignored. But if we are interested in a reduction of hierarchical social control and if we want to maintain a certain ambiguity to allow opportunities for personal freedom, we have to ask ourselves whether this goal can be achieved simply by constructing different forms of application for available technology or whether alternative technologies and alternative basic models including new forms of hardware and software would be more suitable.

In the energy technology area, concrete alternatives are available, but not in the information technology area. Here we have only general and preliminary proposals, as f.i. the ideas by Mike Cooley (1982) from Britain and the

Scandinavian UTOPIA project, which emphasizes worker qualifications and product quality as alternative objectives for the development of technology (cf.
Ehn et al. (1982)). The UTOPIA project, however, is limited to the development
of alternative software and explicitly recognizes the barriers presented by
todays hardware.

An even more fundamental viewpoint of information technology criticizes the imperialism of formal logic and rationality arising from its application (cf,
Fromm (1968) and Weizenbaum (1976 and 198o)). If we consider that human beings
are not just cognitive information processing units but have feelings and emotions which play an important role in individual and social development, we have
to ask whether it is morally acceptable to actually integrate microprocessors
into nearly every sphere of life. Should we instead oppose the total rationalization of life in order to save some of the basic human capabilities? This line
of thought indicates that participation should also include the possibility of
completely rejecting the application of information technology into certain
spheres of life. But where shall we draw the boundaries and on which criteria
should our decisions be based?

Recent decisions by trade union congresses give examples for considerations in
this direction. Some German trade unions state that they are not generally
against information technology, but do oppose personnel information systems and
intend to fight this form of application. Swedish TCO also states that it is
not generally against information technology but does oppose computer mediated
work in the home. In my opinion it is vital to adopt such a differentiated view
which explicitly defines restrictions in the application of information technology. But which are the criteria determining the restrictions voiced in West-
Germany and in Sweden? Are these differences only the result of different domestic situations or are they just a first step requiring further systematic and
explicit evaluation? If the latter is the case, the development of explicit
criteria for defining restrictions in the application of information technology
should be seen as a major task for trade unions and researchers. IFIP should
also accept the challenge presented by this problem. After all, isn't an awareness for the limititations of one's own specialty the sign of good professiona-
lism?

The questions on the research side discussed here indicate that we have to reconsider our present concepts for analysing the effects of information technology.
I have the impression that we tend to adopt traditional concepts of industrial
sociology which cannot really cope with the specific characteristics of information technology, as f.i. the formalization and abstraction in cognitive work
processes and the substitution of ambiguity, associative thinking, emotions and
feelings, tacit knowledge,shared values, etc. We have to acknowledge that we
know very little about the complexity and functions of human information processing and communication in terms of personal development. And we don't know
very much about the latent functions of communication in connection with the
development of social relations either. Nevertheless it is obvious that communication is more than a formalized exchange of precisely defined data. The
application of "information" technology and new "communication" networks rashly
interrupts these social constituents of life. I find that this situation strongly
resembles the one we had during the fifties and sixties when we knew very little
about ecological interdependencies and accepted serious ecological interventions
by chemical plants and other "dirty" industries. The old wishful thinking which
assumed that nature has unlimited capacities for adjusting to such interventions has finally been identified as a false assumption having far reaching de-
trimental consequences. A comparable form of wishful thinking has apparently
been attached to the application of "information" and "communication" technology.
Human beings and society are assumed to have unlimited capacities for adapting to
technology induced interventions. I find that we should be less naive in this
issue and show more concern for the social ecology of information and communication. This implies that in addition to discussing the effects of information technology in terms of displacement, pay, monotony or technical control,

more attention should be directed to other effects, as f.i. changes in language which is the constituent part of consciousness and social relations (cf. Göranzon(1982)).

Issues of this type raise fundamental questions which go far beyond the traditional conflicts of capital and organized labor. Here, most trade unionists try to adopt a world attitude based on objectivity and formal rationality and try to eliminate ambiguity. They do not view personal feelings and emotions,as central components of the working and living environment or do not consider these issues to be their business. When identifying this problem as a problem of social ecology, we must also take into account that the trade union attitude towards the ecological movement is very ambiguous even though ecological problems are clearly visible. Changes in the information and communication ecology, however, are much less obvious. The discussion of such problems should not be restricted to changes in work processes and working conditions but also include changes in products and their usefullness. This, however, would inevitably result in labor conflicts over job security.

And even though trade unions have not yet assumed an active role in issues of this type, the research devoted to workers' interests should strive to investigate these questions and try to bring them to the attention of the trade unions. I believe that we are dealing with a historical problem here the solution of which may well afford a cultural revolution. The universal application of information technology, likewise advocated by governments and trade unions as a means of regaining economic growth, can be viewed as the manifestation of rationalism in our cultural heritage ("Aufklärung"). If we intend to break the dominance of this special type of rationalism and develop alternative technology, more than just changes in hard- and software will be required. Changes in our dominant cultural traditions will also be unavoidable.

In fact, a recent German publication even deplored the formal logic inherent in information technology as a form of violence which people have to revolt against in order to save their individual personality (cf. Hartmann 1981).

Even if this attitude appears somewhat odd at first glance, we shouldn t ignore the argument but rather examine the reasoning behind it and discuss the implied consequences. This could be helpful both in identifying the necessary restrictions for the application of information technology and in designing appropriate supplementary measures for acceptable forms of application requiring appropriate counteraction. If considerations of this type could be brought into public discussion and raise the consciousness of workers as workers, consumers and citizens policy makers may be motivated to reconsider their concepts and strategies. Such a process may then lead to the development of alternative technologies - in whatever form they will finally appear.

CONCLUSIONS

The most important point I had wanted to make is that recent research indicates that the issue of user participation in system design touches a larger spectrum of problems than just the question of who should participate in what stage of the design process. If participation is viewed as a means of producing systems better adjusted to workers' interests profound changes will have to be initiated. Research theory, however, has not yet identified these necessary changes precisely. At present, we are just beginning to describe and structure the problems discussed here, the major part of the research task lies ahead and be a challenge to scientific efforts.

With regard to the structure of participation, i.e. the question who participates in which decisions, it should be obvious that participation should include both workers and their representatives. When considering the content of

participation it should have become clear that is has to go beyond of ergonomic aspects, job content, pay and job security. If the available hard-and software play an important role, participation is necessary in investment decisions
and in political decisions about the funding of the development of new technologies. Because there are links between work processes and products participation should also be concerned with product policy. This seems to be of special
importance in those companies, where information and communication technology
is produced. Finally participation should not be confined to workers as workers
but should incluse workers as consumers and citizens as well.

Analogies to the ecological and the peace movement may be helpful in clarifying
such a broad conceptualization of user partizipation. Everyone is affected by
large computer systems and the wide range of products based on microelectronics.
Many politicians believe that a boom in industrial and private demand for
information and communication technology is the only chance for accelerating
economic growth and solving todays social problems. Even the vaguest of doubts
about information technology, specifically doubts about applying technology in
certain spheres of life, justify an in-depth pursuance of the question raised.
Research about user participation so far has not contributed much to clarifying
these questions. Rather a narrow concept of participation fosters the illusion,
dangers for the working and living environment could be avoided by the participation of workers and/or representatives in single design processes. Overcoming such a narrow conceptualization of participation seems to be the first
necessary step for achieving a more realistic view and for identifying additional strategies.

The questions raised have also implications for trade unions and computer specialists. For trade unions it seems necessary that they enter a discussion
about technology policy and be not confined to the control of negative side
effects. Computer specialists in my opinion no longer can neglect the responsibility for the effects of the application of the products they help producing.
Participation understood in a broad sense may mean short term problems for the
profession. But it may also mean a step towards a deliberation of the computer
specialists in the longer run. For building trade union strategies for technology policy, however, it seems crucial that computer specialists be integrated
in the debate.

  These short hints should make clear, that the question of user participation
on the research side should not just be viewed as an academic subject which has
to be analyzed in objective or neutral terms. Participation and participation
research are highly political issues. Only Scandinavian cooperation projects
between trade unions and scientists have explicitly taken such a view. The limitations of these projects mentioned above now can be viewed as challenges for
future research. My final conclusion is that despite of ten years of research
about user participation we are far from having answers to most questions. In
fact, we have not even decided which of the questions are the crucial ones, and
much less how they can be defined more precisely. But to me it seems that an
increasing number of researchers in this area is now wondering whether the research questions pursued in the seventies are still the right ones. From my
point of view this is a very positive sign. This conference is a good opportunity for critically reflecting the present state of the art and for discussing
different directions for future research. Therefore I hope that the proceedings
of this conference stimulate a broader discussion. I also hope that IFIP will
not be satisfied to have conducted this conference but will meet the challenges
for the profession of computer specialists implied by the issues discussed here.

FOOTNOTES

1) I am grateful to Brigitte Pool-Brosi for helping to improve my English. However, I may have made new mistakes in the final revision of the manuscript.
2) These three phases correspond with different stages in my own research work (cf. Kubicek 1975 und 1979, Kubicek et al. 1981). I have carried out research projects in the three areas outlined here and am presenting arguments based on personal experience. Subsequently, my personal research experience may have shaped my perception of the overall development. Therefore a possible bias in the following description is explicitly acknowledged.

REFERENCES

(1) Bjørn-Andersen, N., Public participation in research projects, working paper (Information Systems Research Group, The Copenhagen School of Economics, Copenhagen 1981).

(2) Bjørn-Andersen, N., Participation/democracy in organizations, paper prepared for the EEC-FAST-conference on "information technology - impact on representation and sharing of power" in Copenhagen, 9-11 November 1981.

(3) Bjørn-Andersen, N., Earl, M., Holst, O. and Mumford, E. (eds.), Information society, for richer, for poorer (North-Holland, Amsterdam, 1982).

(4) Blegvad, B.-M., Undersoegelse vedroerende beskyttelsen af arbejdstagerne i tilfaelde af rationalisering af virksomheden med henblik pa et bedre kendskab til de ved lov eller kollektiv overenskomst fastsatte bestemmelser i medlemsstaterne, rapport til Kommissionen for de Europaeiske Faelleskaber (Koebenhavn, 1981).

(5) Briefs, U., Arbeiten ohne Sinn und Perspektive? Gewerkschaften und "Neue Technologien" (Pahl-Rugenstein, Köln, 1980a).

(6) Briefs, U., The impact of computerization on the working class and the role of trade unions. In: Bjørn-Andersen, N. (ed.), The human side of information processing (North-Holland, Amsterdam, 1980b).

(7) Briefs, U., "Neue Technologien". Neue Aufgaben und ein neues Potential für die Verbesserung der Arbeitsbedingungen, WSI-Mitteilungen 34 (1981) 82-9o.

(8) Briefs, U., Computernetzwerke und andere "neue Technologien" - Zwischen universeller Rationalisierungs- und Überwachungstechnologie und bewußter Nutzung durch die Beschäftigten, WSI-Mitteilungen 35 (1982) 246-257.

(9) Docherty, P., User participation in and influence on systems design in Norway and Sweden in the light of union involvement, new legislation, and joint agreements, in: Bjørn-Andersen, N. (ed.), The human side of information processing (North-Holland, Amsterdam, 198o).

(1o) Ciborra, C.U., A contractual view of information systems, paper presented at the EEC-FAST-conference "information technology - impact on representation and sharing of power", Copenhagen, 9-11 november 1981 (to be published in the proceedings).

(11) Ciborra, C., Bracchi, G. and Maggiolini, P., A multiple-contingency review of systems analysis methods and models, in: Lucas, H.C. Jr. et al. (eds.), The information systems environment (North-Holland, Amsterdam, 198o).

(12) Coleman, R.J. and M.J. Riley (eds.), MIS: management dimensions (Holden Day Inc., San Francisco, 1973).

(13) Cooley, M., New technologies - some trade union concerns and possible solutions, in: Bjørn-Andersen, N. et al. (eds.), Information society, for richer, for poorer (North-Holland, Amsterdam, 1982).

(14) Davis, G.B. and G.C. Everest (eds.), Readings in management information systems (McGraw Hill, New York, 1976).

(15) Ehn, P. et al., The Utopia project - on training, technology and products viewed from the quality of work perspective (Arbetslivscentrum, Stockholm, 1982).

(16) Evans, J., Negotiating technological change - a review of trade union approaches to the introduction of new technology in Western Europe (European Trade Union Institute, Brussels, 1982).

(17) Fjalestad, J. and Papo, A., Die gesellschaftlichen Auswirkungen der Informationstechnologie. Norwegische Forschungsstrategien. In: Kalbhen, U., Krückeberg, F. and Reese, J. (eds.), Gesellschaftliche Auswirkungen der Informationstechnologie. Ein internationaler Vergleich (Campus, Frankfurt am Main and New York, 198o).

(18) Friedrichs, G., Computer und Angestellte, Band I und II (Europäische Verlagsanstalt, Frankfurt am Main, Nachdruck, 1971).

(19) Fromm, E., The revolution of hope - toward a humanized technology (Harper & Row, New York, 1968).

(2o) Göranzon, B. et al., Job design and automation in Sweden - skills and computerization (Center for Working Life, Stockholm, 1982).

(21) Gullers, P. et al., Datorn kommer: Bildbok om yrkeskunskaper och datorisierung (Tjänstemännens Bildningsverksamhet (TBV), Stockholm, 1981).

(22) Hartmann, D., Die Alternative - Leben als Sabotage (Initiative Verlagsanstalt, Tübingen, 1981).

(23) Heibey, H.W., Lutterbeck, B. and Töpel, M., Auswirkungen der elektronischen Datenverarbeitung in Organisationen (Bundesministerium für Forschung und Technologie, Forschungsbericht DV 77-ol, Eggenstein-Leopoldshafen, 1977).

(24) Kubicek, H., Informationstechnologie und organisatorische Regelungen (Duncker & Humblot, Berlin, 1975).

(25) Kubicek, H., Informationstechnologie und Organisationsforschung. Eine kritische Bestandsaufnahme der Forschung, in: Hansen, H.R., Schröder, K.T. and Weihe, H.J. (eds.), Mensch und Computer (Oldenbourg, München and Wien, 1979).

(26) Kubicek, H., Interessenberücksichtigung beim Technikeinsatz im Büro- und Verwaltungsbereich. Grundgedanken und neuere skandinavische Entwicklungen (Oldenbourg, München and Wien, 198o).

(27) Kubicek, H., Berger, P., Döbele, C. and Seitz, D., Handlungsmöglichkeiten des Betriebsrats bei Rationalisierung durch Bildschirmgeräte und computergestützte Informationssysteme (Arbeitskammer des Saarlandes, Saarbrücken, 1981).

(28) Kyng, M. and Mathiassen, L., Systems development and trade union activities, in: Bjørn-Andersen, N. et al. (eds.), Information society, for richer, for poorer (North-Holland, Amsterdam, 1982).

(29) Lucas, H.C., Why information systems fail (McGraw Hill, New York, 1975).

(3o) Lucas, H.C. Jr., Land, F.F., Lincoln, T.J. and Supper, K.(eds.), The information systems environment (North-Holland, Amsterdam, 198o).

(31) Mumford, E., Towards the democratic design of work systems, Personnel Management 8 (1976), No.9.

(32) Mumford, E. and Henshall, D., A participative approach to computer systems design (Associated Business Press, London, 1979).

(33) Mumford, E. and Sackman, H. (eds.), Human choice and computers (North-Holland, Amsterdam, 1975).

(34) Mumford, E. and Ward, T.B., Computers: Planning for people (Batsfords, London, 1968).

(35) Mumford, E. and Weir, M., Computer systems in work design: the ETHICS method (Associated Business Press, London, 1979).

(36) Nygaard, K. and Bergo, O.T., The trade unions - new users of research, Personnel Review 4 (1975), No. 2.

(37) Sandberg, A. (ed.), Computers dividing man and work - recent Scandinavian research on planning and computers from a trade union perspective (Arbetslivscentrum, Stockholm, 1979).

(38) Sandberg, A., Trade union oriented research for democratization of planning in work life - problems and potentials, Journal of Occupational Behaviour 4 (1983).

(39) Sedeno-Andres, F., Wendt, M. and Knetsch, W., Bildschirm-Arbeitsplätze - Vergleich geltender Betriebs- und Dienstvereinbarungen (Gesellschaft für Informatik-Anwendungen und Wirkungsforschung, Berlin, 1981).

(4o) Skouenborg Rolskov, B. and Vedel, E., Skandinaviske love og aftaler med betydning for systemudvikling (DAIMI, Aarhus, 1981).

(41) Trautwein-Kalms, G., Zur Auseinandersetzung um Bildschirmarbeit am Beispiel betrieblicher Vereinbarungen, WSI-Mitteilungen 34 (1981) 9o-99.

(42) Weizenbaum, J., Computer power and human reason (W.H. Freeman and Company, San Francisco, 1976).

(43) Weizenbaum, J., Human choice in the interstices of the megamachine, in: Moshowitz, A. (ed.), Human choice and computers 2 (North-Holland, Amsterdam, 198o).

(44) Williams, R. and Moseley, R., The trade union response to information technology - Technology agreements: consensus, control and technical change in the workplace, in: Bjørn-Andersen, N. et al. (eds.), Information Society, for richer, for poorer (North-Holland, Amsterdam, 1982).

SYSTEMS DESIGN FOR, WITH, AND BY THE USERS
U. Briefs, C. Ciborra and L. Schneider (editors)
North-Holland Publishing Company
© IFIP, 1983

Participation in System Development.

The Tasks Ahead.

by Kristen Nygaard,

Norwegian Computing Center and University of Oslo.

INTRODUCTION

This conference addresses itself to the subject of "participation"
in system development. Many papers, even other conferences have
described their subject matter by the same term - "participation",
without dealing with the issues which are at the center of interest
at this conference. The slogan "System development - for the
user, with the user, by the user" obviously is an attempt at
emphasizing the "user"- but who are "users"?

The explanation of this equivocality is, of course, that most people
hesitate, in a field with predominantly natural science paradigms,
to state clearly that conflicts of interests very often are essential features of system development processes. In fact, most
people find it comfortable or advantageous to shut their eyes to
this aspect of system development.

The majority of the papers at this conference fall into a different
tradition, started by the Norwegian "Iron and Metal Workers'
Project" - a tradition which has been described by the other
keynote speaker, professor Herbert Kubichck. Within this tradition,
conflicts of basic interests are regarded as an obvious aspect of
system development and permanently organised interest groups as
main actors as well as management.

SOME IMPORTANT LESSONS

I will start my lecture by reminding you of a few lessons learnt
from the "Iron and Metal Workers' Project".

Around 1969 when we realised that the trade unions had to build
up knowledge about information technology, we did not start by
going to courses or reading literature aimed at programmers,
engineers, sales people or managers. All knowledge is organised
and presented from a perspective reflecting the "view of the
world" of the authors and the intended target group. Taking over
the existing courses and literature would imply that we brainwashed
ourselves, understanding the new technology in terms of concepts
and values different from those on which the trade unions base
their "view of the world". We realised that we had to start by
building our own platform for understanding, starting from the
jobs, the workplace, from solidarity as a basic value.

This we did, and using that platform we could examine individual
pieces of facts and relate them to our way of understanding the
technology.

I feel that this point should be kept in mind by all groups who try to understand and get some control over the impact of information technology upon their interests and life situation.

A second lesson learnt was that it is not sufficient to get some researchers to acquire insight "on behalf of" the unions (or any other interest group). The new technology is infiltrating production and administration to an extent which make it impossible to rely upon some centrally located "experts". Understanding must be built up locally, on the floor.

This is also necessary for another reason. An increasing proportion of key decision problems in company (and institutional policies will relate to new technology (and thus to information technology). If workers are to influence these decisions, they must understand the implications of the technological choices. And if the trade unions are to create a new policy for the development of working life through a democratic process, it is also necessary to create a knowledge building process with participation from all levels, from the shop floor to the central union echelons.

SYSTEM DEVELOPMENT AS A DISCIPLINE

Some people want to define informatics (computer science) as a formal science akin to mathematics. In our opinion (quoted from Nygaard and Håndlykken, 1981, slightly modified) informatics should be defined in the same way as e.g. physics, geography and botany: as a science having certain aspects of a class of phenomena as its subject of study. Our definition is as follows:

<u>Informatics</u> is the science which has as its subject of study the <u>information aspects of phenomena</u> in nature and society:

1. their identification and properties.
2. how they may be understood and described.
3. how they may be designed, implemented, controlled and modified.
4. their interaction with other aspects of reality.

The four components listed are common to most natural and social sciences. Component 1) is the phenomenology of the science, component 2) is analysis, 3) is synthesis, the contructional or technological insight acquired, and 4) constitutes the interdisciplinary knowledge.

Most sciences have a long history and have based its main body of technologically useful knowledge upon analytical insight, in its turn based upon study of phenomena. Informatics started a few decades ago by the development of a very powerful tool for construction of information processes: the computer. The first and overwhelmingly important task was to develop tools for the process of constructing information processes, or, in other words: tools for the development of information systems.

Analysis did not become an important part of informatics until the late 1960-s, and phenomenology is still today a very much neglected part of our science. This is very unfortunate. In my opinion the study of the properties of actually operating information systems and ongoing system development processes should be regarded as perhaps the most important area of research in informatics in the future.

One deplorable consequence of this tradition of construction without empirical insight is that most methods proposed (and said to be used)

are unrealistic in their assumptions about the properties of
actual system development processes. Also, most attempts at understanding and describing (analysing) the system development process
are linked to methods proposed and based upon their concepts and
assumptions. Only recently are method-independent concepts being
proposed, making possible e.g. comparison between methods
(Mathiassen, 1981).

Mathiassen points out that a method for system development is
described by:

1. Its area of application (by what kind of organisation for what
   kind of system).
2. Its perspective or "world view" (consisting of assumptions about
   the nature of systems, organisations, the surrounding society, and
   the purpose and values of the local organisation.
3. Principles for organising the development process (splitting it
   into tasks specifying partial processes, assigning resources,
   supervision of the processes etc.).
4. Techniques of work used in the various tasks.
5. Tools used in the application of the techniques.

It is important to observe that the perspective of methods proposed
for system development are almost never explicitly stated. In
fact, a basic requirement for all education given in system development should be a thorough training in establishing the perspectives
embedded in the methods, techniques and tools which are taught.

Methods for system development obviously and necessarily adopts a
system perspective upon the organisation of which the new system
is to become a part. (The implications of a "system perspective"
are discussed in e.g. Holbæk-Hanssen, Håndlykken and Nygaard,
1975 and Mathiassen,1981).
For the employees whose working situation are going to be changed
by the new system it may be completely unnatural to adopt a system
perspective upon their everyday work. And a number of very relevant
points, seen from an interest group perspective, are not usefully
discussed within a system conceptual framework (Nygaard and Håndlykken, 1981):

- Which economic benefit will we (the group) get from the system?
  (As employees, middle or top management, employers.)
- To which extent may we exercise control (power) over the system?
- How will the system influence the working environment?
- Will the social network in the enterprise be changed to our ad-
  vantage or disadvantage?
- What is the relationship between the objectives of the system and
  the objectives which we feel should direct our society?

The enforcement of one's own perspective upon another interest
group is a major achievement if manipulation is the purpose.
Contrarily, being able to extract and comprehend the perspectives
used by the other actors in the development process, and the
capability of maintaining one's own relevant perspectives is a
main assumption for real participation. Consequently, the study
of perspectives and communication tools related to these perspectives
are vital to the subject matter of this conference.

System development (of the kind of systems discussed at this
conference) is a new discipline, sometimes frowned at (and sometimes with reason). This part of informatics also relates to
social processes, and social sciences provide useful information.

We should in the years to come within the academic world:
- Establish the study of system development as an important, integrated and accepted part of the science of informatics.
- Establish the links to the relevant parts of the social sciences. Establish social science curriculae within education in informatics.
- Inspire social scientists to take up information systems as their field of research and to learn what is necessary of informatics to carry out this research in a qualified and nontrivial manner.
- Try to establish respect among "traditionalists" in informatics for the quality of insight gained in the social sciences.

THE NEW TECHNOLOGICAL SETTING

The main emphasis in system development is upon the development of programs, or the programs plus the immediate man/machine inter-faces. (One speaks about "Software Engineering" and "Programming Environments", not about "System Development Environments".) However, most systems to be introduced in production and administration will be networks of human beings, various kinds of equipment, information processing equipment, linked by communication channels.

In this situation the programs which coordinate the function of a (changing) collection of concurrently operating equipment may be regarded both as an operating system and as an important part of the work organisation.

When the information processing and communication equipment grad-ually penetrate the whole organisation, it is becoming increasingly important to understand the properties and capabilities inherent in human and interhuman information handling. (An example illus-trating this point is given in Nygaard and Håndlykken, 1981, p. 163.) System specialists should have sufficient knowledge (which they lack today) to be able to build human information processing components into systems to give them improved performance, in-stead of only priding themselves on eliminating people.

In the future, interaction with information systems will be important in the practice of most professions and crafts. The tools for interaction should be developed as languages and not as the very primitive and poor set of transactions usually offered the users today. And the languages should relate not to one job only, but rather to a family of jobs constituting the domain of a profession. The mastery of the language will then be an essential part of the competence and qualify for a career within that profession. The design of such languages will influence the definitions of future professions and also their life span.

It is intolerable for a profession to let computer manufacturers or software companies be in control of the language(s) related to their work and their future. The profesions' organisations must get control over their respective languages.

A profession oriented language must contain concepts and con-tructs relating to several "process-structure"-levels:

- concepts *for* understanding the structure and functioning of the systems being used. Concepts and tools for interacting with the components of the system and for extracting and inserting information.

- concepts and tools for adding new concepts, new procedures and new kinds of components to the system (adding new structures, corresponding to programming).

- concepts for understanding, discussing and contributing to the continued development of the system.

A profession oriented language, as I have described it above, will also contribute to a knowledge-building process which is decentralised and open for participation and competition between alter native views. It should enhance a free diffusion of competing facts and perspectives.

The current version of the "yellow peril" is called "the fifth generation (Japanese) computer". The Japanese envisage so called "knowledge based systems" as a main application area for their planned supercomputers of the late 1980's or early 1990's. These systems are also named "expert systems", and they are intended to contain all important information about some field of expertise, organised by a "knowledge representation" making it possible for the system to make inferences and give answers to questions.

The proponents of expert systems seem to be highly aware of the commercial possibilities of such systems, but rather uninterested in their potential impact upon the structure of the knowledge building processes within the related professions.

The risks are, of course, that instead of enhancing e.g. a physician's competence, the (IBM or Stanford Research International?) "medical expert system" will substitute that competence. Also, the system manufacturers will control what input should be given to the system (e.g. about what brands of drugs to be used in the treatment of patients?) etc. Corresponding dangers exist in most crafts and professions, and constitute a new and very serious threat not only to trade unions but to all professions.

The notion of "profession-oriented languages" represent an approach to "expert systems" which intends to create a situation avoiding these dangers.

THE NEXT GENERATION TRADE UNION PROJECTS

The first generation trade union projects created platforms for understanding of the new technology, based upon a trade union perspective. They provided a wide range of cases illustrating how information technology impacted upon workers' interests. They resulted in agreements and laws securing rights to information and participation. They started important knowledge-building processes.

In spite of these successes, the situation regarding participation in system development today is rather dark. What we are doing is relevant, gives results, but is not enough. The rapid restructuring of the production system of the world (also called "the economic crisis") is strongly dependent upon information technology for two major purposes:

1. Competence may be built into the production equipment, thus making the employers independent of the existence of a qualified work force.

2. Competence in administration may be centralised in corporate
    headquarters of transnational firms. State information may
    be collected and control information given by the aid of
    modern communication networks.

As a result production may be moved to profitable areas quickly,
exploiting unqualified, unorganised labour if possible, and under-
mining the position of the trade unions in industrialised countries
- even playing them against each other ("We must not price ourselves
out of the market by increasing salaries or keeping people employed
when new technology make it possible to do without them".)

In a situation with increasing unemployment, the current strategy
for participation may easily seem to be of marginal interest, a
kind of luxury activity when the existence of large number of
jobs is at stake.

It is necessary to relate the current strategy to a more active
strategy aimed at developing an increasing amount of cooperation,
also at the tactical level, across international borders.

Since the Third World countries are important in the current
restructuring of the production system, the problems of their
people become just another aspect of the problems which face the
populations of the industrialised world. If we are going to solve
our problems, we must find solutions - and perhaps difficult
solutions - which at the same time are acceptable in the Third
World.

The first trade union related project on a "profession-oriented
language" is conducted by the unions of the graphical workers in
Scandinavia. The project is named UTOPIA and will be presented at
this conference.

A second project in this area "System Development Environments
and Profession Oriented Languages", will start in Oslo in 1983 in
cooperation with researchers from Sweden, Denmark and USA. The
hospital professions will be used as a frame of reference.

The PUMA project in Denmark represents a different approach. In
this project, conducted at the Technical University of Denmark
and financed by the Department of Labour, information leaflets
are prepared, containing information about all new production
processes and equipment in the metal processing industries. The
leaflets are written by experts, for trade unionist at the company level, making them aware of alternatives and trends.

The PUMA information may, of course, also be made available as an
electronically stored data base, accessible through a data network. It is also easy to conceive a number of other data bases of
great use to trade unionists, made available through an international trade union data network. (Requiring a solution to problems of many different spoken languages.) Examples would be data
bases on hazardous chemicals and on laws and agreements.

The development of closer international cooperation needs the
support of a highly efficient communication infra-structure: once
again, a modern data network.

The concept of such a network has been introduced and given the
name "Union Net for Information, Teamwork and Education", (giving

the English acronym UNITE and UNITÉ in French). The Norwegian Federation of Trade Unions has obtained initial funding for a design study of such a network, with particular emphasis upon the terminals' capabilities. The study will be conducted in close contact with unions in other countries.

COOPERATION

This conference presents a considerable number of papers building upon a trade union oriented perspective. Most other conferences are so completely dominated by the employers "or the system specialists" perspectives that the bias is not perceived by the participants. In fact, the introduction of trade union points of view at such conferences is often resented as being "political" as opposed to the "objective" and "neutral" majority view.

This conference is, in my opinion, an important event and gives us the possibility of establishing a network of cooperating researchers sharing a common perspective.

When this conference is finished, we will know each other. But we will need means for staying in contact, for distributing relevant information: important resolutions case studies, research reports, surveys of events in each country. We need perhaps a publication series which could (perhaps) be named "Materials And Reports on COmputers and Society" (MARCOS). Not a flashy journal run for business purposes by some publisher and for prestige reasons by us – but a series of various kinds of publications appearing in a modest format when information needs to be distributed. Associated with MARCOS we could provide a contact service to assist people with common interest to reach each other.

I mention these ideas now, at the start of the conference, hoping that they will be discussed between you in the days to come. This conference should be both a milestone and a starting point.

References

Holbæk-Hanssen, E, Håndlykken, P and Nygaard, K, 1975: "System Description and the DELTA Language". Norwegian Computing Center, Publ. 523, Oslo 1975.

Nygaard, K and Håndlykken, P: "The System Development Process – Its Setting, Some Problems and Needs for Methods". In "Software Engineering Environment", ed. H. Hünke, North Holland 1981.

Mathiassen, L: "Systemudvikling og Systemudviklingsmetode", 1981, in Danish. ("System Development and System Development Method".) DAIMI PB - 136, 1981. Department of Computer Science, University of Århus, Denmark.

CONTRIBUTIONS TO A
THEORETICAL FRAMEWORK
OF PARTICIPATIVE
SYSTEM DESIGN

SYSTEMS DESIGN FOR, WITH, AND BY THE USERS
U. Briefs, C. Ciborra and L. Schneider (editors)
North-Holland Publishing Company
© IFIP, 1983

THE DESIGN PROCESS:
FRAMES, METAPHORS, AND GAMES

Giovan Francesco Lanzara

Istituto di Scienze dell'Informazione
and
Istituto di Studi Politici
Università di Bari,Italy

A perspective on the design process is here presen=
ted and discussed which emphasizes design as a pro=
blem-setting activity. It is argued that the functio=
nal analysis and the problem-solving models of de=
sign do not give account of some of the most crucial
aspects of a designer's work. Design is here conside=
red to be a process of creative inquiry taking place
through transactions and conversations among multiple
social actors in cooperative or competitive situations.
Cognitive activities such as framing,evoking,metaphor-
making,and behavioral strategies such as bargaining,
concerting,reconciling,transacting are shown to be
relevant to a sound design theory and practice.

INTRODUCTION

My purpose in this paper is to propose a view of the design process
which is in many respects different from the current view of instru=
mental rationality held by most design theorists and practitioners.
My argument is that most designers,though competent and effective at
solving the problems that they are given,do not know what they are
really doing when they are involved in a design process. Though
skilled at producing all kinds of artifacts,they do not seem to pay
to much attention to their own human behavior. The abstract image a
designer holds of that process very little resembles the concrete
phenomenology of his real-life activities,of how he actually proceeds
in designing. According to that view the design process is seen as a
technical activity by which a designer starts up with a clearly sta=
ted problem and explicit objectives,then looks for the best means to
achieve the objectives and solve the problem,proceeding along the
steps of a procedure. Most manuals and handbooks of system design
and development contain formal methods and recipes which are all
structured and organized,except for minor variations,like steps that
a designer is asked to follow if he wants to realize his final pro=
duct. At the core of these methods,that I take as a unique general
methodology,is the idea that a complex problem or reality is best
understood,and hence controlled or solved,when it is subdivided into
smaller pieces. Once that the problem has been broken into simpler
components,one can tackle and solve the components separately,then
proceed to a global solution just by re-composing the components.

Here the "analytic knife" is at work: the designer's skill is skill
to use that knife (Pirsig,1974). For example,if you are given the
task to design an information system for an office,you analyse offi=
ce work by splitting activities into functions,like budgeting,plan=
ning,purchasing,inventoring,registering,advertising,etc.,then fur=
therly splitting these functions into elementary tasks. What a desi=
gner designs are simple procedures to realize the tasks and functions.
The set of procedures,variously composed and combined,is the office
information system, a whole supposedly re-composed by putting toge=
ther isolated procedures.

DESIGN AS FUNCTIONAL ANALYSIS

The attempt to turn design into a scientific discipline,based on
formal rules and procedures independent of the "think-so" of the
analyst or the practitioner,has led to a broad family of methods and
techniques,which can simply be named <u>functional analysis</u> or <u>functio=
nal strategies</u>. Functional analysis has been widely applied - and it
is still being applied - in many fields,particularly in industrial
production,in architectural and environmental design,in management,
in policy planning,and in the development of information systems.
According to functional analysis a final product or artifact is de=
signed first by de-composing it into its constituent parts,then by
re-composing it into a final form: every component has a function
that must be precisely described. By a process of hierarchical de=
composition a tree is generated,the <u>design tree</u> or <u>functional tree</u>:
going down to the bottom of the tree (branching) one describes sim=
pler and simpler functions to the most elementary ones,then going up
back to the roots,the functions are coordinated and the components
assembled. Functional analysis consists in buiding that tree(Alexan=
der,1964).

In all functional methods the design tree coincides with the functio=
nal structure of the artifact. Functional analysis allows for an
exact product definition through a systematic screening of product
features,in order to make the product structure clear. Form perfect=
ly matches function,and the artifact is "rational" or "optimal" be=
ing the result of a design procedure which is internally coherent.
Evaluation criteria coincide with functional requirements and design
goals are nothing else but detailed descriptions of the alternative
options. Several assumptions characterize the method of functional
analysis:

a) goals are given explicitly at the start,and cannot be modified
   during the process. Also,alternative means for achieving the ends
   and criteria for evaluating performance are given as distinct
   from ends;
b) the design process is a process of selecting means for achieving
   given ends. In the process the <u>best</u> solution is achieved by a
   one-shot strategy;

c) there is an explicit isomorphism between the morphology of the
   design process and the morphology of the artifact. Because of the
   assumed isomorphism, the artifact "naturally" embodies rationality;
d) the designer is an abstract individual - idealtypic - having a
   completely rational behavior. He has perfect information on en=
   vironmental parameters and design variables; his basic skills
   consist in being able to assign utility and preference values to
   outcomes, and his discipline is economic calculus.

In this view of design the environmental context is fixed, the pro=
blem is clear and unambiguous, ends and means are given, and the de=
sign process consists in a formal technique to make the internal
structure of the artifact coherent. As Herbert Simon has remarked,
the analytic method applied to design rests on the assumption that
a variety of _possible_ worlds can be reduced to _one_ _normative_ world,
to an "ought-to-be" statement (Simon,1969). As it can be easily un=
derstood, this is a stance toward design that has very little to do
with real-life problematic situations or design contexts, where pro=
blems are not clearly formulated but must be set, environment is fuz=
zy and uncertain, ends are vague, shifting, or conflicting, means and
ends are nor given or cannot be easily distinguished from each other.

DESIGN AS PROBLEM-SOLVING

With his principle of _bounded rationality_ and his empirical observa=
tions on "satisficing" behavior Herbert Simon (1969) has introduced
a remarkable innovation in design theory and method, generating a
whole new family of design strategies based on learning and adapta=
tion (Simon and Newell,1972). Design is essentially "finding solu=
tions to problems", but the designer, as any other observer or actor-
in-situation, does not have absolute rationality and perfect informa=
tion. He may only find a "satisficing" solution to his problem at
hand by exploring and using the additional information contained in
the environment at each step of the process. In other words, the de=
signer can _learn_ from the context how to structure his search and
how to proceed to the next step. The context contains _cues_ that may
help the designer toward a solution. The resulting artifact is al=
ways an _interface_ between an internal structure and an external con=
text. A stable but flexible shape of the interface - a form - is a=
chieved by a _learning strategy_, by a step-by-step adaptation. The co=
re of the design process is a complex interaction between the search
process, which, according to Simon and Newell, is governed by simple
rules, and the structure of the environment. Search is an _open_ strate=
gy, going from possibilities to a solution, which opens up to further
possibilities and to further decisions and solutions, and so forth.
But search is limited by time and money, **and** the final solution is
just _one_ among the many that are feasible, not the unique and optimal
solution to the problem.

As a problem solving strategy design is a heuristic process to col=

lect information on the structure of the problem,not just a formal
technique to select best means to achieve given ends. Even if the
means-ends pattern is maintained in Simon and Newell's search proce=
dures,ends can be incrementally changed along the way and adapted to
varying situations; informations and alternative courses of action
which do not get used don't get lost but are stored and may be even=
tually used later on to build new problem representations. Thus,the
terminal state of the process,and the path and time to get there
strictly depend on the designer's evaluation criteria and discretio=
nary judgement. The image of the designer shifts from the rational
economic man's,executing formal mathematical calculus,to the infor=
mation processor's,carrying out intelligent search and able to learn
from his own search. The designer performs basic cognitive activities:
screening,scanning,coding,memorizing,retrieving multiple choice op=
tions. The currently used metaphor for this perspective on design is
"maze-running".(Simon,1956).

I believe that the most fundamental tenets of the problem-solving
model of the design process,namely bounded rationality,satisficing
behavior,open strategies of heuristic search,learning,still hold.
But this problem-solving model seems to catch only some aspects of
the design process,neglecting others which seem to me to be at least
as important. What Simon and Newell assume to be a general informa=
tion processing model is only a particular way of processing infor=
mation,applicable to rather well-structured problems. The problem-
solving protocols that Simon and Newell have analysed in Human Pro=
blem Solving (1972) are just a particuler case of a larger family of
design protocols.

Here are some of the most critical points:

a) the empirical protocols concern an individual problem solver who
   faces and solves problems individually in a structured situation.
   The problem is given and is generally well-formed: chess playing,
   theorem proving,logic calculus,puzzles,etc.;
b) the design process consists,in Simon's view,of two distinct pha=
   ses: generation and selection of alternatives. The selection pro=
   cedure takes place after the generation and independently of it.
   The designer generates,randomly or systematically,a range of de=
   sign options from which he then selects a satisficing one through
   heuristic search and computation;
c) the generation/selection occurs within a decisional structure or
   or basic design structure,consisting of nodes and branches arran=
   ged in a tree pattern (possibilities,decisions,and links between
   them) and given a priori. Even here the tree pattern seems to be
   the archetypical representation of the design process;
d) alternatives are generated as a combination and composition of
   simple elements,which are treated as independent of the decisio=
   nal structure and are considered to be of minor importance with
   respect to it. A solution,then,is achieved through a process of
   generation/selection of complex combinations of simple elements.

Solutions vary from each other and are changed one into another
by incremental changes,by variations or substitutions of simple
elements,or else by minor corrections.

My argument is that this <u>representation</u> of the design process as an
individually-centered process of generation/selection of alternatives
on a given design structure falls short in giving account of some of
the most interesting features of design situations. Recent research
and findings on the phenomenology of human behavior and of decision
processes have shown that a large part of the design activities and
efforts concern the creation or the modification of the decisional
structure. Crucial aspects of design,of which very little is still
known,have to do with problem setting,with the definition of the pro=
blematic situation,and they cannot be understood and properly descri=
bed within the framework offered by instrumental rationality,be it
optimizing or satisficing.

DESIGN AS PROBLEM SETTING

In most real-life situations (organizations,teams,governments,offices,
policy-making,etc.) design is a process of collective inquiry and
search taking place through transactions and conversations among se=
veral actors in cooperation or competition,or with mixed interests
over the problem at hand. The most general and interesting design si=
tuations are concerned with the setting of the problem. Designers in=
volved in a typical design situation most of the times have trouble
to design not because they are unable to find out specific technical
solutions but because they do not know much about what the <u>real</u> pro=
blem is,or else because they cannot agree with their partners on
what the problem is,or even because they are misguided by the decep=
tive behavior of their partners. Design is difficult not because of
the internal technical complexity of a given problem,but because peo=
ple do not agree on what to do (contextual complexity). Design situa=
tions are generally confused,puzzled,troubling,characterized by un=
certainty and by conflicting frames and views. What lacks and needs
to be created is what the problem solving model takes for granted,
that is the decisional structure,an appropriate problem representa=
tion (Schon,1974).

Problem representation is not context-free but largely context-sensi=
tive. It certainly might take a tree-shape in the end,but it still
needs to be understood how it is built and especially how comes that
designers frequently switch from one representation to a completely
different one in the same design process. If the representation (a
coherent organization of symbols by which the problem is structured,
or in simpler words: how one sees the problem,what one sees of the
problem) determines the range of possibilities and solutions (or,more
precisely,of what is considered to be a possibility and a solution),
and if it influences the style of research and the organization of
the design process,then an essential part of design theory should

concern the knowledge of how representations are constructed and how
they affect solutions (Newell,1982). And an effective design practi=
ce is affected by the designer's skill in creating appropriate,ima=
ginative representations.

In the following section,drawing on recent work on design theory de=
veloped in various fields as artificial intelligence,cognitive sci=
ence,organization theory,educational sciences,I shall advance some
ideas both on the nature and on the context of the design process.
(Argyris & Schon,1978;Crozier & Friedberg,1977;Dewey,1949;Minsky,
1975;Rein & Peattie,1981;Ortony,1977;Schon,1977 & 1980).

FRAMES, METAPHORS, AND GAMES

In the analytic "scientific" view of the design process the designer
regards the design problem or situation as a case for which standard
rules and procedures apply. Design is seen as a formalized or forma=
lizable activity,where formal thinking is at work,except for the ini=
tial intuition (the idea!) and the final evaluation. The problem is
somewhat an external entity (it is there) that is to be processed by
formal "neutral" operations in order to be transformed into a soluti=
on. The designer is simply a spectator or manipulator of the problem.

But as empirical research has shown in real-life situations the desi=
gner experiences the problem as a unique situation,characterized by
uncertainty and ambiguity,for which there are no recipes ready. In a
puzzling and troubling situation the designer works on a what if ba=
se: "what if I thought of it this way? what if I used this plan,
tried this theory of action,adopted this model of the phenomenon,
chose this way of framing the problem or the role ?" (Schon,1980).
He tries to reduce ambiguity by constructing a virtual world,i.e. "a
world constructed to represent a real world of action,but at the same
time relatively free of the constraints and costs of real world in=
quiry"(Schon,1980).

In doing that,he does not apply standard categories and operations
to objects or classes of objects but rather frames and scripts to si=
tuations. He tries to generate "situation-specific variations of fa=
miliar themes" constructed from a memorized repertoire of exemplars,
precedents,metaphors,cases (Schon,1980). What the designer seems to
be doing (before eventually proceeding to more formal thinking) is
evoking some "exemplar" or "precedent" situation and assuming a simi=
larity between the precedent and the situation in which he is perso=
nally involved. In different ways Thomas Kuhn and Sir Geoffrey Vi=
ckers have given some attention to the process of "thinking from
exemplars" or "from precedents",but also Miller,Galanter,and Pribram
have remarked some years ago that new plans often originate from old
plans,and not always by applying formal procedures or from scratch
(Miller,Galanter,Pribram,1960).

While working toward setting a problem a designer continuously pro=
duces examples,picks up instances,draws analogies,shapes virtual
worlds (as if...). Let us look more closely at this process. On what
base a designer can assume a similarity between the previous and the
present situation ? What kind of similarity is there ? Schon suggests
that a situation or a problem is recognized as having a family re=
semblance,in the sense of Wittgenstein's (1953),with other situations
or problems in which the designer has already been involved and of
which he has previous experience. Not the two problems have all the
same features,but together with differences they share some simila=
rities,that the designer picks up and that might be helpful to bring
the problem to a solution. The designer's competence and ability
seems to consist in <u>seeing</u> a situation <u>as</u> another for which a cer=
tain kind of solution was adopted that might prove appropriate to
the present case. Several studies have been made on the generative
and structuring power of these activities of <u>evoking</u>,<u>seeing as</u>,<u>tran=
sposing</u>,<u>enacting</u> , which can be usefully denoted with the term <u>meta-
phor-making</u> (Schon,1977;Ortony,1977;Weick,1979;Lanzara,1982).

It is crucial to understand that the ability to see a situation as
another is not at all an analytical ability: the process of SEEING
AS is not realized by taking situation A,breaking it into simple
pieces,then by taking situation B,breaking it into simple pieces,and
and then by checking if they perfectly match or belong to the same
classes of objects. Briefly,the two situations are not analytically
comparable. On the contrary,metaphor-making has to do more with <u>fi=
gurative</u> thinking,with the ability to think in terms of images that
are powerful,metaphorically meaningful,and generative of virtual
worlds; images that are simple but have the capacity of connecting
and conveying complex relationships and meanings. After all,that is
the etimological sense of thinking: generating visions.

Metaphors verbally expressed in design conversations and stories
and communicated by dialogue may generate frames,images,patterns
useful for design. Generative metaphors are a hybrid of simplicity
and complexity. They are familiar ideas,implicit in spoken language
or in common sense experience,that are transposed and applied in the
new situation. Consider for example the couples of ideas: fragmenta=
tion/coordination,flexibility/rigidity,whole/parts,tree/network,ma=
chine/organism,etc. The search for a bridge between what is already
known and what it is still unexplored is less of a search among the
branches of a tree leading to a solution,and more of a search for
ways of framing and of designing structures that might prove appro=
priate to the problem. Interestingly enough,that search not only
shapes a design structure but also surfaces some basic alternatives
at the same time. The generation of alternatives seems neither a to=
tally random process nor a totally systematic one but a work of in=
quiry and communication taking place within a dialogical,interactive
context. And the options available for decisions are not combinations
of simple elements all independent from each other but alternative
states of the whole system (Schon,1974),connected by systematic re=

lationships and submitted to restrictions which an experienced desi=
gner can easily grasp in his mental and professional work.

What Simon calls "the elements of design" are not peripheral and in=
dependent from the structure,but may be complex segments of it: most
often the design units a designer deals with are structures or com=
plex segments of a structure. One cannot generate a decision stru=
cture without at the same time articulating the decision options.
Sometimes the emergence of a new element may drastically modify the
structure: metaphors,for example,may originate from simple associa=
tions and generate whole new frames. Frames used by designers con=
tain both facts and values,both rough descriptions of the problem
and criteria for its solution,both anticipations and remembrances,
habits and innovations,styles and standards,in a complex that cannot
be analytically separated. Finally,frames implicitly embed interests
and stances toward a situation or a goal (Minsky,1974;Schon,1977;
Rein & Peattie,1981;Dewey & Bentley,1949).

As a nice example of how frames and metaphors may overtly or tacitly
influence design methods let us briefly consider office work and of=
fice system design. In a very familiar frame office work is <u>seen</u> <u>as</u>
a set of procedures and tasks which are manipulated or executed by
single individuals across a hierarchy of levels. An office is a te=
chnical-functional artifact to realize a mission. In this functional
frame analysts see a system of components: functions,machines,equip=
ment,paper,space,roles,and relations of roles to the components. Of=
fice work is complex and,in order to reduce its complexity and to ma=
ke it more efficient and productive,must be subdivided into functio=
nal and hierarchical levels. The unit of **analysis** and design is the
<u>function</u>. Leading metaphors embedded in this frame are: "office as a
machine",or "organization as a tree",or else "top/bottom lines". The
"hierarchy"metaphor seems to be so deeply embedded in our language
and culture that,as we step into an office,we usually happen to ask:
"who's the boss here ?". Associated to that metaphor is a specific
way of thinking about reality and a specific organization of work:
we see office work as accomplished by adding one task after the
other in a sequential order. People attend individually to each sin=
gle task and assume specific roles. Rules for work are generally
established at the top of the hierarchy (Hammer & Zisman,1979).

But,alternatively,one might <u>see</u> office work <u>as</u> a bundle of conversa=
tions and transactions taking place among people. From a more anth=
ropological point of view, the office can also be seen as a communi=
ty where a microculture grows. Office work carry out their work col=
lectively and creatively by **conversations**,transactions,bargaining,
mutual arrangements and agreements,day-by-day committments,engage=
ments and decisions,which are not necessarily structured as procedu=
res. On the contrary they depend for a **large** part on the discretio=
nary judgement and on work attitudes of the persons involved in con=
tingent situations. The metaphors evoked and draped in the language
are here "office as a market",or "office as a network",or else "of=

fice as a folks'group". A group of intelligent and autonomous persons
collectively deals with instances and solves problems in a world of
interpersonal relationships and communications that must be meaning=
ful to themselves in the first place. Informal activities and local
person-to person transactions play the same role - if not a more re=
levant one - than formal-procedural ones: in any case they cannot be
easily distinguished. Rules for work are the result of many local ne=
gotiations,modifications,and adaptations (Wynn,1979).

Thus,depending on whether one brings to the foreground either formal
functions or informal interpersonal interaction - either the "machine"
aspect or the "community" aspect of an office-,different and non-com=
parable segmentations of the office world are produced. In the for=
mer the object of design is <u>functions</u>, a system of procedures, in the
latter is <u>conversations</u> and transactions,i.e. a network of communica=
tions among people. In the functional frame emphasis necessarily falls
on the design of specific functions and of ideal "mainline" procedu=
res that the worker,once they are implemented,is asked to follow ca=
refully. Attention focuses on analytical exactness,on exhaustive de=
scription of procedures and tasks,and of eventual exceptions. Con=
cern with atomistic specification of procedural steps becomes almost
obsessive. As it is well known side-effects of this approach are fra=
gmentation of work,growing distance between the worker and his task,
loss of meaningfulness of work,loss of problem,loss of competence,
loss of effectiveness. System design and development tend to be a
process producing the system as its final product. Then the system is
"sold" to the user,be it in a market place or in a political arena,
and must be plugged into a specific organizational setting and cultu=
re. Whether the system is actually bought or not by a user,and whe=
ther it really works or it does not,it is not a matter of much concern
for the designer.

In the transactive frame emphasis falls on the design of people's re=
lations and of a communication network to carry out such activities
as contracting,concerting,bargaining,agreeing/disagreeing,informing,
choosing,dialoguing,deciding,etc. As Schon (1980) has remarked,a good
conversation cannot be completely described or designed by an external
observer nor by a participant in it. It is indeed an open enterprise
conducted by partners or counterparts interacting within a situation.
Within this frame there is not such a thing as a final product origi=
nating from a procedural design process and subsequently "thrown" in=
to the organizational or market or political setting. The actors them=
selves are involved in the design and implementation of the system.
Criteria applied to evaluate the design performance and the"goodness"
of the product are not the same of the functional frame. Issues of
intersubjective validity,of collective agreements,of liking/disliking,
of iterative testing,of inquiring into other actors' intentions and
attitudes,become dominant in the process.

The illustration of the different views of the office shows that in
its problem setting phase but also - and very much so - in its imple=

mentation phase,the design process consists in framing and reframing
a problematic situation which escapes a stable "once-for-all" defini=
tion: there is interaction,exchange,conflict among frames. Frame in=
congruence is a matter of course in real-life design: different indi=
viduals or groups may frame a situation in different ways which might
be incompatible with each other. A large part of the design process,
especially in large-scale projects and organizations involving seve=
ral actors,is not dedicated to analytical work to achieve a solution
but mostly to efforts at reconciling conflicting frames or at tran=
slating one frame into another. Much work of the designer is less
concerned with finding a solution to a specific problem than with de=
fining collectively what is the relevant problem,how to see it.

Designers do not work in vacuo,sitting on the top of an ivory tower.
In the most common situations,problem-setting is essentially a tran=
sactive process,where different actors communicate,exchange,argue,and
bargain their perspectives,values,and (even!) facts. They may enact
very differentiated strategies leading to failure or success: avoi=
dance,coercion,bargaining,promise,persuasion,pre-committment,decep=
tion and self-deception,opportunism,collective inquiry,mutual under=
sta,ding,etc. When "the designer" is a design team many insights on
the process should be given by the study of group and interpersonal
dynamics and by collective decisionmaking: how decisions and choices
are taken collectively ? Who or where is the "rational" designer ? Is
there a collective rationality ? Who is entitled to have voice on a
problem and influence the solution ? Who is supposed to do what ? By
framing,discussing,and negotiating rules of mutual behavior and inte=
raction,designers first of all design their own "design setting".
They play games with the situation they are inquiring and of which
they are a part. They play games with the actors involved in the same
situation and engaged in the design process. That introduces new so=
urces of uncertainty in the process,due to the fact that the actors'
behavior may be variable,ambiguous,deceptive,basically unpredictable.
All these games and strategies of behavior are inevitably a part of
the design situation,and affect problem definition and solution. They
cannot be considered simply as an externality in the process. Problems
dilemmas and goals are defined in this process of transaction,and in=
quiry proceeds through these games, which are not simply disturbances
or deviations to the mainline but an essential feature of any colle=
ctive decisionmaking endeavour which is not trivial. A design project
feeds on the unique and peculiar features of a situation. It might
begin with one definition of the problem and end up with a completely
different one,that better responds to a changed or changing context.

CONCLUSION

Concluding these sketchy remarks,the core message I intend to push
through is that design is both a process of creative inquiry and
construction and a process of political transaction conducted by so=
cial actors who may be competitive or collaborative,or having mixed

interests. It is a generative process by which new forms of the world are created and new perspectives on the world come to existen= ce. We still know very little about the cognitive work and the stra= tegic behavior involved in a complex design process,about the frames and the games enacted and played by designers and other social ac= tors. Certainly more study is needed on these aspects, if we want to be more effective in our design profession and if we want to make it more relevant and useful for society.

REFERENCES

/1/ Alexander, C., Notes on the Synthesis of Form,(Harvard University Press,Cambridge,1964).

/2/ Argyris ,C. and Schon,D.A., Theory in Practice: Increasing Pro= fessional Effectiveness (Jossey Bass Publ.,San Francisco,1978).

/3/ Bamberger,J. and Schon,D.A., The Figural/Formal Transaction, DSRE Working Paper,M.I.T.,Cambridge,1979.

/4/ Ciborra,C., Information Systems and Transactions Architecture, Journal of Policy Analysis and Information Systems,vol.5,no.4, december 1981.

/5/ Crozier,M. and Friedberg,E., L'acteur et le système,(Seuil,Paris, 1977).

/6/ Dewey,J., Logic. The Theory of Inquiry (Holt and Co.,New York, 1949).

/7/ Dewey,J. and Bentley,A.F., Knowing and the Known (The Beacon Press,Boston,1949).

/8/ Goffman,I., Forms of Talk (University of Pennsylvania Press,Phi= ladelphia,1981).

/9/ ISFOL,Rapporto su "Progettazione di nuove tecnologie e qualità della vita di lavoro",chapt.1 and 2, Rome,1982.

/10/Lanzara,G.F., Ephemeral Organizations in Extreme Environments: Emergence,Strategy,Exstinction, Journal of Management Studies, Special Issue on Organizational Learning,Argyris & Schon editors, Oxford,1982 (forthcoming).

/11/Miller,G.A.,Galanter,E.,Pribram,K.H., Plans and the Structure of Behavior (Holt and Co.,New York,1960).

/12/Minsky,M., A Framework for Representing Knowledge, in : Winston, P.H.,(ed.) The Psychology of Computer Vision (McGraw-Hill,New York,1975).

/13/Newell,A., The Knowledge Level, Artificial Intelligence (Jan.1982)

/14/Pirsig,R., Zen and the Art of Motor cycle Maintenance (By R.Pir= sig,1974).

/15/ Rapoport,A., Fights,Games and Debates (The University of Michigan Press,Ann Arbor,1960).

/16/ Rein,M. and Peattie,L., Action Frames and Policy Setting,mimeo, Dpt. of Urban Studies and Planning,M.I.T.,Cambridge,1981.

/17/ Ortony,A., Metaphor and Thought (ed.)(Cambridge University Press Cambridge,U.K.,1977).

/18/ Schon,D.A., The Design Process, mimeo,Dpt. of Urban Studies and Planning,M.I.T.,1974.

/19/ Schon,D.A., Generative Metaphor: A Perspective on Problem-Setting in Social Policy, in: Ortony,A. ref. /17/.

/20/ Scon,D.A., Converstional Planning, An Essay in Honor of Sir Geoffrey Vickers, DRSE,M.I.T.,Cambridge,1980.

/21/ Schon,D.A., Reflection-on-Action, mimeo, Dpt. of Urban Studies and Planning,M.I.T. Cambridge,1980.

/22/ Simon,H.A., The Sciences of the Artificial (MIT Press,Cambridge, 1969).

/23/ Simon,H.A. and Newell,A.,Human Problem Solving (Prentice Hall, Englewood Cliffs,N.J.,1972).

/24/ Simon,H?A., Rational Choice and the Structure of the Environment,(1956)

/25/ Tversky A. and Kahneman,D. The Framing of Decisions and the Psychology of Choice,in Science,vol.211,453-458,Jan.30,1981.

/26/ Weick,K., Enactment Processes, in: Staw and Salancik,(eds.), New Directions in Organizational Behavior (St.Clair Press,Chicago,1977).

/27/ Wittgenstein,L. Philosophical Investigations (Mac Millan,New York,1953).

/28/ Wynn,E. Office Conversation as an Information Medium, Phd. Thesis,Dpt. of Anthropology,University of California at Berkeley, 1979.

/29/ Suchmann,L. and Wynn;E., Procedures and Problems in Office Environment, Xerox Advanced Systems,April 1979.

/30/ Hammer,M. and Zisman,M., Design and Implementation of Office Information Systems,in: Proceedings of the New York Conference on Automated Office Systems,New York,may 1979.

SYSTEMS DESIGN FOR, WITH, AND BY THE USERS
U. Briefs, C. Ciborra and L. Schneider (editors)
North-Holland Publishing Company
© IFIP, 1983

THE SOCIAL COSTS OF INFORMATION TECHNOLOGY
AND PARTICIPATION IN SYSTEM DESIGN

Claudio Ciborra

Dipartimento di Elettronica, Politecnico di Milano

Dipartimento di Organizzazione Aziendale,
Università della Calabria, Cosenza

Information technology generates externalities or
social costs for the large community of users. These costs
are difficult to assess and allocate among the interested
parties. Allocation can only take place through the bargain
ing of the rights to define systems. Various contractual arrangements can regulate the involvement of users in technical
change: latent bargaining, agreements and legislation. Effi -
ciency reasons would indicate that alternatives be compared
and evaluated in order to determine the best participation
strategy in each specific system development project.

INTRODUCTION

Since its beginning user participation in systems design was a "moral issue". Con
scious systems designers looked critically at their past practice and recognized
their own imperialism towards the user.

Progressive managers and consultants wanted to apply a socio-technical approach to
the design of information systems and work organization, yet sticking to humanistic
values (Mumford, 1981).

Unions initiatives aimed at organizing the solidarity of members in front of a
potentially menacing technological change.

Sometimes efficiency arguments justifying user participation were raised: users are
those who in the end consume the systems output: systems have to be "friendly",
otherwise the risks of underutilization plainly have to be faced. But such argu -
ments might sound very mundane, when a moral issue is at stake! Most of the   ap -
proaches to user participation have been strictly normative. Depending too much on
a normative perspective leaves too many problems unresolved, however, especially
where one wants to choose between different alternatives, ranging from state legislation to benevolent managerial support or manipulation.

A less shaky ground on which to compare, evaluate and develop alternative approaches
to user participation and, even more basic, a grounded theory to justify partici -
pation itself are badly needed. More precisely, an advancement in devising strategies for user participation could benefit from a comparative institutional assessment of the governance structures of technological change within organizations.
The assessment should firstly point out why participation is necessary, if it is pos
sible to by-pass moral considerations; and secondly what are the best ways to organize it given specific sets of circumstances.

In order to deal with these questions, although in a preliminary way, this paper
applies the theoretical apparatus provided by the New Institutional Economics (Wil
liamson, 1975, 1976, 1979). While the main concern of such a discipline is for the
efficiency of economic organizations, interest for the bargaining process and a

realistic view of organizations are all germane to it.

The discussion is carried out as follows. Firstly, the design and implementation of information systems are regarded as processes generating social costs. Regulat ing the externalities of pollution falls in the same class of problems as regulat ing computerization. Secondly, bargaining technological change is considered as an inevitable process of internalization of the social costs through the exchange of property rights in organizing work and designing systems.

Then alternative governance structures are evaluated on the basis of their effi - ciency in securing the internalization of social costs. The evaluation is not ulti mative, but should provide methodological hints to overcome the strong reliance on normative recipies. Finally, reference to the results of an empirical investig - ation on system design in regulated organizational contexts exemplifies and justi- fies the theory.

THE SOCIAL COSTS OF INFORMATION TECHNOLOGY

Technological change in production and administration carries externalities, or broadly speaking, social costs. That is, an economic agent applying for its pro - ductive purposes a new machine or system may affect in an uncompensated way other agents, who are in direct or indirect contact with that machine or system(Arrow, 1970; Dahlam, 1979). Pollution is a well known case of externality provoked by in- dustry. Typical question marks related to externatility are: who is liable and should pay for the damage? What is the best solution to reduce the damage (to in - troduce an air cleaner; a tax; a new zoning scheme)?; How and through which organ- izational arrangement can individuals affected react? (Salomon 1981). The point of view assumed here is not that all such problems are easily cleared away by market forces or simply by letting the "pollution agent" pay for the damage. The question is much more intricate and warrants attention to the bargaining processes neces - sary to allocate the social costs among the parties involved. (Stone, 1982). The problem of social costs has a reciprocal nature. In devising and choosing between different solutions one should take into account the "total effect", i.e. what are the costs and benefits which have to be borne by all the parties and what are the specific costs of the social arrangement selected (Coase, 1960).

Information technology is not an exception. Many of the negative consequences ori- ginated by the introduction of computer systems can be regarded as externalities. Consider, within an organization which uses a computer, the effects on decision making, control and autonomy (Whisler, 1970) or on qualifications of blue and white collar workers (Bravermann, 1974), or on pace of work and health and safety at the terminals. Or, in a wider context, consider the consequences of computerization on employment (Briefs, 1980) and privacy.

Many of the negative effects are borne by people outside the computer-based organ- ization, in the following we are mainly concerned with the internal environment of the firm. There, the main impact of systems is on the key contractual relation of the hierarchy: the employment relation (Ciborra, 1981).

The employment relation is governed by a contract according to which the employee accepts to give up the right to govern his/her productive behaviour during the working day and accepts for that period the authority of the employer to sequen - tially specify the actions he/she must perform, to control that actions are carried out according to plans in exchange of a set of tangible and intangible re- wards. Computer-based information systems, no matter what they are dedicated to, allow the employer to perform more sharply the planning, monitoring and controlling of work, thus altering the implicit or explicit balance (or equity) embedded in the execution of the traditional employment contract.

THE INTERNALIZATION OF SOCIAL COSTS

General

The preceding section has shown how a factor of production such as information technology may have harmful effects or social costs to be borne by different indivi -
duals.

These costs may be paid implicitly given a set of property rights (i.e. a given
social arrangement). For example, a firm which employs slaves does not take into
account the full cost of its own activity, because it can rely on the availability
of cheap slave labour paid at a subsistence level. If the legal system of slavery
is abolished, slaves can bargain with their owners offering an amount of money to
buy their own freedom. Such a sum becomes an "opportunity cost" for the firm to
use slave labour. In this way, a cost emerges explicitly in the use of the labour
factor. The bargaining process which makes a cost explicit, which is allowed by a
change in the system of property rights, is called internalization of social costs.
Internalizing social costs scattered among various individual means converting a
cost, which is difficult to fix and allocate, into something measurable and allo-
cable at a sufficiently low bargaining cost. Usually, the internalization of social
costs occurs through a change in the property rights, either because a legal system
is changed or because property rights themselves are object of trade among the interested parties (Demsetz, 1967).

Given a set of social costs the problem of internalization is to find the best institutional arrangement of property rights which allows the allocation of costs
such as the total product yield by this arrangement is maximum. It is not guaran -
teed that the optimal arrangement is going to be reached: the exchange of rights
might be very difficult and not get through. The economic analysis distinguished
two cases:

- in a world where transaction costs are zero, i.e. where negotiating and exchanging rights can be performed at zero cost, thanks to a frictionless market, the
  end result in the allocation of social costs will be independent of the legal position of the parties. The initial delimitation of rights does not matter: whe -
  ther it is the "emittor" or the "recipient" of the externality who has the liabi-
  lity to carry the cost of the harmful effect, an optimal bargain will be struck
  by which parties take into account the harmful effect and value of production is
  maximized (with a corresponding fall in the value to pay the social costs).

- but a world without friction is just a textbook fiction. In real situations,
  transaction costs differ significantly from zero. In fact, there are costs to
  discover the parties with whom to exchange, to conduct negotiations, to draw up
  the contract, to control its execution, to enforce modifications, to maintain
  the exchange relationship (Coase, 1960).

These costs, which are due to imperfect information present in an exchange between
opportunistic parties, can prevent certain bargains or trades which would be mutually beneficial if carried out. Two consequences obtain: for one thing,the optimal
pointed out by the frictionless market is not reached in practice, because   the
costs of the negotiation of the rights is so high to outset any internalization of
costs; for another, when there are transaction costs and informational differences
between opportunistic traders, then it matters a lot to whom liabilities and rights
are assigned (Dahlam, 1979). In such an environment, the analysis and choice of policies come to the forefront: i.e. which is the best rearrangement of liabilities
and rights to achieve a higher valued global output?; how much the moving to such
new rearrangement costs? and how much it costs to operate it compared to the costs
to be internalized? (there are various policy alternatives: agreements; agencies
or arbitrators to govern contracts; legislation and an enforcement apparatus; the
establishment of appropriate markets etc.)? At the worst, if bargaining costs off-
set the social costs, no internalization will take place, and the <u>status quo</u>   is

maintained until impediments to trade are eliminated or reduced.

Bargaining costs in the case of information technology

For the case of information technology, transaction costs cannot be ignored. This
means that policy issues, property rights etc. are a relevant factor and, in the
case of the firm, that the existing modes of representation such as unions can
play an essential role as bargainers of technological change.

First, there is an inertia factor of organizational nature. Organizations, both
private and public, will work for reduction in social costs only under limited con
dition. i.e. they have no incentives to reduce the external costs of their pro -
ductive processes, nor to search for and identify the depth and extent of external
costs borne by individuals within and outside the boundaries of the organization.
Management is not likely to respond favorably to efforts to alter behaviour, rules,
structures in system development when such changes imply increases in costs of sys
tems. If this is true for any technological change, it is even more relevant for
the case of system design, where both a new technological core is introduced into
the organization and the rules of running the organization itself are affected.
The interests of individuals and groups bearing externalities will be taken into
account only to the extent that the organization is exposed to the demands of those
individuals and to the degree that some influence can overcome the incentives of
organizations buffer to demands fro change. Influence can be exercised either
through environmental factors, such as legislation and/or through exercising
"voice" or collective action (Marchand), 1977). We can conclude that at least one
important actor, management factor, is prone to behave opootunistically and so in
crease the costs of bargaining technological change.

A second factor is due to the nature of social costs in the specific case of in -
formation technology. They are reciprocal, difficult to assess and talk about. It
is often the case that a new system brings both benefits and costs to management
and workers, and it is difficult to separate them. For example, a production control system can allow better production scheduling and smooth production runs, so
reducing the amount of overtime required at the expense of increased monitoring
of individual effort. Costs often are also subtle, "costly" to identify and com -
municate information about. For example those related to the organizational impacts
of computers on decision making, centralization, certain forms of de-skilling,
etc. Especially when an investigation has not been carried out before the system
is implemented, it is difficult to identify and account for such effects.

Information and language asimmetries are another feature arising during system development. For those potentially affected by informatics it is not only a matter of
ignoring relevant information on systems, but of difficulty in receiving, evaluating, discussing and communicating such information. It can be mind boggling to extract from a flow chart or a structured tree describing the main system functions,
what will be the consequences on skills job content, social contact, etc. This is
due to the fact that while education for users is often inadequate, education for
specialists is mainly centered on the machine rather than its social and organiz -
ational consequences. The provision included in Scandinavian agreements that all
information regarding systems must be in an understandable form to non specialists
is a crucial step to reduce friction in bargaining due to language barriers.
(Nygaard, Bergo, 1975).

A fourth element is technological progress itself. Information technology is   a
highly uncertain bargaining subject. New hardware, new software, new design strate
gies, new organizational solutions are coming up at a very fast rate. This requi -
res continuous learning, adaptation, appropriate bargaining strategies and means.

Finally, various difficulties arise from the need of collective action. Given the
diffuse character of social costs, a brief analysis is warranted of the conditions
under which collective action of individuals and groups bearing external costs can

be expected and the conditions under which the representation of the interests in reducing external costs is likely to be effective. Systems users face various impediments. They need to coordinate their voice to change an integrated system: but they are dispersed horizontally and vertically in the hierarchy. Moreover, reduction of social costs is a collective good: the "free rider" problem arises as a consequence; there may be incentives for some individual users or groups not to reveal their true attitude towards a system so that others will bear the costs of trying to change it to the benefit of the whole user community. (Olson, 1965).

For the broader publics of customers and citizens outside the organization, information asymmetry, impediments to collective action are even worse. In what follows, however, focus is on the problem within the firm. There, problems related to col - lective action can be solved efficiently by employing the existing union machinery. Unions permit to supersede to individual or group interests of users; unions dispose of a structure ready to deal with problems of representativeness and so are the best mechanism to exercise voice to influence the allocation of costs falling on a large group of users. Unions also deal with various aspects of the employment relation, through collective bargaining agreements and all the relevant adaptative mechanisms regarding wages changes, labour adjustments, assignment changes, refinement of working rules, qualification structures etc. (Williamson, 1980).

FORMS OF PARTICIPATION IN SYSTEM DESIGN

It is now possible to reconsider the issue of participation within a broader context, the one of internalizing social costs.As explained above, internalizing social costs requires bargaining among the parties affected: management and   employees, the latter organized by unions (Brooks, 1981).

Out of the various possibilities, three situations can be illustrated with references to the European environment (Evans, 1982):
- no explicit bargaining
- explicit contracts, outcome of bargaining between unions and management
- state regulation.

The alternative forms can be compared on the basis of their efficacy and efficiency as contractual arrangements dedicated to the governance of technological change.

The "no formal bargaining" alternative corresponds to the case where the existence of social costs due to information technology is not acknowledged; the right   to use informatics lies exclusively in the hands of managment, who dispose of its con sequences by fiat: to the employees adaptations are required to follow instruc - tions from the top regarding changes in their work organization. This was thought to be the most efficient solution for introducing computers before the user parti cipation theme was ever played. At the extreme, it was claimed that computers had no impact on work organization, qualifications, employment etc. But inefficiencies emerged under the forms we all know by now: user resistance; adaptation problems; local and/or global conflicts during and after computerization; slow downs in pro ject execution and so on. Frequently such problems were attributed to the user's psychology, outside the doamin of rational organizational behaviour that could be controlled by specialists and management.

In the perspective here outlined, these are all inefficiencies related to the rational process of internalization of social costs (recall also the slavery ex   - ample, where cheap labour went along with low productivity). As mentioned above, informatics affects the balance embedded in the employment relation. If equity does not obtain anymore, then employees withold effort in various ways, mainly exploiting uncertainties around the new technology. For example, they can refuse to tap their knowledge and skill to the formal procedures running on the new system, so hindering its efficacy. The opportunistic use of job knowledge is a rational reaction to the perception of unequity in the employment contract, brought by the increased sharpness in monitoring and control.

Resistance can then arise in any point of the organization: individuals, groups or
organizational units can block the whole system, or more frequently can lower its
efficacy. As a consequence, individual bargains regulated by ad hoc contracts must
be continuously struck by the organization with different parties to continue to
develop the system. Bargaining and implementation costs rise as a consequence.

The second contractual alternative portraits a variety of solutions. Only a couple
of them are discussed in the following. The need of explicitly bargaining the consequences of systems is acknowledged and a formal machinery is set up between
unions and management, usually in connection with collective bargaining agreements,
at company, industry, and national levels (see the Scandinavian experiences as an
example, Nygaard and Bergo, 1975). In the present perspective, the object of the
contracts is to achieve a rearrengement in the property rights (management preroga
tives) related to systems and data. More specifically, the property rights concern
(a) the system development process and (b) the use of the system once implemented.

How the rearrengement is to be carried out in practice is a complex task, given
the high transaction costs previously discussed.

By examining the Norwegian case (see below) two basic approaches have been singled
out: an ex post and an ex ante bargaining process. Both are applied within the
same framework of the national data agreement between the employers confederation
(NAF) and the unions(LO).
Ex post contracts are of a contingent claim type: once the new system is operat -
ing, unions and management strike a bargain at company level concerning its modes
of usage. Items included in the contract are: scope of the system; operating modes;
user training; qualifications; use of personal data filed into the system; work
organization. Such "system contracts" are easy to draw up and enforce, because
they can be based on a joint description fo the system characteristics and effects
as evaluated by those who directly operate it or use it. And any uncertainty about
the social costs can be reduced, if not eliminated, by investigating the features
of the system while it functions.

The bargaining machinery needed is rather slim. A (data) shop steward can collect
information about the system, about the attitudes and interests of its direct
users, and take them at the bargaining table. The users are a rather well defined
group both because of the boundaries set by the system and because of union member
ship.

Object of exchange are not the rights of desinging the system but of using it and
designing the work organization surrounding it. Such contracts become of a recur -
rent type as more and more systems are implemented. Parties have the opportunity
to successively develop their own bargaining experience and competence in system
use, so being able to draw up realistic contingent claim contracts. Some inadequacies are however present. First, the scope of the changes is limited, and only a
part of the social costs can be internalized. On the one hand, it would be too
costly to find alternative designs of the system which would eliminate sources of
costs once the system is already designed. On the other, it would be excessively
expensive to negotiate the modification of an already existing software (there is
an exception to that, which is widely used in ex post contracting: the exclusion
from operation of routines originally designed into the system: an example is
given by routines for the monitoring of individual performance included in pro -
duction control systems). Second, the user community is too narrowly defined. A
production control system can have interdependencies with administrative departments, or inversly, a financial system can have an impact on the way operations
are organized. In both case, ex post contracting tends to disregard cross-effects
which overcome organizational boundaries or union membership. All this makes narrow and inefficacious the internalization of costs when integrated, or at the opposite, highly decentralized systems are implemented.

Ex ante contracts are of a more general, longer term type. They can be of a con -
tingent claim type, where both parties try to specify all the features of the new
system, its consequences, the reciprocal behaviour when the new system will be
adopted and the modification plans; or more open contracts as far as the system
characteristics are concerned, but with specific clauses regarding the modes of
participation during system design.

With the former approach a risky forecasting exercise is needed to anticipate and
agree on the future system; in the latter procedural rationality is employed so
that the framework for a bilateral relation is established during system design:
in that process the parties find solutions, negotiate and execute them as specific
events and choices unfold. What is traded in the latter approach are the rights to
influence decision -making related to system development, and via this to influen
ce the system itself and its consequences. Given the high degree of uncertainty
and specificity of system development, it is obvious that a contract that includes
the second approach is to be preferred because it allows more adaptive decision
making.

Costs between alternatives should be compared; a longer design process versus hag-
gling around contract execution and control when a system is designed. The complex
ity of the system could discriminate between the alternatives.

Finally, regulation through legislation. Reference is made here to the legislation
regarding the organization of work and system design (the Norwegian Work Environ -
ment Act is a good example). First, given the high bargaining costs related to
technological change, regulation does have an impact on the application of compu -
ters and the organization of computer-based tasks. Establishing regulation should
be made taking into account the economic impact of the resulting legal arrangement.
Making the employer (the employees) totally liable for externalities might not be
the optimal (from a global point of view) solution.

In the case where organizations do not have incentives to reduce social costs
borne by individuals inside and outside the organization, regulation is a means of
forcing them to alter their structures, rules and norms so as to better inter -
nalizethose costs. This role of regulation is important especially in those cases
where (a) because of the "public good" or "bad" character of the consequences of
the technology, i.e. the impossibility to exclude anyone from the impacts (e.g.
privacy of the citizen's personal data), and (b) because of the gap in resources
and information between organizations and the public, it would be difficult to
initiate and maintain a coherent collective action by citizens, employees etc.
aimed at influencing the use of computers.

Regulation is the means to modify the status quo, the inertia due to the impossibi
lity of large groups influencing organizations. But there are difficulties in us -
ing regulation for that purpose. For one thing, regulation is emanated by a politi
cal body, and the representation of interests within this body can be problematic
and the difficulties in organizing a collective action may be shifted from the
economic arena to the political one. For another regulation may be too general,
and in many cases, generic, because of tis comprehensiveness. In fact, either very
specific aspects are regulated because of the existence of minimum standards (e.g.
working time at VDUs), or simply "principles" are stated, the detailed application
of which has to be carried out by other contractual arrangements (e.g. participa -
tion in system design as stated in par. 12 of the Norwegian Work Environment Act).
Aslo, regulation is rigid. The time needed to prepare, implement and evaluate
rules is longer than the pace of technological change. So regulation implicitly
valid for a large, centralized edp center may be totally irrelevant for a distri -
buted office automation system. Finally, costs of enforcement have to be faced.The
establishment of clear-cut standards and an enforcement apparatus is required (e.g.
special units in the Labour Inspectorate dedicated to information technology). New
bureaucratic agencies have to be created, external to the organizations to be monitored. More resources have to be employed than in the case of an internal

control apparatus (like the data shop steward).

Empirical evidence

A recent investigation carried out in Norway[1], the country which has had a wide
application of agreements and laws regarding system design since the middle 70's,
seems to confirm some of the points discussed above.

By examining the pattern of system development of nine large organizations in dif
ferent sectors and so the agreements and the legislation "in action", it has been
found that :
- the existence of agreements and laws has unfreezed the present arrangement of
  rights regarding system and organization design. These are no more exclusive management prerogatives; but this is just an opportunity to be exploited through
  effective bargaining between management and unions. This happens only in a minori
  ty of cases.

- the ex post model is the most frequently followed, because it is the easiest to
  apply in situations where both parties lack knowledge and experience on system
  development. "Systems contracts" scattered all over the organization are the
  usual arrangements. It is the competence, bargaining strenght of the unions and
  the type of system which determine the effectiveness of a contract. The more ex
  perience is accumulated by drawing up such contracts, the more the unions seem
  to prefer the ex ante model.

- the ex ante approach was found in two organizations which have a long experience
  in system development. Its application seems to be exposed to the perils of in -
  competence, manipulation and failure. Nevertheless, this model gives the unions
  opportunities for timely intervention and influence on system development.

- participation is costly The ex ante approach is more costly that the ex post.
  System development is slown down; systems or part of systems are not used; bar -
  gaining and control apparatus are necessary to apply the agreements; considerable
  resources have to be spent for training and education etc. Most probably, the
  costs which surface with the agreements come from the accounting and internal -
  ization of those social costs normally ignored in traditional, non regulated sys
  tem development. On the other hand, systems, once implemented, seem to be produc
  tive and show a good level of utilization.

- regulation not supported by agreements is not effective in impacting the practice
  of system development. The enforcement apparatus (Labour Inspectorate) is too
  small to dedicate sufficient resources to the problem. All its resources are concentrated on other priorities, such as those health and safety clauses where
  clear-cut standards can be defined at low cost.

- high uncertainty stems from continuous technological and organizational change.
  Decentralization of systems and organizations; new technological models, new
  project management methods; subcontracting system development etc., are factors
  which compel parties to start from scratch in bargaining a system contract or
  drawing up an ex ante contract. Resources to be employed into negotiations in -
  crease as a consequence.

CONCLUDING REMARKS

The impacts of information technology have been reexamined in an economic and bar
gaining perspective. Participation in system design, besides a moral and normative
preoccupation, is a means to achieve the internalization of social costs caused by
technological change under specific contractual arrangements.

Some of the possible arrangements have been appraised (neglecting social costs altogether; ex post and ex ante agreements; regulation). The appraisal has not stated ultimatively what arrangement is the most efficient and effective at internal -
izing social costs. It all probably depends on the contingencies related to the de

velopment of a specific system. What is certain, I argue, is the inefficiency of disregarding a detailed comparative analysis, in a specific situation, of the alternatives available. Economic forces at work around the issue of participation should not be ignored. One of the first important consequence of considering them is to establish that bargaining technological change always takes place under one form or another, if social costs obtain. Secondly, that given the high bargaining costs stemming from the parties'conflict of interests and uncertainty of the tech nology, agreements and regulation. All these factors have an impact on the allo cation of social costs and the global production yield generated by employing a new system. Maintaing the status quo is one of the alternatives, but there is a presumption that this alternative is more costly to implement than others which explicitly recognize bargaining, again only if the hypotehsis that information technology brings considerable changes and uncompensated side effects is valid.

Further research is needed to support the theory outlined here. First, empirical research on system development, its outcomes and costs under different contractual arrangements.Then, research on the nature and variety of costs generated by information technology. Even the rearrangements of rights provoked by the edp should be systematically studied.

All this can lead to devise better methods for project management (understood in the broad sense of social project management).

What emerges also is the need for a better integration of approaches and disciplines: legal experts should work together with economists, sociologists, edp specialists, union and management experts to look at the issue of technological change in a global perspective, even when examining problems arising at company level.

FOOTNOTES

(1) Research carried out by L. Schneider and the author during winter 1981. For more detailed results see L. Schneider, C. Ciborra in this volume.

REFERENCES

Arrow, K.J., Political and Economic Evaluation of Social Effects and Externalities, in the Analysis of Public Output, J. Margolis (ed.) National Bureau of Economic Research, New York, 1970.

Bravermann, H., Labor and Monopoly Capital, Montly Review Press, New York, 1974.

Briefs, U., Arbeiten ohne Sinne und Perspektiven?, Köln, 1980.

Brooks, H., Science, Technology and Society in the 1980s, in Science and Technology Policy for the 80s, OECD, Paris, 1981.

Ciborra, C., Information Systems and Transactions Architecture, International Journal of Policy Analysis and Information Systems, 5, 4, december 1981.

Coase, R.H., The Problem of Social Cost, Journal of Law and Economics, 15 (1), 1960, pp. 1-44.

Dahlam, C.J., The problem of Externality, Journal of Law and Economics, 22, 1979, pp. 141-162.

Demsetz, H., Towards a Theory of Property Rights, American Economic Review, vol. LVII, 2, 1967, pp. 347-359.

Evans, J., Negotiating Technological Change, ETUI, Brussels, 1982.

Marchand, D.A., Criminal Justice Information Systems and Information Policy: the Politics of Social Costs and Technological change, PhD Thesis, UCLA, Los Angeles, 1977.

Mumford, E., Participative System Design: Structure and Method, Systems, Objectives, Solutions, 1, 1, 1981.

Nygaard, K., Bergo, O.T., The Trade Unions, New Users of Research, Personnel Review, 4, 2, 1975.

Olson, M., The Logic of Collective Action, Harvard University Press, 1965.

Stone, A., Regulation and its Alternatives, Congressional Quarterly Press, Washington D.C., 1982.

Salomon, J.J., Prométhée empetré, Pergamon Press, Paris, 1981.

Schneider, L., Ciborra, C., Bargaining technological change, in this volume.

Whisler, T.L., The Impact of Computers on Organizations, Praeger Pub., New York, 1970.

Williams, R., Mosley, R., Technology Agreements: Consensus, Control and Technical Change in the Workplace, EEC/FAST Conference on Transfer to an Information Society, Selsdon Park, January 1982.

Williamson, O.E., Transaction-cost economics: the Governance of Contractual Relations, Journal of Law and Economics, Oct. 1979, 22 (2), pp. 233-61.

Williamson, O.E., Franchise bidding for natural monopolies-in general and with respect to CATV, Bell Journal of Economics, June 1976, 7, 1, pp. 73-104.

Williamson, O.E., Markets and Hierarchies: Analysis and Antitrust Implications, The Free Press, New York, 1975.

SYSTEMS DESIGN FOR, WITH, AND BY THE USERS
U. Briefs, C. Ciborra and L. Schneider (editors)
North-Holland Publishing Company
© IFIP, 1983

CONSULTATION WITH USERS :

A NEW PARADIGM AND A NEW CULTURE

Jean-Louis RIGAL

Professor at the University
of Paris IX Dauphine

Emphasising the users' wishes and inventing the socio-technico-organisational alternatives necessary
for producing the goods or services this requires
implies a major educational effort, for each person
must learn to use his imagination and his means of
expression to the full, must learn to create new
criteria for evaluating utility and organisational
methods, but also learn to invent new paradigms and
to extend his temporal perspective. Organisational
problems concern therefore the cultural domain much
more than the technological one - and this will
become more and more true as time goes on.

1 - THE PARADIGM THAT REFUSES TO GO AWAY

When new forms of technology are introduced into an organisation,
the classical method is to start from what the scientists can do, to
produce the corresponding products, and to promote their sales, but
without taking the time to ask the question : "WHAT WILL THEY BE
USED FOR ?". The undeniable acceleration of technological progress,
contrasting with the slowness of advance in the knowledge of social
systems, contributes to such an order of events, for "the only real
problems are the scientific, technological and industrial ones" -
especially given that, however difficult these problems are, they
are relatively measurable and controllable, and we have been trained
only to solve them[1] by all our history since Plato, Gahlee, Laplace,
Taylor... But the very success of this method leads to another question : "SHOULD PRODUCTION BE AN END IN ITSELF OR SHOULD IT BE APPLIED
TO SOME OTHER AIM ?" Such a questioning underlay the events of May
1968, but was at that time premature and could not be expressed clearly ; it came into its own in the crisis of the 1970s, which was a
specifically CULTURAL crisis, caused by the discovery of the number
of "needs" - very often created by new media or semply by the fact
that elementary needs were satisfied, at least in western-Countries.
"Needs" requiring the invention of ever more numerous techniques and
forms of technology, AND NOT ONLY IN THE MECHANICAL OR PHYSICAL SPHE-
RE.

*Observing one of the "needs" is clearly equivalent to concluding that
the process of work is undemocratic, and that it is impossible to
understand the managerial system (unless one is actually a manager);
in a word, more education and more transparency are required. And
also, as far as the users are concerned, producess that are less complicated, more resistant, more convivial, and more useful.*

2 - BUT WHAT THEN ARE THE WORKERS, THE CITIZENS, THE USERS LOOKING
    FOR ?

Our culture has learnt to control the physical world of matter, of
space, of time and of mass almost as much as it wishes(1). The result
is modern technology both in its material aspects, like the physical
tools on which modern industry is based, and in its intellectual aspects, the concepts and paradigms employed. It has thus largely solved the problems of agriculture and hence those of famine and of many
diseases.

*This was a necessary stage, for basic needs must have priority. But
the very success of modern technology makes it now possible to consider other needs that are less easily defined and measured, and to
have some hope of satisfying them. Man is more than a behaviorist mon-
key, more than homo economicus.*

Two problems still remain :

a. <u>Do needs even exist</u> ? And if so, what are they ? How are they to
be defined ? Who has the power to define them ? (It is clear that
being able to define needs - in however implicit a fashion - is perhaps the subtlest but the purest form of power). This problem is thus
essentially a political one, one that amounts to the overall choices
made by society but also to the very exercise of power.

b. <u>Are the present paradigms sufficient to meet the challenge of the
future</u> ? Are current material technology and the conceptions gover-
ning it sufficient, even with adaptations ? Or should other means be
created ? If so, FOR WHOM, BY WHOM, HOW, AND AT WHAT PRICE ?

What are the workers, the citizens, the users then looking for ? How
can one obtain an answer is a difficult question.

<u>First response</u> : To ask them the question and analyse their replies.
This is an interesting method ; and even the elections even those
that are apparently the most political (in the narrow sense) deal
with the major choices of society, the priority of expectations and
needs. But it is also a fragile method. Any sociologist knows that
questions influence the answers, and that the whole of our production -
obsessed and mercantile culture twists it even further (POWER IS THERE-
FORE, IN THE LAST ANALYSIS, THE ART OF ASKING "THE" RIGHT QUESTIONS).
Moreover, the overwhelming majority of citizens and workers cannot
even as we will see below imagine alternative ways of life and alternative needs (it is no coincidence that the debatable method of
"scenarios" is reserved for "experts"). The only replies are then
"A BIT MORE OF EVERYTHING, and a BETTER QUALITY", or "TOTAL REVOLU-
TION". Both are excuses for conservatism ; they also ignore the opportunities offered by the new forms of technology.
It goes without saying that laziness, conservatism and fear fuelled
by unemployment and bu the short-term predictability of socio-economic perspectives do not encourage people to devote a greater energy
to imagination, fun, and freedom. Which of us don't imitate the
Great Inquisitor's(2) reaction of Christ, and don't place our trust
in the ability of technostructure to produce bread (at the price of
a loss of freedom) ? The advertising industry - whose functions are
to sell, with varying degrees of success, what has been produced and
to invent dreams helping people to accept everyday reality - is hardly concerned with needs ; except in order to create new ones in line
with the product being sold.

Second response : to ask through some DELFI method, the technocrats.
("These people generally rich, at least in sociocultural terms -
know better than others what they need.") But such a method leads to
similar dead ends, the only difference being that technological
breakthroughs are easier to take into account, and that we have thus
given mixed responses.

Third answer : to pay no attention to the question. This method results
in the manufacturing of goods and services without any regard to
their use or social utility, according to the customary justification
that this method is the only one that is fast enough to be able to
compete with the dominant-Anglo-Saxon or Japanese - industry (and
therefore culture) on their own terms. This produces the well-known
consumer society, whose limits are all the better demonstrated by its
frenetic pursuit of over-exploited lines but also by its neglect of
other lines that would be useful and therefore economically profitable. But this is precisely where we think that the French (the European) genius is best able to hold its own, for we are in our own culture, amongst human and personal concerns, and not in the domain of
the latest Taylorist fads thrown up by the Gury of Boston.

The concept of need is thus ambiguous, and one could also talk of social expectation, of social lacks to be catered for, or of potential
to be developed. In any case we saw that it is linked with our culture. This is all the more relevant because meaningful communication
between individuals and social partners and participation in satisfying work seem to be essential needs. This applies to both the European area and the countries of the Third World (a greater number
of cultures killed by contempt than by guns).

Modern man is subject to three psychological blocks (to use yet another term) :

. Work thought of as a sanction and no longer as creative for the
workman, as a punishment rather than as a means of personal achievement and of production. The origins of the vocabulary of work are
very revealing in this connection (1),(3).

. Contempt for everything which "cannot" be stored in a computer's
memory (4), because it can't be reduced to space, time and mass, and
thus is not of a physical nature. We are muchless capable of producing a social balance-sheet than an accountant's one (even if it is
clear that the meaning and interpretation of the latter are very
ambiguous, and largely subject to the intention of the persons producing and interpreting it). The only social balance-sheet we have
is a stereotyped one, imposed from above, with only numerical va-
lue(s), and therefore rarely consulted and taken into account.
KNOWING HOW TO READ EXISTING DATA, KNOWING HOW TO READ ALTERNATIVE
DATA ARE THE VERY LOCUS OF POWER and consequently the locus where
conflict and consensus are really situated

.The absence - unfortunately only too characteristic of France - of
any consultation at the appropriate moment concerning the processes
of work, of production or of their aims and evaluation.
(Ledren's paper will insist on it).French Cartesianism and Napoleonic
centralisation combine here only too well with the mechanisms of Taylorism.

Once more, we notice the preeminence of culture. The blocks, which
seem psychological, are in fact - culturel ones (we have also shown-

(3) that its apex is the concept of time and duration) :

Il is difficult to participate in a prospective of planification if we are not able to consider alternatives ways, and their possible evolution in the years to come, if our "temporal horizon" is short.

3 - CONSULTATION AND PARTICIPATION

Planing doesn't consist of in accumulating hypercomplex mathematical models that are incomprehensible even for their constructors, but of encouraging discussion of aims. If the models of Operational Research are necessary to optimise the functioning of a complex organisation with multiple and unanalysable interactions, there remains one problem : OPTIMISING WHAT ? The essential question is here, prevailing or preceding all the others. The rest is mere fine-tuning! Planning, then, on all levels, in all directions, for any stretch of the future ; by everyone, either directly or via representatives (some reality must often be sacrified and betrayed by mediation but for the sake of greater cohesion and coherence. A point that can be debated, given that the problem does not have a unique solution)

Experiments are also necessary, taking into account the following two risks :

1. An experiment on a localised area may be far from reflecting the general situation.
2. A great deal of time may be lost. THERE IS ALSO THE DIFFICULTY OF KNOWING HOW AND BY WHOM THE RESULTS SHOULD BE ANALYSED.

Difficult problems indeed, but primordial ones. It is often better to take one's time to produce a really useful object than to keep "sprinting" in order to turn out things that will be as usless as turned out by others and end up on a rubbish dump, for they are more cumbersome than useful for human communication...
Concorde is not the only example here ; one can quote ready-to-use factories as well as gadgets that are more unwieldy than useful for human communication.

One can also only wonder why firms have been so little studied (especially in France). Certainly, much has been written on unskilled workers (at a moment when their number is reducing, at least apparently) and on their alienation ; BUT LITTLE ON THE RELATIONSHIP BETWEEN CULTURAL MODELS, MANAGEMENT METHODS, AND WORKING METHODS. And yet this is near the heart of the matter. The most limited survey - 8 days in Tokyo and 8 in Silicon Valley - has demonstrated the basic fact, too often ignored, that a good organisation is one that is modelled on the dominant culture(s).

More specifically :

a) A single model does not exist : *our civilisation should be defined by its capacity to adapt methods to cultures.* In other words, people living in differend cultures should be helped to produce their own organisational models (from which they will deduce the sorts of technology they have to - whether it be material, structural or conceptual).

b) *In particular, neither the Harvard model (reproduced throughout the French educational system), nor the model of the mythical Japanese Industry and Employment Ministry is well adapted to our skill ;*

*thus the model to imitate or even to transpose does not exist. And
here we are at the very nub of the problem :*

4 - THE INTERACTION BETWEEN CULTURE, TECHNIQUES, ACTORS, AND ORGANI-
SATIONAL METHODS

No technique is ever neutral, for there is always the preponderant
influence of a culture and an organisational method.
Certainly, as Toffler has shown(5), the tremendous progress in the
technology of information processing - and in particular that of
computers - allows organisations to be run in a rich and decentralised manner, and allows various aspects of reality to be studied (unlike the first-generation computers, with their pitiful thousands of
memories). But is that sufficient, even with the help of "American
good sense", to guarantee that the "Third Wave" will be characterised
by self-management and happiness, as Toffler believes so whole heart-
edly ? Technological progress in hardware (and, to a lesser degree,
software) implies such a radiant future ; but without organisational,
social, cultural, political and psychological conditions, technology
will not lead to the free expression and full participation of each
individual in his destiny(6). One example will be sufficient to show
this : it has often been said that power derives from knowledge even
more so nowadays than from the accumulation of capital (even if those
in control of power are more or less the same in both cases), and
particularly from the art of defining and interpreting data/models.

This is certainsly true if by "interpreting" we mean the attempt to
really understand data/models, to detect the underlying hypotheses, to
know which aspects of reality have been emphasised and which ignored.
But "interpreting" also means the attempt to write and to speak in
terms of other constraints and other aims than those promoted by 2000
years of Platonism and scientism. *(I do not believe that science is
evil : what is dangerous is a false scientism claiming that the results
of a "calculation" follow automatically - by mathematical or algorithmic Divine Right - without any consideration of the underlying
hypotheses).* Language, and in particular its mathematical variety, is
therefore an essential tool for understanding and acting, provided
that it is not the unseeing language of a purely formal grammar, for-
malided in such a way as to rule out automatically any human and social meaning (as the French information-processing school tries to
do). "Interpreting" does not mean merely "decoding a message the meaning of which escapes us". It means, understanding its clearly and
fully.

We have just spoken about "culture". It is clear that the very nub of
the whole question is a cultural one, insofar as it concerns what
should be considered as the most important aim, and insofar as it involves our whole history, our whole tradition, our whole education,
on a deeper level our whole method of rationalising (as shown by
Weissenbaum, Bjorn, Anderson, Gailbraith, J.L. Rigal and a large number of other publications, well known to the members of W69-I).

5 - A MAJOR FORM OF TECHNOLOGY : SEMANTICS AND CULTURE

*I would like to emphasise here that if "technology" means any exten-
sion of our body leading to a better understanding and better action,
there are many sorts of technology going from the most material ones
(telescopes, computers) to the most intellectual ones (software,
data/models, organisational methods, paradigms..)*

Even thus culture can be considered not only as linked with technologies but to be by itself a technology.

It is perhaps the intellectual ones, being the closest to the human
and social worlds(8), which require most participation from everyone(9).

We have thus already established an inventory of some of the obstacles
preventing the users from expressing themselves.

Expression is rarely allowed (in France). Or - if it is - it is as a very
recent development, and one is obliged to use the same semantics, the
same data, the same method of rationalisation as the producers and
the creators of industrial paradigms. We cannot therefore expect very
much, as long as the users have not been educated (or self-educated)
to see further than the immediate perspective. Of course, they must
participate   in adequate educational system, or otherwise they will
be mentally strait-jacketed from the beginning.

6 - THE SITUATION IN FRANCE

An almost complete lack of negociation/industrial democraty/consulta-
tion/participation (the terms are permutable). Why ?
Three reasons may be evoked :

. The Mediterranean preference for conflict rather than consultation
(even if "talking-shops" are very often used in the South of the
Mediterranean area) ; we may add that it is particularly difficult
to establish a consensus in a country where there is so much social
inequality : power, money, knowledge and education are all in the
same hands.

. The above point is especially important : even now, there is no
educational system at all by with   for the workers (or trade unioners)
or by the users. Comparison with other countries or with other experiences - quoted throughout this Congress - would be too horifying
to contemplate here.

. Because of the lack of responsability and education, it follows
that perhaps the most important obstacle to both more equality and
more industrial participation resides in inequalities in the ability
to contemplate extended perspectives - in both space and time. How
can one propose a substitute for production-lines, other socio-
technico-cultural modes, if one cannot see further than the compart-
mentalised and repetitive work that occupies all one's time, if one's
perspective is foreshortened ? This would seem to be the major point,
and our whole system of education (including the education that consists of participating in the work-process) must have as priority
to meet this challenge, which once again is an educational one (but
which means a better distribution of power and the right for each
person to be different).

The recent "SCIENCE OF ORGANISATIONS MEETING" we organised in Paris
in November 1982 proposed such a methodology (priority to expectations/
needs over technological/scientific problems : how to educate citizens,
workers and users to accept progressively the theory and practice of
democracy and participation in system design by, with and for the
users). The route towards such a result was shown to be long and difficult... : it was decided to create a large number of committees,
and these will make suggestions in their own good time, with the result that the present industrial structure will still prevail for a
long while ! (This consultation may fall into the trap of resembling

the caricature of consultation at Velizy - but that is another sto-
ry !) As the crux of the matter is cultural, it will take a long
time for change to be visible in people's mentalities, in theoretical
paragdigms and in practical methods : but at least the bell has
been rung now. If the bell is not to fall on deaf ears, enlightened
users must try to convince the technocrats that the problems is urgent and that it cannot be solved by were administrative and technocratic methods.

7 - SOME KEY PRIORITIES IN RESEARCH AND DEVELOPMENT(7) :

a) *To draw up an inventory and analyse various aspects of reality*,
taking into account the fact that the myth of the single model is
the arch-enemy (What is known as the "one best way" in Taylorism -
or neo-Taylorism).

b- *To obtain new data, in line with new constraints or new expectations, which also serves to get rid of part of the wasteful redundancy of present data and models.*

To improve the semantics of each organisation, by appointing specialists in what could be called "data administration"(9), would seem
essential, both in order to avoid the expense of redundancy and in-
coherence and to allow each participant, each social partner to define, the "data" that conform to his own aspirations and to see them
accepted. This should be possible without one's being always obliged
to take into account the dominant data, whose limits and limitations
we have already seen. A long and difficult task, it is true ! But
one that is essential to "industrial democracy"(10), which we all
hold dear. And which assumes that each person accepts that responsible for, his work, his "production", and his temporal perspective.
He himself getsresponsible for his destiny (must be autonomous).

c) *In order to permit such a freedom, an educational system must be
set up catering for both full-time and professional students*
- Allowing each person, citizen and worker, to free himself from the
jargon used by technicians (everybody does economics and management
without thinking about it) and too create counter-languages and coun-
ter-models, as well as socio-technico-organisational alternatives(12)
(all the better given that technical objects are so cheap and so flexible now that they are becoming, or will become, more and more accessible). That is, a system which will replace the Napoleonic centralisation by a situation where everyone is encouraged to communicate and
express himself. "Being able to read oneself and express what we are,
as in the title of a Master's Degree in Information Processing Applied
to Management(9) which is just starting at the university of Dauphine,
after nearly ten years of hesitation.

d) *Making communication easier is primordial.*(11) This implies an effort at lucidity by the specialists, so that they can isolate from
their techniques the way in which they translate/transform reality problem
to be solved - in short they must TO MAKE THEIR HYPOTHESES ABSOLUTELY
EXPLICIT. Technology that is regarderdin this way, that is stripped of
its high level of technicity, becomes a science that is easy to understand ; an effort at popularisation is moreover necessary, especially
in the form of television programmes (general system,or for circula-
tion within the company) and written material. "Each one of us exercises management all the time without thinking about it". THE ESSEN-
TIAL CHOICE IS THAT OF AIMS AND THEIR COMMUNICATION, RATHER THAN THE
LONG JUSTIFICATORY CALCULATIONS THAT FOLLOWS THEM (to say this is not
to underestimate the role of calculations and their difficulty, but

to simplify their control by all and for all).

5) *The role of the managers (and we are all managers) is decisive here.* Each person must be assessed not only in terms of his command of a more or less highly specialized form of technology and of his passion for keeping knowledge secret. HE MUST BE ABOVE ALL ASSESSED BY HIS CAPACITY TO LISTEN TO OTHERS AND TO PARTICIPATE IN THE SETTING UP OF TECHNOLOGY DERIVED COLLECTIVELY FROM ALL THE VARIETIES OF KNOW-HOW, WHICH MUST NO LONGER BE CONTROLLED BY THE HARDWARE MANU-FACTURERS, BUT MUST BECOME THE PROPERTY OF E VERYONE(12)

8 - PATIENCE ... AND BOLDNESS

Of course, all this implies long negociations and necessary and legitimate conflicts : it implies also the birth of a new science, and a new system of organisation. No participant must see his rights infringed, or be rejected on the pretext that he does not speak "correctly(13). We must therefore first learn how to listen, at the risk of recreating the Tower of Babel, (which incidentally was n ot entirely a bad thing ; and indeed are we not already all in a Tower of Babel where nobody understands anybody, except perhaps for a few initiates who master the dominant language ?). And first, let the least semantically favoured people be able to co-opt experts. Even if these experts need to be found and trained. In the same way as it is necessary to train researchers who are multidisciplinary because they are not enslaved by a single dominant culture and who are on the service of the users. Which implies first a reform of the Boards of Direction of firms at all levels ; and a reform of the whole system of Teaching and Research. But this also implies a r eal desire by a large enough number of researchers, especially coming from the trade-unions (unfortunately in France there is not even a union-financed labour research centre !) - to pursue a career which at present cannot be recognised as "serious", because of the ways in which researchers are assessed (that is number of publications in "serious" periodicals, or string-pulling by well-placed people).

REFERENCES :

(1) - J.L. RIGAL, Faits et données de la Civilisation Occidentale, Lesseps, 1978.
(2) - DOSTOIEVSKY, The legend of the grand inquisitor in "The Brothers Karamazov (1880)
(3) - J.L. RIGAL, Le temps du travail, 1983.
(4) - Colloque International C.N.R.S. : "La Quantification en Sciences Sociales" (1978, Brive-la-Gaillarde)
(5) - TOFFLER : The Third Wave
(6) - J.L. RIGAL, Gérer... enfin, Revue Terminal n° 9, 1982.
(7) - Assises des Sciences des Organisations, Paris, 1982
(8) - J.L. RIGAL, La régulation socio-culturelle, Publ. Collège de France, Paris, 1978.
(9) - J.L. RIGAL, La fonction "administration des données", Lesseps, 1981
(10)- J.L. RIGAL, Brave New Dataware, IFIP, Tokyo/ Towards Data cons-cious citizen (IFIP Melbourne) 1980.
(11)- Colloque Informatique et Travail, Lesseps, Paris, 1980.
(12)- Mike COOLEY, The bee and the architect
(13)- G. ORWELL, 1984 (and its definition of Langsoc) Londres, 1944

EXPERIENCES WITH GENERAL USERS' PARTICIPATION

SYSTEMS DESIGN FOR, WITH, AND BY THE USERS
U. Briefs, C. Ciborra and L. Schneider (editors)
North-Holland Publishing Company
© IFIP, 1983

SYSTEMS DESIGNERS AND USERS IN A PARTICIPATIVE DESIGN PROCESS

SOME FICTIONS AND FACTS

Peter Mambrey and Barbara Schmidt-Belz

Gesellschaft für Mathematik und Datenverarbeitung,
St. Augustin, Schloß Birlinghoven,
Federal Republik of Germany

In a commonplace twist of rethoric, the world is always divided into
two classes of people. I have heard, for example, that there are those
who count beans and those who grow beans.
(Edward Wenk 1982)

Usually, in the literature of participative systems design chances and
problems are discussed theoretically, or with respect to a specific case
procedures, methods etc. are positively described. This paper is to look
behind the scenes of a design process. It will still be a rather unstructured report on a variety of actually experienceable problems
turning much that is traded as facts into fictions. For the present we
shall confine ourselves to systems designers and users (persons affected).
This report is intended to be input to an exchange of experience at
practical level.

INTRODUCTION

The discussions on participation of clients and employees in systems design use to lead
to the call for better approaches, tools and methods of systems design (Hawgood/
Land/Mumford 1978) and the call for increased codetermination of users (e.g.
technology agreements) (ÖTV 1980). These calls are certainly justified, but one should
be well aware of the fact that users and systems designers do not fully utilise existing
rights or available facilities.

Within a systems development we - the design team - attempted to carry out a participative design with the goal to enable the users within the existing formal codetermination facilities in West Germany to exert an optimum influence on the course and the
result of the design process. It was not intended to prove that the existing codetermination rights were sufficient, but to gather experiences in the application of participative methods and tools. This experiment was financed by the GMD (Governmental
dp-research organisation) as a research and development project. The goal was to
develop an information system to assist the administration of a school and to
implement a prototype. This should be done by permanent involvement of those, who
are affected (secretaries, teachers, school-mamangement, parents and pupils). The
system should a) improve the working-situation for the administrative staff b) reduce
administrative tasks of the teachers c) quickly provide actual information for planning
and organisation d) and improve services for the pupils and parents
(Breiling/Haunhorst/Mambrey 1980). During the development process, the users
participated by direct interaction, group discussions, works councils, attending
information events of various kinds (regular meetings, presentations etc.).
Furthermore there was a representative of the users who, following the idea of the
advocacy planner (Davidoff 1965), was a member of the project team and was paid for
this additional work.

Attempts of the project team to shift contractual responsibilities from the management to the users failed for legal reasons and as a result of the opposition of the management. Nevertheless we considered the attempt to carry out the project even under these conditions to be of practical use. Users often realise too late the fact that they are affected, they are rarely active and frequently leave the representation of their interests to the trade unions. Our work aimed at informing the users themselves permanently so that they would early realise their state of being affected, that they would be able to form their own opinion about the innovation and its impacts and that they would use the facilties of participation provided or find their own forms of action. If the users themselves safeguard their interests, it is to be expected that this will support their representatives and lead to the call for a greater amount of influence. In its very essence the approach aims at a close cooperation and communication between users and systems designers and constitutes a grass-root-oriented approach with a small number of formal bodies for decision making.

From the variety of the experiences so far collected we like to put stress on one aspect which seems very important to us and which the discussion on participative systems design has so far considered too little: the systems designers in interaction with the users.

We assume that in a participative design process it is heavily dependent on systems designers whether and to which extent users are able to influence the development. Despite of all analysis and programming rules the systems designers do not only carry out a plan, but usually organise the development process and design the system and its environment in accordance with their own environment, knowledge, ability, and ambition. They have freedoms of design, and it is necessary to increase the control by users and clients so that a system corresponding to their wishes will be created. Based on actual experience it is shown clearly which difficulties systems designers meet in a participative design. Furthermore, it is indicated why systems designers act in a participation-stunting or -supporting manner.

IDEAS AND ATTITUDES AT THE OUTSET OF THE PROJECT

In the phase preceding the cooperation with the users the systems designers met for discussing basic objectives of the project. There were computer scientists, management scientists, and social scientists. Soon it was agreed upon that in most systems design processes the requirements of the users had so far been considered too little. It was assumed that the projects were fixed only to management aims or technical aspects. Therefore, the wish to involve the users permanently was recognized. Participation would ensure that the users would be able to introduce actively their requirements and interests into the design process and therefore the system would be more in accordance with their interests. It was assumed that the opportunity of participation would be welcomed by the users.

The existing possibilities of participation and the additional participation procedures should allow an articulation of interests and should be used in conflicts between users and management for reaching sound agreements. Some designers understood themselves as mediators between users and mangement, others as advocates of the users thus having a strong user bias.

The joint transformation of the approach into a work plan showed diverging ideas among the project team. Attitudes ranged somewhere between three extreme positions: The theory of planning considered it possible to place all tasks to be accomplished in a project into neatly bundled work packages whose relation to each other were of a temporal (before, after, in parallel) or logical (subtasks, no relation), at all events, clear nature.

The division into phases, milestones, mechanisms of documentation and control as well as a set of methods and a variety of forms should complete planning and secure a successful project. This was in contradiction to another theoretical orientation that required discussions towards the objects of the project, the approach, and group dynamic aspects. Study of literature and reference to experiences gathered by other projects seemed necessary. Methods should be selected in accordance with the objectives and they should not correspond to the usual patterns. Processing according to a fixed plan would be inconsistent with the necessity of flexibility being a prerequisite for any consideration of user requirements. Another strongly pragmatical attitude existed among the project team according to which it was useless to make detailed plans and it would be better to begin working practically. In the course of the discussion, a compromise including elements of all three positions was found. This compromise turned out to be successfull and now nobody of the team would agree to one of these extreme positions.

In the discussions problems of interdisciplinary work became evident. Apart from the lack of understanding there was an overestimation of the other sciences. The reason for many misunderstandings was that the colleague from another discipline did not provide the expected achievements, e.g. the social scientists said: "In view of the state of the art this realisation should not be difficult at all", the computer scientist said: "As social scientist one should simply know how to settle this conflict".

These problems resulted from the different background of experience, the different discipline-related interests but also from political attitudes. In the course of time it was however possible to reconcile the different viewpoints considerably.

Research findings and experiences of other systems design groups being available in literature were considered sceptically. This might be explained by the fact

- that frequently only positive experiences with methods, tools or strategies of participation are described and that in view of the expected problems the reported positive experiences were not believed.

- that portability was not realised since the situational factors, the environmental conditions in general, were quite different (the organisations, user groups, hardware, system goals etc.). Systems design was regarded as an original act of creation.

- that the prevailing idea of division of labour was in short as follows: The natural scientists are concerned with hard facts = technical problems (hardware + software) and the social scientists treat soft facts = social problems (users, organisation of work and decision-making). This initially rigid separation was quickly abandoned and only occured again in the programming phase against the desire of all. Those who began with programming had no longer the time to carry out field-related activities. As a consequence some new problems appeared, e.g. reproaches towards the analysts. It was said that they elaborated the requirements of the system unprecisely, for example, in the case of repeated revision of programs.

For some members it was unusual at the outset to have a political discussion on information processing and its impacts. Initially there were different evaluations in this respect, namely regarding the influence systems designers may exercise and their responsibility. They considered themselves competent and responsible for technical quality, e.g. of software production. With respect to applicational conditions the responsibility was assigned to the management and the users or the representatives of the latter. It was said that these were rather political issues which were hard to influence. In the course of the discussion it was however agreed upon that this should also be a subject of the design process. An early problem reduction and a quick acceptance of supposed or actual constraints would constitute a substantial shortcoming. This would stunt creativity and reduce the chances of finding actual alternatives.

This was the reason why at the outset and in the course of the project non-project-specific questions of computer application were also discussed. The systems designers assumed an affirmative, but very critical attitude towards information processing: Are we abused for opening up new applications to information technology without an actual need, but only for selling products? Do we design a well working and accepted product with the support and by the users, which later on will then be imposed on other users? May we or the users influence the future conditions of application? What will come after the project when the innovation will have been performed. To what extent is it possible to define the future working environment? What are the advantages or disadvantages of the system from the user's point of view? Are we allowed to design without being sure that the advantages prevail?

The discussions in the project reflected the discussions in society on the chances of office automation but also on its negative impacts such as unemployment, dequalification, smaller salaries, taylorism etc.. These controversial and critical disputes made it later on hard for the project team to do persuasive work as promotors. The reactions of the users to critical statements were fairly negative: everybody is promising something positive and they are doubting themselves, probably they are unexperienced!

EXPERIENCES WITH USERS

The approach to involve the users in all phases of system development was not demanded by them. It was put forward by the project team. We met quite different reactions of the users to this proposal. The decision makers (management) took that for granted. Without their expertise it would be impossible to develop this system, furthermore they would be formally responsible anyway. Among the other employees quite different opinions were expressed. This reached from goodwill through lack of understanding to criticism. They were all sceptical, criticism was prevailing. In our opinion this was to be explained by the fact that participation was not in accordance with everyday experience, in particular, with the decision-making in the organisation. Decisions were taken by the management. Employees being of special expertise were consulted if required. Therefore, participation was understood as "being consulted".

The criticism was explained quite differently:

1) Participation would be useless since you cannot exert any influence anyway. In this context we found out that the lower the status was in the hierarchy the less was the assessment of possible influence.
2) Extremely few users would have the competence to take appropriate decisions, they lacked the knowledge required for having a say. This was imputed to users by other users, but also said as self-assessment. Both groups would prefer that the management decided as it did in the past.
3) This was also preferred by users who feared that the individual interests of dominant persons would be considered to a greater extent. For these users the management guaranteed the overall interest.

In a more generalised way, the experiences are as follows: Only a small number of users and the representative of the secretaries regarded participation in the whole process as important, but almost all wanted to participate in the decision whether the completed product would be used or not. The indication that then the point of no return would probably be already past was accepted, but the attitudes remained unchanged. First the project team interpreted these attitude as "typical consumer behaviour". Certainly, this was one of the influencing factors, but the reasons may rather be found in the non-perceived state of being affected, the refusal of technology and its application or simply the disinterest. An aspect which is of central importance to the systems designers is often only a marginal problem among many others for the users.

This was still increased by an understanding of division of labour which was inconsistent with any close cooperation. The systems designers were regarded as experts who had to solve this problem on the basis of their expertise, exactly in the same way as any other person being responsible for his functional area.

Whether these attitudes changed, can be reported only with respect to those who entered in active cooperation.

The first discussions with user groups were intended to deal with general goals, task areas affected and special requirements of the information system. This was however impossible. Initially the users discussed with us quite generally problems of privacy, rationalisation effects of industrial robots, enslavement of people by machines and cost aspects, e.g. the money required for computers should rather be spent for helping aged persons. Then the project team was asked for details, e.g. how a DP support would look like for them and which improvements could be gained. Altogether, they expected to be confronted with a detailed plan (systems requirements) whose advantages and disadvantages could be discussed. That this plan should be the result of joint efforts, was accepted, but the project team was accused of lack of conception and experience. It would have been easy to present plausible examples of positive DP impacts. However, the project team feared that such examples anticipated future system goals to a too great extent. This fear proved subsequently to be justified. The only example we presented, the printing of certificates by means of computer, was again and again discussed controversially and passionately though afterwards nobody mentioned this as a requirement of the system.

The systems designers considered the first discussion a smaller disaster. They were forced into the role of describing the future system positively not yet knowing which activities should be supported by the system, which hardware would be available, how the work could be organised and so on. Global objectives, such as enlarged jobs for the secretaries, were not sufficient for satisfying the information requirements and for forming an opinion on the side of the user. The users wanted to know in a far more concrete manner whether and how their activities might change. Since we did not intend to proceed like salesmen, and since we wanted to inform in a realistic way we could answer many questions only very vaguely or not at all. The promise to answer these questions at a later time and the argument that many of the questions asked at the moment could only be answered as a result of joint work satisfied the users insofar as they did not boycott further cooperation. Why didn't they boycott? For the first time the designers realised a fact, which became evident again and again during the design process: the lack of methods, mistakes, or "bad work" of the team met the good-will of the users. The reason for this good-will is, that the interaction between users and systems designers has been transformed during the development to a personal relation.

In the further cooperation, i.e. analysis and design of system requirements, choice of hardware, contracts to protect the secretaries against deterioration, implementation, training and system revision, mainly those people participated whose activities were changed by innovation, furthermore, the formally responsible decision makers (management and representatives of secretaries), employees and clients being active in other school matters as well or being technically interested.

In the course of the design process we were repeatedly confronted with difficulties the users had: Users could not understand why a design process takes quite a long time. In particular, they regarded the period between first discussions, analyses, selections of alternatives, and realisations as too long. Thus we could not rely on an increasing amount of information on the side of the users, but the information had to be supplied again and again. On the other hand, many users felt overloaded with information. In particular, it was difficult for the users to select alternatives. They wanted to know from the experts which alternative would be the best. In difficult problems all participants were happy if they were able to agree upon one solution though it could not be checked if it was the best one.

The assumption the users would introduce their requirements and interests by participation also proved to be too naive in our opinion. The users feared the transparency of their interests, they did not only consider and express their own interests, but vicariously they also looked after supposed or actual interests of other persons and groups. Furthermore, we gained the impression that often ideals or modern topics were formulated, but not one's own needs. The "altruism" of many users was surprising. Though presenting individual needs, they never neglected the overall objective of the organisation (efficient provision of services) and introduced it everywhere. The requirements to be met by the system seemed to be a tradeoff between these two factors worked out in the head of the user.

The willingness of the designers to consider the requirements and ideas of the users led to a constant increase of the expectations some users placed in the system and its organisational integration. In our opinion some requirements were of an extremely high standard both with respect to their realisation and their subsequent handling.

Altogether, it could be stated that by the good cooperation between all parties a relationship of personal confidence in the systems designers had been established. This had a limiting effect on active participation. As a consequence the users thought that the systems designers would inform and invite them for negotiating if something important was under consideration. Thus, the users became rather passive and reacted only to inputs delivered by the team instead of participating actively. The control of the systems designers by the users was thus reduced. The team did not know how to react. Should it provoke a conflict, should it produce uncertainty?

SYSTEMS DESIGNERS AND PARTICIPATIVE APPROACH

After this description of the atmosphere prevailing among the users we would like to deal with the systems designers in more detail.

At the beginning of this paper we reported shortly on designers' discussions on IT and its social evaluation. The attitude of the project team was initially of a rather defensive nature. First of all the designers wanted to avoid negative impacts and then to make specific proposals (participation, user friendliness, job enlargement etc.) feasible and to prove this feasibility.

Furthermore, and that was certainly of equal importance, the whole task was considered interesting and regarded as a chance of advancing one's own career. This orientation, the self-interest, had strong effects on the approach. Since the systems designers thus felt firmly connected with the achievement of the goal (=good system, satisfied users), the critical problems discussed within the team were formulated as input for the users in a reduced form only or not at all. Another consequence was the specific preparation of decision-making. It always aimed at reaching a suitable compromise for further work and not to push forward specific interests. Frequently the interests of the users and the management were anticipated and a compromise was formulated as proposal instead of showing actual alternatives. Apart from the decisions on general concept, requirements, and hardware it was difficult to show all points of decision to be discussed alternatively. The whole development process turned out to be a permanent decision-making on details whose future importance to the development was partly unclear. Just this permanent decision-making on details, which was often done uncritically by the systems designers since it was not realised at all that the specific problem constituted a point of decision, characterised system development and its result. We think that in this context the very preparation of decision-making is of great importance and constitutes the system designer's freedom of design.

For reaching the goal, namely the implementation, the approach pursued was more similar to an appeasement than to a strategy of systems design evocating conflicts. It was however not only the success-oriented self-interest of systems designers which influenced the approach, but also ideals being specific to their profession. The requirements of the users were sometimes regarded as being very simple, and the designers shrinked from realising such "primitive, short-sighted and obsolete solutions". This was still increased by another consequence of the same cause: Partly there was a tendency to solve problems perfectly or to realise advanced software technology ideas with great efforts so that the aim of merely realising user ideas was sometimes likely to come second to identified new and technically interesting tasks.

The professional socialisation of systems designers had still another disruptive effect on the participative approach. Superficially it could be regarded as difficulty of understanding among users and systems designers. Exaggerating we could compare the situation of an external systems designer in an organisation with respect to his contacts with the users to the problems of a European ethnologist among Eskimos. But unlike the latter case the two groups speak the same language. The designers perceived these difficulties of understanding in a quite different way. Two examples are to illustrate it:

a) To our questions we received answers we could not make suitable as input to the design at all or only with great difficulties.

b) The reactions of the users to actions or results were often rather surprising for the designers.

What was the reason for these difficulties which we could partly reduce only after a longer period of cooperation.

Case a) it may be assumed that systems designers have quite specific ideas of the quality and the precision of an answer. They ask questions in order to get information input for a specific, well-defined aspect, e.g. a working process. This thorough differentiation of individual segments was not familiar to the users. In their answers they described a mixture of overall contexts and individual aspects and explained relations which were not asked by the systems designers since they were not required for their task.

Case b) used to occur when the systems designers presented a suggested solution or a specific programme after lengthy, troublesome preparations and were confronted with disinterest, acceptance of the work as being trivial or criticism of marginal details as reactions of the users. The users seemed to ignore the work involved and instead of receiving appreciation the systems designers were confronted with new requirements or problems. The consequence was a temporarily deep frustration among the designers about the "ignorant" users.

What is behind these difficulties of understanding? It has to be stated that there is no identity of interests among systems designers and users. The interest of designers is focussed on the design of the system and its environment while the interest of the users is concentrated on increasing the convencience and satisfaction of their work. Though information technology changes the way of working, it is, as tool, only of marginal importance to the understanding of the user. At his office desk the user, for example, regards the writing of letters or the preparation of statistics as activity and not the handling of a system.

During the whole development process the systems designers had, futhermore, to struggle with rather methodic problems for which little or no information on how to act was available: Interest and competence of acting as well as technical knowledge by the participants are not given a priori, but have to be initiated or furthered by learning processes. Hardly any practicable methods are known. This is still complicated by the fact that individual clients are quasi beyond the reach of the systems designers. Additionally in the early planning phase the state of being affected has to be anticipated by the users.

Problems of understanding among designers and users have already been mentioned. But there are some more: Apart from giving vague scenarios or assumptions it is almost impossible for the designers to assess future impacts of the system precisely and in relation to a person or group of persons. By that we do not mean the economic cost-benefit analysis, but statements on rather qualitative aspects and the further development in the organisation.

Another still unsolved problem is how to achieve participation over a longer period of time and not only sporadically. The undeterminacy of objectives and the duration of the participative development process are in contradiction with the users' needs for concrete information about the system and its functions and impacts on him and with respect to the quick realisation of solutions.

This is still aggravated by the fact that even by participative systems design the general problem of software production, namely the quick aging of software and the software revisions, cannot be reduced. A direct realisation of the system-related users needs can further lead to a status-quo-orientation of the product. By the temporal difference of analysis and implementation one may obtain a product which is already out of date when it is installed.

CONCLUSIONS

As a conclusion of our experiences we want to point out two problem areas, which cannot be solved solely by improved methods and tools and by giving more rights to the users.

This includes

a) problems of interaction between systems designers and users which do not only constitute a matter of good methods or tools but which rather are severely dependent on personnel and quality factors, such as involvement, style, interest, professional ideals, social competence, social responsibility, creativity, willingness to learn and ability to critisise mentioning only some of them.

b) environmental influences in terms of social policy related ideas of information technology and working environment which are not realised as such or which are not discussed in development. These determinants restrict the design process and lead to conventional solutions without requiring precise target data or decision-making by the management's veto which would have to be counterbalanced by increased codetermination. The environmental influences consist in overall society ideas of the goals of techno-logical innovation (increased efficiency or humanisation of working environment), the reasons for technological innovation (problem solution or profiteering), the kind of production (individual or social benefit) etc.

It should be the goal of future approaches to enable the users to play an active and predominant role in the design process. But improved methods and tools and technology agreements are not sufficient. Nowadays we realise a lack of development, discussion and establishment of qualitative targets, e.g. for an alternative organisation of work. Alternative to taylorism, "which devalue the human contribution, reject human skill, and attempt to set up systems from which human intervention is excluded" (Rosenbrock 1980, p.9). Job enlargement or job enrichment only minimises the negative impacts of fragmented and trivialised jobs on the users. To find new targets and solutions seems for us to be an important task for the future.

REFERENCES

Breiling, Adolf/Hubert Haunhorst/Peter Mambrey (1979):
Partizipative Entwicklung eines schulinternen Informationssystems zur Unterstützung schulischer Arbeitsbereiche durch Datenverarbeitung.
Birlinghoven.

Davidoff, Paul (1965):
Advocacy and Pluralism in Planning, in Journal of the American Institute of Planners, XXXI (Nov 1965), pp. 331-338.

Hawgood, John/Frank Land/Enid Mumford (1978):
Training The Systems Analysts Of The 1980's: four new design tools to assist the design process, in Impact Of Science On Society.

Langenheder, Werner (1980):
Wirkungsforschung - Modethema oder Forschungsgegenstand mit Zukunft.
Birlinghoven.

ÖTV (1980):
Leitbeschlüsse des ÖTV-Gewerkschaftstages 1980 zu Rationalisierung, Humanisierung, technischem Wandel -
öffentliche Forschungs- und Entwicklungsförderung.
Stuttgart.

Rosenbrock, H. H. (1982):
Technology policies and options.
Paper to be presented at EEC FAST Conference on "The Information Society: the distribution of benefits and risks associated with microelectronic applications",
London, 25-29 Jan 1982.

Wenk, Edward (1982):
Growing beans or counting beans, in Impact Assessment Bulletin 1(1982)3, p.1.

SYSTEMS DESIGN FOR, WITH, AND BY THE USERS
U. Briefs, C. Ciborra and L. Schneider (editors)
North-Holland Publishing Company

INITIATION AND ACCEPTANCE OF THE PARTICIPATION
OF PERSONS AFFECTED IN SYSTEM DEVELOPMENT

Reinhard Oppermann, August Tepper

Gesellschaft für Mathematik und Datenverarbeitung
Institut für Planungs- und Entscheidungssysteme
Schloß Birlinghoven, (D) 5205 St. Augustin

The problems involved in the realisation of participation also continue after the management's fundamental consent. A first, very important difficulty consists in gaining a sufficient number of staff
members for the participation in system development. Various
barriers to participation and possibilities of supporting the
motivation to participate are discussed.

1. INTRODUCTION

The realisation of participation concepts for those concerned raises a number of
initial problems. The main reasons for the failure of experiments are often to
be found in an insufficient clarification of open questions or latent interest
conflicts during the initiation of participation (an example is described in
detail in KUBICEK et al. 1980). Moreover, participation has to be newly
organised in addition to usual organisation. The experience required for this
exercise is often not available. Quite far-reaching decisions are taken in the
phases of problem definition and preparation of target concepts, i.e. at the
beginning of a reorganisation measure. Under the perspective of a quick
effectiveness it would be desirable that qualified staff with highly developed
goal-orientation participate in this activity. Above all in the initiation phase
these functional demands on the selection of especially qualified staff for
participation is in a state of tension towards the acceptance of participation
among the personnel, because acceptance is mainly based on voluntary
participation and the confidence the participating staff enjoy in the personnel.
Especially qualified members may, but need not, enjoy the confidence of the
colleagues.

A somewhat more extensive description of the decision field characterised by the
conflicting requirements of initiation and acceptance should indicate points
where it is possible to influence the most important prerequisites of a successful participaton, namely which persons intend to or actually participate. Our
considerations are primarily based on experiences collected in a current
research project with the municipal administration in Unna and the results of a
questionnaire of 223 of its staff members [1]. There follows a short description

of this project. The various problem levels and approaches to solving problems
during the initiation of participation are indicated in the following chapters
step by step.

2. SHORT PROJECT DESCRIPTION [2]

The basis of the project is a pilot project "Offenes Rathaus" (open town hall)
which the town of Unna started in 1978 and which introduced first ideas how to
realise a greater amount of citizen-orientation in local government (cf. UNNA
1980). Since autumn 1980 a project "Bürgeramt" (citizen office) has been conducted as joint research project by the Gesellschaft für Mathematik und
Datenverarbeitung (GMD), St. Augustin, and the town of Unna. The background of
this work are changes in the relationship of citizens and administration which
have led to claims for a more "citizen-oriented administration" (cf. GRAMKE
1978, HEGNER 1978, BRINKMANN/GRIMMER/LENK/RAVE 1974 and BREUEL 1979). The concepts of a citizen-oriented administration developed in Unna focus on the
following:

o a reorganisation of administration aiming at reduced specialisation of
   agencies, those tasks which are today fulfilled in different agencies to be
   accomplished by any clerk in the Bürgeramt (task concentration and non-
   specialised counters). This measure is to reduce the efforts the citizen
   requires for settling his matters. Furthermore,
o an advisory and information service shall increase the transparency of
   administration from the viewpoint of the citizen.

It is hoped, that through an early participation of persons concerned internally
and externally (staff members and citizens) the planned Bürgeramt will meet the
interests and requirements of a maximum number of persons. The participation of
staff members which is the main object of this paper shows different levels and
types (cf. multilevel concept WALKER 1975; KUBICEK 1981; cf. detailed description of the participation concept of the project in MAMBREY/OPPERMANN/TEPPER
1982). The first level provides a direct contact between staff members and
project group members for discussing problems of a specific job. Group discussions serve to identify problems and the formation of opinions on the level of
working groups. An intensive influence on project work from the employees'
viewpoint is performed by a personnel working group; some 20 members of the
administrative personnel have volunteered for this group. The inclusion of the
Personalrat (elected personnel representatives) and trade unions serves, in
particular, to coordinate the employees' overall interests. A discussion of

required decisions in a so-called advisory body shall finally secure that the decision makers will take their decisions on an agreed basis thus considering the interests of those persons concerned who are formally not entitled to decide.

It is to be noticed that a legally secured participation in decision-making in the sense of a codetermination is not feasible in a public administration, in particular, on account of the competences of the democratically authorised Council and the legally defined responsibility of the heads of administration. Because of this lack of formal decision competences a consideration of interests has all the more to be based on a substantiated argumentation, the information of all staff members affected, and the coordination of various groups of persons concerned.

3. INTRODUCTION OF THE PROJECT INTO THE ORGANISATION

Often it is useful to have a look at the history of an organisation if the evaluation of a project and its aspect of participation is to be understood. In the predecessor project "Offenes Rathaus" the Stadtdirektor (chairman of the administration) tried first to realise the idea of a more citizen-oriented administration by using staff provided by a job-creation measure. There are various reasons why the work of such groups is depreciated; they are regarded as fill-ins and remain outside the usual organisation. Other, in some opinions much simpler, concepts of a more citizen-oriented administration were also discussed, e.g., it was suggested to give the clerks just more time for serving the citizens. Other groups however supposed wrong goals in the current project "Bürgeramt" only on account of the participation of some organisers in the advisory body. The project is partly at issue and partly not taken seriously.

Thus the idea of the Bürgeramt has been partially discredited. This has impacts on the initiation of concrete participation. Except for the fact that the Personalrat of the municipal administration of Unna gave his consent to start the research project, the staff members themselves did not demand the introduction of a regulated participation. The necessity of an increased participation was especially emphasised by the development team since they had a research interest in it. The details of the organisation of participation were elaborated by the development team and presented to the staff members via the Personalrat and in group discussions.

According to our experience it may be said that some shortcomings in the initial phase of projects are based on the fact that the initiators of a project do not try hard enough to reach a more general agreement on the necessity of change. In particular, the staff members are not asked to develop proposals from their own viewpoints (e.g. DP support for specific working processes). The start of a reorganisation measure is thus the outcome of an outside decision. In DP projects this situation is still aggravated by the frequently mentioned problems in relations beween user department and DP department; from the staff members' viewpoint, project organisation could well be put aside.

4. PROBLEM PERCEPTION AND INVOLEMENT

It is not only important how the staff members rate the importance of the project's underlying ideas or how convincing these ideas are supported by a proper organisation, but the perception of positive or negative impacts is also of great importance to the initiation of participation. The staff members com-bine rumours, opinions gathered from colleagues, official information and their own experiences into a picture against which they see their current situation and from where they derive assumptions about improvements or deteriorations. The following table shows the rating of those positive and negative impacts by staff members.

Table 1: Average impacts of the Bürgeramt supposed by the respondents

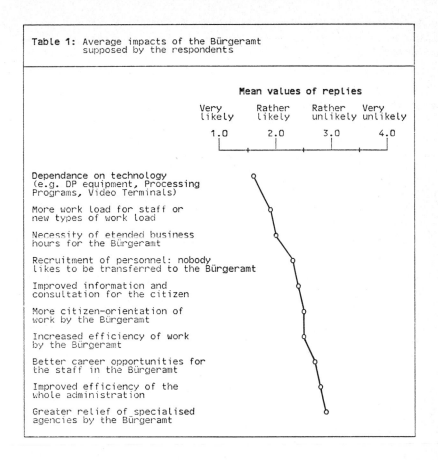

The table shows that staff members expect a dependence on technology involved in the introduction of DP into the Bürgeramt, increased work loads as well as extended business hours in the Bürgeramt. This emphasises the negative aspects; positive impacts of the Bürgeramt (e.g. career opportunities and more citizen-orientation) are considered to be somewhat unlikely. In the opinion of many staff members the negative expectations become marginal problems since they think that other jobs and staff members will primarily be involved. To the question "Do you expect that YOUR job will be changed by the planned Bürgeramt?" only 5% of the interviewed staff members replied that they were likely to be affected very much and 8% said that they were likely to be affected relatively seriously. In contrast, 78% thought that they would be affected little or not at all by changes in their job. In this context it is interesting that in the department which has been considered to be the centre of the Bürgeramt from the very beginning the recognition of the state of being involved is twice as high

as in the other areas. This shows the necessity and importance of clear information to a realistic recognition involvement.

Apart from the large group of staff members with mainly negative expectations we
would like to mention another group of staff members who see advantages in the
development of the Bürgeramt. This groups comprises especially those staff
members who critisize the insufficient career opportunities within the
administration. Some additional replies allow the conclusion that these staff
members consider the present administration to be antiquated and out of date.
They think that improved services for the citizen are connected with useful
changes in the organisation of administration in which they are interested.

5. GOALS AND ORIENTATION OF PROCEDURE

Another condition for participation is that the persons concerned should have
their own objectives with respect to the participation subject or that they
should at least develop them rapidly. An influence on the problem definition and
target concept of project work is otherwise not feasible. The staff interviews
showed that relatively general orientations, such as "call for further improvements for the staff", are commonly shared. This orientation however hardly sup-
plies a basis for concrete, subject-oriented goals (e.g. identification of
qualifications to be maintained or reorganisation of specific working
processes). There is a particularly helpless attitude towards the question of
the social progress allowed by technical progress. Experiences gained from
current project work show that the width of attitudes varies from an evaluation
of technology as a pure tool for increased efficiency to an evaluation of technology as a basis for qualified jobs. Thus, the participation groups reflect the
discussions on the role of technology as they are conducted in literature, in
public media, political parties, trade unions etc. (cf. e.g. LEISTER 1982, RIS
1981).

The lack of developed objectives may reduce the readiness to participate. If the
individual staff member cannot answer satisfactorily the question "What do I
want to achieve?", there will hardly be any readiness to participate. Possible
experiences later in project work are very likely to be frustrating events if
the existing and frequently quite different individual opinions are to be combined in one common strategy of participation.

6. SCOPE OF PARTICIPATION AND CHANCES OF SUCCESS

Another problem of participation is the scope and the protection of influencial opportunities. The staff members do not only want to be informed, but they want to participate in decision-making. A reduction of their participation, e.g. to the submission of proposals, is rejected by 66% of the respondents. 79% of the staff members however advocate a joint discussion of proposals and 74% even demand a joint decision-making.

As against this high claim with respect to participation in decision-making the chances of success are on the other hand rated quite low. Thus, 64% of the staff members think that the heads of administration will finally prevail. Only 5% think that staff members will prevail. Less than 1% think the Personalrat capable of doing so.

Both the demand for a formally protected participation in decision-making and the predominance of the administrative heads in the process of decision making show the importance staff members attach to the forma power of decision. The influencial opportunities (available to experts, to those concerned in all hierachical levels to administrative heads, and local politicians) of influencing the project-related argumentation are often over-looked. This perhaps reflects the difficulties of argumentation caused by the absence of a concrete goal orientation. The seemingly resigned evaluation of their own chances of success is for those concerned an important detraction from their readiness to act. 62% of the respondents say that the absence of opportunities to influence decision-making based on formal rights is an important or rather important reason for their non-participation in the development of the Bürgeramt.

The sceptical evaluation of one's own opportunities is still increased by the expectation that the impacts of the introduction of the Bürgeramt will be mainly negative. The minor perception of advantages is a barrier to the readiness to participate insofar as possible improvements are likely to have a more motivating effect than the mere resistance to negative impacts. On the other hand, in the light of strongly emphasised disadvantages a participation may appear inevitable. There is however the danger that the disadvantages seem to be so serious that their expected marginal reduction is not considered worth the effort to participate, especially when combined with the perceivable lack of influencial opportunities.

7. THE IMPORTANCE OF DIFFERENT MOTIVES FOR PARTICIPATION

A number of further questions help us to identify the goals the staff members
intend to achieve by a participation in the planning of the Bürgeramt. The
"demand for further improvements" is of maximum importance to the staff members.
The "maintenance of present working conditions" is also rated very highly.
Another strong motive for the participation in planning is the opportunity "to
do something decisive for the citizen". These instrumental orientations are of
greater interest than motives with immanent orientations which are directed to
the specific development of personality, such as "to train personal behaviour in
groups" or "participation brings credit".

The problem of such an orientation is that possibly a disregard of social and
group dynamic abilities attends the under-estimation of social motives. The experiences with participation processes however show that corresponding social
and group dynamic abilities are required for instrumental goals of
participation.

It is interesting that neither the instrumental orientations so strongly emphasised in this context nor the social orientations contribute considerably to the
readiness to participate. Statistically significant relations between
participation motives and readiness to participate only apear in the motives
"interest in new topics, e.g. data processing", "the study of new problems
enables one to acquire new qualifications" and "the discussion with experts of
the problems to be solved". Certainly these motives are in a close substantial
connection with the participation in system development. If compared with instrumental orientations the absence of goals directed to the purpose of
participation becomes obvious.

8. WILLINGNESS TO PARTICIPATE AND INTENSITY OF PARTICIPATION OF VARIOUS GROUPS

Some 25% of the respondents were willing "to be more intensively concerned about
the problems of organising a Bürgeramt". The form of involvement was not defined
by the question so that the participation promised here might vary greatly in
the individual case. Almost 25% of the respondents clearly refused any
participation. The remaining 50% did not refuse participation so obviously, they
intended just to "think participation over very carefully".

For completing our picture of the personal readiness to participate and its realisation in the personnel working group we asked how strongly relevant groups should join in the development of the Bürgeramt. The following table shows the corresponding institutions in the order of the mean strength of participation required in the opinion of the respondents.

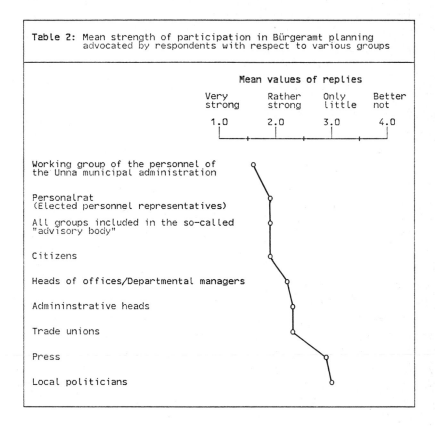

Table 2: Mean strength of participation in Bürgeramt planning advocated by respondents with respect to various groups

This table shows the special emphasis placed on the participation of staff members in the personnel working groups and (somewhat reduced) the participation of the Personalrat. The joint work of the various groups in the "advisory body" also enjoys great confidence among the staff members and even ranks before individual groups also represented in the advisory body (citizens, office managers, administrative heads, trade unions). The press and local politicians should be less concerned with the Bürgeramt.

If comparing these expectations with the readiness to participate as outlined above, it becomes obvious that many staff members shift the commitment on to

other staff members and bodies. For example, 85% of the respondents demand a
strong or rather strong commitment of the personnel working group mentioned
above. But only 25% however were willing to participate themselves.

Furthermore, the above table indicates a different evaluation of more direct and
more indirect forms of representation. The first example of this different
evaluation is to be seen in the greater weight attached to the personnel working
group when compared with the Personalrat. This weighting however is not
necessarily to be regarded as criticism with respect to the Personalrat, but
rather as today's usual preference of direct as possible form of interest
representation. The second example of the different evaluation of indirect and
direct forms of representation is the different weighting by citizens and local
politicians.

9. SOCIAL PREREQUISTIES FOR THE READINESS TO PARTICIPATE

In the above chapters we indicated various factors which impede participation
and which occur within an enterprise or an administration. In addition we would
like to indicate some factors which are based on general conditions; their
relevance to the readiness to participate, identified in the individual
organisations, has been already included in the difficulties so far described.

Because of their living and working conditions most workers and employees are
only able, with great effort, to care about new developments in our society.
Strict work schedules and a stream of necessary matters to settle in free time
leave little time for such intentions. Furthermore, the generally limited
knowledge of individual persons limits the group of persons capable of
participating in a specific matter. Division of labour and specialisation have
brought about, on the one hand, the reduction of the amount of experience and
knowledge which the individual possesses. The individuals know little about
situations and developments going on beyond their own living and working
environment. On the other hand, division of labour and above all specialisation
in economy and society has increased the awareness that there are special
responsibilities for all problems and that those having these responsibilities
have to discuss and solve the problems. Apart from the appearance of technical
experts we have to mentioned the professionalisation of politicians, trade
unionists or personnel committee members. Only if experts fail, a commitment of
their own is taken into consideration by the staff members.

We have already mentioned the effect that these general factors have when reporting on the inclination of staff members to shifting the commitment to groups already institutionalised. General conditions form a framework which restricts individual projects and which can be influenced only marginally, e.g. by in-organisational training and information (cf. BALLERSTEDT 1971). A consideration of this important aspect will avoid any over-estimation of possible influences on the readiness to participate.

10. REALISATION OF READINESS TO PARTICIPATE

An empirical evidence for the realisation of this general readiness is to be seen in the number of staff members volunteering for participation in the personnel working group. Despite the efforts of the project team only 20 out of a staff of about 450 were willing to participate. Even when reducing the personnel to the staff actually concerned, e.g. 150 to 200 members involved in approx. 80 tasks which are in principle suitable for the Bürgeramt, the above number is rather small. In reality this number is further modified by the fact that on average about 10 staff members participated in the meetings of the personnel working group.

If staff members themselves tried to explain this situation, they mentioned the lack of time. Because of their workload many staff members think that they are not able to participate in the working group twice a month for two hours. Another reason for non-participation mentioned by the staff is the fear that a participation in system development may support a rationalisation measure which will finally kill their own jobs.

Considering the variety of barriers the staff participation achieved is to be rated positively, especially since during a period of nearly one year the number of registered members has increased to 26, among them 6 members of the Personalrat, during a period of nearly one year.

11. SUMMARY AND CONCLUSIONS

The various barriers to participate contribute in different ways to that potentially useful opportunities of participation are not used sufficiently or not correctly. Our results on the integration of a project into the overall organisation, problem perception and problem suppression, insufficient develop-

ment of objectives, increased expectation with simultaneous pessimistic assessment of actual opportunities of influence and the support of a strong
participation of third parties, show that only a minority of staff members wants
to participate to a greater extent and that an even smaller number is actually
participating.

The originally conflicting requirements of participation-initiation and
participation-acceptance can hardly be satisfied as optimum so long as
participation has not become a usual component of organisational development. We
therefore recommend are extension of the group of staff members willing to
participate, thus securing the possibility of an argumentatively well-founded
selection of participants.

Based on these weaknesses we want to recommend the following measures as examples for improving the readiness to participate:

o An early as possible information about those concerned to show them that they
  are included in the reorganisation measure.

o Activation of as great a number possible of persons concerned for
  participation. The necessity of participation should be explained in detail
  and the readiness to participate should be promoted.

o Argumentative discussion on possible disadvantages and advantages of a development indicating the opportunities of influence provided to the staff
  members. Freedom of action should be outlined for staff members, and formal
  and informal opportunities of influence should be illustrated.

o Supply and promotion of possibilities to submit one's own proposals for
  advancing the work system. Staff members should be able to suggest in the
  project definition phase those subjects of their field of work which in their
  opinion require improvement (e.g. DP assistance), but also those which should
  remain unchanged.

o Discussion of motives for participation and qualifications required for
  participation. It should be indicated that any motive for participation is
  justified, that the importance of social abilities to participate is often
  under-rated and that missing subject-oriented or technical qualifications can
  be introduced by other staff members or that external working goups can make
  up for this lack.

o Elimination of any barriers of participation by appropriate measures, e.g.
  provision of the time required for participation.

o Appropriate integration of the project into the organisation. A relatively
  great responsibility of the user department seems desirable to us since the
  orientation to working goals would here be on a more reliable basis. In any
  case, a clear decision-making has to be secured so that the agreements
  reached in the individual project phases be binding.

If it is correct to assume that in principle the employees have quite a number
of chances to act, but that these chances however are currently buried, one must
ask who should carry out the measures suggested for unburying them and who
should provide the required support. This should primarily be done by the
representative bodies of the employees. Unfortunately their readiness to provide
support in structuring the qualification-oriented and organisational
prerequisites is relatively small for various reasons. Many personnel committee

members resign themselves to a small participation since they know from experience the extent of grassroot support. The trade unions (e.g. the German Civil
Service Union - ÖTV) are heavily urging that technological development in
organisations be controlled by commited members. A stronger committment of trade
unions in individual reorganisation measures is however not advocated. On the
one hand, they are afraid of an identification of personnel committees and trade
unions with the disadvantages of a possible trade-off on account of their
participation. On the other hand, a stronger inclusion of interest representing
institutions seems undesirable since a shifting of involvement to the trade
unionist is to be expected.

Currently this attitude however means a stagnation of any development of
participation. The employees themselves are by far overstrained by the complexity and rapidity of development. Despite almost 20 years' history of computer
utilisation in public administration the employees are for the first time confronted with this utilisation at their workplace. Therefore they are not informed sufficiently to influence the development by early and well-founded ideas
of alternative technological design. Preventative training and qualified education of individual employees are not available. Greater willingness of personnel committee members and trade unions, namely the readiness to a more case-
oriented commitment and the introducing or supporting supra-organisational and
continuous forms of cooperation, will give an important contribution to the
solution of problems of initiation.

---

[1] The survey took place in February 1982. 450 employees in the main depart-
    ments were asked to answer the questionnaire, of which 50% returned the
    questionnaire.

[2] Additional members of the project team are Ehrenberg, Fix, Heckmann,
    Jörissen, Kaeton-Ammon, Krause, Liedtke, Noltemeier, Schubert, Schulze,
    Seidel, Tuner, Welke.

Literature:

Ballerstedt Eike Ballerstedt: Soziologische Aspekte der innerbetrieblichen
Partnerschaft. Das Ahrendsburger Modell, München 1971

Brinkmann   Hans   Brinkmann,   Klaus   Grimmer,   Klaus   Lenk,   Dieter   Rave:
Verwaltungsautomation, Darmstadt 1974

Breuel   Birgit Breuel: Den Amtsschimmel absatteln - Weniger Bürokratie, mehr
Bürgernähe, Düsseldorf-Wien 1979

Gramke   Jürgen Gramke: Praktizierte Bürgernähe, Köln, Stuttgart usw. 1978
(Kohlhammer), 2. Auflage

Hegner   Friedhart Hegner: Das bürokratische Dilemma, Frankfurt und New York
1978

Kubicek   Herbert Kubicek, Lothar Bittner, Gisela Finke, Henning Schirner,
Dieter Seitz, August Tepper: Humanisierung durch Partizipation?,
Band   1   (Konzeption,   Erfahrungen   und   Konsequenzen),
unveröffentlichter   Projektbericht   (Veröffentlichung   in
Vorbereitung), Trier 1980

Kubicek   Herbert Kubicek: Zu den Schwierigkeiten im Reden über "Partizipation
bei der Systementwicklung", Birlinghoven 1981, Interner GMD-Bericht
IPES 81.208

Leister   Rolf-Dieter Leister: Der Weg zu einer humanen Produktivität. In:
Office Management, 30. Jg, Nr.3/1982, S. 226 ff.

Mambrey   Peter Mambrey, Reinhard Oppermann, August Tepper: Partizipation von
Betroffenen bei der Einführung neuer Technologien in der
öffentlichen Verwaltung, überarbeitete Fassung eines Referates auf
der DVPW-Fachkonferenz vom 1.   - 2. Oktober 1981 in Essen,
unveröffentlichtes Manuskript (erscheint voraussichtlich im Herbst
1982)

Ris   Alexander Ris: Aussteigen ist nicht so einfach. Gespräch zwischen
Gewerkschaftlern und Mitarbeitern in alternativen Projekten. In:
Eberhard Knödler-Bunte (Hrsg.), Was ist heute noch links?, Berlin
1981, S. 15

Unna 80A   Stadtdirektor der Stadt Unna (Hrsg.): Bürgernähe in der
Kommunalverwaltung - Das Einwohnermeldeamt als Ausganspunkt einer
Organisationsentwicklung   zu   einem   Bürgeramt,   Unna   1980
(Eigenveröffentlichung der Stadt Unna), 2. Auflage

Walker   Kenneth F. Walker: Mitbestimmung im internationalen Vergleich, In:
Soziale Welt, 26. Jahrgang 1975, Nr. 2

A STRATEGY FOR USER PARTICIPATION IN

THE DEVELOPMENT OF FUTURE

NON-COMMERCIAL SERVICES

Carol Smolawa, Armin Toepfer

Project CIT (Computer Assisted
Interpersonal Telecommunications)
University of Bremen
Bremen
Federal Republic of Germany

The development of telecommunication services in the non-
professional area requires special participation strategies.
The work presents a method of citizen participation without fixing the development by an application of large technical systems. The involved citizens have therefore to be
enabled to take up qualified positions. This has been done by
discussions with groups of citizens. First results show that
it is possible to achieve results which lead to a design of
beneficial telecommunication services.

Introduction

The introduction of new information technology does not only involve commercial users
but also the private user. The forthcoming introduction of BILDSCHIRMTEXT (the German
interactive videotex service) may serve as an example. BILDSCHIRMTEXT applications in
industry and business rationalize the internal communication paths and, moreover, are
means to get external low-cost capacity.

On the other hand, BILDSCHIRMTEXT also affects the non-professional user at home.
When a bank offers its services via BILDSCHIRMTEXT the people concerned are the
office clerks of the bank (internal effect) as well as private people at home using the
bank-service on their own TV-set instead of going to the bank-office directly (external
effect).

In view of this situation, private users as well as office clerks, should be involved in the
participatory process of introducing new information technology. The present market
research of BILDSCHIRMTEXT and the planned pilot projects of two-way-cable-TV systems
are not good examples of participation of private users. The participants in these field
projects are confronted with a ready-made technology, so they don't have any chance to
intervene.

Possible users of future telecommunication services ought to be involved in the definition,
planning and realization places of future services. Our project CIT has developed and
applied a strategy for the participation of potential non-professional users in the development of future inerpersonal telecommunication services. The non-professional users were
citizens of Bremen selected by a random sample.

The method is characterized by

- thorough information and demonstration of new information technology
  on an easy to understand level;

- discussion of advantages and disadvantages of new services for individual users.

The first step of this participation strategy (the limitation of the service area on a general level) has been finished. The next step (definition of services) enters a new planing phase.

Experience with our strategy shows that participation of non-professional users in the development of future telecommunication services is possible.

PREVIOUS PARTICIPATION CONCEPTS

For a couple of years the insight has been growing that, for the introduction of new technologies, it is not sufficient to consider economic aspects alone, but there is also a need for user oriented development planning.

Among the first studies of the development and utilization of new communication technologies are the 1976th reports of the German "KtK" commission (Commission for the Extension of the technical Communication System). The commission recommended pilot projects to explore the acceptance and the need for the new information technologies. Previous experience with such pilot projects shows, however, that this method is inadequate for the goal of actice citizen participation in the design of future systems and services.

The current runs with BILDSCHIRMTEXT in West-Berlin and Düsseldorf are accompanied by acceptance explorations. The findings of these studies are applied to support the decisions to introduce BILDSCHIRMTEXT.

But even before those large scale pilot runs are finished, we have to realize that:

- the final introduction of BILDSCHIRMTEXT has already been approved
- the findings of the explorations cannot really influence the details of the service
- because of the large amounts of capital already invested in this technology, there is an enormous pressure to introduce BILDSCHIRMTEXT
- the question is neglected whether the intended positive effects can be reached by different means, not necessarily technical ones
- there are no technology assessment studies concerning BILDSCHIRMTEXT

Pilot projects of the kind practised up to now are no road towards a user orientation of technology development because the accompanying social research is based on a given technological concept without any chance for fundamental modifications. /10/

A way open for user participation would be a psychological exploration /7/ which, by means of intensive interviews, investigates the attitudes of people towards new communication technologies. Certainly the involved citizens have no influence on the use of the results after the inquiry is finished. But one advantage of this method is the possibility to explore the prospective consequences of technologies. When applying this method it is important to inform people before and about possible effects of the technologies in question.

It seems, however, that this procedure is more suitable for the evaluation of clearly defined services than for the design of new ones, because the imagination of the citizens is limited and usually fixed to their own concrete experience.

Participation models like the GMD-project "SCHULIS" involve future users earlier, i.e. in the phase of technical design, thus avoiding one grave shortcoming of pilot projects. "SCHULIS" is a project for developing and testing EDP assistance for a clearly defined scope in school administration /6/. The users of the new system take part in all phases from problem identification and first design to the final implementation of the developed system. This project is based on the - rarely realistic - assumption that in an introduction to EDP is similar, or, at least, able to compromise, among users, developers and management /1/2/4/. As with pilot projects the required investment is very high, so that an introduction of a readily developed system is likely, despite foreseeable (possible) negative effects. In particular, non-professional applications will require high costs to provide the technical equipment for a number of participants large enough to simulate complex communiation structures. In view of this, it is most important ot get reliable forecasts of the expected effects <u>before</u> the development and implementation of technologies.

PARTICIPATION IN THE PROJECT CIT

The project CIT explores existing and possible developments of telecommunication and attempts to design socially beneficial services.

This will be done without fixing the development by an application of large and expensive technical systems. To solve social probelms, non-technical solutions should be considered as well as technical ones. Telecommunication services will be designed with participation of potential users and, eventually, be experimentally realized in a later project phase. So it seems guaranteed, that:

- the interest of potential users will be regarded in the first design phase before the design and realization of a certain system
- no technical structure is built up in the early phases that could prevent a necessary abandonment of the technical development.

The following steps are necessary for the development of non-professional telecommunication services with the aid of participation:

- Analysis of private information and communication needs
- Definition of socially beneficial applications
- Design of future services
- Realization of new services in a pilot experiment.

Before realization of the pilot experiment there must be the possibility to break off the the system development.

The requirements and conditions of participation in the non-professional sector differ in many aspects from those in the professional sector (Fig. 1).

Fig. 1

Participative system and service design in the

professional sector   vs.   non-professional sector

---

system design

is related to given goals like rationalization, improving working conditions etc.	needs specification of goals

analysis

of different articulated objectives of involved groups	of potential private requirements and needs

involved persons

number of involved persons in limited	everybody is potentially involved

involvement

is manifest and conscious	private persons are not necessarily conscious of being affected by new services

participation

the dialogue can utilize existing structures	a framework for the dialogue must be built up

---

Most of the involved citizens have too little knowledge of the variety of possible applications of telecommunication in the non-professional area, so that a mere survey would not make much sense. The participants therefore have to be enabled to take up qualified and reflected positions. The CIT project has designed for this reason a participation model consisting of three phases:

PHASE 1 (OUTLINE OF SERVICE REQUIREMENTS)

The definition of areas of potentially relevant services is the goal of this phase. The technical dimension is considered only to exclude entirely unrealizable services, but not to prescribe specific paths of development determined by existing technical services. The citizen participation comprises the following cycle:

- Introduction of technical possibilities. Model systems are presented to and operated by the participants. The project staff gives a survey of possible applications and services.

- Discussion with groups of citizens about possibilities, requirements and effects of future telecommunication services.

- All participants are interviewed on the discussed topics.

The interpretation includes external evaluations such as studies and other literature. The number of citizens involved in this phase, however, will be too small to yield statistically representative results in a strict sense, so that considerable differences to the results of other studies may occur.

The participants receive a summary of the main results and are given the opportunity to evaluate these in a final discussion.

PHASE 2 (DEFINITION OF SERVICES)

By the same method, but with a demoscopicly representative number of citizens, detailed requirements for services are developed. According to these, requirements for the technical telecommunication systeme are derived, so that a pilot system for socially beneficial services can be proposed. If it should occur that no relevant or useful services can be found the system development will be stopped.

PHASE 3 (PILOT EXPERIMENT)

The prestructured useful services will be implemented, tested and further developed for a demoscopicly representative number of citizens who are able to communicate. Services that turn out to be useful in this pilot experiment can be proposed for a general introduction. If no proposal will prove useful in the pilot run, the system development will be stopped at this stage.

PREVIOUS RESULTS

Phase 1 of the above presented CIT-program has been finished. Phase 2 will start in autumn 1982. Hitherto a probability sample of 2.2000 telephone subscribers were invited to take part in the citizen dialogue. Altogether 75 citizens in 6 groups were present. Every group had three discussions on future services.

The method of alternate information, demonstration and discussion of new services led to good results. Participants who at first had only ideas about new services, after a short time were able to express well founded and distinctive statements.

The citizens willing to participate either showed a critical interest in new communication technologies or were supporters of technical innovation. In any case, they were presumably more concerned about this issue than the majority of the population. Hence the participation results are not representative, but they show the whole spectrum of different opinions.

In the citizen dialogue the following points were investigated in greater detail:

- improvements of the telephone, electronic mail, picture-telephone
- shopping, ordering and booking systems, tele-banking, public services
  with telecommunication assistance.

Since detailed results are contained in /9/, we can restrict ourselves to give a summary only in the present paper.

The most frequently pronounced needs aimed at a further development of telephone services, like advance-calling services, telephone auto-answer equipment, automatic dialling, wireless telephone etc. Electronic mail services are considered hardly significant for private applications, for the traditional services telephone and letters are sufficient in the participants' opinion. In the semi-professional area, i.e. communication between private persons and the administration or firms, electronic mail is better accepted.

There is a significant demand from private persons for complex individual information services which surpass the information supply usually accessible today and for tele-banking. Services like elcetronic mail ordering, booking, ticket reservation are regarded critically because of the difficulty of testing articles, loss of hands-on experience at shopping and the presumed monopolization tendencies in the retail business.

Services for education and training are only accepted for special applications like re-training or highly specialized courses but cannot replace personal tuition by a teacher.

To sum up: there is a demand for more comfortable telephoning, but any more advanced telecommunication services seem to make sense only for a few very special applications.

The participating citizens feared that after the installation of new services the traditional services could be reduced, e.g. by shut-down of bank branches or reduction of letter delivery. The social impacts were, in the opinion of the citizens, increasing loneliness and loss of social contact. The costs of such services were suspected to rather lead to "unequal chances" because the poorer part of the population can probably not use these services. Another undesired effect is the danger of total supvervision if access to data bases containing information about private communication behaviour is not effectively controlled.

INTERRELATIONS OF THE PRIVATE AND PROFESSIONAL SECTORS

There is strong interaction between the development of telecommunication systems for he private domain on one hand and for the professional sector on the other hand. A 'ide-spread telecommunication network for private use will make possible, for example, 'ectronic mailing between private individuals and companies thus accelerating the deve-pment of an electronic infrastructure within companies that allows automatic processing. Vice versa, an advance professional EDP structure in connection with electronic communi-cation facilities will be a stimulus for private people to purchase their own terminals. Thus, traditional communication structures will be changed fundamentally. The organi-zation of companies and public institutions, especially in the area of customer services, will have to be modified when private people communicate on-line with the EDP of such institutions.

The EDP-assisted communication network will be a tool for the rationalization and de-centralization of some typical office activities. Consulting can be displaced to the clients' home; the professional work itself can be done at home at the "information technology assisted home working place".

These few examples of interrelations show that neither the private nor the professional sector can be regarded in isolation when planning or developing telecommunication systems.

PARTICIPATION IN THE PRIVATE AND PROFESSIONAL AREA

It is necessary to develop special and problem-adapted participation strategies for the private and professional area respectively.

Telecommunication services for purely in-house professional applications involve, first of all, the office clerk in the organization, who in most cases can make use of formal and informal structures of communication and interest representation, e.g. the shop committee. Shop committees and shop stewards are the natural base for the formation of working groups to articulate and realize employees' interests. Participation models need not establish new particiipation structures with the aim to promote the advancement of self-organization /3/.

As for purely private applications, two probelms are encountered. The set of users is not well defined, nor have the citizens any structures available to articulate and represent their interests. For this reason the development of adequate participation structures must be the first aim. Traditional pressure groups and political parties should not be included as institutions in order to guarantee direct participation of the involved citizens and to prevent a domination of these participation structures by organized interests.

Commercial services for private use, e.g. home banking, affect the private as well as the professional sector. Therefore, a combination of organized interest representation in the professional area and individual participation of the private users has to be found.

PROBLEMS OF REALIZATION

In case of commercial applications of telecommunication systems, any participation that intends more than a mere economic optimization is confronted with resistance by the management. The company will only be interested in taking advantage of the employees' accumulated knowledge for the system development. Goals other than re-organization and rationalization have no chance to be realized under those conditions. The projects of the West-German "Humanisierung der Arbeitswelt" program are good examples for this. In these projects the aims of rationalization and re-organization clearly dominated to the aim of creating better working conditions /4/8/.

Results and recommendations of participation projects which get in conflict with the motives of the management for introducing new information technologies are not carried out; in such cases the project is condemned to fail.

Citizen participation projects in the above described field cause some additional problems. To the average citizen it may not be evident that he could be affected by new services. For this reason the first important step must be to provide all necessary information and produce a feeling of involvement without which an engaged participation is not possible.

To generate insight into the objective involvement is an information problem. This means that qualified information about possible impacts of future communication systems has to be published. Only profound information independent from the interestbound information policies of the companies and the state can lead to an engagement that is prerequisite of participation - a statement that is valid for the professional domain, too.

Detailed information will probably bring about the need for discussions of this issue. These discussions need not to be done exclusively within the context of research projects but in an informal way as well. A base of discussion will help to curb the danger of expert dominance. Unfortunately, our proposed model of user participation indicates no more than a possibility whose chances of being realized are small with respect to the fact that important decisions about the introduction of telecommunication systems have already been made.

Literature

/ 1/   N. Bjørn-Andersen, F. Borum
       Demokratisierung der Gestaltung von Informationssystemen
       In: H.R. Hansen et al., Mensch und Computer; München 1979

/ 2/   A. Breiling, H. Haunhorst, P. Mambrey
       Partizipative Entwicklung eines schulinternen Informationssystems
       zur Unterstützung schulischer Arbeitsbereiche durch Datenverarbeitung;
       GMD, Birlinghoven 1979

/ 3/   U. Briefs
        Gewerkschaftliche Vorstellungen zur "Partizipationsforschung"
        bei der Systementwicklung
        In: P. Mambrey, R. Oppermann, Partizipation bei der System-
        entwicklung; GMD, Birlinghoven 1980

/ 4/   J. Fjalestad
        Some Factory Affecting Participation in Systems Development
        In: P. Mambrey, R. Oppermann, Partizipation bei der System-
        entwicklung (Part 2); GMD, Birlinghoven 1981

/ 5/   J.A. Hartwig
        Eine "öffentliche Verbeugung vor der Demokratie"
        Media Perspektiven, S. 562 - 568, 8/1981

/ 6/   P. Mambrey
        Partizipative Systementwicklung
        In: P. Mambrey, R. Oppermann, Partizipation bei der System-
        entwicklung; GMD, Birlinghoven 1980

/ 7/   A. Müller
        Einstellungen der Fernsehzuschauer zur weiteren Entwicklung
        des Mediums Fernsehen
        Media Perspektiven, S. 179 - 186, 3/1980

/ 8/   F. Naschold
        Probleme gesellschaftlicher Kontrolle der Arbeitsbedingungen
        In: D. Janshen et al., Technischer und sozialer Wandel
        Königstein 1981

/ 9/   C. Smolawa, A. Toepfer
        Beteiligung Betroffener in der Entwicklung fortgeschrittener
        interpersonaler Telekommunikationsdienste für den privaten
        Bereich (will be published in ntz 1/83 and 2/83)

/10/   M. Széplàbi
        Sozialwissenschaftliche Technologieforschung
        In: D. Janshen et al., Technischer und sozialer Wandel
        Königstein 1981

EXPERIENCES WITH PARTICIPATIVE SYSTEM DESIGN IN DIFFERENT SECTORS AND FUNCTIONS

SYSTEMS DESIGN FOR, WITH, AND BY THE USERS
U. Briefs, C. Ciborra and L. Schneider (editors)
North-Holland Publishing Company
© IFIP, 1983

TECHNICAL, ORGANISATION AND POLITICAL CONSTRAINTS ON SYSTEM RE-DESIGN
for machinist programming of nc machine tools

Dr Bryn Jones

School of Humanities and Social Sciences
University of Bath
Bath
ENGLAND

User-oriented re-design of the computerised systems for
'small batch' metal machining in Britain and the USA could
achieve devolution of programming tasks to machinists.
This change is prevented by: 1) managers' technical and
commercial objections; 2) political and organisational
divisions amongst the work-force. Smaller machine shops'
use of CNC systems shows 'craft' machining skills can be
combined with programming tasks. But larger organisations
are centralising programming functions and disqualifying
machinists, accentuating bureaucratic divisions and competing
spheres of trade union interest. Specific re-designs to
meet technical objections thus depend also on de-bureaucratising
re-organisations of occupations.

INTRODUCTION

Conceived as a purely technological problem the design of computer-based systems
which make allowance for the thousands of production workers in metal machining
to express skills and discretion is a feasible engineering project. But to be
acceptable within the actual production enterprises such systems will have to take
explicit account of two major types of constraint. The most obvious of these is
that for the foreseeable future engineering expectations are slanted in the direction
of managers' anxieties about the unreliability of delegated production responsibilities.
These pre-judgements of the conditions of engineering specifications can, I will
suggest below, be countered with highly specific technical re-designs. The second
constraint is much more fundamental and complex.

For actual production enterprises vary between countries in terms of the
organisational constitution of employees' interests and in terms of the political
strategies which arise on the basis of these social divisions. So to be realistic
about achieving system re-design for the users it is necessary to think first about
the possibility of changing the organisational structuring and 'political' regulation
of actual and potential workers' skills and responsibilities.

The nature of these kinds of issues and a demonstration of their importance will
be attempted by considering the patterns of usage and worker responsibility that
have grown up in the British and American firms. In their machine shops Numerical
Control systems of metal machining are planned, programmed and operated by employees
whose trade union traditions and representation vary and conflict with each other.
To begin with (in Section I) we need to consider what the NC principle means, in
general, to the deployment of human skills and levels of decision making in the
machining of the 'typical' short runs - or 'small batches' - which predominate
in this branch of metal manufacture. After that the ways in which managers define
technical engineering obstacles to a more rational extension of decision making
in job-programming amongst machinists is described and evaluated (Section II).
In the third part of this paper the relevance of plant administrative organisation
and trade union representation of interests are explained in terms of the political

constraints that they present to re-organisations of decision-making in computerised
metal machining. As a possible way toward resolving the constraints outlined,
it is suggested in conclusion that there are a number of measures by which NC systems
could be re-designed to meet the allegedly technical engineering objections of
managers. But in addition a much more fundamental re-organisation of occupational
functions ought to be perceived, agreed and pursued amongst trade union representatives
in order to challenge the computerised constriction of a range of engineering tasks
by which the major firms threaten to outflank unions' current tactics for control
of NC work in the UK.

I.   Recent Developments in the Computerisation of Metal Machining Expertise
     via NC Systems

Because the bulk of components machined in metal working industries are required
in short runs or "small batches" of 1 to 200 the 'automation' of human tasks
has differed significantly from manufacturing activities where larger numbers
of standard products has allowed 'dedicated' machines and a virtual elimination
of processing decisions by operators. Instead general purpose machine tools
have prevailed and the switching of the required metal removal routines between
one order ('job') and another presumed a range of understanding of tools,
techniques and metal performance by the individual machine operators (or some
other experienced individual in the machine shop itself).

The automation principles of mass manufacture involve the removal of 'strategic'
decisions about method and planning of production processes from the production
process itself. One way of viewing the application of modern information
processing technology to work processes is to note that it too often has the
purpose of leaving the immediate worker with a narrower range of decision making.
Discretion is limited to minor operating decisions within the overall framework
of strategic decisions that others program into the system.

One purpose of numerical control is to achieve the same principle for the
machining of a particular sequence of metal removal operations. The machine tool
itself carries through different operations that are activated by servo-mechanisms
under the control of electronic circuits which themselves respond to individual
programs written away from the work shop by technicians called 'part-programmers'.

Because the programs specify tooling choice, the configurations of cutting,
dimensions and the overall sequence of movements together with the appropriate
speeds at which metal and tools are to come together, strategic decision making
is confined to the technicians in the planning department. Or at least this is
the theoretical principle. The same principle envisages the operator as simply
monitoring for mishaps and errors, changing components and, sometimes, re-setting
the tools.

However the dividing line between strategic decisions in the techniques of metal
machining and the operational decisions by which minor adjustments of the final
process actually occur has, in practice, proved difficult to maintain with NC.
The lengthy preparation period for planning the running characteristics of a
mass manufacturing process (plus the opportunities for 'de-bugging' faults before
final operation commences) normally allow errors and weaknesses in product
specification and the processing plans to be rectified in advance. With NC on
the other hand, without dedicated machines and with product types changing from
day to day, strategic decision making on the final relationship between product
specification and machining technique is less easy to finalise in advance of the
operations which are supposedly only a routine processing phase. Either the part
programmer extends his responsibilities into the final machining phases, or the
operators extend their range of discretion to re-specify some aspect of the

operation (the dimensions, speeds, or timing of cuts for example) which prove to be problematic on either quality, cost or time grounds.

Thus the division of labour that accompanied the spread of NC from the late 1950's onwards has been far from unambiguous. The enhancement of the auxiliary technology has in some respects favoured the concentration of programmed decision making, yet also, more recently, allowed the possible extension of the discretionary judgements of the machine tool operators.

Cutting tool manufacturers have been supplying standardised data on recommended capacities for their products, so simplifying the experience and judgement of the programmers. Programming departments build up 'stocks' of programs which are proven and ought to require only slight modifications for adaptation to new work. The cheapening of microprocessor facilities provides 'automatic' computational aids for mathematical calculations. Computer Numerical Control (CNC) provides the possibility of a shorter gap between the basic programming work and the operational refinements that iron out errors or achieve more effective machining techniques. With CNC the programmer can re-program directly into the control cabinet on the machine itself. For this now has inter-active input facilities, a memory for holding several programs, and the capacity for issuing the paper tapes which were the original medium of NC records of programs.

The cheaper computing costs and 'distributed' solid state memories of CNC provide the technological core for two distinct modes of organising the combination of strategic with operational decision making for small batch metal machining. In the version favoured by promoters of a high technology, centralised production control logic, machining units with CNC capacity are on-line to a central program store (mainframe) which delegates programs to the units (individual machine tools or 'cells' of these) and monitors their progress. Production support for tooling and materials is also computer planned and the pre-production functions of design and process planning are undertaken via Computer Aided Design and Computer Aided Manufacture systems. Centralised programming and monitoring, known as DNC (Direct Numerical Control) has so far proven the most widely used commercial element of this complex. But each of the other constituents are under trial or operation in various parts of the world. By implication the effect of this total development of Computer Integrated Manufacture is to inter-mesh strategic decision making and monitoring to such an extent that the numbers and quality of supplementary 'operational' decisions are minimised. So too with the operational decision makers: the publicity label for CIM is 'the unmanned factory'.

The other, more pragmatic, mode of exploiting CNC since its commercial market entry in the mid-1970's stands (in many cases of application) in direct contrast to the DNC - CIM route. For the smaller machine shop establishments, with whom CNC has proved most noticeably popular, often push (or retain) the decision making boundary in the opposite direction: by making operators and other machining personnel - not technician-level part programmers - responsible for many of the programming decisions relating to machining technique. Such CNC usage can be interpreted as the commercial corroboration of alternative system re-design approaches. For it seems to fly in the face of the emerging production engineering consensus on metal-working automation by emphasising user involvement in programming decisions and the enhancement and satisfaction of the immediate worker's skills and work tasks.

With CNC it is possible to insert new instructions within a particular program which do not require an understanding of the programming language. For example changes in the speed, or depth of the cutting action, or in the rate of 'feed' of the material. Depending on the character of the modifications made it is possible for machinists to effectively 're-program' jobs.

Such a devolution of strategic decision making runs counter to the high-level

automation technological strategies just mentioned. For the advocates of this
development it would be regarded as an inappropriate regression to increase user
involvement in this way. Because operator programming contradicts both the
hierarchisation of decision making (which is seen as implicit in the NC principle)
and also the principle of replacement of human processes and problems by technical
ones through capital investment. We can return to the particular engineering
objections raised against operator discretion in NC programming in the next section.
For the moment it should be noted that there is nothing in NC technology itself
which demands that it has to be developed in the direction of hierachised decision
making, or that it can be most effectively used when operator involvement is
minimised.

It should be recalled that NC machine tools themselves were only widely adopted
in the USA by aircraft manufacturers because of massive US Air Force financial
incentives. An alternative automatic control to NC was available at the same time
in the early 1950's. This 'record playback' system however required a machinist
to accomplish the first operation for a new batch along the same lines as some
modern robotic devices. It has been argued that the extra security and financial
considerations of the Defence industry led to the diffusion of NC at the expense
of record playback, (Noble, 1978). At the moment Professor Rosenbrock and
collaborators at the University of Manchester are developing a control system for
an automatic machining cell of machine tools and robot which centres upon interactive dialogues between a skilled machine operator and the computer facility
rather than pre-programmed decision making away from the machining operation(1).

A final point on the utility of operator involvement is to note the reasons for
the marked success of smaller establishments in gaining new market opportunities
and competitive positions in relation to major firms through use of CNC. In part
this is because of their familiar advantage in having lower cost overheads. But
it is also because CNC is used to enhance labour flexibility by devolving and
sharing programming responsibilities amongst the machine shop workers so that
innovation in techniques for different orders is rapid, (Sorge et al. 1981; Brusco
1982). What then are the obstacles to this alternative approach in the larger,
more capital intensive metal machining establishments?

II. Clarifying the Importance of Production Engineering Criteria

The results of a recent cross-national study of CNC usage in British and West
German establishments shows that it is not simply the technical imperatives of
metal component manufacture that influence production managements to 'dis-qualify'
(2) machinists from using NC capacities to make their own judgements. The Anglo-
German study found that in both German and British plants where batch sizes were
large the technical opportunities for operator discretion was reduced. Where the
components produced required complex programming operations and consequent inter-
dependence of the constituent elements there was, similarly, limitations on the
discretion allowed for operators in both countries (Sorge et al. pp. 181-187).
It should be recognised, however, that the influence of such apparently technical
obstacles is over-ridden by social and organisational factors. For even where
German and British firms were matched in terms of product character, size of
business organisation and size of batch the British firms were much more inclined
in general to formalise programming decisions, away from shop floor personnel,
in specialised departments.

In order to consider the objections to more machinist involvement in programming
that are alleged to inhere in the technicalities of production engineering let
us evaluate some typical arguments that have been made to myself in the course
of visits to firms in the UK and the USA (3). The general theme voiced by
managers is that post-planning modification to the relevant program should be
minimal in order to guarantee a standard quality and reliability of each component.
This theme is composed of separate sub-arguments:

i) NC is particularly suited to the machining of complex configurations (using up to five axes of cutting) in the kind of 'exotic' metals required in industries such as aerospace. Uninformed interventions risk scrapping such high cost components.

ii) Only the programmers involved at the planning stage of a machining operation fully appreciate the inter-relationship of all of the constituent specifications. A machinist may improve one of these elements but unwittingly upset one of the others if he is allowed to modify the programs.

iii) Operators and planner/programmers have conflicting objectives when there is a possibility of varying the rate at which a job is machined. If operators are paid output bonuses they will want to exceed the specified machining time in order to increase their earnings. But conversely, where there is no financial incentive operator discretion would lead them to slow down the rate of work below the economic optimum prescribed by planners and programmers. These objections are raised against letting machine operators vary the rates at which the cutting tools are applied to the workpiece, or the latter is fed to the cutter.

iv) Dangerous discrepancies in the dissemination of knowledge in process modifications are also diagnosed by production managers. The operator on one shift may re-program some aspect and fail to inform his successor on the next shift. As a consequence incorrect tool or workpiece settings may be made which result in collisions or cutting errors. Similarly without an amended record of the changes made, a part-programmer may later 're-issue' a program for a job which he thinks that it is suitable for, without knowing that critical aspects have been changed.

In essence all of these objections derive from the problems of communicating technical information between occupations that have been organisationally segregated. Consequently it is necessary to consider solutions not only in terms of changes to the information processing equipment itself, but in terms of the additional constraints deriving from the organisational characteristics discussed below. However, the essential fragility of these objections as insuperable obstacles can be established.

Even without a major re-design of the software it should not be too difficult to overcome objections (i) and (ii) by allowing a general operator the right to make certain kinds of modifications unless programmers or managers wrote in either a bar to changes on certain complex jobs, or a threshold to the level of modification that was possible. These checks would then be automatically called up when operators requested clearance for modifications.

The objection on changes to speeds and feeds ((iii) above) is internally inconsistent because it recognises that operators have the skills necessary to raise rates when this is 'authorised' by appropriate bonuses but not the all important responsibility to balance quality against output. Financial incentives are a poor regulator of machinists' abilities (Burawoy, 1979). What is required is that planner/programmers and machinists are able to pool knowledge and expectations about quality/output trade offs. The final objection concerning inadequate recording of shop floor modifications simply suggests the inadequate design of current systems in terms of a 'top down' communication of information. The possibilities for inverting this arrangement are outlined in the conclusion of this paper.

III. The Relationship Between the Administrative Regulation of Occupational Responsibilities and the Definition of Trade Union Interests

Unlike Europe countries such as the Scandinavian societies, trade unions in the U.S.A. and U.K. have confined their explicit policy on technological changes of

production methods largely to contesting with management over the effects on the
conditions of employment rather than the character of changes to working tasks.
Thus interest has focussed on preservation of individual job security, health and
safety and compensatory rates of pay. This focus is partly a result of the past
traditions and politics of trade unionism in both countries. But the case of the
representation of occupational interests in British metal-working engineering
industry suggests that an equally important independent influence is exerted by
the managerial practices: for administrative organisation and regulation of
diffe.ent occupations; and for recruiting individuals into these positions. In
a nutshell, unions' policies and strategies are channelled by the very conditions
of occupational regulation which lie behind the problem of technical change against
which they struggle.

The 'conditions of employment' perspective on technical change taken by U.S.
unions is most certainly maintained by the legal restrictions on the conduct of
bargaining and the sphere of negotiable issues. These serve to preserve managerial prerogative over changes in the organisation of production (Jones, 1982 b).
In Britain the preservation of such management rights has rarely taken direct legal
form. It is the continuous establishment and revision of informally recognised
'custom and practice' in work places which has influenced the main machinists'
union (now the Engineering Section of the Amalgamated Union of Engineering Workers
- AUEW (ES)) to leave the disputation of technical change largely to the traditional 'craft' tactics of local work-place branches.

The central logic of these tactics has been to retain the ultimate right of use
of the machine for the notional craft-trained union member. Thus NC equipment
has not been resisted per se only the prerogative of final responsibility for
mechanical operations. As a result NC machine tools are each normally attended
by one AUEW (ES) member who starts and stops the machine's operations while the
'setting up' of tools and work pieces is done either by that machinist, or in
conjunction with another (possibly more competent) shop floor worker. These
tactics have been successfully pursued by union representatives in plant-level
bargaining in as much as they have: slowed down the reduction in numbers of
machinists employed as a result of NC productiveness; left machinists with clearly
defined tasks and jurisdiction over the mechanical aspects of machining; and
preserved/enhanced the levels of earnings (up until the recent deepening of the
recession).

But as NC control systems have become more reliable and able to automate remaining manual tasks (such as automatic tool changing and work-piece rotation around
multi-function 'machining centres') so the NC part-programmers in the larger
machine shops have come to be seen as the effective controllers of the machine
tools. After disputes between machinists and part-programmers, official AUEW(ES)
policy has changed. ES local representatives have been instructed to bargain for
an agreement that machinists should input data into CNC control cabinets instead
of part-programmers. (Financial Times, 23rd April 1982).

In taking this step the Engineering Section comes into direct conflict with the
technicians' union the Technical and Supervisory Section - organisationally part
of the same AUEW grouping, but having, like the ES, considerable executive
independence. The ES change of policy gives explicit recognition to a divergence
of occupational interests between the technicians and machinists. Part-programmers
(who if unionised are normally members of TASS) are classed as technical staff
which in Britain means payment by salary rather than wages (as with production
workers) and terms and conditions of employment typical of the managerial and
professional 'staff' sphere. From the point of view of these workers the
programming and adjustment of machining jobs is an extension and realisation
of the design and planning process (with which they are organisationally grouped)
rather than a usurpation of machine operation decisions. Sandwiched between the
shop floor and production planners and designers (whose own tasks are being
reduced through CAD and CAM) part-programmers are unlikely to look favourably

on work and skill enhancement for machinists which involves the straightforward transfer of 'their' programming tasks.

It is important, when considering radical re-designs of the hierarchy of decision making in NC systems, to recognise that it is mainly administrative organisation and definition of the different occupational functions just referred to that separates them and leads to the ensuing conflicts of interest over re-allocation of responsibilities. In Germany, Sorge and his colleagues found that rigid departmental distinctions of occupation by either machining expertise or formal engineering training were much less in evidence than in the comparable British firms. A few examples from cases studied in Britain by myself will confirm how the structure of administrative regulation departs from efficient co-ordination of production engineering expertise in metal machining and acts as a strait-jacket upon efficiency.

Heads of programming departments, both in the U.K. and U.S.A., conceded to me in interviews that the crucial practical training for a part-programmer was experience of metal machining operations in order to be able to 'visualise' the various movements which had to be calculated in the form of the particular programs. Astute managers have chosen to acquire this capacity in their staff by recruiting mathematically inclined ex-machinists away from the shop floor and into the planning and programming staff. But these ambidextrous individuals cannot be in two places at once. In one firm studied machinists had taken to consulting informally with programmers when deficiencies, or unforeseen problems, arose in a program that had been put into operation on the machine tools. Management then decided to re-impose a formal communication procedure via departmental heads in order to control programmers' work allocations and ensure departmental accountability. The result was that machines lay idle for periods whilst the paperwork was processed between individuals and departments.(4)

The technocratic bias that often accompanies the departmental specialisation and recruitment of formally qualified technical staff blinkers production managers to the discrepancies in the sharing of the necessary expertise. In the machine shop of a transmissions plant graduate engineers and mathematicians had been recruited to staff a part-programming office. Lacking almost any machining experience these young men explained to me how they had surreptitiously to learn machining techniques in the exchanges with operators at the 'prove out' (test run) stages, before they could write programs with any degree of confidence.

Administrative development of engineering functions for small batch machining followed a Tayloristic pattern in the earlier years of this century as organisational forms were adopted to make up for the eclecticism of the production process by formalising the pre-production decisions of planning and design. The arrival of information processing technologies has been received by attempts to incorporate the ensuing strategic decision making tasks into these departments. But since, as with CNC, these systems now implicitly relocate many areas of decision back with the machining process the administrative structures constitute bureaucratic obstacles to a more co-ordinated sharing of decision making between occupational functions and a more participative and productive use of individual's skills and capacities(5).

IV. Conclusion: Two Paths of Development for Allocation of Computerised Decision Making in Small Batch Machining Systems

At the extremes the next twenty years should see a polarisation of the experienced metal machinists' responsibilities and expression of skills. In smaller firms producing small batches the trend to operator involvement of different levels of CNC programming decisions should continue. With further simplifications of interactive programming the 'skill' of converting machining expertise into programs should diffuse through the small-producer sector. In the larger shops, especially where batch sizes are at the higher end of the 'small batch' ranges and where technologist-managers have access to capital finance and knowledge of 'state of the art' developments, combinations of the higher automation modes of computerised engineering referred to above in Section I seem likely to be introduced (I. Prod. E. 1980).

The effects of the latter path on the unionised strongholds of the larger producers in the U.K. and U.S.A. is difficult to predict. On balance however the previous experiences and the conflicts of occupational interest between technical and machining workers suggests that on present policies of unions and managers there is more likely to be a hierarchisation of decision making beyond even the present categories of programming staff and a consequent contraction of skilled participation in the running of more pre-programmed systems. In order to counter these possibilities, and the attendant diminution in numbers of members and skills employed, policies aimed at reforming the bureaucratic divisions referred to in the previous section would form a necessary first step in the direction of a more participative form of involvement and a lessening of conflicts of interests between worker groups.

Two inter-related types of policy to enhance participation and overcome inter-work group conflicts of interest seem to be called for. To begin with sympathetic technologists must generalise from the lesson of CNC that the technological potential is there for reliable and efficient enhancement of operator responsibilities - to meet the kind of management objections outlined in Section II. Additionally, but hand in hand with system modification, must go a de-bureaucratisation of occupational functions in a way which retains scope for various degrees of aptitude and qualification.

The objectives of the specifically technological exercises would be firstly to combine a respectable measure of operator innovation within the parameters of more basic product specifications; and, secondly to foster a more 'permissive' climate for such innovations by incorporating systemic mechanisms for the recording and open communication of improvements to original job plans. At the University of Manchester in England Professor Rosenbrock and his colleagues are already experimenting with executive programs which could meet the objections anticipated by the first objective. Operators have to 'satisfy' the controlling program that both safeguards and consequences to the original machining plan have been anticipated in the modifications that are being proposed. The operator issues commands and receives back queries and confirmations through a 'conversational' interaction with the CNC memory(6).

The objections which were shown in Section II to cluster around inadequate recording and communication of alterations to program specifications could be met by inverting the information-transfer process of DNC systems. In these, it may be recalled, a central mainframe computer issues instructions to separate machining units as to which programs to commence machining from. The central store receives, in return, up to date information on progress, the occurrence and nature of hold ups etc. If the DNC centre were converted into acting as a central 'clearing house' for keeping all relevant participants updated on modifications to particular operations (or even of the 'fleshing out' of rudimentary product plans into machining processes) then it could not be claimed that discrepancies in recorded information about program characteristics militated against machinist innovation. It goes without saying, perhaps, that some safeguards would be necessary under this kind of arrangement to ensure that 'open' reporting of interventions was not utilised as a device for penalising genuine errors.

We have already drawn attention to the occupational prerogatives on NC functions that define different groups of workers' interests as opposed. The kinds of system changes just mentioned would require more fundamental changes in occupational organisation in order to transcend these differences and to create an atmosphere in which devolved decision making was seen as desirable by management and different occupational groups. If, as is claimed,(7) CNC and its auxiliary technologies allow the machining area to return to the centre of the production decision-making process (with design and planning functions in more of a service relationship to it) then why not re-organise the technical and machining occupations into a non-departmentalised set of definitions?

There could be a loosely graded set of occupational categories with different levels of decision-making responsibility divided, not monolithically by the technician-machinist definitions, but incrementally according to mixed quanta of experience in machining work and short training courses in basic information processing or work planning techniques. In this way individuals could progress between different kinds and levels of work either through an agreed promotion scheme or through forms of job rotation. But there need be no division by departmental status. All could be machine-programming workers within a more fluid production and product planning area in which computer aided pre-programming overlapped with machine programming work. This suggested occupational re-organisation is similar in some respects to the 'Professionalita' schemes of the Italian steel workers in the 1970's and might be assessed in the light of those workers' experiences(8).

The package of measures suggested here is ambitious. But it has certain advantages over the alternatives. It seeks to augment technological re-design aimed at an enhancement of user involvement by suggesting attention to the organisational obstacles which might preclude the commercial receptivity to such measures. Under the present conditions of the politics of trade unionism dilution of occupational boundaries is not likely to have an immediate appeal to trade union representatives. But the currently emerging collision course between technical and machine workers seems unlikely to deal with the longer (or even medium) term changes to their work roles.

For this is a dispute over responsibility for the existing definitions of pro-gramming tasks. But in the next stage of automation, which the larger companies are already planning to introduce, the integration of various computerbased engineering functions will be designed with the explicit intent of further centralising individual-machine programming tasks. If successful it seems likely that this path of development will make it possible to eliminate the separate detail-programming tasks which are currently being contested and so undermine the main functions of both part-programmers and machinists occupations.

FOOTNOTES

(1)   Private communication from Professor H. Rosenbrock, University of
             Manchester Institute of Science and Technology. A form of 'Record
             Playback' is planned for this system.

(2)   The term 'disqualify' seems more appropriate than the frequently
             used 'de-skill'. For at least in NC machining it is not the
             elimination of practical knowledge of metal cutting that takes
             place: for this is still required at critical junctures. This is
             re-distributed to other occupational roles and the machinist
             loses the opportunity to engage skills by being disqualified from
             utilising the control system by administrative and technical devices.
             cf. B. Jones, 1982a.

(3)   Fieldwork research funded by Social Science Research Council in
             Britain and by the Nuffield Foundation in the United States.

(4)   This pressure for administrative control by managers can be also a
             strong underlying influence on the design and choice stages of system
             development. Thus the technical potential of information processing
             may be deformed by concerns for bureaucratic control. As Ulrich
             Briefs has pointed out to me this aspect is a far more general system
             design problem than just the NC principle in 'small-batch' metal-
             machining.

(5)   On CNC machines introduced into one Midlands machine-tool manufacturer
             in Britain operators took to converting ther own judgements about
             machining improvements into new paper tapes which were then hidden
             away from part-programming staff in the operators' lockers! Here
             operators took the initiative in compartmentalising the knowledge
             which under a less divisive organisation could have been shared to
             enhance efficiency. (Communicated to me by K. Grainger of Coventry
             Workshop, Coventry, England).

(6)   H. Rosenbrock and J. Davies in a proposal for a Project on "A Flexible
             Manufacturing System in which Operators are Not Subordinate to
             Machines".

(7)   Sorge et al., p. 201.

(8)   Barisi, 1980.

BIBLIOGRAPHY

Barisi, G.   La Notion de Professionalita Pour Les Syndicats en Italie,
                      Paper at the Colloque Politique d'Emploi et Rapports
                      Sociaux du Travail, December 1980.

Brusco, S. and   The Artisanal Firm and Economic Growth in F. Wilkinson(ed)
Sabel, C.   The Dynamics of Labour Market Segmentation, London, 1982.

Burawoy, M.   Manufacturing Consent: Changes in the Labour Process Under
                      Monopoly Capitalism, Chicago/London, 1979.

I. Prod. E.   (Institution of Production Engineering) Technical Policy
                      Board, Current and Future Trends of Manufacturing and
                      Technology in the U.K. The Institution of Production
                      Engineers, London, 1980.

Jones, B.   Destruction or Redistribution of Engineering Skills? The
                      Case of Numerical Control, in S. Wood (ed) The Degradation
                      of Work? London, 1982.

Jones, B.   Differing National Constraints on the Use of New Production
                      Technology, (Final Fieldwork Report to the Nuffield
                      Foundation), 1982, School of Humanities and Social Sciences,
                      University of Bath, Engand (mimeo).

Noble, D.   Social Choice in Machine Design: The Case of Automatically
                      Controlled Machine Tools and A Challenge to Labor,
                      Politics and Society, 8, Nos 3-4, pp. 313-347, 1978.

Sorge, A. and   'Microelectronics and Manpower', IIM/LMP Discussion Paper
Hartmann, G.,   81-16 Wissenschaftszentrum, Berlin, October 1981.
Nicholas I.,
Warner, M.

SYSTEMS DESIGN FOR, WITH, AND BY THE USERS
U. Briefs, C. Ciborra and L. Schneider (editors)
North-Holland Publishing Company
© IFIP, 1983

EFFECT OF THE INTRODUCTION OF THE CAD SYSTEM UPON
ORGANIZATIONAL SYSTEM AND PROFESSIONAL ROLES

O. Marchisio, G. Guiducci

Gruppo ANSALDO
Genova
ITALIA

The application of Cad System involves changes both among the
roles and within the roles, so possible hypotheses of
organizational roles should be defined on the ground of the
various working factors. The structure of previous roles, the
outline of technical system, the typology of designing flows,
the management subjective choices are the working factors which
may affect the organizational plan.
It is obvious that the "freedom degree" in organizational
choices depends upon the quality or work pursued by the Company
as well as on Trade Union interventions.

1.1 Introduction of CAD

Any changes in the organization and in the occupational functions correlated to
the introduction of new technologies cannot be totally explained based upon such
new processes.
This is due to the fact that the previous "state of art" as well as overall
organizative processes are interacting with the new variables. From methodologic
al viewpoint, it is therefore extremely interesting to investigate whether the
various variables can be isolated and highlight the "weight" ot the new technolo
gy in determining the modifications.

On the one side, we have the new technology which changes the conventional
draftsman's job "contents" while on the other the division of work between sistem
engineer, design engineer, chief draftsman, draftsman and tracer depend on the
previous division together with the share in the work to be allocated to the new
"draftsman" figure. The various interlaced levels of the variables require a
definition of hierarchy of the causes as well as an interaction model capable of
"supporting" this complexity.

1.2 Composition of Knowledge Distribution in the "corporate" System "CAD"

The process we want to explore is regarding the transfer of Informative System
nowledge conveyed through the social or corporate system to the machine built-in
intelligence system.

An ever growing amount of knowledge is being incorporated in the machine system
and this transfer is performed at an ever higher speed.

In the specific CAD sector, design, information system and drawing are the channels through which corporate knowledge composition is implemented. There is indeed a new and different "distribution" of project flow knowledge as well as of the interaction between the various channels of the corporate information system. This means that the transformation of information technologies in the specific design area first of all requires not only a transformation of that particular sector but also its upstream and downstream "connection" to other information systems. In other words, the introduction of "CAD" has its greatest significance in the absolute need for a complete transformation of the "data bank" and of the information system to which the various corporate users have access.

Not only this, but language "code" standardization required by the new data processing model also requires translation procedures, i.e. "symbol standard - ization" directly involving the draftsmen's operating conditions. This has a double impact on knowledge and on "language code" contacts, both regarding congruency of "translation" with the new technology and engineering language homogenizing.

In other terms, the functions of the draftsman and the rôle of the design and engineering information system in the overall corporate system are both redesign ed.

1.3 Organization Levels involved in CAD

1)   Impact on work (job) layers: 1.2 qualitative redefinition

2)   Impact on rôles   1.1 Redefinition of job descriptions
                                     1.2 Redefinition of management criteria

3)   Impact on organization unit   3.1 Redefinition of operating criteria
                                     3.2 Redefinition of corporate goals

2.   ORGANIZATION ANALYSIS STAGES FOR THE INTRODUCTION OF "CAD"

2.1 "Environment" Typology

We can assume the presence of different macro-structures and different "technic- al culture" levels in the sectors into which "CAD" is to be introduced.

Obviously, the "environmental" typology will affect or condition the conditions and the path along which "CAD" is to be introduced in particular its more or less actual utilization.

We may assume "informal organization" types and with a high percentage of work stages translated into procedures, i.e. the former informal and unstructured, modelled on routine and the other on non-routine. The variables determining both contexts may be multifarious, but the overall "state of art" and their relation- ship with the market are no doubt determinant for the different organization forms.

2.2 Design and engineering flow typology

When considering the different electrical, mechanical and electronic contexts involving design and engineering activities, it will be possible to identify their direction of development.

The determination of design sub areas and the specific phases of such sub-areas will permit the identification of one or more flow models. Once the design flow configuration has been finalized, an estimate can be made of the share already systemized and hence easily automatizable of the drafting stage. This will enable us to define the optimum relation between the introduction of the CAD system, the possible saturation of the system and the organization of the design and engineering flow.

2.3 Organization typology

The introduction of the CAD system causes inter-rôle and intra-rôle modifications so that it will be necessary to define all possible organization rôle scenaries based upon the involved variable hierarchies. The structures of previous rôles , the configuration of the engineering system, the design flow typology, subjective management "choice" are the variables affecting the configuration of the or-ganization structure.

Obviously "the degree of freedom" in management "choice" is also a function of the criteria involving the corporate pursued job quality and of possible Trade Union actions.

2.4 Hypothesis of Organization Relations (after the introduction of CAD)

1) Scenary A: machine/operator/design engineer
   Scenary B: machine/design engineer
   Scenary C: machine/operator/design engineer machine/design engineer.

These three scenaries are obviously affecting: system optimization, flexibility/ rigidity of the design and engineering sector, costs, parcelling, job quality and of course occupation.

Therefore, an analysis of present Ansaldo scenaries may constitute an interesting "observation point" for the processes now developing to a larger extent in other areas.

2.5 On the subject of dialogue

The specificity of graphic systems lies in their interaction dimension, in machine /operator dialogue. "Dialogue" typology is one of the system's critical moments and the overall productivity of the engineering flow depends on the quality level of the interaction between the various language levels.

Possible interaction models can be synthetized as follows:

1) interaction A: design engineer/"typist"/"typist"/machine
2) interaction B: design engineer/machine
3) interaction C: "typist"/machine

2.6 Rôle typology in design and engineering

When analyzing the specific rôle of the design engineer and the possible reactions
to the introduction of the "CAD" system, some critical variables emerge regard -
ing the "composition" of the job description of draftsmen/design engineers, chief
design engineers and tracers as well as their career and their seniority in age
in length of service.

A timely and point by point check of the attitude and reaction modalities should
not be made only in the Ansaldo context but it is at least an "indication" for an
understanding of the subjective dimension achieved ir the design and engineering
sector.

3.   CASE ANALYSIS

Let us consider the introduction of CAD in a specific corporate context to verify
the truth of some of the foregoing hypotheses.

The placing and applicability of an empirical analysis can not be defined once
and for all, but despite their multifarious dynamics between definite and
abstract, we want to state some paradigms to which reference is made while out -
lining, on the other hand, the relationships from which the empirical protocols
must be chosen and read.

The analysis of a "case" has thus a control and ascertaining function of the set
up hypotheses rather than confirming or negation of the same.

The case in question is regarding an engineering Firm belonging to a large
Italian Concern.

3.1 Context

In the design and engineering area of this Firm, the introduction of the CAD
system so far affected activities related to flow charts, functional and electric
diagrams; in particular we can note the interaction between the new system and
some areas such as DSA (Auxiliary Systems Department) belonging to DME (Thermo -
mechanical Processes) and like DAC (Dynamics and Control) belonging to DDR
(functional Analysis).

Both areas are organization segments of the "Systems and Components" sector, the
very heart of engineering.

3.2 Management relation typologies

For the above mentioned areas we find elements belonging to scenery C, since both
the simple interacting "machine/design engineer" and the composite "machine/ope -
rator/design engineer" are involved.

There can be no coubt about the fact that the introduction of automatic drafting
and even more CAD strongly affected the operator/machine systems modifying their
previous man/tool relationship. It should be stressed that the relation between
operation and information flow in the manual versus the "automatic" context is
.

reversed by the very diversity between tool and "machine". In the latter case we have a technological "prius" imposing greater restraints than required by the technigraph. While establishing the "technological" standardization for the simple as well as for the composite system, we must highlight at the same time the differentiated impact on both cases.

In the DSA area (auxiliary systems) where the "composite" system is active, impact of the CAD system was not very strong (see diagram n° 1). Distribution of effects is rigidly separated between the objectives of the design engineer and the operator's task, with a clear-cut division between the "station" environment and the environment of the involved area.

This gives the impression of a still rather "limited" utilization of the CAD system capacity, since automatic drafting tasks are prevailing over file and data bank for design purposes. In this area, where 60% of the drawings to be produced for the commissioned Nuclear Power Plant is entrusted to the automatic drafting service, no significant transformation in the activities of the design engineer can be noted.

When considering the rôle of the design engineer in this specific context we note that neither the output nor the input of his activity have been affected for the moment by the introduction of the new technology.

When considering the restraints and objectives of the Customers Specifications and "Requirements" as inputs to be met by processing and design of a congruent output, we immediately note that this information system is still wholly tradi - tional and entursted to "Paper" and "verbal" supports. The fabrication process of the congruent output by the design engineer or group of engineers finalized towards a horizontal objective with respect to the distribution of competences is hinged on a communication system interacting with the knowledge file, i.e. with the "data bank" built into and accessible in the corporate system. This critical phase is also conveyed on a "traditional" information system; the various "per- sonnel", "group" files, the "licence" file are stored on "paper carriers" or "verbal" media and access modalities are determined by the formal organization and informal processes juxtaposed during the implementation of the various Orders.

In particular only part of the "licence" file is linked up to the availability and formal access, whereas consolidation and specialization of the documentation are entrusted to informal and personal circuits based on travels or contacts activated with the licensing Company.

Inputs and files as elements constituting the design engineer's activity still remain outside the new automation system while the main modifications occur during the output phase.

The design output mediated by the draftman's activities includes the flow process charts, the component list, the line list and valve list and this is the area "processed" by the automatic drafting. The conditions for a different "operator/ design engineer" information interchange are determined by this new output medium, often superimposed on the filtered communication line of the Chief Draftsman as well as for the development of the characteristics of these new media. Two major elements are induced by the new automatic processing of the iconic and alphanume- rical information; the former concerning the standardization while the latter covers the planned accumulation of a file segment. The former and latter are both correlated structurally to the new system, i.e. they are indispensable elements of this system up to the point that the system would be inefficient without their application.

Furthermore, standardization, i.e. the construction of one single code for the iconic and alpha numerical symbols triggers a homogenized language process well beyond the automatic drafting action range, thus reaching current conventional communication systems through a modifying action. As to the building of a file to be activated by macro-symbols, this is the specific activity on which the dif - ferent productivity automatic drafting system can be checked against the traditional drafting system. Filing on tapes or discs of drafting secrets thus becomes the main carrier, reducing the operator's direct activity.

Standardization and automatic filing, although limited to handling of the final product of design engineering activities are prefiguring processes that might also involve other activity segments.

This prefiguration is perhaps increased by the simple "design engineer/machine" system as shown in the DAC area (Dynamics and Control area), where the design engineer is directly interacting at the station and is directly incorporating the draftman rôle.

In particular, for a desalination plant (see fig. 2) there was a first direct experience for a design engineer in absorbing this segment of drafting activity. On subjective level, the results also express the doubts and criticisms from those who had no specific knowledge about drawing and machine, but had to acquire a fast acculturation, spending more time on it than required for the usual hand sketch. There can, however, be no doubt about the fact that the direct mediation of the design engineer between machine and "knowledge" (data) file reduces the control and regulation circuit of any possible variances to real time execution.

There is no longer any information chain between design engineer, chief drafts-man and tracer, but the design engineer directly corrects and adjusts any errors displayed on the video. For this specific order, much time was especially saved during the revision stage of the drawings since the design engineer could directly act upon the corrections made by the Customer, by changing the draiwing on the video. It is also obvious that filing of the drawings as well as of any other specifications would permit on a sufficiently large market to improve the performance efficiency in subsequent orders. The simple interaction system is thought as a possible systems engineering relation in which standardization and automatic filing will be at stake to measure the reduced amount of work, i.e. the increased productivity of paperwork.

4.   TRE DRAFTSMAN: DEQUALIFICATION OR NEW RÔLE

"Yes, since capability is certainly expressed by the drawing", according to the unanimous comment of all people who were interviewed during the survey; but this loss of so called "hand", i.e. of the specialistic partiality can not be deemed negative in itself.

The measuring device for professional skill cannot be defined statically start-ing from the previous drafting job description, but must be seen as a dynamic calculation of an exchange between previous and present professional capabilities.

In this dimension, it will not be easy to detect an univocal trend towards either dequalification or professional enrichment pole.

Table A shows sufficiently clearly that the new job description in automatic drafting requires a greater involvement of the draftsman in the activities of the design engineer, as well as with the activities of the "information" staff who introduced the CAD system. This dual reference of the new draftsman will gear the "resources" for possible organization configurations towards thorough modifications of conventional work division within the engineering sector. The need to optimize the exchange between the two different universes of knowledge, i.e. information and design engineering (drafting) may well make the new rôle of the draftsman more complex than before.

With other words, the interaction between the two activity axes or more exactly between a knowledge content and a different availability of the suitable process ing language code (in this case formalized language) will create the conditions for the presence of the expected as well as of potential variances.

As a matter of fact, the interaction between two different level variances creates a "noise" of a more complex degree, difficult to foresee and to adjust except by the "historical" process.

From this stage onwards, it will be possible to remodel vocational capability segments apt to absorb growing shares of complexity or more exactly of the potential variance spectrum.

Along this course, technology will require integration and hence complexity to which the organization still responds with static and rigid feed-back models.

TABLE "A"

	Conventional draftsman	Automatic Drafting Draftsman
Activity	1) translation of the processor's sketch into drawing	translation of the processor's sketch into automatic drafting
	2) copying of the "draft" into clean "drawing"	translation by "automatic" drafting into "clean" drawing
	3) preparation of "component list"	automatic compilation of the component list
	4) revision of the drawing and of the Component list.	automatic revision of the drawing and of the list of components.
capabilities (skills)	1) graphic "skill" the so called draftman's "hand"	no graphic skill is required but the attention remains
	2) -	capability of using and creating new integrative drafting information processes.
knowledge	1) necessary knowledge about drafting symbology and techniques	knowledge about symbology
	2) low accumulation degree of "design" knowledge	knowledge about "machine" interacting procedures
	3) -	knowledge about control/regulation circuits
	4) -	increased direct interaction with the processor; possible increased design knowledge
	5) -	possible increased knowledge about information systems.
Training	minimum time	- co-operation will be possible after 3 months - autonomous after 6 months
Autonomy	in corporate context the Chief draftsman is a total filter, hence low autonomy	increased direct interaction with the processor, hence growing autonomy. He is depending from the CAD center and no longer from the Chief Draftsman

	Conventional draftsman	Automatic Drafting Draftsman
Repeatibility/ variability	The arrangement of the drawing and the "hand" are the variability parameters while the symbology and object of the drawing are strongly repeatable.	The arrangement of the drawing remains to be chosen by the draftsman.
Information system	Sole unidirectional channel from the Chief draftsman to his draftsman.	Extension of the draftman's information channels towards the processor as well as towards the CAD Service.

	ACTIVITY	TIME	VARIANCES	CONTROL-ADJUSTMENT
Conventional draftsman	transfer from sketch to drawing		- possible interpretation errors - possible symbology errors - drafting quality (poor)	- Chief draftsman is the controller and most often the adjuster of variances
	Copying		- possible simbology erros - drafting quality poor	= =
	Preparation of component list		- listing errors	- control and adjustment by the Chief Draftsman
	Revision of "drawing" and "list"		- conceptual and transcription errors during manual modification of the drawing and all lists	- control and adjustment by all users - control and adjustment by Chief Draftsman

	ACTIVITY	TIME	VARIANCES	CONTROL – ADJUSTMENT
Automatic drafting Draftsman	1) Translation of the sketch into automatic drawing		– possible interpretation errors	– interaction with the processor to check and adjust any interpretaticn variance
			– "machine" variances	– control and adjustment by draftsman
				– according to the seriousness of the error, action is taken by the CAD service or producing firm
	2) Reduction of a draft into automatic drawing		– "machine" variance	– control and adjustment by draftsman
				– according to the seriousness of the variance, action is taken by the CAD service or by the producing Firm
	3) Automatic compilation of the list	strongly reduced time	=	=
	4) Automatic revision of drawing and list	=	=	=

A SWEDISH MODEL FOR SYSTEMS DEVELOPMENT
IN PUBLIC ADMINISTRATION

Barbara Klockare & Kerstin Norrby

The Swedish Agency for Administrative
Development (SAFAD)
Statskontoret,
Stockholm
SWEDEN

In Sweden the implementation of new technology is to some extent
controlled by labour legislation and governmental bills. The
opportunity for user participation is dependant on the decision-making process and on the document bases used. The outline
for system development is also based on this decision-making
process. The "specification of user need" and the "assessment of
effects" are both documents serving as bases for the decision
between the stages of "Systems Analysis study" and "Systems Design Phase". The SAFAD-method to assess effects of computerization takes into account both tecknical and other effects. Our
experiences using this method have proved it to be useful.

INTRODUCTION

The consequences of computerization and the role of computerization are issues
that are widely discussed in Sweden. With increased utilization of computers in
governmental administration, certain weaknessess and disadvantages have been in-
dentified. But it has also been argued that it is necessary to improve planning,
control and co-ordination of ADP in public administration. Anothermain question in
this discussion concerns the opportunity for the end-users and others involved to
influence and control the use of computers.

In response to this the Government/Riksdagen in 1979 passed a bill on the utilization of automatic data processing (ADP) in the governmental administration. The
bill underlines the need for a formalized procedure for decision-making with regard to major computer applications. The need for documentation as a basis for
these decisions should also be more complete.

Furthermore, the bill states that the use of data processing is a tool for improving public administration. Computers must be used in a way that enables a more
efficient use of available resources or leads to other benefits. It was also suggested that members of parliament should participate directly in important systems
development projects, e.g in reference groups.

As a result of the bill, a special committee has been created to follow the consequences of computerization in the Swedish society at large. It is made up of
members from the political parties, the labour unions, the employers organizations
and local Government authorities.

A new bill has been passed this year outlining the Government's interest in coordinating and controlling the use of computers in Swedish society. In the bill, the
Government has spelled out measures regarding education and research.

In addition to these bills, two laws protect the employee when changes are made in
hisworking routines.

These laws are:

- Act on Employee Participation in Decision-Making (1977),

- Work Environment Act (1978).

Both are general laws supplemented by collective agreements between employers and employees.

The Act on Employee Participation in Decision-Making is applicable to the relation between employers and employees. It contains fundamental rules on the right of participation and negotiation, collective agreements, the right to information, and so on. The employer is obliged to inform and negotiate with the union before taking decisions about any major operational changes. This applies to major changes in working conditions for any individual employee, including implementation of new technology.

The first employee participation agreement was concluded in 1978 for the civil servants. The participation agreement gives employees influence in three important areas: planning, organization and staffing policy.

The Work Environment Act defines the general demands which can be made with regard to working conditions. The Act states, for example that work must be planned in such a way that it can be carried out in a healthy and safe environment. Hence, focus is put on the working premises, its equipment, techniques and working methods.

In the 1979 bill, the Government/Riksdagen spelled out the necessity of improved procedures for decision-making and more complete documentation as a basis for decisions regarding computerization. Thus the "Regulation on investments in public ADP-systems" was issued in 1981. In the regulation it is specified:

- that the systems development process shall be divided into stages,

- which documentation shall be produced in the different stages, one of these being assessment of effects,

- that decision-makers have the opportunity to gradually - after each stage - be more explicit in defining the goal and level of ambition of the proposals,

- criteria selecting those ADP-investments which are to be scrutinized by the parliament and cabinet under this special regulation.

In exceptional cases, for example when using new techniques and experimental methods, the Government is able to make an exception from this rule. In such case the authority concerned has to suggest an alternative decision-making process which gives the Government the possibilities to control the development.

These directives are based on a model that already was in use at SAFAD (the Swedish Agency For Administrative Development). Now, all authorities normally have to use the same decision-making process.

The rest of this paper will be devoted to three areas where SAFAD is engaged in developing new methods. The three areas include an outline of the decision-making process, the specification of users´ needs, and a method to assess effects of computerization.

OUTLINE OF A DECISION-MAKING PROCESS FOR SYSTEMS DEVELOPMENT

The decision-making process is based on the assumption that the process of the systems development is divided into the following major stages: initiation, fea-

sability study, systems analysis, system design or system construction, implementation, and operations and maintenance. Furthermore, a post-evaluation should be
carried out when the system has been running for some time.

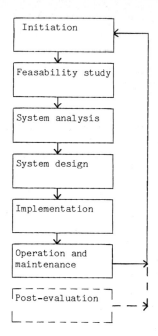

Between each stage, a major decision about whether and how to proceed must be
taken. The quality of the documentation to be used as a basis for these decisions
is therefore of great importance. Before each decision, the authority concerned
and the local trade unions have to negotiate about the proposals in accordance
with The Act on Employee Participation.

The initiation stage consists of collecting and roughly evaluating different
ideeas and alternative solutions. The terms of reference, given by the Government
or by the authority concerned, include expected results, organization and methods
etc.

During the feasability study, the important strategic decisions are taken, for instance whether to computerize or not. The problems at hand are analyzed   in
depth and possible solutions are identified. Different proposals for solutions
must be compared to a zero-based alternative and for each alternative there has to
be an assessment of effects and cost-estimates.

Based on this documentation, decisions are made regarding which alternative is to
be studied in more detail in the next stage, whether the feasability study should
be carried on further, or whether the project should be discontinued.

The systems analysis study, which can be divided into several steps, aims at identifying problems and solutions in greater detail. Now the proposed system, the
organization for which it is intended, and the manual routines should be worked
out and described. As a result of the proposed system, certain effects for end-
users and others are expected to appear. These effects, together with cost-estimates, have to be described in more depth than during earlier stages.

The project work must be arranged in such a way that end-users and others involved
get an opportunity to take an active part in the outline of the system, for instance, end-users may join the project group or form a group of reference.

The following documentation should be prepared during systems analysis stage:

- A specification of users' needs, including the users' demands of the system, the
organization and the routines, the demand on input/output, and the demand for
flexibility in the system. The document will serve as a receipt for the users' demands and as a guide for the technical design of the system. It must also be easy
for users to read and understand.

- A crude technical specification, based on the specification of the users' needs,
including a description of the computer application. This technical specification
also forms a basis for purchasing equipment and service.

- An assessment of effects and cost-estimates of the proposal compared to a zero-
based alternative.

- Plans for system design and implementation stages, including information and
training activities, design and test, equipment, other resources etc.

This documentation should serve as the basis for a decision to stop the project or
to continue according to the directives set down for the design stage.

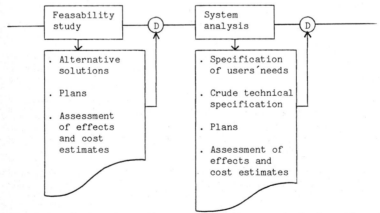

During the system design stage, the manual and the computerized routines are
worked out in detail and the whole system is tested. Rules for implementation and
operation are documented.

Implementation of the new system includes activities such as training, creations
of new files, parallel running, and allocating the responsibility for the day-to-
day running.

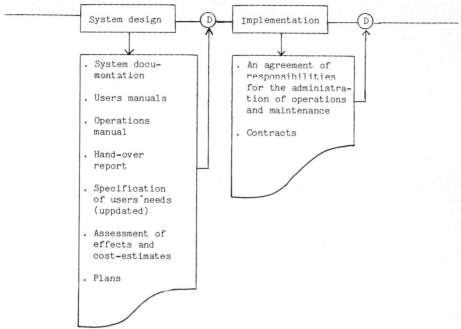

<u>Operation and maintenance</u> are regarded as part of the normal activity of the orga-
nization. Special rules may be needed for decisions regarding maintenance and
changes of the ADP-system.

When an extensive or a specialized follow-up of the system is of interest, the
<u>post-evaluation</u> is carried out as a separate project.

A SPECIFICATION OF USERS´ NEEDS – A BASIS FOR DECISION-MAKING

The most important decision, whether to continue the development of a proposed
system or not, is taken between the stages of systems analysis and system design.
Before this decision-point it is not possible to see how the system is going to
function in detail, what the effects for the users and other groups may be and how
much it will cost. Until now, there has only been limited expenditure compared to
the costs that will occur during the system design or later.

The users´ demands, technical possibilities, effects and costs are all examples of
important factors that should influence the final system. The specification of the
users´ needs is successively worked out during the systems analysis stage. In order to make sure that the proposed system is technically and economically viable,
you must work with crude technical solutions and assessment of effects including
cost-estimates at the same time. Nevertheless it is important that the technical
solution is based on the specification of the users´ needs and not the other way
around. These three documents depend on each other and neither of them can be
finalized before the others.

The specification of the users´ needs shall describe the proposed system from the
users´ point of view. The end-users must therefore play an important part in the
preparation of the specifications. They could do most of the work themselves. In
doing so they need time, education and most likely help from the project group.
When analyzing their needs and discussing possible solutions, they are really able

to influence the outline of the new system. The technical solutions are, as mentioned earlier, described separately in the crude technical specification.

The settlement of the specification of the users´ needs forms a transition from the systems analysis stage to the design stage. An important aspect of the document is then that it should serve as an agreement between the decision-maker and the project group. The document also serves as a "receipt" for the users´ demands. During the proceeding work, it is important that the document is updated as soon as any changes are decided on.

Many organizations have started to use the concept "specification of users´ needs". The quality of the documents produced differs of course. But the content of the documentation of different proposals has become more uniform, and therefore easier to read by end-users and decision-makers. It has also become easier to compare one investment to another.

The contents of the specification of the users´ needs can be grouped under these following headlines:

- description of problems

- assessment of the future development in the area of change

- aims and demands

- brief description of rejected solutions

- a zero-based alternative to compare with

- the proposed system is described in detail

    . organization

    . the main working tasks, their relationships, which decisions are made based on which information etc

    . demands on personnel, rooms and computerbased routines etc

    . manual routines including how the routines at and around the terminals are going to work

    . social environment

A METHOD TO ASSESS EFFECTS OF COMPUTERIZATION

It is often said that ADP is a tool for information processing with very special characteristics. Many have experienced that new information systems lead to both expected and unexpected effects, some wanted and some not. In many systems development projects, the description of expected effects, monetary and nonmonetary, is neither complete nor easily accessible.

In recent years, however, there has been some improvement in the bases for the decision-making, largely because decision-makers have requested it. Also, the labour unions and the public have taken greater interest in the effects of computerized public service, thus influencing systems analysts to describe expected effects.

In order to take into account not only technical, but also other effects, SAFAD has developed a method to assess the effects of computerization.

In the Participation Agreement (MBA-S) between Government and trade unions the following definition is found:

"By effectivity is understood that each authority should achieve the aims of its activities

- through good utilization of resources,

- in regard to demands of service, access to public records and legal security

- in regard to the employees need for job-satisfaction, good working environment, security of employment and the opportunity for participation in decision-making and personal development."

In accordance with this definition the effects of a proposed administrative change can be divided into five major effect areas:

- "Which effects will the proposal have on the tasks performed (activities) within the authority, that is on the service rendered to the public, other authorities or enterprises?

- Which effects will the proposal have on the working conditions of various categories of personnel?

- Which effects will the proposal have on the demands by the public, the press and others for service, access to public records and legal security?

- Which effects will the proposal have on the economy and utilization of resources of the authority and others?

- Which effects will the proposal have on the possibility to change and develop authority in the future?"

With these questions in mind, the actual work of analyzing and documenting effects of the proposal takes place.

The method for assessing effects includes:

- six working steps to be followed

- the check-lists to be used in each step. This facilitates a systematic identification of changes that are expected and the effects that might occur

- the effects are assessed and documented into five major effects areas. These areas are in accordance with the definition of effectivity above.

The six working steps are as follows:

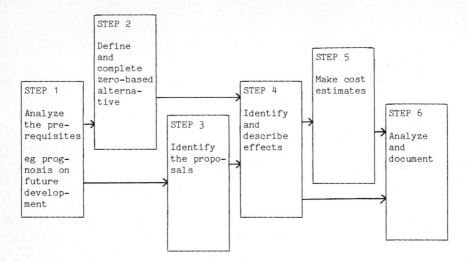

The actual work of assessing the effects of a proposal starts with analyzing the prerequisties of the proposal. This work is done in three first steps.

In "STEP 1" the prognosis of future development within the area of change is checked and if necessary, it is completed.

In "STEP 2" the zero-base alternative is checked and completed. The zero-base alternative equals the expected development if the proposed changes are not implemented. This alternative is used as a point of reference.

To enable the actual identification and documentation of the effects of a computer-based system, the latter has to be rather detailed. By using the check-lists of "STEP 3" the proposal is examined, and if necessary further investigations are done. Documentation often concentrate on the technical system, while the working conditions, the organsiation and the social environment tend to be discussed superficially.

STEP 4 involves the actual analysis and description of effects of both the zero-based alternative as well as the proposal(-s). The effects are divided into five major effect areas mentioned above.

The process of assessing the effects can be schematically described as follows:

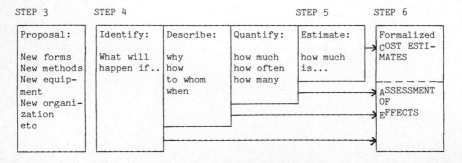

In "STEP 4" you identify the effects of the zero-based alternative and the proposal. To simplify this work, checklists have been worked out. Beginning

- What will happen ...?

When you have identified the effects you describe them, by asking:

- Why, how, to whom, when ...?

After that you quantify the effects, if possible, by asking questions such as:

- How much, how many, how often ...?

For each of the major effect areas you use the same process. And for each effect area it is important to clarify which organizations, groups and individuals that will be affected.

All effects that can be measured in monetary terms are formalized into estimates in "STEP 5". These estimates are of three types:

- a project estimate, which includes costs related to the development and implementation of the proposal,

- a profitability estimate, using present value, which will compare the proposal with the zero-base alternative,

- a budget estimate, which will show the actual flow of money for the years concerned.

These steps (1-5) influence the investigation and proposed solutions iteratively.

In "STEP 6" - the final analysis of the effects is made. The result from this analysis is documented both verbally and as cost estimates. This document serve as one of the bases for decision-making.

"Working conditions" - one effect-area - An example

As mentioned, before you group the effects into five major effect-areas, one of them being the "working conditions", an answer to the following question is of interest:

- Which effects will a proposed computer-based system have on the working conditions of various categories of personnel?

First of all you have to know which various categories of personnel will be affected by the proposal. For each of these categories, the effects must be assessed. In examining what the change implies and how it will influence the different groups, you use the check-list. Not only do you have to know the factual change and the effects that occur. You also have to get an impression of how these various groups will experience the changes that might occur.

The work of assessing the effects in the area of working conditions must be done together with the users. Check-lists facilitate this co-operation.

In order to illustrate the contents of the check-lists, a short extract of the questions in the checklist concerning "Working-conditions" is given here.

- The aim of the work, e.g, will the proposal lead to improved service to the public?

- The organization of work, e.g, will the proposal change the hierachy of the organization?

- Contents and methods, e.g, will the work become more repetitive or more specializqed?

- Volume and resorces, e.g, will the proposal lead to staff changes?

Who will do the assessing?

Whether the work of assessing effects should be done by people outside the project group or by those working in it has been discused. We don´t think that the question is an either-or but rather a both-and.

On several occasions, important decisions are made, which most certainly influence further work. At these decision points, it is crucial that the basis for decision-making is complete and of high quality. Thus, we consider the assessing of effects to be an integral part of the studies made during the systems development process.

This SAFAD-method is primarily designed for those working specifically with assessments of effects. Of course, anyone or any group, e.g, trade union, with special interest in a specific project regarding computerization can use the same method.

When should the assessing be done?

When planning the assessment you also have to choose the level of ambition at which the assessment should be done. This choice depends on how great the expected change is, and on the stage of the process.

Becouce the purpose is to improve the basis for decision-making, the assessment should be performed before starting each new stage in the system development process as described above.

Experiences of the SAFAD–method in a project

This SAFAD-method has been tested in several projects. The experiences so far show that the conditions for working according to this method and the ambition in this work are quite different.

Recently a systems analysis study was finished at one of our state authorities, the National Housing Board. The board had been studying the prerequisites for exchanging their computer-based system. The proposal was that their 14-year-old ADP-system for the management of loans should be replaced by a new system. The change also involved decentralization to the regional administration.

The proposed system, its functions and effects have been documented in a "Specification of Users´ Needs" which includes the assessments and cost-estimates as well as in a "Crude Technical Specification". All groups involved wish to see this new system implemented. The Government hasn´t decided yet whether to continue the work.

During the systems analysis study the local trade union took active part. From the beginning the trade union had demanded a "local collective agreement" covering how the study should be carried out. The local collective agreement covered the staffing of the project organization. The users should be represented in the project group as working members, as well as in the managerial group and in reference groups:

It was also agreed:

- on how to divide the responsibility in the project organization,

- that informations about the project was to be distributed to all employees,

- that all documents given to decision-makers were to be circulated for comments among employees concerned,

- which system development process to be used,

- that the assessment of effects and cost-estimates should be documented and the SAFAD-method for assessing effects should be followed.

Both management and the unions were pleased with this agreement, and they started the system development with a common framework.

In the study of assessing effects, the project-group followed the SAFAD-method step by step.The check-lists were used for each step. Both the employees and the trade union took active part. Their participation show a high degree of ambition.

Having already decided at an early stage which method to use, the investigator could concentrate on the problems of assessing and estimating. The methodological discussions could be left behind. This was considered an advantage.

Of course, some problems occurred. There were some difficulties in interpreting the method and the check-lists.

While assessing the effects the group soon discovered the benefits and costs of their proposed system. For example, the cost-estimates showed that the chosen technical equipment made the whole proposal unprofitable. Another feasable technical solution was found. It was economically viable and more adjustable to the "needs" as specificated both in the directives and in the "Specification of Users´ Needs".

To sum up: The participants in the project group and those responsible for the assessment agreed that the SAFAD-method was very useful. They were convinced that the documentation had become both more comprehensive and correct.The checklists were considered a great help in identifying effects. Methodological support from SAFAD was useful.

SYSTEMS DESIGN FOR, WITH, AND BY THE USERS
U. Briefs, C. Ciborra and L. Schneider (editors)
North-Holland Publishing Company
© IFIP, 1983

TECHNOLOGY ASSESSMENT
OF
EDP-TECHNOLOGY IN CONNECTION WITH NURSING IN HOSPITALS

Arne Kjær

Computer Science Department
Aarhus University
Ny Munkegade
DK - 8000 Aarhus C
Denmark

Peder Grotkjær

The Danish Nurses Organisation
Vimmelskaftet 38
DK - 1160 Copenhagen K
Denmark

1. INTRODUCTION

This paper describes a project aiming at developing methods that the
employee can use to assess technology at work. It is a collaborative
project to be carried out by a group which includes nurses, computer
scientist and sociologist. The subject matter of the project is to
assess the development and application of EDP-technology, and the
changes for the staff and the patients caused by this development
and application. Technology assessment is the central concept we will
use in our discussion of the changes.

The project has three purposes. Two of these have a methodological
character. First of all, we want to set up general proposals for the
elaboration and subject matter of technology assessments. These
proposals should be useful for the employee at the hospitals and
their organizations. Therefore, as a second purpose, we want to develop and try out working forms that improve the possibilities of
the employee to elaborate, to participate in, and to use assessments
of EDP-technology. To fulfil these two purposes, we are going to
assess EDP-technology within the project. And this leads us to the
third purpose of the project: to carry out assessments of existing,
scheduled, and prospective EDP-technology. We want to assess both
the EDP-based systems themselves, as well as the way in which they
are developed and maintained.

The paper describes the background for the project, the activities
in the project, as well as the research method we will use. Finally,
the different types of expected results and the application of these
results will be discussed.

An application for resources to the project has been made, and it is
the plan to start the project in the spring of 1983.

2. BACKGROUND

The background for the project is outlined in a description of the
development of EDP-technology within the hospital sector, of activities within the Danish Nurses' Organisation, and of activities in
relation to technology assessment in Denmark.

2.1. Development of EDP-technology within the hospital sector

The hospitals in Denmark are with few exceptions financed by the
public sector. The hospital sector is mainly financed at the county
level. A minor part is financed by the state and the municipalities.

During the last 10 - 15 years, efforts have been made to reduce the
growth in the public expenditure within the health services. About
3/4 of the resources allocated to the health services is spent within
the hospital sector. Therefore, the hospital sector has been the
target for political demands for a more effective utilization of
resources. About 3/4 of the expenditure within the hospital sector
comes from staffing costs. A more effective utilization of the resources therefore means a more effective utilization of the manpower.

This situation has created a need for effective tools to control the
hospital sector. One of the important tools has been the development
of EDP-based hospital information systems. An EDP-based hospital
information system will be able to perform two main functions, namely a recording function and a communication function. The recording
function is performed by recording systems for information about the
patients, and recording systems for information about staff resources.
The communication function is performed by systems for transmission
of information between the various departments in the hospital. The
primary aim of these systems is to be used in the planning and control
of the hospital sector.

The nurses are in a central position as intermidiaries of information
within the existing hospital information system. The introduction of
EDP-based systems therefore means changes in the working situation
of the nurses and the other staff involved. The systems are not yet
fully developed, and with few exceptions, there have not yet been
implemented special EDP-based systems within the field of nursing.
Until now the systems are primarily implemented as separate applications for recording and communication. But it seems that the separate
applications are going to be integrated to more powerful tools for
planning and control. And the changes for the staff will therefore
become clearer as the systems are further developed.

The initiative to introduce EDP-based systems comes mainly from central authorities, that is the Ministry of the Interior and the Association of County Councils. The main EDP-applications within the
Danish hospital sector are supplied by the municipal EDP-service
bureau called "Kommunedata", which is a partnership between the
Association of County Councils and the National Association of Municipalities. The strategy of Kommunedata is to develop a common information system which can be used by all counties. Until now,
Kommunedata has supplied more than a third of the counties with a
common-on-line information system used for patient recording. And
other counties have planned to implement the same system. A few of
the counties have based their use of EDP-technology in hospitals on
systems developed in their own local EDP-department.

2.2. Activities within the Danish Nurses' Organization

The EDP-based hospital information systems implemented until now
have already caused such problems for the nurses working situation
as inappropriate working procedures, less direct contact with staff
from other departments, and tighter constraints on the collective
planning in the individual departments. However, the overall problem

for the staff until now has been the lack of influence on the design of the systems. It has been very difficult for them and their shop stewards to even establish reasonable preconditions for the assessment of the systems. Lack of information from management, and lack of resources to assess it from the staff's point of view are some of the problems. Therefore, it is difficult for the staff to be aware of the consequences and to gain influence.

The Danish Nurses' Organization has initiated some activities which should place the nurses in a better position to gain influence over technological changes together with other groups of employee. Some important activities are:

- formation of working groups both at the local and at the central level,

- publishing an EDP-handbook for nurses and other pamphlets,

- establishing EDP-education as a part of the shop steward education,

- negotiating technology agreements.

The process of planning this research project has also been an important activity.

The formation of working groups started at the local level with a group of ten nurses from two hospitals and three computer science specialists. This group tried to understand the impact of EDP-technology on the nurses working situation and use this knowledge to gain more influence over the development and application of the EDP-based systems. One result is the "EDP-Handbook for Nurses" [1], written by the group. Since the publication of the EDP-Handbook, other working groups have been established in a number of local Branches of the Danish Nurses' Organization, as well as a working group at the central level of the Danish Nurses' Organization.

The "EDP-Handbook for Nurses", published by the Danish Nurses' Organization, is used as educational material in the courses for shop stewards and as background material for working groups in the Branches. Other material has also been published to support the shop stewards in their efforts of gaining influence.

EDP-education for shop stewards was established to make them aware of the trends and enable them to initiate activities and actions concerning the development and application of EDP-technology. The EDP-education is spread over six hours and is performed by a computer science specialist employed by the Danish Nurses' Organization, together with a nurse, who has been involved in activities in the local Branches. In addition to the education for shop stewards, there are also one-day-courses within the local Branches. These courses have not only been for shop stewards, but also for ordinary nurses, including those participating in development groups appointed by the management.

At the central level, technology agreements has been negotiated within the municipal area for several years without any result. Since agreements have been settled within the private area and the state area, efforts are now being made from the trade unions to force the municipal employers to make an agreement.

2.3. Technology assessment in Denmark

Two years ago a committee appointed by the Council of Technology under the Ministry of Industry, worked out a report about publicly financed "Technology Assessment in Denmark" [13]. The members in the committee represented the interests of the central public administration, the employers and the employees. The report contains, among other things, the committee's considerations concerning

- fields of application of technology assessment,
- organization of technology assessment.

In the report, the committe suggested a very broad definition of technology assessment. This definition says

"Technology assessments should comprise a systematically and generally oriented assessment of the consequences of using a definite technology, understood not only as a technique, but also as the combination of the technique and the organization belonging to it." [13]

The assessments should include the human, the social, the financial, and the environmental consequences.

Concerning the fields of application the committee suggested that technology assessments should include nearly all kinds of technology. Production technology, infra-structure and communication, global and transnational technologies, as well as products and consumer goods should be included. And the technology assessment should take place both at the level of the individual companies and at the society level.

Concerning organization, the committee suggested the establishment of a Council of Technology Assessment to coordinate the activities. It also suggested that the total financial grant should be divided into the following four fields:

- superior long-term technology assessments,

- technology assessments attached to professional organizations and citizens' movements,

- interest oriented technology assessments attached to the interests of employers,

- interest oriented technology assessments attached to the interests of employees.

The publishing of the committee report caused strong reactions from industrial organizations and associations of employers. They were dissatisfied with the suggestions concerning the division of the total grant between interests of employers, employees, and citizens movements, and the assessment of products at the level of individual companies. The result was that the Council of Technology recommended the report to the Minister of Industry without the above mentioned suggestions. The minister has taken no further initiatives.

In the meantime, the Council of Technology has granted a number of projects, which have status as experimental technology assessment. This is the situation where the Danish Nurses' Organization, among

other trade unions, finds it relevant to gain experience with technology assessment, which can be of use for the employees.

3. DESCRIPTION OF THE PROJECT

In this section, we present four characteristic features of the
project, which separates it from other ongoing technology assessment
projects in Denmark. Then, we will describe how the project is organized, and outline the main activities in the project.

3.1. Some characteristics of the project

Firstly, the project is going to contribute to the development of
methods, perceived as guidelines for work processes. The project is
concerned with methods for technology assessment, both in general
regarding the superior guidelines, and concretely regarding guidelines useable for the trade unions. This project will make proposals
for the elaboration and subject matter of technology assessments.
These proposals should take into account, who is going to use the
proposals, and which processes they are going to be incorporated in.
As it appears in the report from the Council of Technology [13],
there are not sufficient well-developed methods to carry out technology assessments. Therefore, an important task in this field is to
develop such useful methods.

Secondly, the project will investigate, how a systematic use of technology assessments can affect the development of EDP-based systems.
Thus, the project is going to deal with necessary changes in existing
system development methods to take into account the need for technology assessments.

Thirdly, the project is occupied with both assessments of the products: the EDP-based systems, and assessments of the process: the
development of these systems. It is especially important to include
assessments of the process, because the project is concerned with
prospective applications of EDP-technology and different trends in
these. The ways in which system development methods handle the
choice between these prospective technologies is also critical.

Fourthly, nurses are going to participate in the implementation of
the project on an equal basis with the academic staff. This means
that the project has better opportunities to benefit from the professional knowledge of the employees. This should result in more qualified assessments. Involvement of the professional knowledge of the
employees is also recognized as an important problem in many newer
system development methods. Methodologically, this participation is
a further development of earlier projects: e.g. the Norwegian "Iron
and Metal project" [11, 12], the Swedish "Democratic Planning and
Control in Working Life" [12], and the Danish "Development, Democracy
and EDP project" [4, 6, 7, 12]. From the staff's point of view, this
participation makes it possible to build up knowledge and experience
about development, use and assessment of EDP-technology, which may
improve the possibilities and assumptions to influence the development and application of EDP-technology.

3.2. How the project is organized

The project includes a project group, a steering committee, and some
working groups.

The <u>project group</u> carries out the daily work in the project. The project group is composed of two nurses and two academics, full-time. Further an EDP-consultant employed by the Danish Nurses' Organization participates on a part-time basis. This participation makes it possible to have better contact with nurses in hospitals, a better utilization and quicker dissipation of the results. Finally, a secretary participates in the project group. The qualifications in the project group includes nursing, computer science and sociology. There are possibilities for involving consultants with expertise supplementing that of the project group (e.g., consultants with expertise in economics). The composition of the project group reflects the essence of the project: the connection between nursing and the use of EDP-technology at the hospitals.

The <u>steering committee</u> follows the project, and guides the project group in its work. The steering committee is composed of two representatives from the Danish Nurses' Organization and one representative from each of the two research institutions who have been involved in the start of this project: one from the Computer Science Department, Aarhus University, and one from the Department of Information Research, the Copenhagen School of Economics and Business Administration. Various institutions and organizations also participate as observers in the steering committee.

The <u>working groups</u> are appointed in one part of the project to complement the work of the project group in this part. The working groups are composed of two representatives from the project group, one graduate student, and about ten employees at hospitals. The latter have or may have contact with the EDP-technology which the working group is going to assess.

3.3. Activities in the project

The project starts with the changes caused by the development and application of EDP-technology, especially those which affect the work situation of the employee. The main task will be to investigate the application of EDP-technology in connection with nursing and the changes that may result from these applications. The activities in the project are divided into three phases. The first and the second phase are planned to take 15 months, and the third phase 6 months. Next we will outline the activities in the three phases of the project.

In <u>the first phase</u>, information will be collected about:

- the EDP-based systems used in connection with nursing
- the system development methods used to create these systems.

Our aim is to produce an overview of how and to what extent EDP-technology is used in connection with nursing. We will also assess the extent to which existing system development methods would accomodate the participation of hospital employee in technology assessment. In the selection of EDP-based systems, we will choose places, where the applications reflect different trends.

In gathering information about the applications of EDP-technology, we will concentrate on applications in foreign countries. It is our impression that one finds more advanced applications of EDP abroad than in Denmark. Secondly, EDP-based systems are transferred between countries, either as standard systems or as know how, the trend in foreign

countries may influence Danish EDP-based systems, used in connection
with nursing.

In gathering information about system development methods, the main
investigations will take place in Denmark. First of all, because
the overall features in the methods are widely used across frontiers.
Secondly, because the state of the labour market in the different
countries determines the specific elaboration of the methods.

In order to get an overview of the applications of EDP-technology in
connection with nursing and existing system development methods, we
will make some study-travels to foreign and Danish hospitals.

In the second phase, the project group will elaborate assessments of
selected EDP-technology in connection with nursing. The assessments
of the systems may comprise, for instance, changes in working conditions, employment, education, qualification structure, patient care,
and economy of the national society. An important condition of the
elaboration of qualified assessments is the establishment of a
number of working groups, approximately four, at different work
places. The task for these working groups should be:

- to experiment with the elaboration of technology assessments,

- to contribute to the assessment of the individual EDP-based
  systems and the trends these systems reflect,

- to develop and try out new working forms that employees can
  use in their work with technology assessments,

- to investigate how work with technology assessments may be
  integrated with local trade union activities.

The assessments of EDP-based systems and the trends in these, may
comprise the same fields of consequences as mentioned above. The
information and experiences collected in the first phase is used in
the working groups. This creates possibilities to form ideas of
different trends of development.

Besides this, the project group does research about the trends in the
application of EDP-technology in the health service in Denmark.
Among other things, this can support work with technology assessment
in the working groups, as well as the total technology assessment,
which is elaborated in the third phase.

In the third phase, the project group documents the project as a
whole, including:

- a total assessment of the application of EDP-technology in connection with nursing at hospitals.

- the drawing up of general proposals for the elaboration and
  subject matter of technology assessments.

- a description of the work forms used in the working groups and
  a discussion of the circumstances under which they may be used.

- reflections on the requirements the use of technology assessments put to the system development methods.

- a discussion about whether and how technology assessment may
  be integrated in trade union activities both at the local and
  at the central level.

4.   DESCRIPTION OF THE RESEARCH METHOD

The research method is based on the methodological experience from
the DUE-project, a Danish acronym for Democracy, Development and
EDP [3, 4, 5, 6, 7], and a collaboration project between nurses and
computer scientist in 1976-77 [1, 8]. Furthermore, it is inspired
by the work of Bergo & Nygaard (1975), the work of Freire (1970),
and the work of Negt (1972). The research method may be characterized
as action-oriented, interest-based technology assessment. The method
will be presented and discussed in terms of the three key-words:
interest-based research, technology assessment, and action orientation.

4.1.   Interest-based research

Trade union research and influence over technological development is
limited if the trade unions first have to compromise about goals,
research activities, results of the research, and the like, with the
employers' associations.

Trade unions also have interests in the development of methods when
technology assessment is to be a part of the change process. They
have, for instance, interests in:

- how the goal of the technology assessment process is defined,

- which activities the process includes,

- what the results of the process will contain,

- how the process is going to be carried out, i.e. how the
  process can be integrated into the trade unions' activities
  both on the local and on the central level.

Therefore, one of the main aims of the project is to develop methods,
so the trade union, both on the local and on the central level, may
elaborate, participate in, and use technology assessment as a part
of their activities.

Furthermore, in interest-based research you may distinguish between
research _for_ the trade unions, research _with_ the trade unions, and
research _by_ the trade unions.

By research _for_ the trade unions, we perceive that some specialists
are doing the research. It could, for instance, be a computer scientist, a sociologist, and an economist, who is going to assess the
changes caused by the application of an EDP-based system. The assessment may be based on analyses in the information flow, and changes
in the work situation based on managements' description of the
work routines. Furthermore, it may include considerations about the
employment, and the financial situation of the organization. And
there may even be some interviews with the employees. The research
is characterized by producing some results, useable for the trade
unions in a negotiation and a bargaining situation with the employers'
associations.

By research <u>with</u> the trade unions, we perceive that some specialists together with representatives from the trade unions are doing the research. And the representatives have a professional education and are not specialists.

This is the approach we use in this project, and in section 4.2 we will discuss, how technology assessment may be organized, if the users are going to take part in this. The advantages of collaboration is the involvement of the professional knowledge of the users, which creates better possibilities to assess the changes in the work situation of the staff. Through a research process like this, the trade unions will build up knowledge about experiences with possible changes caused by the application of technology. In the DUE-project they also did research with the trade unions. But the representatives in the project group only used 1/6 of their working time in the project. This participation did not give the same possibilities, as we intend, to withdraw the professional knowledge of the staff in order to make more qualified assessments.

By research <u>by</u> the trade unions, we perceive that some representatives from the trade unions are doing the research. The representatives have a professional education and are not specialists. To do this research, it is necessary that the representatives have some experience with changes caused by the application of EDP-technology and knowlege of the possibilities the technology offers. In the research it may be necessary for the representatives to call in some specialists to analyze technical descriptions. As a result of the project, the trade unions should, at least to a greater extent than today, be able to carry out technology assessments themselves, both at the local and at the central level.

4.2. Technology assessment

One of the main activities in the project group and in the working groups is to assess how the use of EDP-technology may change the working conditions, the employment, the qualifications needed in the jobs, and the education of the employees. Furthermore, both the consequences for the patients caused by changes in nursing and the economic implications of the use of EDP-technology for the society will be investigated.

These activities may be characterized as development of professional knowledge. The development process is described in figure 1.

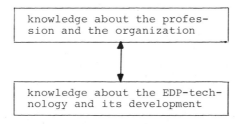

Figure 1
Development of professional knowlege

The arrows in figure 1 cover the development process, and they have
the following meaning:

↓ knowledge about the profession and the organization is necessary
  in order to be aware of important consequences of the application
  of EDP-technology.

↑ knowledge about the EDP-technology and its development is necessary in order to be aware of the professional and the organizational changes, which are influenced by the introduction of EDP-
  technology.

One point in figure 1 is, that the technology is assessed in relation
to somethings other than the organizational change as a whole, namely
the qualifications needed for the jobs. Another point is, in making
the assessments, you have to incorporate a detailed knowledge about
how the work is carried out.

This leads to the following two principles after which we may organize
the technology assessment:

Firstly, the knowledge of the employees (users) has to be involved in
the investigations of the consequences. It is necessary to involve
professional and organizational knowledge of the employee in order
to investigate and assess the consequences of EDP-based systems not
yet introduced. Furthermore, the knowledge of the employees is necessary in order to develop the professional knowledge which creates
possibilities to use technology in another way.

Secondly, interdisciplinary work is critical. When we assess EDP-
technology, it is important not only to include technical knowledge,
but also knowledge of sociology and economics because the technology
affects many different sides of the organization.

These two principles are considered in the composition of the project
group and the establishment of working groups in the second phase of
the project.

4.3. Action orientation

By action orientation we mean that the development of professional
knowledge and actions must interact.

With the development of professional knowledge, as described in section 4.2, figure 1, one acquires a certain knowledge about EDP-
technology. This knowledge may act as the basis for discussions and
clarification among employees. Furthermore, meaningful actions are
necessary in order to change the present ways of using EDP-technology.

Consequently, we may talk about two types of actions:

- actions among employees, e.g. discussions about changes in the
  work situation,

- actions in relation to the employer, e.g. in order to change
  the actual work situation.

One result of the actions may be changes in the use of EDP-technology.
Furthermore, they may uncover lack of knowledge, and consequently,
lead to new investigations and a development of professional knowledge.

The relationship between the development of professional knowledge and actions can be described as in figure 2.

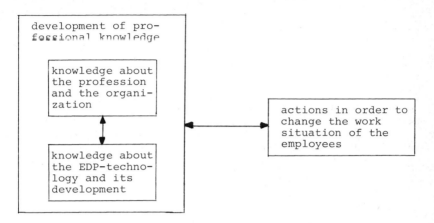

Figure 2
The relationship between the development of professional knowledge and actions

The arrows in figure 2 have the following meaning:

— the development of professional knowledge, especially about the relationship between the application of EDP-technology and the work situation of employees is a necessary precondition starting meaningful actions to change the application of the technology.

— the actions may either lead to actual changes in the application of EDP-technology in the organization, or to new knowledge, e.g. about possible changes and the power of the staff, which both may be used as input to the process of developing professional knowledge.

The action orientation leads to the third principle, according to which we may organize the technology assessment:

The investigations should be a part of a process in the trade unions, both at the local and at the central level. The third principle makes the results useable for the trade union, and it is considered in the composition of the project group and the establishment of the working groups in the second phase. Furthermore, it will, of course, be important <u>where</u> the working groups are established and <u>which</u> applications they investigate.

5. ABOUT THE APPLICATION OF THE RESULTS OF THE PROJECT

In this section, we will give a summary of the application of the results in relation to activities within the trade unions, and activities within the research and educational institutions.

5.1.   In relation to activities within the trade unions

As described in the background section of this paper, there is a
great need for knowledge about the consequences of the development
and application of EDP-based systems. There is also a need to try
to influence this development in order to control it in a more
democratic way.

One of the principal aims of the project is to make the application
of the results an integral part of the project. In the second phase,
the project group will work together with working groups at selected
workplaces. This means that these working groups can use the project
group's knowledge about the specific problems at the workplaces.
Thus, the working groups will have more resources at their disposal,
which should place them in a better position to gain influence.

The knowledge and experience gained from the project, should not only
be used during the project period, but also be kept and utilized after
the project is finished. The participation of two nurses and the EDP-
consultant at the central level of the Danish Nurses' Organization
should ensure that the project will contribute building up permanent
resources within the trade union.

One way to utilize the project is to integrate the results and the
experience from the project in educational activities both within the
Danish Nurses' Organization and in the trade unions as a whole.
Furthermore, the results should be used to support other local activities, and to improve the advise given by the Danish Nurses' Organization. In this way, the project should help to create better conditions for the employees to influence the development. And in the
long term, they may also help to set up alternatives to the existing
development which are based on the interests of the employees.

In the light of the experiments with technology assessment, the project should set up general proposals for the elaboration and subject
matter of technology assessment. Therefore, the project can also be
used to influence the public resources for technology assessment in
order to make it useful from the employees' point of view. In this
way, the trade unions as a whole, should be able to benefit from the
project.

5.2.   In relation to research and educational institutions

Four kinds of results should be outlined here. The first two have
a methodological character.

Firstly, the methodological experience we gain in the project concerning collaboration with trade unions may be of great value for
collaboration in the future.

Secondly, in the project we will discuss which demands a systematic
use of technology assessments may make on existing system development methods. This can be a part of the more theoretical work about
the system development process taking place at the Computer Science
Department, Aarhus University.

Thirdly, the assessment of EDP-technology in connection with nursing
may be used in the definition of professional oriented computer languages. We are in contact with K. Nygaard, Department of Informatics,
Oslo University, who is the director of a project. The objective of
this project is to develop computer language for professionals to-

gether with the staff at the Rikshospital in Oslo. This research project is planned to show special interest to nursing.

Fourthly, the project will lead to results about how the EDP-technology may change the organization and the work situation of the employees. In this connection, it is of special interest, that these changes will also say something about the development and application of EDP technology.

REFERENCES

[1] EDP-Handbook for Nurses (The Danish Nurses' Organization, Copenhagen, 1982). Distributed by the Public Services International, Feltham, Middlesex.

[2] P. Freire: Pedagogy of the Oppressed (Herder and Herder, New York, 1970).

[3] F. Kensing: The need for alternative methods. Preprint, Computer Science Department, Aarhus University (Nov. 1981).

[4] F. Kensing: The trade unions' influence on technological change. Computer Science Department, Aarhus University (Aug. 1982).

[5] A. Kjær, L. Mathiassen: Klubarbejde og edb på Postgiro (Local Union Work and EDP at the Postgiro Office). DUE-note 13, Computer Science Department, Aarhus University (Nov. 1979). In Danish.

[6] Klubarbejde og edb (The Local Unions and EDP). DUE-report 4, Computer Science Department, Aarhus University (Jan. 1981). In Danish.

[7] M. Kyng, L. Mathiassen: System Development and Trade Union Activities. DUE-report 3, DAIMI-PB-99, Computer Science Department, Aarhus University (June 1980).

[8] A. Munk-Madsen: Systembeskrivelse med brugere (System Description with Users). DUE-note 9, Computer Science Department, Aarhus University (Jan. 1978). In Danish.

[9] O. Negt: Sociological Fantasy and exemplified Learning (EVA, Frankfurt/M, 1972).

[10] K. Nygaard: Kundskabsstrategi for fagbevægelsen (Strategy of Knowledge for the Trade Union). Nordisk Forum hæfte 2, vol. 10 (1975). In Norwegian.

[11] K. Nygaard, O. T. Bergo: The trade unions: new users of research. Personnel Review, vol. 4, no. 2 (1975).

[12] Å. Sandberg (ed.): Computers Dividing Man and Work (Arbetslivscentrum, Stockholm, 1979).

[13] Teknologivurdering i Danmark (Technology Assessment in Denmark). Report given by a committee under the Council of Technology, Ministry of Interior (Copenhagen, June 1980). In Danish, but with a summary in English.

MODELS AND METHODS
FOR PARTICIPATIVE
SYSTEM DESIGN

SYSTEMS DESIGN FOR, WITH, AND BY THE USERS
U. Briefs, C. Ciborra and L. Schneider (editors)
North-Holland Publishing Company
© IFIP, 1983

SOCIO-TECHNICAL PROBLEMS OF SYSTEM DESIGN METHODS[1]

Reinhard Budde, Heinz Züllighoven

Gesellschaft für Mathematik und Datenverarbeitung (GMD)
D-5205 St. Augustin 1
F.R. Germany

This paper focuses on the development of dp-systems as the
technical part of information systems. It faces the problem
that user participation does not automatically lead to better
(more user-friendly) dp-systems. This leads to several issues
regarding the relations between system design methods and the
means and ways of user involvement. An attempt is made to
answer the central question whether strategies for participation are invariant with respect to methods of dp-system design.

INTRODUCTION

Design of dp-systems within a socio-technical system (an existing organization) is
a process which involves at least two different worlds - the dp-oriented world of
system developers and the application-oriented world of the users. It has often
been said that the crucial point of system development is rooted in the differences between these worlds. Thus it is that researchers and practitioners
analyse and try to find solutions for the communication problems of developers and
users, or try to bridge the gap between so-called informal requirements of users
and formal system design.

Criticising development strategies which are centred on the dp-professionals
and taking the users' point of view has led to a new approach: different
strategies of user participation or involvement have been proposed. First empirical results of participation projects raise more or less high hopes. But working
in the field of concepts for system development we note that these strategies of
participation concentrate on the organizational aspects of user involvement and
neglect to a considerable degree the more technical methods of system design and
construction.

This observation leads to the issues of this paper:

- Are strategies for participation invariant with respect to methods of system
  design?

- If not, are there methods and tools which are more favorable for participative strategies than others?

- Which structural differences determine the worlds of users and developers
  (i.e. system designers, programmers, etc.)?

- Which social and political attitudes of whom influence participative system
  development?

INTERLUDE

Development of information systems is first of all development of models. Models depict reality. We start by presenting three pictures.

Methodology of System Design:

We would like to pick up the idea of an ambitious colleague. Just imagine this:

Design of a methodically thoroughbred car at the research institute "Future Cars Ltd." The expert team at its first brainstorming. "Well, a car decomposes into body, drive, four wheels and steering system"; the system analyst develops the overall concept. "Which leads to our first essential problem", interposes the system designer. "What should the steering system look like?" "When I was with General Mobiles, we always did it like this: four wheels, one steering wheel", a veteran constructor (a former machine fitter) puts in. Some subtle smiles cross the faces of the car-technologists and a young graduate technologist counters: "The car of the future will have four wheels and four steering wheels, one steering wheel each." "Now that has to be analysed methodically", interposes the chief designer. "Well", says the veteran constructor, "one could drive pretty well with a single steering wheel." "But the solution with four wheels is more general; it includes the traditional solution as a special case, if you just synchronize the two front wheels and keep all rear ones constant," the young graduate technologist ponders. "Do we have an application where four steering wheels are superior to the traditional solution", the chief designer reasons. After a moment of silence the system analyst says: "In case of an emergency braking one could position all four tyres crosswise with those four steering wheels, that would be an ideal solution - and then imagine parking in the city: every wheel adjusted separately and you will pull into a parking space to the fraction of an inch.

This breaks the spell. Champagne corks, slapping of backs, and now a brilliant idea follows the next: "In order to improve the user friendlyness we will show the position of the wheels in grade on a colour bit-map display on the dashboard!" "Why not take eight wheels instead of four and increase reliability." "What we really need is a reset button for the starting position." "An undo-switch for driving faults!" And it becomes a very nice evening...

Communication Problems in System Analysis:

You are feeling sick and pay a visit to your doctor. Leading you into the pre-examination room the nurse secretary provides you with a bulky questionnaire, writing utensils and a book of rules on how to conduct the pre-examination. You start filling the questionnaire. Carefully you answer fill-in-the-blanks questions like "What is your respiration rate?" or "State your complete blood count!" Sometimes you have to consult the medical library on the wall and glance over a short treatise on electro-encephalography or gastroscopy before you know how to conduct these as self-analyses in a well-equipped laboratory next door, guided by the book of rules. After the successful completion of the pre-examination you press a button and the doctor himself enters. He takes the filled questionnaire and says: "Well, now we will start designing your health."

On User Interfaces and Important Principles of Implementation:

The following picture we have borrowed from McCracken and Jackson/1/:

I left my car in the car park of the supermarket and entered one of the doors over which was written "Customers' Requirements Specification". When one of the small cabins which filled the giant hall like telephone boxes was vacant I entered it. The beaming face of a clerk smiled at me from a big colour screen on the wall when I sat down on the stool. "Your requirements please", he said. Immediately I named a few goods I wanted to buy: milk, tea, sugar, a dozen eggs. When I thought of the vegetables for dinner, I stopped my specification of requirements. "What kind of vegetables do you have?" I asked the friendly face on the screen. "You have put the wrong question", he said. "The only thing of interest is what vegetables you want." "But if exactly that vegetable is out of stock?" I reasoned. "Then we will find an optimal solution for you according to our eminent experience with customers and our knowledge of the supermarket", was the still friendly answer. "And if I don't know exactly what kind of vegetable I want to cook for tonight, would it then be possible to have a quick look   " "Sir!" the face interrupted quite harshly, "we operate according to the most advanced methods: 'information hiding', 'abstract order types', 'general product theory', etc., etc. Thereby we have relieved our customers from all the superfluous burdens. What's the use of the exact knowledge of our department structure, the long access paths to the shelves, the retrieval of the right product, the knowledge of types of packing. What our customers really want is the satisfaction of their needs and wishes. Why bother them with the How, the internal structure of our supermarket?"

Later on at the counter a glossy made up parcel waited for me. "This one?", asked the cashier. I nodded, for the numbers on the parcel matched with those on the receipt of my order specification. At home when I began to open the parcel the first specification error hit my eyes: it was true that I had ordered a kilo of sugar, but why the hell did I forget to specify a paper bag?

QUESTION 1:   <u>Are strategies for participation invariant with respect to methods of system design?</u>

Usually software engineers will design a dp-system according to traditional system development strategies (called "life cycle models") in a top-down sequence like this:

1. step: Requirement Specification (in our terminology: problem-oriented models).

2. step: System design (in our terminology: design-oriented models)

3. step: Coding and implementation (in our terminology: implementation-oriented models).

Those traditional life cycle models take for granted that implementation-oriented models are derived from "higher level" design- and problem-oriented models, and that design-oriented models are derived beforehand from problem-oriented models. Any influence going the other way round is not permitted. This means: The system requirements determine the system design, which for its part determines the implementation. A reaction e.g. from system design on the setting of the problem (maybe by learning processes of the users) is not taken into account. In our opinion this approach is wrong. This is indicated by the many problems encountered during the assembly phases (subsystem and system integration, installation).

It has been stated frequently that users are normally unable to describe all relevant aspects of a future system at the beginning of the development, i.e. during requirement analysis. Exceptions to this general statement can be found only with certain types of systems:

<u>Trivial systems</u>: Complexity is so low that they can be constructed as a whole. <u>Well-known systems</u>: All relevant aspects can be derived by analogy with existing systems. <u>Standardized systems</u>: All relevant aspects can be taken from a standard specification.

If the object of development is not of one of these simple types we will call it a <u>complex system</u>. In developing complex systems users and engineers have to elaborate both the description of the problem and the solution in parallel. This means, that problem and solution will influence each other. In other words, we may say that implementation-oriented models have an influence on problem-oriented models.

   Users and software engineers have to model their reality in order to have a basis for discussions on present and future working situations. This modeling process is not at all "objective" - it is determined by the experience, contents of work, interests and aims of the different people and groups.

   We may derive from existing models additional models by way of abstraction or concretization. All models have a more or less close connection with reality, they are more or less understandable, they are more or less granulated, etc.

   All traditional life cycle models prescribe the following development sequence, at least in principle (cf. figure):

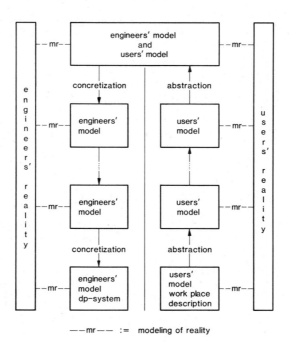

—mr— := modeling of reality

Figure: The Modeling Process of Traditional
        System Development

The users develop a sequence of models of increasing abstraction. The users and engineers then select a model as frame of reference. Finally, the engineers con- vert this model into an operative system by stepwise concretization within their world.

This means, that

-   in the course of development the models disappear more and more from the conception of the users; they become less understandable,

- the operative system is the first contact that the users have with the dp-system, i.e. this system interferes with their reality. If the model conceptions of the engineers have meanwhile diverged from those of the users, the users will conceive this part of their reality as a sudden chaos, i.e. they will have severe troubles in recognizing the dp-system as a "model" based on their former work place description.

Thus this is one reason why a user is unable to describe his or her goals and even his or her working situation sufficiently in the beginning of a development process, namely, because he or she does not yet know which of the specific interpretations of reality will influence the development process. (A more detailed discussion of modeling problems may be found in /2/).

What do we mean by this statement in view of the question, whether participation is dependent or independent of the methods of system development?

First of all we have said that models on the different levels of abstraction influence each other, or to put it in other words that the realization of dp-systems will influence the problem situation.

We then have analyzed that the coordination of different models belonging to one complex system cannot be accomplished by the developers alone. It seems to be necessary to integrate the users into the whole process of system development, in order to discuss and modify the various models according to the different views.

Following these assumptions it should be quite clear that the methods of system development have an essential influence on strategies of participation, because

- Methods of system development influence problems and aims of the users and thus become an object of participation.

- Methods of system development determine the visibility of system aspects; they, so to speak, put spotlights on selected characteristics of a system. Thus certain attributes of a system will become objects of communication while other attributes will be visible only at the end of the development process or during application. In this way methods of system development will limit the possibilities of participation.

- Methods of system development support communication between users and developers to a varying degree, because they will lead to more or less understandable system models thereby influencing basic means of participation.

QUESTION 2: <u>Are there methods and tools which are more favorable for participative strategies than others?</u>

We see the following approaches towards a solution of the communication problem.

1. The users are <u>involved during the whole development process</u> in designing the system. The views of developers and users must be represented in the design documents. This approach is greatly complicated by the little knowledge at hand about structure and content of documents representing different views.

2. The users should form an idea about the product by means of <u>prototypes and simulations</u>. Without going into details we may state here that this approach looks promising for a wide range of applications. Nevertheless this approach is neither without problems:

- Frequently the users have no ideas about the technical possibilities, and thus stick too close to the features of the first prototype. They lack

"phantasy". In this case details of minor importance are discussed too
early.

- A lot of concepts which are not visible at the user interface are thus
  hidden from the users, in spite of their importance for the evaluation of
  the system (e.g. transaction mechanisms of data bases, recovery features of
  hardware).

3. The users get an insight into a <u>similar system within a comparable organisational context</u>, thus acquiring knowledge about what the consequences of the
   various technical features are. Problems similar to prototyping are
   encountered. In addition to these the users will get no idea whether the future
   system meets their expectations until it is finally delivered.

4. The use of <u>program generators</u> will permit the generation of a dp-system with
   moderate effort based on a rather expensive problem-oriented specification.
   This specification may eventually be set up by the users. By comparison, this
   approach leaves no uncertainties whether a prototype (cf. 2.) or a similar system (cf. 3.) differs from the final product. The drawback of this approach can
   be seen in the very narrow application fields ("software for the bookkeeping of
   moving companies").

QUESTION 3:   <u>Which structural differences determine the worlds of users and
              developers?</u>

Reality is not perceived as a chaos, but purposeful human acting structures the
cognition of our reality. Thus reality can never be perceived objectively but is
always seen from a certain point of view. Attempting mechanistically to remove
these subjective parts from different views in order to get an "objective" picture
of reality will always be useless and perspectiveless.

   We learn by general system theory and epistemology that human beings structure
their reality as a set of states and changes. They themselves produce changes by
actions. States and changes are closely connected.

What do we want to say by this general introduction?

   We start from the assumption that information systems are linguistic systems
which comprise the linguistic world of the users as well as the "language" of a
formalized dp-system. Given this, the approach is at hand to analyze how "normal"
end-users apply their natural language in order to describe their working situation, and then to analyze whether there are differences between the structure of
these descriptions and the constructive characteristics of traditional dp-systems.
That is, we hold that linguistic research can indicate principles of system construction.

   On a general level linguistics provides the proposition that all natural languages, despite their differences on the conceptual level, show certain structural
similarities. Most general is the distinction of noun and verb; or in other words
the distinction of objects, actions and relations between them. Universal, too, is
the structural division into sentences. A central linguistic operation is the
transformation of basic patterns into derived strings (cf. /3/).

   We may well conclude from these statements that human beings structure their
reality (especially their working situation) according to objects, operations on
these objects, and relations between them. This assumption can be supported and
detailed by research activities on natural language descriptions of working
processes (cf. /4/ /5/):

A special stress is put on operations on complex objects (seen as functional units like "filing box" or "appointment book"); without interest are control structures in the fashion of traditional programming languages like Fortran:
"Open the file box; start with the first index card; repeat; stop."

Operations are normally applied to the object as a whole, not stepwise to its elements ("search file box"). Conditional statements in a traditional dp-oriented sense ("if-then-else") do not occur, neither do unconditional jumps like "GOTO". Very frequently objects are referenced in a highly context sensitive way:
"I take it up and put it on top of the larger one."

It is a characteristic of the structure of natural languages, that action statements are followed by the neccessary conditions and limitations, while traditional programming languages are structured the other way round:
"Search the file until you have found a certain index card."
instead of
"While file box not empty and selected card not equal wanted card, search file."

Hence it follows:

The structural way in which users think and describe their reality shows essential differences to those representations which traditional dp-systems and programming languages expect and support. But instead of teaching the users ways and means to apply this different linguistic world, it seems more appropriate to demand that dp-systems should be constructed according to the structures users are familiar with. As we have indicated that the different models of a system are closely interrelated, we may conclude as well that not only the user interface but all system models should show these structural characteristics. Again it should be pointed out that an object oriented approach based on the fundamental terms "objects", "operations", and "relations" seems to be a feasible solution. Contextual knowledge should be integrated into the construction of a dp-system or, what seems to be better, contextual knowledge should be introduced to the system by its users. This indicates a new application field for expert systems. Algorithmic control structures should be kept as far away from the users as possible.

Finally, linguistic research gives an additional clue: Formal systems have only very limited means to capture the contextual knowledge of users in complex situations and to cope with the human ability of meta-communication.
A simple example: "Wet hair, apply shampoo, rinse, and repeat."
Without contextual knowledge ("which action is appropriate in a situation like this") and the ability of meta-communication ("I will ask someone who knows") a "user" of a shampoo bottle with these instructions would go on washing his or her hair till eternity.

This is why a traditional requirement analysis, which during a pre-study expects the users to describe their working objects and activities in a complete way, will on principle run into difficulties.

QUESTION 4: Which social and political attitudes influence a participative system development?

The development of information systems in Europe has various social roots:

- The separation of producers and users has led to a separation of software production and information needs.
  Problems and the know-how for their solution have drifted apart. The solutions are split into separate parts, which then are handled by specialists. The end-users are suddenly in a weak position - they hold only a marginal position in the development process.

- Military and industrial software production especially in the U.S.A.
  dominate the methods and concepts of software engineering even in Europe.

- Technical embedded systems, i.e. systems with mainly technical interfaces
  (e.g. auto-pilots), for which nearly complete formal specifications can be
  defined at the beginning of development.

- Logistic (military) systems without major participation or acceptance
  problems, because of a hierarchical command structure and distribution of
  competence the solutions of problems are given clearly.

- The principle of "hire-and-fire" and an obvious trend towards dequalification dominate the methods of system development.
  A catchword like "expert systems" will mean in this context: Substituting
  the experts by a dp-system.

These tendencies are opposed by efforts to develop systems on a different
basis. Here we find the Scandinavian countries in the lead. Their approach is
based on the assumption that in developing information systems various factors
have to be considered for decision processes. In addition to traditional economical categories like cost-benefit calculations a stress is put on social and
political issues. The discussions on co-determination and participation in the development of working processes as well as efforts to increase the quality of work
and the motivation of qualified personnel are here of importance.

DIRECTIONS FOR FUTURE WORK

Following this what we like to call human-centred approach of developing dp-
systems we want to underline that various, often conflicting dimensions of decision have to be considered. Traditional management strategies fail to cope with
this situation, especially when trying to apply quantifying methods to reach an
optimal solution.

Two strategies to overcome the problem seem to be impractical:

- Reduction to only one (strictly economical) dimension.

- Evaluation of all possible alternative solutions.

The arbitrary reduction to one dimension of decision increases the risk of
overlooking side-effects and conflicts of farreaching importance; the evaluation
of all possible alternatives goes beyond the borders of practicability.

Our suggestion is in line with the idea of H. Simon that a solution for socio-
technical problems need not be optimal but sufficient, i.e., sufficient for all
interest groups involved. This also means participative system development. In
order to reduce the still prevailing complexity of problems and to foresee the
effects and sideeffects of a single decision a stepwise (incremental) approach is
recommended.

Remember! We do not postulate a fixed form of participation strategies; this
will strongly depend on the social and institutional distribution of power and on
the actual process of negotiations of every system development. What we want to
stress is the fundamental importance of participative and stepwise development
strategies if the target is a sufficient solution instead of a fictitious optimal
one.

In more detail: If we have a realistic look at the possibilities and the practice of information system development in Europe we find the prevailing strategy of introducing a dp-system "top-down" applying methods to increase acceptance as a type of lubrication. This is one end (also the dominant one) of a scale called "integration of all parties involved". Frequently postulated but rarely applied in practice is a system development based on the principle of consent. This means that all parties involved should establish their own rules according to which they then will discuss the relevant alternatives of decision and elaborate a sufficient solution.

The more radical approach of developing a system for settling conflicting points of view has been, to our knowledge, only conceptually outlined (cf. /2/ /6/).

Looking at these three strategies of system development we may well say that traditional development and decision models favour a hierarchical development process. The consideration of different viewpoints (interpretations) even according to the principle of consent will go beyond the scope of traditional models. The representation of conflicting processes, despite their creative value according to epistemology and social sciences, is completely beyond the reach of all models we know. But to think beyond these borders seems necessary.

----

1   This paper describes work being done as part of the joint research programme Specification and Development of Software Systems of GMD, Bonn and NCC, Manchester, sponsored by the Commission of the European Communities and national governments.

LITERATURE

/1/ McCracken, D.D., Jackson, M.A., Life Cycle Concept Considered Harmful, Software Engineering Notes Vol. 7 No. 2 pp. 29 - 32 April 1982.

/2/ Budde, R., Züllighoven, H., Some Considerations About Modeling Information Systems and an Interpretation of the PSC Model, in: Goldkuhl, G., Kall, C-O. (eds.), Report of the Fifth Scandinavian Research Seminar on Systemeering (Department of Information Processing, Chalmers University of Technology and University of Göteborg, 1982).

/3/ Simon, H.A., The Sciences of the Artificial (M.I.T. Press, Cambridge, Mass., 1970).

/4/ Miller, L.A., Natural Language Programming: Styles, Strategies, and Contrasts, IBM Systems Journal, Vol. 20 No. 2 pp. 184 - 215, 1981.

/5/ Shniderman, B., Software Psychology (Winthrop Publishers, Cambridge, Mass., 1980).

/6/ Rittel, H.W.J., Kunz, W., Issues as Elements of Information Systems, IGP S-78-2 (Institut für Grundlagen der Planung, Universität Stuttgart, 1970).

SYSTEMS DESIGN FOR, WITH, AND BY THE USERS
U. Briefs, C. Ciborra and L. Schneider (editors)
North-Holland Publishing Company
© IFIP, 1983

SYSTEM ANALYSIS WITH USERS

Andreas Munk-Madsen

Dansk Datamatik Center
Lundtoftevej 1C
DK-2800 Lyngby
DANMARK

This paper presents guidelines and techniques for
a system analysis process that can be imbedded in
larger processes such as trade union activities or
usual system development.

The guidelines propose (among others)

- that analysing the users' work and their
  organisation and describing the edp-based
  system should be done simultaneously,

- that a structured description of the edp-
  based system must be built from a concrete
  description of the edp-system as seen from
  the present work of the users,

- that the analysis of the users' work and
  their organisation must be performed in a
  dialogue.

SYSTEM ANALYSIS WITH USERS

This paper presents some guidelines (a partial method) for conducting
system analysis with users. These guidelines should be useful
whether the system analysis is part of a traditional system development project or part of trade union activities.

First a few definitions are necessary. The fundamental concept is
work process. "Work process" applies both to what the users normally
do and to the (in this respect meta-) process of changing their work,
i.e. system development.

Definition 1   A work process is conducted through time by people
               having certain qualifications.

               A work process has two fundamental (almost orthogonal)
               abstractions:

               - the function, which describes the relationship
                 between the situation before and after the work
                 process has been carried out (or before and after
                 the work process has been conducted through a time
                 interval),

- the <u>method</u>, which describes <u>how</u> the work process
  is performed.

A work process may be split into <u>partial processes</u>,
that interact mutually. The same process may be split
in different ways, if different aspects are studied.

A work process may be regarded as <u>part</u> of a larger
process where it interacts with other processes.

<u>Definition 2</u>   A method consists of

- the <u>application area</u>, i.e. the type of work processes, where the guidelines can be used,

- the <u>perspective</u>, i.e. the implicit or explicit
  assumptions about the nature of the surrounding
  organisation,

- the <u>guidelines</u>, which consist of

  - <u>techniques</u> for conducting partial processes.
    A technique describes how to perform a spe-
    cific work process. The technique normally
    disregards the constraints imposed on the work
    process,

  - <u>tools</u> that improve the performance in the
    partial processes,

  - <u>principles for organizing</u> the work, taking into
    account the various constraints imposed on the
    process. These constraints include the expec-
    tation of a certain quality of work, the
    limited available resources and the fact that
    several persons with different qualifications
    have to cooperate. (Mathiassen-81).

With these definitions it is possible to be more precise about the
system analysis process.

<u>Definition 3</u>   The <u>system analysis process</u> is conducted by computer
experts and the potential users of an edp-based system.

The <u>function</u> of the system analysis process is to
improve the understanding of

- the work processes that the users are involved in

- the function of a (proposed) edp-based system and
  its consequences for the working conditions of the
  users.

This understanding may be materialized in a <u>system
description</u>.

The system analysis process may be part of

- a traditional system development process, which should improve the efficiency of the concerned organisation through a better adapted edp-based system,

- and/or a trade union activity, which should increase the influence the users have on their working conditions.

Within this framework the first statement about the function of the system analysis process can be made.

Thesis 4   It is important for the system analysis process to consider the future by including plans and visions of future edp-based systems.

The reason for this statement is that work processes and technology are constantly moving while at the same time the system developers are trying to implement changes. This may seem an obvious statement, but many system descriptions present the work processes of the users too statically. The system to be implemented is presented as though no future changes will occur.

An important principle for organizing the system analysis process is the following:

Thesis 5   The system analysis process contains two important partial processes relating to the definition of the function:

(1) analysing the work processes of the users and the organisation they are part of,

(2) describing the function of the edp-system and its interaction with the work processes of the users.

The two processes should be conducted <u>simultaneously</u> in order to support each other.

The partitioning of the system analysis process is based on the amount of input from the users and the computer experts, respectively.

It is commonly acknowledged that you should not develop systems without having done some analysis, so thesis 5 is merely saying that you should not analyse without knowing why.

Many problems in system development projects are due to neglecting this rule. Typically the users' work is analysed and then the system is designed. Much later, deep in the system construction it becomes apparent that the analysis was not good enough. At this time it is very costly to redo the whole process.

Researchers involved in trade union activities also tend to make this sort of mistake. They misinterpret the slogan "starting from the situation of the users" by omitting the functional details of the edp-system and concentrating on the details of the users' work.

Taking a closer look at the partial processes of the system analysis
process will make this more clear.

Definition 6   The <u>function</u> of the partial process (1) is to impose a
                <u>relevant structure</u> on the description of the users'
                work. This structure should help in clarifying the
                consequences of changing the edp-system.

An important principle for organizing the process is the following:

Thesis 7   The partial process (1) should take the form of a
               <u>dialogue</u> between the users and the computer experts.
               It is important that the computer experts acquire a
               good working knowledge of what the users do.

An example of violating this rule is the case of full-time user representatives in project groups. The user representatives relieve
the computer experts from the tediousness of collecting details
about the users' work. However, in presenting the details to the
computer experts they impose their own structure on the information.
This hinders the computer experts in using their skills to create a
relevant structure. The typical result of having full-time user
representatives are mountains of low-quality documentation and nothing more.

Definition 8   The function of the partial process (2) is to give <u>a
               concrete and structured description</u> of the edp-system.

               From this description it should be possible to derive
               the consequences of implementing (or changing) the edp-
               system.

               These consequences particularly relate to

                   - the working conditions of the users,

                   - the function of the organisation they are part of.

               Furthermore, this description should be the basis for
               any system construction that may occur.

A fundamental technique in this partial process is:

Thesis 9   The structured description of the edp-system should be
               built from a concrete description of the edp-system
               based on examples relating to the present work of the
               users.

Not using this technique, but assuming that the users are incapable
of understanding details of the edp-system, results in general, tame
descriptions from which no consequences can be derived.

An interesting question is how to go "the other way" in definition 8.
That is, given a set of desired consequences, how should a system be
designed in order to realize them. There may be no simple solution
to this problem. The practical solution is that the computer experts subsequently generate a set of solutions. These solutions are
subjected to the process of system analysis to see whether their consequences match the desired consequences.

A final statement about the environment of a system analysis process:

Thesis 10   The system analysis process is a learning process which makes the interaction with the action-oriented processes it supports important.

This is simply stating that an isolated system analysis process has little prospect of success.

CONCLUSION

Although the definitions and theses above only are fragments of a method for system development, I think they represent the sort of ideas that are needed to reach an improved understanding of the development of edp-based systems.

REFERENCE

(Mathiassen-81)   Lars Mathiassen, "Systemudvikling og systemudviklingsmetode", Datalogisk Afdeling, Aarhus Universitet, 1981, (written in Danish).

ADAPTING SOFTWARE DEVELOPMENT
FOR SYSTEMS DESIGN WITH THE USER

Christiane Floyd and Reinhard Keil

Technische Universität Berlin
Institut für Angewandte Informatik
Franklinstr. 28/29, D-1000 Berlin 10

In the context of developing DP-systems which are to be
embedded in the work processes of people, we consider the
conventional phase-oriented approach to software production
problematic. In order to achieve DP-systems which are adequate as tools for their users we must re-think software
engineering-methods, tools and forms of organization. As a
first step in this direction we propose a process-oriented
approach, which views software development as a sequence of
cycles: (re-)design, (re-)implementation and (re-)evaluation.
The approach takes into account the contribution of the user
to software development as well as that of the developer. In
this approach, the base documents for software development
have a well defined role in communication. We identify problems arising when specifying DP-systems with a view of adequacy
and we propose some solutions.

1. INTRODUCTION

This paper presents some ideas on software development quite different from those
found normally in the software engineering literature. It is part of an ongoing
effort at the Technical University of Berlin in which we are attempting to re-think
software engineering-methods, tools and forms of organizations-with the aim of
doing justice to such software which is to be embedded into the work processes of
people. For programs of this kind we feel that the basic assumptions of software
engineering:

- that requirements for software can be determined and fixed in advance

- that bulky documents describing software formally are sufficient as a primary
  means of communication between the software developer and the user

- that there is essentially one system to produce and that its initial design
  should determine the system's basic structure throughout its lifetime

are highly problematic. We therefore began by challenging the conventional phase-
oriented approach to software development and instead proposed a process-oriented
approach (Floyd (1981a)), which sees software development as a sequence of cycles:
(re-)design, (re-)implementation and (re-)evaluation and which takes into account
the contribution of the user to software development as well as that of the developer. The process-oriented approach will also be presented in this paper in its
current, slightly modified form.

As a project model for software development, the process-oriented approach, like
the phase model, serves several purposes:

- it provides a basis for supplying well defined intermediate results which can
  be used in contractual agreements

-   it offers guidelines for planning, budgeting and supervising

-   it serves as a framework for discussing methods and tools for software develop-
    ment.

As software engineering researchers, we are interested primarily in working on
methods and tools which support software development according to the process-
oriented approach. This has been dealt with earlier to some extent (Floyd (1981a)
and Floyd, Keil (1982)). We feel, however, that this line is in keeping with the
topic "systems design for the users, with the users, by the users". After presenting the process-oriented approach, we will therefore discuss some aspects relating
to

-   the responsibility of the user and the developer in systems development as we
    see it

-   requirements on formal specification aids with a view to the communication bet-
    ween developer and user

-   adequacy of data processing (DP) systems, i.e. the suitability of the DP-system
    as a tool for people to perform their work tasks with.

As to the maturity of our approach, we will honestly admit that we have so far had
no chance to try out these ideas in actual systems development outside the university. To the extent that we have empirical evidence for their workability, it has
been obtained from projects that we have carried out with students or from software
we have developed for internal use, so that the user community was reachable within
the university.

Though we have worked quite independently and our points of departure were different,
we found our results to be highly compatible with those put forward by Kyng and
Matthiassen (1979). In fact, we hold that our process-oriented approach is a suitable
alternative system development method which is relevant wherever system design whith
the user is seriously considered.

2.   DP-SYSTEMS AND THEIR USAGE CONTEXT

With Kyng and Matthiassen (1979) we see the system development process "as a partial
process of organizational development which is the process of consciously changing
organizations to improve the organization's ability to pursue specific goals". In
this process, the development of the DP-system plays a small but important part: it
serves to embody far reaching decisions, such as the number of employment possibilities or the working times for the employees, and so on. These decisions, however,
are taken before or outside the development of the DP-system.

The scope of our approach is much more limited. We cannot hope to alter the basic
decisions of an organization by changing software development methods, and we do
not see our approach as a tool for manipulating users. Therefore, what follows is
only applicable in situations where the overriding decisions in systems development
are being made openly in such a manner that the prospective users can see themselves
as partners and not as victims in system development. This will be the tacit assumption from now on.

What we can influence, however, by DP-systems (more concretely by software) development is the usage context of the DP-system. By this, we mean the work and communication processes of the users and how they are affected by the system (see Figure
1). In particular, we consider users

-   working alone

-   cooperating with others

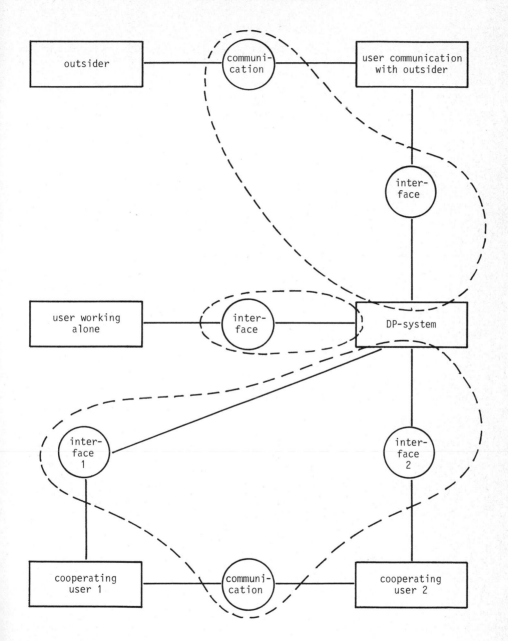

Figure 1: Usage context of DP-system

-    communicating with outsiders such as clients in the course of their work.

Since programs are concerned with information processing, system developers tend
to find information processing aspects of the users work tasks important and relevant, whereas they tend to abstract from other aspects which they consider irrelevant. As we know, the users, who judge the DP-system as a tool for performing their
work, have an entirely different perspective.

Software development begins with requirements analysis. We will <u>classify</u> <u>require-</u>
<u>ments</u> into the following categories:

-    <u>functional</u> <u>requirements</u> describing the desired output to be produced for a given
     input

-    <u>performance</u> <u>requirements</u> stating the resources available to achieve these func-
     tions, and

-    <u>handling</u> <u>requirements</u> defining the manner in which the system is to be embedded
     in the work and communication processes of its users.

The adequacy of DP-systems is crucially dependent on handling and performance requirements being recognized and satisfied. Our experience shows that handling requirements (such as suitable man-machine interfaces or the possibility of intervening with the system in the case of unexpected events) are exceedingly difficult to
relate to the usage context on the basis of defining documents alone. This observation motivated us to look for alternative system development methods.

3.   THE PROCESS-ORIENTED APPROACH TO SOFTWARE DEVELOPMENT

3.1 Overview

The process-oriented approach is a general purpose project model for software development. Unlike the well known phase model, it does not rely on phases such as
design, implementation or maintenance as a primary means for structuring the software development process in time. Instead, it views software development as a sequence of development cycles, in which developers and users cooperate. The object
of each cycle is to produce a version of the system which can be evaluated. The
transition from one development cycle to the next is initiated by a revision of the
current systems version based on the results of the evaluation.

The process-oriented approach is shown in Figure 2. Here, a box (☐) stands for
an activity or a set of connected activities. A circle (◯) represents a document (a program is considered as a document). An arrow from box to circle (☐➔◯)
means "produces" or "leads to", an arrow from circle to box (◯➔☐) means "is input to".

Before we explain the basic concepts of the process-oriented approach in more detail, we would like to point out its essential differences from the phase-oriented
approach:

-    it models the responsibility of the user together with that of the developer

-    it defines intermediate results which can be evaluated by the user (i.e. tried
     out when performing actual work tasks)

-    it does not separate what is commonly called maintenance from software produc-
     tion, instead it integrates the two in a sequence of development cycles

-    it can be used for developing a new system as well as for enhancing an existing
     system.

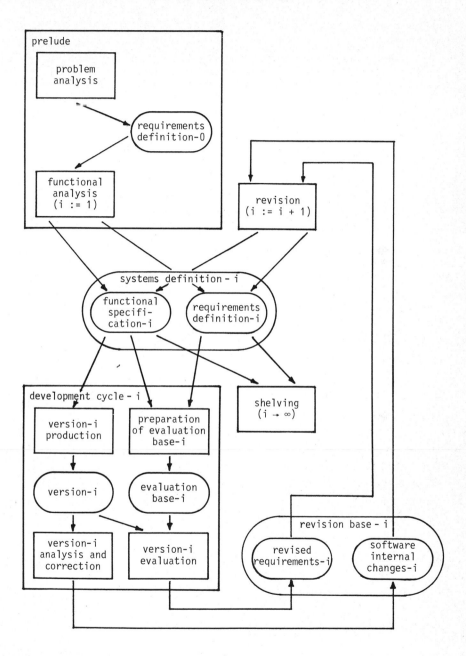

Figure 2: The process-oriented approach to software development

The process-oriented approach is primarily geared to systems development processes where there is one well defined user community, and where developer and user can expect to be linked throughout the expected lifetime of the system. This kind of setting for systems development arises, for example, when user and developer belong to the same company or when a user organization has a contract with a consulting company over a considerable period of time. With some modifications, which we will not consider in this paper, the process-oriented approach can be extended to cover other systems development settings as well.

3.2 Defining documents and their role in communication

Because of the connection between the DP-system and its usage context, the system definition should consist of two documents, which must both be evolutionary and which must be clearly related to each other.

The requirements definition describes the usage context, i.e. the work tasks that the system is supposed to support. This document must be structured according to connected work tasks and it must describe different views of the system as perceived from the point of view of the various user groups. In order to be useful in the communication, each system view should

-    be expressed in the technical language of the user and make use of formalizations familiar to the user

-    aim at describing the system in terms of the work tasks of this user and refer to the work of others by stating how it affects the work of the user under consideration

-    pinpoint where and how the DP-system is to be embedded in the work processes, but not describe solutions

-    state justified long term goals and wishes irrespective of their feasibility

-    include aspects of the work processes not related to information processing, such as the time and the place, the work rhythm, communication with other people, and so on.

The functional specification describes the functions of the DP-system, i.e. its input-output behaviour, its user interfaces, its base machine and its decomposition into subsystems. This document must be structured according to connected system functions. It is based on a compromise reached by weighing the interests of all parties and the exigencies implied by limited resources. It states product goals that have been agreed upon and which are binding for a limited period of time. It must clarify which functions are related to which work tasks, which requirements can or cannot be met. It may include a plan for enhancing the DP system according to a list of priorities.

Both documents are valid for one cycle at a time, the functional specification being the basis for the production of the system version, whereas the evaluation of the system version must be based on the requirements definition as well. At the end of each cycle both documents are subject to revision as described in section 3.4. We feel that, in view of the use of these documents in communication, it would be disastrous to require that they should be entirely formal. They should, however, contain formalized parts, wherever this proves helpful. Section 4 discusses some blessings and some pitfalls inherent in using methods of this kind.

3.3 System versions and work tasks

All long life DP-systems exist in versions, which often come into being late in the development as a result of approaching deadlines, unfulfillable hopes and detected errors. By contrast, we propose the planned use of system versions as an aid in design and communication. As has been pointed out elsewhere (Floyd (1981b)), this use of versions is related to, but not identical with, the idea of using prototypes in software development.

When explaining our version concept, we will refer to the prelude shown in Figure 2; we also talk about early, middle and late development cycles. The reader accustomed to notions of the phase model is invited to associate the early cycles with design, the middle cycles with implementation and the late cycles with maintenance. Note that in the process-oriented approach we do not propose to stop designing, but to combine iterative, incremental design with the early production of system versions for controlled experiments with the user which we call evaluation. For planning system versions we propose the following guidelines.

In the prelude start by evaluating a version 0, which may be an antiquated program already available on site or a similar system that can be examined at a different installation. If the expense is justifiable, make a prototype, but be sure to place the emphasis on its systematic evaluation rather than insisting on its full functional scope.

In the early cycles we see system versions primarily as an aid to communication. The idea is to try out first crucial design decisions, which pertain to the embedment of the DP-system in the work tasks.

Important considerations are:

- the user interface in the widest sense

- the availability of all information the user is accustomed to have access to

- the possibility of interfering with or reshuffling partial system functions to fit the needs of specific work tasks

- the interplay between worksteps that are supported by the DP-system and other worksteps that are independent of the DP-system

- the matching of system performance to the work rhythm

- the interruptibility of working with the DP-system.

Many of these points are elaborated for example by Mehlmann (1981). In the middle cycle system versions might correspond roughly to successive extensions of an already existing kernel of the final DP-system. The idea here is to tie the planning of versions carefully to a stepwise progression in supporting connected work tasks. Because a revision of the evaluated system version is included after each cycle, each successive version must be expected to be a revised extension of its predecessor.

In the late cycles, the degrees of freedom for change will naturally be much smaller, yet changes have to be expected due to changing requirements. Though we have no empirical evidence to corroborate this at the present time, we are confident that the very fact of the DP-system having been planned as a sequence of versions implying, for example, that the programmers had to revise their own programs several times from the start and that the documents where revised along with the programs from cycle to cycle, will mean the adaptation of the system to new requirements will at least have been better prepared than it tends to be in conventional software development.

3.4 Evaluation and revision

By evaluation we mean a systematic use of currently available system versions to determine the adequacy of the system functions in connection with the user's work tasks. Evaluation is not the same as testing. Whereas in testing the goal is to establish whether the system processes all conceivable input data correctly, in evaluation the goal is to establish whether the system fits into all conceivable work tasks in a desirable manner. Neither test nor evaluation can be carried out in an exhaustive manner. Very much like a successful test, an evaluation needs to be prepared and planned.

The evaluation should be based on evaluation criteria that are agreed upon and that are, themselves, subject to revision. Evaluation criteria should be based on the goals of the users as stated in the requirements definition, taking into account the restraints stated in the functional specification. Because of the connection between system versions and work tasks described in section 3.3, it is possible to concentrate on one set of connected work tasks at a time. The evaluation serves several purposes:

-   determining whether the stated requirements have been met

-   finding errors and misunderstandings in the requirements

-   completing the requirements for this set of work tasks.

Note that errors and misunderstandings may have occurred on both sides, user and developer, and these should be clarified, before their correction becomes outrageously expensive. The evaluation also serves to establish whether priorities stated in the functional specification are in keeping with the actual needs of the work tasks.

Since exhaustive evaluation is impossible, care should be taken to include routine work processes as well as carefully selected special cases in the evaluation base.

Revision refers to both requirements definition and functional specification. The requirements definition may have to be changed

-   as a result of the evaluation of the current system version

-   as a result of changes in the user organization

-   as a result of the DP-system's creating new demands.

The functional definition may have to be changed

-   due to changes in the requirements definition

-   because of errors or inadequacies detected in evaluation

-   according to a given (or revised) plan of system enhancement.

In order to make these revisions feasible, we need to develop techniques for writing documents which can be changed incrementally.

4.   SPECIFYING FOR ADEQUACY

This section serves to identify important aspects in using methods for requirements analysis and specification in connection with the process-oriented approach. Since we do not propose a method of our own at this point, the aspects mentioned here can be used

- as a help in judging the suitability of existing methods when making a choice which method should be used, or

- as guidelines for how to use whichever method is available.

Our comments are adressed to semiformal methods available for practical use today. In spite of their many differences all these methods have important points in common: they all rely on a combination of semantic language concepts, structuring primitives and graphics, they all claim to be applicable for the defining documents mentioned in section 3.3, and none of them has been designed so as to support the process of communication and incremental change made explicit in the process-oriented approach.

Our comments will take the form of stating problems and point to some solutions.

1) The problem of reduction

In programming we have to reduce the semantic richness of reality in such a manner that we eventually find data structures and algorithms that can be embodied in programs. While this reduction is useful and inevitable, it should be restricted to the DP-system. The danger is, that the reduced model will be the basis of system development as a whole.

In the context of methods of the kind mentioned above, we see the following specific dangers:

- equating people with things (people as data sources or receivers) or with computer programs (people as information processors)

- reducing objects to data about the objects (for example a book to data about a book)

- reducing goal-oriented action carried out by people to the processing of symbolic information.

For example, describing a work process in terms of actions carried out on objects is highly useful, but there must be a possibility of relating this reduced description to aspects such as time and place, cooperation with others, context information that we are accustomed to have access to and so on.

Possible solutions to avoid this danger are

- to enrich descriptions written according to the method (for example diagrams) by additional information

- to use several kinds of diagrams describing different aspects of the system and contrasting them

- to choose one's own semantic primitives and map them onto the concepts offered by the method.

2) The problem of separating concerns

Though most methods provide means of structuring descriptions such as refinement, and some explicitly refer to different perspectives, they offer few guidelines on how descriptions should be structured to be useful in discussions, where the interests of several user groups must be taken into account.

One important structuring principle is according to connected work tasks, where each partial description aims at giving a coherent view of the system as perceived by one prospective user group.

It offers the advantage of being able to discuss with the user groups one at a time. Contrasting different group-oriented views helps to detect misunderstandings and conflicts of interest in time.

3) The problem of complexity

The number of individual items and the number of relations between items must be kept very small. This calls for design criteria such as stepwise refinement and modularization akin to those used in designing software, but which have not yet been sufficiently established on the level of requirements definition and specification.

4) The problem of incremental changes

The structure of the description must be such as to permit the exchange of parts of a solution in favour of a new solution as a consequence of evaluation and revision. Since we do not wish to loose the connection with the usage context, this implies:

-   connecting partial descriptions of system functions to the corresponding work tasks

-   when replacing system functions rechecking the connection to the work tasks

-   checking for inadequacy with respect to other work tasks.

This list is probably not complete, but it does pinpoint how difficult the problems are. Clearly the difficulties lie both in finding structuring criteria and in applying them in a given project.

5. CONCLUSIONS

Ending a paper with an enumeration of serious, open problems leaves the reader uneasy. What we have to offer at this point is an alternative model for software development, which provides an organizational framework - no more. What we need to develop are methods and tools to fill it in, including a suitable specification method as an alternative to existing ones, which should take the problems of communication and change better into account. We need to develop criteria to relate system functions back to the work tasks which they support. We need to gain experience in using the process-oriented approach. There is still a long way to go. Even so, we hope that our approach is a step in the right direction.

REFERENCES:

Floyd, Christiane (1981a), A Process-Oriented Approach to Software Development, Systems Architecture, Proc. of the 6th Europ. ACM regional Conf., Westbury House (1981) 285-294.

Floyd, Christiane (1981b), On the Use of 'Prototyping' in Software Development, invited lecture at the HP 3000 - International Users Group Meeting, Technical University of Berlin (Oct. 1981).

Floyd, Christiane; Keil, Reinhard (1982), Softwaretechnik und Betroffenenbeteiligung, in: Betroffenenbeteiligung bei der Informationssystementwicklung, ed. P. Mambrey, R. Oppermann (Campus Verlag, Frankfurt, to appear).

Kyng, Morten; Mathiassen, Lars (1979), A 'New Systems Development': Trade Union and Research Activities, in: Computers Dividing Man and Work, ed. Ake Sandberg, Arbetslivscentrum (Stockholm, March 1979).

Mehlmann, Marilyn (1981), When People Use Computers, (Englewood Cliffs, 1981).

CONDITIONS AND TOOLS FOR AN EFFECTIVE NEGOTIATION DURING
THE ORGANIZATION/INFORMATION SYSTEMS DESIGN PROCESS.

F. De Cindio, G. De Michelis, L. Pomello, C. Simone

Istituto di Cibernetica - Università di Milano
Via Viotti 5   20133 Milano

An effective negotiation of the organizational change (mainly if it is
connected to the application of computer based technologies) needs that all
the involved parties reach a conscious agreement about the expected
behaviours of the whole organization and of the subsystems constituting it.
It needs, therefore, more formalization (in the mathematical sense) and a
closer attention to the communication problems inside the organization.
In this paper Superposed Automata Nets are proposed as a formal and
communicable tool for designing and discussing the organizational change.
Their application in a negotiation context is presented by means of an
example taken from a working group conducted by some of the authors with the
workers of a large Engineering Company.

FOREWORD

Some recent approaches to organization analysis, mainly focused on clerical work
analysis, decision support systems and office automation design, claim that the
classical organizational theories based on the management sciences approach are
presently inadequate (e.g. (1) and (2)) and, from different points of view,
consider organizations as characterized by their communication networks,
outlining interesting research directions towards a new organization theory
((1),...,(6)).

"Communication Disciplines"(4), and in that framework the "General Net Theory"
defined by C.A. Petri (3),(7) offer a new theoretical background for a formal
treatment of communication networks problems, suggesting that, instead of the
classical communication theory based on the notions of sender and receiver
channel and of speed of transmission, specific disciplines concerning
synchronization, identification, addressing, etc. may result much more fruitful
in capturing the real nature of the communication.

Flores (1) and Grandi(2) apply the Searle's Speech Acts Theory to organization
analysis, as the means to understand the conversations inside the organization;
Ouchi (5), and in his line Ciborra (6), analyze the typologies of the agreements
inside an organization, considering the organization as a steady network of
negotiated agreements regulating a set of transactions between individuals.

Without any ambition of combining these three approaches in a new Organization
Theory, the next section offers some hints derived from them, in order to outline
a context (i.e. a way to look at organization) to discuss both conditions and
tools for an effective negotiation of the organizational change.

THE OUTLINE OF AN ORGANIZATIONAL CONTEXT

The conversations occurring inside an organization consist of assertives,
directives ,commissives, declaratives and expressives (see Flores (1)): they
allow the individuals to undertake commitments, which characterize the
conversations themselves. Commitments define the agreements regulating the

transactions between the individuals.
But the commitments, in their turn, have patterns fixed by some agreements. The network of agreements which regulate both the transactions and the commitments defines the organization.
In other words, any negotiation inside the organization occurs in the frame defined by the preexistent network of agreements and may imply a changement of it.

Any agreement is characterized by three components: the market component (defining which goods and services are exchanged between the parties), the procedural component (defining which roles distribution, working procedures and communications protocols are fixed), the value component (defining which are the general and specific aims to be pursued by the subsystem under consideration and/or by the whole organization).
The proposed agreement components are strictly related to the three control mechanisms identified by Ouchi (5).

While the market component has been for a long time fully formalized, the other two are poorly formalized or not at all.

It is important to specify what here is meant by "formal". "Formal" in this paper essentially means "not ambiguous", i.e. whose semantics is univocally defined. The notion of formality here used therefore refers to the mathematical concept of formality, while, generally, in organizational theories, "formal" refers to the normative, rigid (fixed by law, by hierarchical rules, by a signed contract) character of a commitment.
Thus the two notions are semantically disjoint: an agreement which is highly formalized in the second sense may be informal in the first one (e.g. when the behavioural rules are rigid but not univocally defined, allowing that different individuals give different readings of them) and viceversa (e.g. when the behavioural rules are non-ambiguous and well defined but do not impose rigid constraints to the involved individuals allowing them an high degree of autonomy).

It is clear that, in the context of this paper, the formalization of an agreement has not to be confused with the rigid bureaucracy of its procedural component. In fact, while the formalization of the agreements has the aim to rigorously define the commitment undertaken by the involved parties with respect to their mutual behaviour, a rigid bureaucracy of the organization usually introduces (using the standard socio-technical terminology) an high variance between the real system and the formal system, generally allowing the subjects highly discretional behaviours.
On the contrary, the degree of formalization of an agreement, i.e. of its three components, is strictly related to the transparency of the agreement itself with respect to the involved parties. In fact, in a conflictual context, as offices, firms and companies are, the (partial) informality of the agreements reached via a negotiation directly reduces the effectiveness of the negotiation itself, and allows that relevant changes in the organization may occur whithout any conscious negotiation between the interacting parties.

To improve the effectiveness of the negotiation, then, requires to raise the degree of formalization of the agreements, i.e. of its three components.
The market component, as has been already mentioned, is, generally, fully formalized.

The problems arising with the formalization of the value component are much more complex. The value component of an agreement is, in fact, highly determined by the degree of identification of the involved individuals with the aims, value and traditions of the organization (see about this Ouchi's pages about clan mechanism (5)). It is, moreover, qualified by factors as the image of the organization, its history, its ideology, and so on. It is out of the scope of this paper to discuss deeply the value component, which would require also sociological and psychological analyses of the employees behaviour. It can be observed however that in the value component, as it is presently defined, two kinds of factors are considered. Firstly the factors characterizing the higher or lower adhesion of the individuals to the organization they are part of: they can be considered as creating the conditions for the negotiation and for the subsequent agreement. Secondly the factors characterizing the higher or lower adhesion of the individuals to their roles and functions in the organization: they can be better defined if the procedural component of the agreement is adequately formalized.

Therefore, in order to improve the effectiveness of the negotiation via the formalization of the agreements, the attention has to be put at first on the formalization of its procedural component. This means that the involved parties define in a rigorous and non-ambiguous way the constraints which they impose each other with respect to their behaviour, so that each of them knows the behaviour it accepts to exhibit to the others and that the others are expected to exhibit to it. In the frame of the so defined constraints each individual or group may model his behaviour in any way, only regarding about its consistency with the stated constraints.

A further and relevant consequence of this approach is that the availability of a formal model of the procedural component allows to subordinate, to the organizational choices, the formal specifications (and therefore the implementation) of the computer procedures to be used, and to formally prove their consistency with the constraints defined by those organizational choices. This avoids that computer based technologies impose their logic to the organization because of their strong formalization. In the present situation, computer based technologies are one of the most important means to produce organizational changes, even if people are not fully aware of it, being used to consider computers only as tools able to substitute or integrate human work.

A more adequate computer image has been proposed by Petri (4) who has argued that the definition of the computer as "a generalized communication medium" actually is the most adherent to its use inside the organization. Petri's approach leads to a deeper understanding of the modifications induced by the introduction of computer technologies into the organizations, and of the fact that any computer technology supports different organizational choices.
Its introduction, therefore, has to be negotiated mainly from the organizational point of view, as a part, an important part, of the organizational change.

In the context sketched by the above remarks, the following sections present and discuss some conditions to be fulfilled in order to successfully negotiate (computer based) organizational changes, and some conceptual tools meeting these conditions, also on the basis of a real example.

CONDITIONS

The aim is now to identify some conditions to improve the effectiveness of the negotiation viewed as the main way to control the (computer based) organizational changes occurring inside a firm or a company. First of all,

A formal and communicable model of the matter of the change is needed.

In fact, the object of the negotiation has to be well defined. Two main questions have to be rigorously answered:

a)   which subsystems of the target organization are proposed for a modification? That is, which part of the organization has to be modelled and which part has to be considered as its environment. This restriction may lead to consider some subfunctionalities, neglecting other ones also perfomed by the same executor (individual, group, etc.)

b) at which level of organizational abstraction the organization is affected by the modification? Three main levels may be identified:

.   the behavioural architecture, i.e. the model of the behaviour that the target organization exibits to its environment;
.   the macro-organizational architecture, i.e. the model of the behaviours that the chosen operational units exhibit to each others and to the environment.
An operational unit is a subsystem whose behaviour can be modelled as an autonomous process interacting with the behaviours of the other operational units and of the environment.
A modification can affect the macro-organizational architecture of an organization changing task distribution and interaction protocols between the operational units or, more deeply, changing the choice of the operational units themeselves. It is worthwhile, therefore, to point out that no constraints are posed on the way of choosing the operational units, allowing different macro-organizations, with respect to a fixed behavioural architecture.
At this level some preliminary choices can be made about the subsystems to be automatized.
.   the micro-organizational architecture, i.e. the model of the behaviours that the single employees (their tasks), and the machines (the computer based procedures) of each operational units exhibit to each other, to the other operational units and to the environment.
A modification can affect the micro-organizational architecture of an organization changing the task distribution among the employees and/or the specification of the computer based procedures or, more deeply, modifying the group of the employees and/or the computer systems used in an operational unit.

These considerations identify the need of modelling the object of the change, at the required organizational level. But, as widely argumented in the previous section, only a formal model of the negotiated organization behaviour can avoid ambiguities and misunderstandings in the mutual commitments the agreement implies.

The formal model of each level of the system architecture has to be communicable, i.e. within the reach of all the subjects involved in the negotiation: managers, workers, T.U. members. This means that the model must fit also people who are not skilled in (computer based) organization: the language the model is based on must be therefore easy to learn. Furthermore it is suitable that the model itself allows some use of the jargon typical to the target organization.
The use of a communicable language, for representing the system models, has to be combined with an education program for the management, the employees and the T.U. members in order to ensure that they use a common language analyzing, discussing and modelling the organization.

Some conditions on the formal model

System models of the organization are a useful tool in the negotiation process, if they allow to represent different organizational choices and to discuss them from the point of view of some qualitative aims (e.g. organizational noise and organizational autonomy).

a) Computer based technologies, when introduced into an organization, absorbe some of the human activities and transform the professional skills of the involved individuals. To avoid that the effect of this process is an increasing impoverishment of the professional skills, it is necessary to improve the organizational autonomy of individuals and groups working inside the organization, i.e. their autonomy in managing their work and their interrelations with other subsystems. Computer based technologies, thanks to their flexibility, may support the improvement of the organizational autonomy of the workers.

Therefore, at each organizational level the formal model of the system has to support the discussion on the organizational autonomy of the individuals and groups inside the organization.

b) Since organizational change always involves more then one organizational level, a proof of their mutual consistency with respect to the behaviour they show to the interacting environment is needed. In other words, the interaction protocol of the (sub)system under consideration with respect to its environment has to be an "invariant" during the (sub)system design, from the top level down to its micro-organization.

Therefore a formal notion of equivalence between two models, based on the above mentioned "invariant" property, has to be defined and supported with proof methods.

c) Although till now no notion of productivity has been proposed which is able to exhaustively deal with brain work and, therefore, no measure is available to evaluate on the whole the performances of an organizational system incorporating a relevant amount of clerical work, anyway it is suitable that the formal model of the organizational system supports the discussion of some parameters related to its efficiency. To this aim two parameters seem to be relevant: concurrency and organizational noise.

In fact, on one hand, the amount of activities which can be performed concurrently is obviously related to the efficiency of the organization, in particular at the micro-organizational level where the actual executors and, possibly, the automatic processors are considered.

On the other hand, any obstacle (like hierarchical intervention into an information exchange, lack of knowledge about the information providers) which hinders two subsystems to directly communicate introduces unnecessary steps and intermediators into communication thus producing unuseful organizational noise.

The reduction of organizational noise allows to increase the efficiency of an organization without compress working times.

On the formal model building process

In the reorganization process, users and experts strictly interact: the role of the experts is not to interpret the various, maybe conflictual, needs of users and customers, neither to act as a middleman among them; he has only to provide the different actors, which have the actual knowledge of the problem, with a common field where they can discuss the problem and communicate with each other, and to help them in comparing different issues.

This common field is the model building process itself, mainly for two reasons. First of all, since usually the knowledge of the different users on their work context is highly partial, it is suitable that, in the interaction with the experts to build up the formal model, the different users acquire a more complete and univoque, both detailed and synthetic, knowledge of the organization in which they work.

Secondly, only a direct participation of the users in the model construction, with the help of the experts which are more familiar with the solution of the formalization problems, allows a meaningful negotiation between them during the model construction itself in opposition to the use of discussing a posteriori on a model (even fully formalized) constructed by the experts alone.

From this point of view the negotiation has not to be considered an exceptional fact in the life of an organization, but it has to be considered the basic tool for monitoring it. The model of the target organization, therefore, is neither global neither built up once for all, but its construction is a never-ending process which, turn by turn, via subsequent changes, allows the updating of the agreements concerning the rules which govern the interactions between the different subsystems.

TOOLS

In the frame of "Progetto Finalizzato Informatica" of the Italian National Research Council (CNR) the authors are developing a method for organizational system analysis and design, which fits the above mentioned conditions. The method is based on a formal language defined inside the General Net Theory (7), which is presented here below, while the subsequent section contains the outlines of the main formal and conceptual tools the method makes use of.

SA nets

For a formal and exhaustive definition of SA nets see (8).
Here below the notions necessary to read and understand the nets which will be presented in the next paragraph are only briefly recalled, using these nets as examples.

Let us firstly consider the net of fig.3 . As Petri nets, SA nets are directed graphs composed by two kinds of nodes, places and transitions, connected by oriented arcs in such a way that no two nodes of the same kind are directly connected: places denote states and transitions actions.

A SA net can be considered as the composition of a set of elementary nets (corresponding to not deterministic automata) by means of the identification (merging) of some of their transitions. Elementary nets are characterized by the fact that each transition has exactly one incoming/outcoming arc, and therefore one input place and one output place. The merging operation superposes two or more transitions, each belonging to a different elementary net, the reversal operation is called splitting operation, as shown in fig.1 (a fragment of fig.3).

Each elementary net represents a subprocess. For example, the net of fig.3 represents a possible macro-organization of the target system. It is the composition of a set of elementary nets (subprocesses obtained via the merging of some transitions, namely the Process Department, the Drawing Division, the Projects Engineer Office and the Technological Department subprocesses).
Merged transitions are those having more than one input (output) place and model the interactions among subprocesses; while the 1-1 (one input place - one output place) transitions model the actions that are local to one subprocess. For example, the transitions labelled by 'begin/end process flow diagram' indicate that the accomplishement of such operations needs an interaction (not specified here) with the Drawing Division subprocess. Other examples of interactions are the exchanges of documents (indicated in the fig.3 by the labelling 'exchange of ...'). On the contrary, the transitions labelled by 'begin/end process specification' indicate that, even if these operations are quite complex, they do not need any interaction with other subprocesses. Places having at least two outcoming arcs are called conflict places.

The initial state of the SA net is defined by the initial marking of the set of elementary nets constituting it. The initial marking of an elementary net is given putting one token in its initial place.
A transition can fire if all its input places carry one token, and its firing moves all the tokens from its input places to its output places.

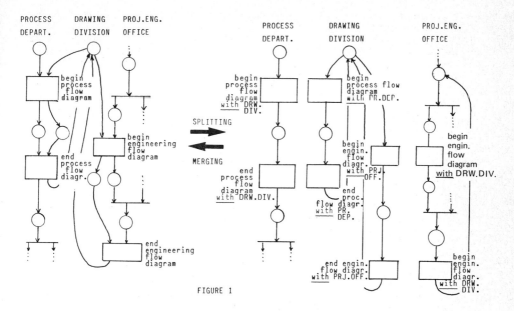

FIGURE 1

The initial places in our example are four, one for each subprocess. Under the initial marking shown in the fig.3, only the transition 'begin process flow diagram' can fire, moving the tokens present in its input places (A, B) into its output places (C, D) one each.

The behaviour of a system can be dynamically simulated by the sequences of transitions firings which can occur starting from the initial state.
The firing of a local transition denotes a state change inside a single subprocess. The firing of an interaction transition denotes a simultaneous change of the state of all the subprocesses involved by the transition. In addition, the model has no global state, but only a collection of local states, one for each subprocess.

The above recalled notions define a subclass of the SA nets class, whose components are C/E systems (7). The modelling power of this subclass is not enough to handle real problems, especially of the micro-organizational level where the power of the whole SA nets class is needed as shown in nets of fig.4.a,4.b,4.c, 5.a,5.b,5.c.
The main difference between the two classes consists in the marking definition. In SA nets, tokens are not undistinguishable as in the above presented subclass; they can be individuals, belonging to predefined domains which carry some structured information. Each subprocess has exactly one domain associated to it as shown in fig.4.a, 4.b, 4.c, 5.a, 5.b, 5.c. Each domain consists of the cartesian product of a colour component (C) which characterizes a single individual with respect to the others flowing in the same subprocess and a <u>data component</u> $D_1 x...x D_n$, which represents the data structure own of the subprocess and which it operates on. When a subprocess has associated a domain whose colour component has cardinality one and whose data component is not empty, it means that this subprocess has a private data structure and that the system contains only one instance of this subprocess. If the cardinality is n>1, the system contains n instances of the same subprocess whose behaviour is modelled by a simple net carrying n individuals. In this case, if the data component is not empty, then each subprocess has its private (with respect to the other istances) data structure.

From the above considerations, it follows that it is possible to require the
presence of some specific individuals in the input places in order to enable the
firing of a transition and it is necessary to specify how the firing of each
transition transforms and distributes the individuals which give concession to
it. Each transition has associated these specifications using the following
pattern:

where $\underline{x}$ is a vector variable belonging to the domain associated to the subprocess
containing t; ($\underline{x}$) is a predicate on $\underline{x}$, which specifies the individuals to be
removed from the input place; the labelling of the outcoming arc specifies which
component of $\underline{x}$ have been transformed by the firing of t. For sake of conciseness,
a notation which avoids the explicit occurrences of $\underline{x}$ is often used, only showing
the $\underline{x}$'s modifications on the outcoming arc.

The initial marking of a generic SA net is defined by the presence of as many
individuals in the initial place of each subprocess as the cardinality of the
colour component of the domain associated to the subprocess.

A last consideration on the net model: when a SA net is composed of C/E systems
the definition of the initial marking and of the firing rule leads each
elementary net to carry only one token. This implies that the state of each
subprocess is always explicitly defined by the occurrence of the token in a
place; allowing an easy monitoring of the system behaviour.
In the case of a generic SA net more individuals flow in each subprocess.
Nevertheless, the definitions of the initial marking and of the firing rule
guarantee that the individuals do not disappear or increase (their total number
remains constant): therefore in this case also the state of each istance of each
subprocess is explicitly defined by the occurrence of the correspondent
individual token in a place and by the value assumed by its data component.

Some outlines of the method

The characteristics of the method are widely influenced by the above discussed
"conditions" both on the modelling language and modelling process: key concepts
are, then, formality, easiness to be used and learned, suitability to discuss
"new" parameters in the organization.
These conditions lead to the definition of a set of formal tools which can be
used in a quite flexible way, under the possibility of verifying (formally once
more) that the way of operating is correct with respect to some predefined goals.

Some tools have been already mentioned.

First of all, the three organizational levels. This scheme helps in focusing the
object under consideration (the target system) and its environment and specially,
in fixing the level at which the investigation is carried on, avoiding to mix
problems at different levels: e.g. the resources allocation with the behaviour
definition, the macro-organization with the technological problems etc. No rules
are given to define what pertains to each level, but the point is made explicit
and the choices, which can deeply depend on the problem, have to be in some sense
justified and then negotiated. (Examples of models of the three levels are given
in the next paragraph discussing a real case).

The second tool is the formal language presented in the previous section. The
few syntactic rules, the naturally associated semantics and a wide number of

experiences of its use by not experts, allow to say that it satisfies the condition related to the easiness of use and learning. Its modularity, the fact that it drives to look at a system as a composition of interacting subprocesses and to formalize the communication protocols between them, makes it easier to discuss parameters as: autonomy, i.e. to what extent the communication protocols impose constraints to the internal (local) behaviour of each subprocess, organizational noise, i.e. the overhead in organization due to unseful communication or control intervention (these two parameters will be deeply discussed in the example of the next paragraphs).

These two tools, the three organizational levels and the formal language to discuss organizational parameters, allow to construct a model of the target system, at one specific organizational level. But generally any intervention has to consider more than one level: hence, which is the relation between two models at contiguous levels? This gives rise to a third tool, or better to a rule: the construction of a model at one organizational level is completely autonomous from the construction of the previous one(s). That is, it is not a matter of derivation (e.g. in a top-down sense) but of a new design, depending on new organizational choices. In other words, at the end of the process there are at least as many models as the organizational levels taken into account, and they are not derived one from the others.
At least as many,since, at each organizational level, more than one model is possible, depending on the different organization choices (for example, in the next paragraph, these possible solutions at the micro-organizational level will be given).

Two contiguous models are autonomous in their construction but are semantically related. Furthermore, different models at the same level have to be compared, to evaluate the implications of different organizational choices. These two facts lead to the definition of a new formal tool, that is, the notion of equivalence among models (nets) which is formally defined in the frame of the general net theory. Two are the proposed equivalence notions: O-equivalence, guaranteeing that equivalent sequences of events lead to equivalent prolongations (i.e. equivalent hystories in the past guarantee equivalent evolutions in the future) and CO-equivalence which imposes the same property to partially ordered sets of events (instead of sequences), taking into account the concurrency among events also.
The O-equivalence notion allows a formal proof of the consistency of two models at contiguous levels. CO-equivalence is used differently: it is related to notions as efficiency and resources allocation, induced by different degrees of concurrency. Then, it can be suitably used in comparing models at the same organizational level.
Note that the construction of the model is fully recursive with respect to the subsystems, these equivalence notions can be used for any subsystem (considered as target system) with respect to its specific environment.

Finally, two other tools can be used which refer to the handling of complexity of real systems. First of all the notion of functional abstraction, related to the traditional top-down method. It can be used for building the system model at one specific organizational level, to avoid details which are at that point not useful in the discussion (negotiation). For example an action (transition) can be refined in a net which defines it in a more detailed way.
The other tool is the notion of simplification.
A complex system can be analyzed building, as a first step, a model relative to a problem that is a simplification of the one under consideration (e.g. the analysis of the behaviour of a complex organization can be carried on building the models of the organization relative to the various processes it executes, without taking into account the connection between all these processes), and then, on the basis of these reduced models, constructing the model of the system relative to the whole problem. An example of this simplification is given in the next paragraph.

The method provides some way to verify if their use, even quite not completely codified, is correct, leading to consistent descriptions. In fact, the level of functional abstraction, quite free in considering a single subprocess or a net of one level as a whole, is bounded: firstly by the merging on the communication transitions, since only transitions at the same level can be identified (merge); secondly, by the use of the equivalence notions, since the equivalence of two nets can be proved only if they consider as basic the same set of actions. Furthermore, there is a formal way for verifying the correct application of the above mentioned simplification notion. The step between the model relative to the simplified problem and the model relative to the whole problem can be formally controlled, if the latter, considered with respect to the simplified problem, is O-equivalent to the first one.

Once more the way in which the tools are used is flexible and not normative, but for the internal consistency of the modelling process, which can be verified using the tools themselves.

EXPERIENCES

The method for organization modelling based on SA nets has been used in different frames to model: a public administration department devoted to handle the residence change of Italian citizens (11); the management system (updatings and inquirings) of a data base containing information on the diffusion of computers in Italy; some of the safety devices used to control the trains traffic in the Italian railways (13). Furthermore it has been used in a set of experiences to make workers and T.U. better equipped when computer based changes occur in the organizations (10).

In this last frame a working group composed by some of the authors and some workers and shop stewards has faced the problem of the introduction of a CAD system into a large engineering company, whose main activity is the design of large chemical plants, in order to support the negotiation of the organizational change the CAD system introduction will provoke.

More in detail, the specific issue was to compare different organizational choices, i.e. the present not automatized organization, and the one proposed by the management when CAD system is introduced, in order to outline and discuss a different possible solution proposed by T.U. giving more guarantees on workers professional skills. The attention was therefore focused on the micro-organizational level. But, following the methodological approach outlined in the previous section, the sketch of the behavioural architecture and of the macro-organizational architecture was needed to define the context in which the different micro-organizational choices could be discussed.

The behavioural architecture outlines the behaviour the company exhibits to its environment with respect to the design process of one single chemical plant, showing the main activities constituting the chemical plant design process and their mutual relations (causal dependency and concurrency).

The SA net model of fig.2 shows a large fragment of the model: the main activities are preparations of documents, diagrams and drawings. In the model each activity has been splitted into two phases (begin ... , end ...) in order to give a finer characterization of the casual dependency between two activities.

The SA net model of fig.2 puts into evidence the partial order among the activities, without paying any attention to the organizational structure of the company.

The fact that more chemical plant projects are usually carried on at the same time is not taken into account. Nevertheless the model of this simplified problem is in this case sufficient to achieve a good knowledge of the process because the activities concerning different projects do not have effects on each other from the information point of view. (This refers to the simplification procedure

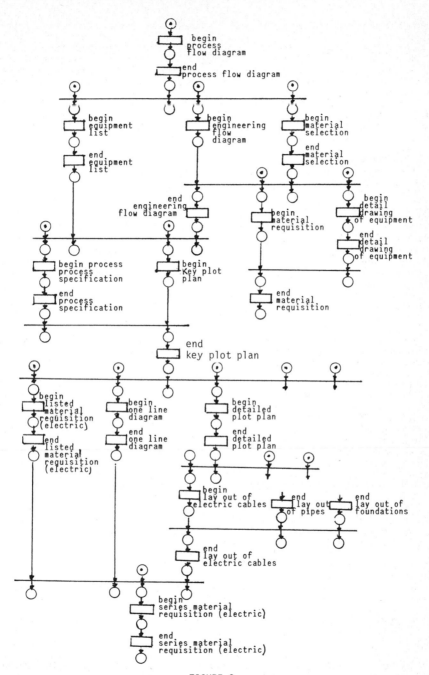

FIGURE 2

THE BEHAVIOURAL ARCHITECTURE OF A LARGE ENGINEERING COMPANY W.R.T. THE CHEMICAL PLANT DESIGN PROCESS.

mentioned in the previous section).

As a second step, the construction of the macro-organizational model of the company with respect to the design process of one single chemical plant is carried out identifying the operational units, and allocating them the activities they perform or concur to perform interacting with other operational units.

The operational units are: the Projects Engineer Office (which defines the main lines of the project and takes the main design choices), the Technical Departments (Process Department, Technological Department, Electrical Department, and some others) and the Drawing Division of the Piping Department which has been taken into account separately from the Piping Department, because it works for other operational units also.

The SA Net model of fig.3 shows a large fragment of the macro-organization of the company with respect to the simplified problem of designing a single chemical plant.

The macro-organizational model does not give a more detailed description of the company behaviour than that one modelled by the behavioural architecture of fig.3. It only shows how the flow of the activities is partitioned among the different operational units and puts into evidence that the behaviours of the various operational units are synchronized by means of direct communications between them.

The macro-organizational architecture of the company, with respect to the set of different chemical plant projects carried on simultaneously in a certain period, can be built up taking the SA net model of fig.3 as a starting point. This step was omitted, because, as already mentioned, the aim was not of designing a new organizational structure of the company, but of sketching it to define the context in which to discuss different micro-organizational choices.
The third step was to build up the models of the different possible micro-organizations, satisfying the constraints defined by the above discussed macro-organization, in order to compare them in particular from two points of view:
a)   the organizational noise induced by the different micro-organizational choices;
b)   the organizational autonomy, and therefore the professional skills, each micro-organizational solution guarantees to workers directly affected by the introduction of the CAD system (in particular draftmen).

The micro-organizational solutions taken into account are three:
a)   the present company organization: draft and counter drawings are drawn by draftmen distributed among technical departments;
b)   the management proposed organization: a unique CAD service department that incorporates all the drawings capacities of the company and serves all the technical departments;
c)   the T.U. proposed organization: the CAD system is introduced into a distributed way allocating to each department its own CAD station.

These different micro-organizational choices were discussed and compared on the basis of some significant fragments of the correspondent micro-organizational models of the company (with respect to the set of different chemical plants design processes).

In this paper the attention is focused on the "One Line Diagram" (OLD) construction process that is a good example of the interactions between the specialist and the draftsman (the CAD operator) during the construction of a graphic document.

Firstly, the present micro-organization is considered: the net of fig.4.a shows

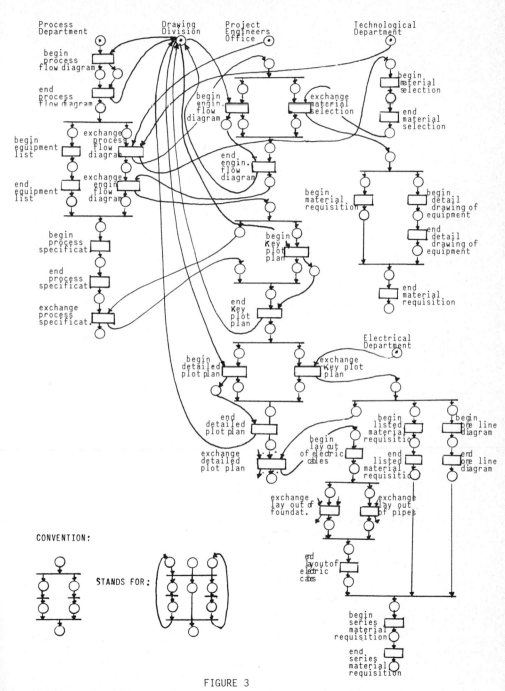

FIGURE 3

A FRAGMENT OF THE MACROORGANIZATIONAL STRUCTURE OF A LARGE ENGINEERING COMPANY
W.R.T. THE CHEMICAL PLANT DESIGN

the behaviour of an Electrical Engineer (EL.ENG) and of a Draftman (DRF.MAN) and
their mutual interactions during the process of constructing the One Line Diagram
concerning a single plant design. Here the principle of simplification is once
more applied since it doesn't affect the subsequent discussion. In fact,
considering more than one chemical plant or more draftsmen and electrical
engineers would issue only in an increased complexity of the domains associated
to these subprocesses, without providing the discussion about autonomy or
organizational noise with further information.

In the net model of fig.4.a, in addition to the conventions already presented in
the previous section, two further labelling simplifications have been introduced:
a) since only one Electrical Engeneer and one Draftman are considered, the colour
components of both their associated domains are omitted; b) the state
modification derived from the firing of a transition is usually evoked by means
of the transition label.
The modification of the value assumed by some data component is formally
described only when these data influence the subsequent evolution of the net (for
example, when the transition labelled by 'new specs request' is fired, the OLD
component of the domain U_D associated to the draftman changes to 'wait': that
implies the transition labelled by 'diagram execution' is not firable).
Using the same conventions of fig.4.a, the net of fig.4.b models the
micro-organization proposed by the management when the CAD system is introduced:
the CAD operator (CAD OP) takes the place of the draftman and a CAD Service
Manager (CAD MAN) appears with an intermediary role in the communication between
the Electrical Engineer and the CAD Operator.

The net of fig.4.c models the micro-organization proposed by the Trade Unions to
introduce the CAD system: it is useful to point out that this proposal was only
briefly outlined when the working group started and it became more and more
defined during the construction of the different possible formal models.

It is easy to see that the management proposed micro-organization increases the
organizational noise with respect to the present organization. In fact in the net
of fig.4.b the communication between the electrical designer, who prepares the
draft of the One Line Diagram, and the CAD operator, who prepares its counter
drawing, is no more direct as the communication between the Electrical Engineer
and the Draftman in the net of fig.4.a. In the management proposed organization
the CAD service manager interventions prevent from direct communication imposing
complex communication protocols between designers and CAD operators.
The T.U. proposed organization (fig.4.c),on the contrary, does not increase the
organizational noise and allows a closer interaction between the CAD Operator and
the Electrical Engineer (they not only speak together but they work together
too!).

The nets of fig.5.a, 5.b and 5.c give a different view of the three different
micro-organizational solutions, focusing the attention on the behaviour the
draftman (CAD. OP.) exhibits when he works without any automatic support or
interacting with the CAD System (CAD SYST.) (fig.5.b and 5.c), in order to
discuss some questions about the organizational autonomy the three
micro-organizational solutions attribute to him.

It has to be observed that the SA net of fig.5.c shows some activities of
updating the CAD system functions ('new electrical design procedures discussing',
'new electrical design procedures development', ...) that were not present in the
SA net of fig.5.a and 5.b, because they are impossible in the present manual
micro-organization, and not assigned to the CAD operator in the management
proposed micro-organization, but to the CAD manager.

The net models show that from the point of view of the organizational autonomy of
the CAD operator also the management proposed option has negative
characteristics.

ELECTRICAL ENGINEER   DRAFTMAN

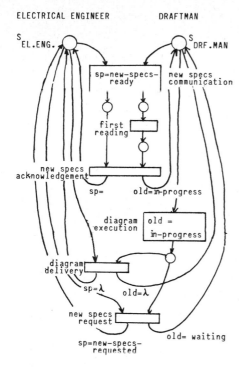

DOMAINS

$D_{EL.ENG.} = \ldots \times SP \times \ldots$, where

$SP = \{$ the set of the possibles states of the specifications SP

new-spec-ready, new-spec-requested, $\lambda \}$

$D_{DRF.MAN} = \ldots \times OLD \times \ldots$, where

$OLD = \{$the set of the possible states of the One Line Diagram =

in-progress, waiting, $\lambda \}$

INITIAL MARKINGS

$m_o(S_{EL.ENG.}) = \langle \ldots, sp = \lambda, \ldots \rangle$;

$m_o(S_{DRF.MAN}) = \langle \ldots, old = , \ldots \rangle$

FIGURE 4.a

LEGENDA

- Only the domain components which determine the net evolution in the conflict situations are made explicit.

- λ means the empty structure; either not already initialized or cancelled, since the information has been still delivered or cancelled.

DOMAINS

$D_{EL.ENG.}$ and $D_{CAD.OP} = D_{DRF.MAN}$

as in FIGURE 4.a

INITIAL MARKINGS

$m_o(S_{EL.ENG.})$ and $m_o(S_{CAD.OP.}) = m_o(S_{DRF.MAN})$

as in FIGURE 4.a

FIGURE 4.c

ELECTRICAL   CAD
ENGINEER   OPERATOR

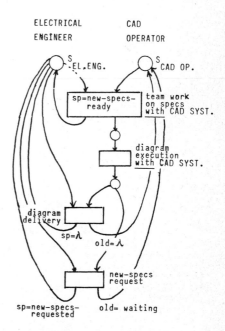

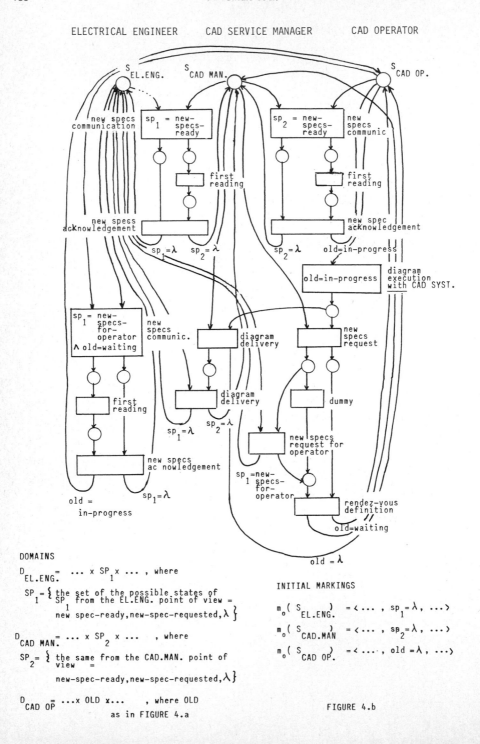

DOMAINS

$D_{EL.ENG.} = \ldots \times SP_1 \times \ldots$, where

$SP_1 = \{$ the set of the possible states of
SP_1 from the EL.ENG. point of view =
new spec-ready, new-spec-requested, $\lambda \}$

$D_{CAD\ MAN.} = \ldots \times SP_2 \times \ldots$, where

$SP_2 = \{$ the same from the CAD.MAN. point of
view =
new-spec-ready, new-spec-requested, $\lambda \}$

$D_{CAD\ OP} = \ldots \times OLD \times \ldots$, where OLD
as in FIGURE 4.a

INITIAL MARKINGS

$m_0(S_{EL.ENG.}) = \langle \ldots , sp_1 = \lambda , \ldots \rangle$

$m_0(S_{CAD.MAN}) = \langle \ldots , sp_2 = \lambda , \ldots \rangle$

$m_0(S_{CAD\ OP.}) = \langle \ldots , old = \lambda , \ldots \rangle$

FIGURE 4.b

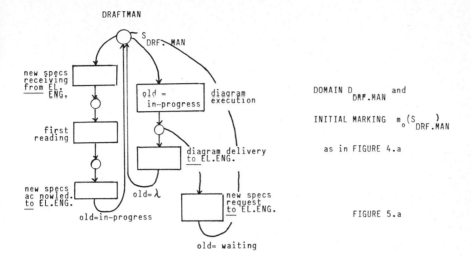

DRAFTMAN

DOMAIN $D_{DRF.MAN}$ and

INITIAL MARKING $m_o(S_{DRF.MAN})$

as in FIGURE 4.a

FIGURE 5.a

FIGURE 5.b

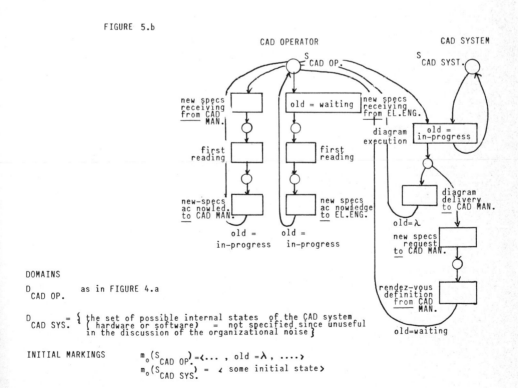

CAD OPERATOR   CAD SYSTEM

DOMAINS

$D_{CAD\ OP.}$ as in FIGURE 4.a

$D_{CAD\ SYS.}$ = { the set of possible internal states of the CAD system
(hardware or software) = not specified since unuseful
in the discussion of the organizational noise }

INITIAL MARKINGS $m_o(S_{CAD\ OP.})$ =<... , old =λ, ...>
$m_o(S_{CAD\ SYS.})$ = < some initial state>

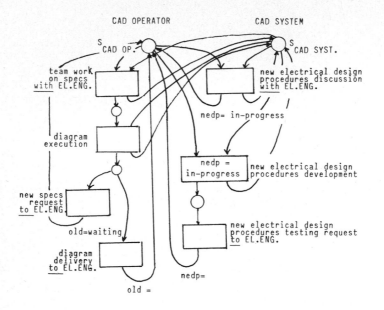

CAD OPERATOR   CAD SYSTEM

team work
on specs
with EL.ENG.

new electrical design
procedures discussion
with EL.ENG.

diagram
execution

nedp= in-progress

nedp =
in-progress

new electrical design
procedures development

new specs
request
to EL.ENG.

old=waiting

new electrical design
procedures testing request
to EL.ENG.

diagram
delivery
to EL.ENG.

nedp=

old =

DOMAINS

$D_{CAD\ OP.}$ = ... x OLD x ... x NEDP x ... , where

OLD   as in   FIGURE 4.a

NEDP = $\{$ set of the possible states of the New
Electrical Design Procedures =
in-progress , λ $\}$

$D_{CAD\ SYS.}$ as in FIGURE 5.b

INITIAL MARKINGS

$m_o(S_{CAD\ OP.})$ = $\langle$ ... , old=λ, ... ,nedp=λ ,...$\rangle$

$m_o(S_{CAD\ SYS.})$ = $\langle$ some initial state $\rangle$

FIGURE 5.c

The draftsman (see fig.5.a) has an high degree of autonomy in doing his job (he decides when to begin drawing the One Line Diagram and how to do it) and has direct communications with the Electrical Engineer, his information provider, but he is not an information provider for this latter (he is subordinate to him).
The CAD operator inside the CAD service department (see fig.5.b) has a low degree of autonomy in doing his job (he executes the drawings the CAD service manager orders to him) and can communicate with the Electrical Engineer only passing through the CAD service manager: his activities are therefore strongly subordinated to a hierarchical control.
The CAD operator inside the technical department (see fig.5.c) has an high degree of autonomy in doing his job and has direct communication with the Electrical Engineer (he interact with him) and also he is an information provider for him (he has the opportunity of improving his automatic tools, of discussing them with the Electrical Engineer, eventually stimulating implementation of new electrical design procedures inside the CAD system which will improve the work of all the electrical CAD operators) and therefore he is not subordinate to the Electrical Engineer, but he is its partner.

Two last considerations on the net model: firstly, it is useful to observe that the degree of autonomy of a subsystem is evaluated analyzing the conflicts that represent decision points (local non-determinism (11)) its behaviour shows and the information flow among the subsystems; secondly, it is also important to point out that the nets of fig.4.a and 5.a (and respectively 4.b and 5.b, 4.c and

5.c) are two partial views of the same micro-organizational SA net model: it is a peculiar characteristic of SA net model to allow, at each time, to consider only the interesting aspects of a model disregarding the details that are not important with respect to a given problem.

For example, the updating activities of the CAD system functions are shown in the net of fig.5.c and omitted in fig.4.c: that is because they are relevant to discuss the organizational autonomy of the CAD operator and therefore his professional skill, while they are meaningless to discuss the problem of the organizational noise.

SOME CONCLUDING REMARKS

All the considerations and the proposals presented in the previous sections presuppose that the users, without transforming themselves into organization experts, increase, both in qualitative and quantitative sense, their ability of analyzing the organization and of communicating about it.

It is, therefore, necessary for an effective negotiation of the organizational change that the workers, the shop stewards, the trade unionists and the management too are involved in a large educational program about the organization and the tools for modelling it.

The experiences carried on by the authors in the last two years in cooperation with the Trade Unions of the area of Milan (see (10)) have shown that a well structured educational program, providing both the basic notions about the tools and the opportunities for using them in concrete cases, gives the participants the ability of understanding the notion of organizational abstraction, of reading, understanding and contributing to build the SA net models of an organization at each level of organizational abstraction, identifying the suitable functional abstraction and discussing with the experts the organizational choices represented by the built models.

The construction of automated tools to support the communicativeness of the language allowing an easy manipulation of the models and the simulation of their behaviour (like, for example, the Net Laboratory (14)) could be an important improvement both of the analysis method and of its usability by not experts.

This research has been developed in the frame of the Progetto Finalizzato Informatica of Consiglio Nazionale delle Ricerche under the contract 81.02524.97.115.11012.

REFERENCES

(1) Flores,F. Ludlow,J.J., Doing and Speaking in the Office, in: Fisk, G. and
     Sprague, R. (eds.), DSS: Issues and Challenges (Pergamon, New York, 1981).

(2) Grandi, M., Problematiche dell'organizzazione e delle professionalità nella
     automazione dell'ufficio, (CEDOS, Milano, 1981).

(3) Petri, C.A., Modelling as a communication discipline, in: Gelembe, E. (ed.),
     Measuring, Modelling and Evaluating Computer Systems (North Holland,
     Amsterdam, 1977).

(4) Petri, C.A., Kommunicationsdisziplinen, in: Petri, C.A. (ed.), Ansaetze zur
     Organisationstheorie Rechnergestuetzer Informationssysteme (R. Oldenbourg,
     Munchen, 1979)

(5) Ouchi, W.G., A conceptual framework for the design of organizational control
     mechanisms, Management Science 25.9 (1979)

(6) Ciborra, C., Information systems and transactions architecture, Journal of
     Policy Analysis and Information Systems 5.4, (1981)

(7) Brauer, W. (ed), Net theory and applications, LNCS 84 (Springer-Verlag,
     Berlin, 1980)

(8) De Cindio, F., De Michelis, G., Pomello, L., Simone, C., Superposed Automata
     Nets, IFB.52 (Springer- Verlag, Berlin, 1982)

(9) Genrich, H.J., Lautenbach, K., System modelling with high-level Petri nets,
     Theoretical Computer Science 13.1 (1981)

(10) De Cindio, F., Pieroni, W., Simone, C., A large education on computer and
     system analysis as a condition to make the negotiation possible, in this
     volume.

(11) De Cindio, F., De Michelis, G., Pomello, L., Simone, C., Real system
     modelling: a formal but realistic approach to organizational design, Proc.
     International Working Conference on Model Realism (Pergamon, New York, 1982)
     (to appear).

(12) De Cindio, F., De Michelis, G., Pomello, L., Simone, C., Equivalence notions
     for concurrent systems, I.C. Internal Report (1982)

(13) Scandroglio, R., Le reti SA per la descrizione di apparati e norme per la
     sicurezza del traffico ferroviario, Tesi di laurea in Fisica, Univ. degli
     Studi di Milano, A.A. 81-82.

(14) Genrich H.J., Shapiro R.M., The GMD Net Editor, Proc. III European
     Workshop on Application and Theory of Petri Nets, IFB (Springer-Verlag,
     Berlin, to appear).

TRADE UNIONS EXPERIENCES WITH NEW TECHNOLOGY

SYSTEMS DESIGN FOR, WITH, AND BY THE USERS
U. Briefs, C. Ciborra and L. Schneider (editors)
North-Holland Publishing Company
© IFIP, 1983

THE CHALLENGE OF NEW TECHNOLOGY
FOR EUROPEAN UNIONS - A COMPARATIVE APPROACH

Anders J. Hingel

Institute of Organization and Industrial Sociology
Copenhagen School of Economics and Social Science
Copenhagen
Denmark

Although the taking up of the technological issue
by unions will probably entail an enlargement of
their bargaining scope, it will also induce more
fundamental changes in industrial relation systems.
Indeed, owing to the complexity and speed of technological development, the latter will launch unprecedented challenges which might lead to notable
transformations in union structures, relations between unions, between unions and researchers, union
and employers, unions and the state as well as between national unions on a cross-national level.
Examples of such changes and an analysis of their
implications are provided on the basis of a comparative perspective.

INTRODUCTION

Most European unions have within recent years adopted a strategy towards new technology which has been marked by a twofold concern: on
the one hand, new technology has been considered as a major remedy
for the creation of welfare, economic growth, social equality and
full employment; on the other hand, new technology has been denounced
as the blameworthy factor in a process of continuous destruction of
working, employment and living conditions. The importance given respectively to each of these two perspectives in a definition of general policy has been varying across unions and countries. But in all
countries, technological issues have been inducing the demand of a
greater union insight and say on decisions related to:

- R & D activities (private/public)
- investments in plants and companies
- the technical organization of production (machines type,
  design, layout etc.)
- products, subproducts, materials
- personnel policy
- training and education
- division of labour
  and various other issues.

The technological issue seems thus to revivify a long-standing union
claim for workers' control over working and employment conditions
(Goodrich (192o);Roth (1974);Vester (197o)).

The ways in which the different unions in European countries have
been facing this technological challenge has become more and more subject to discussion. We will therefore in a first section of this paper examine the major features of the regulatory frame which has been

developing in the field of new technology, in various European countries (Germany, England, France and Scandinavia), and which presently
conditions its introduction and use in production and administration.
In a second section we will analyse the challenges union organizations
are faced with due to the "integration" of the technological issue in
their immediate sphere of concern.

PRESENT REGULATORY SYSTEMS OF TECHNOLOGICAL DEVELOPMENT

In the case of Germany, agreements on consequences induced by technological change ("rationalization") have been signed since the end of
the 60 s' on a national as well as regional level. A strong union demand for influencing state-programmes of R&D in the field of technology and working conditions has, throughout the 70 s' constituted
the focus of unions' technology policy. The programme for humanized
working conditions represents so far the only German state-financed
development programme in which the union representatives have a certain voice (Janzen (1980)).

In spite of a highly centralized union movement and in spite of a
fierce employers' reluctancy to negotiate, local agreements on com-
puter-technology have been reached between the works councils (Betriebsräte) and employers within the plants and companies. A hierarchy of collective agreements appears thus to have developed (Hingel
(1981))[1]. Notwithstanding their shortcomings, the co-determination
Acts of 1951 and 1976 (covering respectively the coal, iron and steel
industries, and large stock companies with more than 2.000 employees),
and especially the works constitution Act of 1972 providing the
works council with numerous information rights and some influence
rights on working conditions and social affairs in firms, have contributed to enhance workers' influence on technology, but have also
clearly circumscribed the bargaining scope on technology in plants
and companies. The present possibilities for concluding agreements on
decentralized levels are becoming extremely limited owing to a reinforced co-ordination of employers' policies regarding technological
development.[2]

In Great-Britain, numerous "technology agreements" have been concluded at plant and at company level between single unions or groups of
unions, and employers (e.g. the agreement between ASTMS/ACTSS and the
firm CPC Ltd, prescribing "joint discussions at each stage of the
company plans for the investigation and introduction of electronic
data processing equipment", or the agreement between the Joint Shop
Steward Committee (TASS, ASTMS, ACTSS) and the Ford company on the
introduction of EDP, agreements signed respectively in 1979 and 1978).
Whereas examples of national industry agreements can be mentioned
(POEU and the Post Office), no agreement has been reached at central
confederation level between TUC and CBI. The breakdown of negotiations
in 1981 was mostly due to resistances on behalf of the engineering employer federation (EEF), but also to the reluctancy of certain
unions to let the TUC play a too prominent role in these matters (In
tersocial, Nov. (1980)). The TUC congress had already in 1956 declared
that the introduction of commercial computers should be controlled,
not restricted. At the congress of 1968 it was confirmed as a TUC policy that all questions such as the introduction of new machines
should be handled on a decentralized level. The shop steward movement
remains thus in Great Britain of crucial importance for workers' influence on technological change and its social consequences in the
firm.[3]

As concerns <u>France</u>, one has to remark that many industrial actions
have been taking place in which new technology was a central issue at
stake. But hardly any examples of technology agreements and negotiations about this domain can be registered. Nevertheless, the major
union confederations (CGT and CFDT), as well as their respective engineer, technician and manager sections representing the "cadres"
(UGICT/CGT and UCC/CFDT) have developed elaborate understandings and
strategies vis-à-vis working conditions, division of labour, technological change and industrial structure. At the annual fair on office
technology in Paris (Sicob), 1979, did CFDT present "9 propositions"
concerning conditions for investments in information technology (informatics) based on the principle that: "we will not together with
new information technology accept the same type of unequivocal tota-
lism as the one followed by scientific management (taylorism)". CFDT
is thus in favour of a critical attitude to new technology and demands
by the "9 propositions" workers' control over investments in information technology (Le Monde, 27 sep.(1979)). In more recent policy discussions within the CFDT a more moderate standpoint has although been
developed, mostly on the basis of pressure from certain member groups
on the local levels. The CFDT is reckoned to play a significant role
in the elaboration and implementation of the industrial policy of the
new socialist government in which "strategic new technologies", e.g.
information technology, are expected to fulfil a major role.

In the past, workers' influence on technology has indeed shown rather
limited in France. But the new law on workers' rights within the firm
(the "Auroux Law") which has been voted in Parliament in June 1982 is
supposed to upon up new possibilities. On one side, the individual
worker has been recognized a right for a direct say on his working
conditions in firms with more than 2oo employees. This right is to be
organized on the basis of the homogeneous work group, and its specific
outline should be left to negotiations between management and trade unions within the firm. Owing to its unprecise legal frame, the outcomes
of this prescription remain however fairly uncertain for the moment
(Lyon-Caen (1981)). On the other side, the works council will have to
be informed in the future before the introduction of new technologies
if the latter bear consequences on employment, qualifications, remune-
rations, training and working conditions (Auroux (1982). The implicit
aim of these reforms is, according to the Minister of Labour: "to reconcile workers with technological innovations which are often perceived as an agression" and further "to create thus new investments opportunities" (Le Monde, 6-7 june (1982)). (4)

Among the Scandinavian countries, the case of <u>Norway</u> deserves special
attention. Indeed, a technology agreement was signed by LO and the
employer organization, NAF, already in 1975 with the aim to regulate
the introduction of "data based systems". Since then, similar agreements have been renegotiated in 1978 and 1981, the latter covering
"technological change and data systems". Outside the LO area, one notices the conclusion of agreements in the public sector, banking and
insurances. On this general basis a substantial number of technology
agreements have subsequently been reached at company or plant level.
One estimates that about 7oo such agreements are presently in force.

In <u>Denmark</u> one registers for the moment less than 1oo technology
agreements on local level. In 1981 a central technology agreement was
signed by LO and DA (the employer organization)-which was in fact an
additional agreement to the Co-operation Agreement of 1977 - and was
followed by a definite reluctancy among employers to discuss any
further local agreements. The number of local agreements between unions
and employers who are not members of DA appear although to be increa-

sing. Similar to the above mentioned central agreement between LO and
DA has a technology agreement been signed in the public sector concerning State-employees, whereas the municipal employees up to now have
rejected such agreements. The unsolved problem has in the latter sector been the demand for information rights and employees' influence on
the highly centralized cross-municipal development of new computer systems.

As regards <u>Sweden</u>, workers' and unions' influence on new technology
has been remaining until now essentially regulated by the Act of co-
determination at work of 1976. Consequently, the Act induced the conclusion of central agreements in the public sector, banking and insurance; more lately, LO and the employer organization, SAF, have, after
five years of fierce negotiations, agreed upon a so-called Development
Agreement (May 1982). The latter is expected to engender local technology agreements in the near future.

However, although employees have, in the three Scandinavian countries,
obtained - at least formally - a certain voice in technology matters
by means of central/decentralized technology agreements, the employers
"right to direct and to distribute work" has been preserved. This is
why unions presume technology and working conditions to be in the long
run transformed primarily by means of the various work environment
Acts and especially by the related directives and regulations, rather
than by means of collective agreements. (5)

CHALLENGES OF NEW TECHNOLOGY FOR THE LABOUR MOVEMENT

Apart form the fact that new technology has been paid great attention
in the above mentioned countries, another common feature is that the
technological issue has to a large extent been treated according to
the specific industrial relation system existing in each country. From
a strategic point of view this seems appropriate and rational given
the immediate demands of the situation. But each industrial relation
system has its "hang ups", and one notices that in each national context traditional, deeply rooted practices very often hinder the carrying out of more innovative and more satisfactory ways of treating the
technological question.

It may thus be relevant to put forward the question whether technology
and technological change are not distinct matters compared to wages,
health and safety items, working hours etc. In other words, does not
the complexity of the social process of technological development and
the speed of present technological change require the setting up of
new control structures and processes ?

If one follows such a logic, the "integration" of the technological
issue in union policies is bound to challenge elements such as:

                   - union structures
                   - inter-union relationships
                   - the union relationship to research
                   - the relationship between unions and employers
                   - the co-operation between unions at cross-national level
                   - union - state relationships.

In no way do we here intend to support the argument of an international convergency of industrial relation systems as a result of technological development: a debate (Kerr & all (196o)), which is taken
up again, this time by marxist orientated authors (Caire (1982)).
Neither do we believe that there is a "one best way" for unions to

deal with new technology. But we do think that new technology constitutes a challenge common to any industrial relation system and that
comparative studies can raise inspiration and provide experiences
about the means, aims and consequences of various ways of confronting
such a challenge.

In this section we will illustrate some of the transformations each
of the previously mentioned elements is presently subject to, as a
consequence of the increasing union activity in the field of new technology.

Union structures

In most European countries we observe centralized as well as decentralized union strategies for the mastering of new technology and its
social consequences (Hingel (1981),(1982)).

Technology agreements on confederation level as we have seen them
in Denmark, Norway and now also in Sweden, and on federation level as
is extensively the case in Scandinavia, Germany and Great Britain,
constitute mostly frames for further decentralized technology agreements to be signed at regional, company and plant level. Decentralized activities are thus often the result of centrally initiated actions, based on a twofold rationality (Hingel (1981)):

> - a technical, economic and social reasoning where the
>   plant (company or region) specific design, use and
>   consequences of new technology make it necessary that
>   "those directly concerned" are actively involved in
>   defining demands founded on concrete technical, eco-
>   nomic and social pre-conditions;
>
> - a union strategic reasoning based on the assumption
>   that the increasing employer mobilization at central
>   levels in all European countries often obliges unions
>   to carry out at decentralized level what connot be
>   achieved centrally. As part of a long term strategy,
>   decentralized results are thus often considered as
>   precedents for a future propagation of union claims.

The respective importance of either level - centralized versus decentralized - can be presumed to influence internal power relations within the single union.

Hence, a different type of union representatives can be supposed to
be fostered as a result of decentralized activities regarding new
technology. Local "technology awareness centers" such as we observe
them in Norway and Germany, or "trade union resource centers" in Great-
Britain, are examples of new union bodies providing economic and technical expertise on decentralized levels. The fact that the TUC for
instance is opposed to such centers because of "the fear of side-step-
ping established hierarchies" gives an indication of possible structural transformations. The open conflicts between IG-Metall and parts
of local works councils in the two companies Daimler-Benz and Siemens
related to the discrepancy between the union policy and employees'
claims concerning the introduction of new data-systems represent other
examples of the sort (Hingel (1981)).

Besides, the specialization of employee and union representatives
(data-stewards, work environment representatives as well as company
board and works council representatives etc.) - although justified
somehow by the necessity of building up sufficient negotiation exper-

tise required by a still more complex, centralized and confidential
information system induced by new technology - will certainly cause a
change in the role distribution within the union and its organizational structure. Such transformations might occur on three levels:

- between union "experts" within the firm and the union
  members where an expertise gap might emerge;

- within the hierarchy of shop stewards within the firm;

- between shop stewards possessing more and more firm
  specific expertise - and firm specific orientations -
  and the union federation/confederation outside the
  firm.

The specific forms of such structural changes and their implications
for the strengthening or weakening of union organizations will differ
from one industrial relation system to another. In countries like Germany with an industrial relation system characterized by union unity
(Einheitsgewerkschaft), industrially organized unions and especially
by highly centralized unionism, such modifications can be crucial and
might well jeopardize the stability of the whole system (Streeck
(1982)). In other countries like France or Great-Britain where union
actions and practices have been marked in the past by a greater dis-
persion between central and decentralized levels, changes in the union
structure will appear less clearly, although one will probably observe at firm level a trend towards more centralized negotiations - with
a shift from plant to company negotiations - due partly to the more
central information systems brought about by technological development.

Inter - union relationships

New technology challenges also in different degrees occupational experiences, skills, employment conditions and career perspectives. For
certain union members new technology might well induce new opportunities for higher salaries, employment security and requalification,
whereas for others it is a threat to each of these three items.
Such consequences are experienced among employees within the firm,
across firms (users and non-users of new technology) or branches
(users and producers of new technology) as well as between nations
each time new technologies are set up. As a consequence, rather narrow
craft, industry or nationally orientated technology policies have, for
the reasons exposed above, caused open conflicts between union members
and/or between unions, in numerous cases.

Such conflicts, resulting directly from technological changes, have
occured for example in Great-Britain between APEX and TASS, or between
TGWU and ASTMS. In Germany, similar fights have taken place between
the printing union, IG-DruPa, and the salaried employees' union outside DGB, DAG, as well as between the union for employees in banking and
insurance,HBV, and DAG. The continual discord between the semi-skilled
workers' union, SID, and the metal workers' union, Metal, in the Danish
case has also recently been accentuated due to different member interests vis-à-vis new technology. The conflicts between occupational
groups, demarcation disputes etc., induced by the introduction of new
technology, challenge thus established power and interest relationships between unions, and exacerbate the competition as regards the
recruiting of members.

Nevertheless, one also registers cases where the difficulties resulting from new technology have produced co-operation between unions.
In Great-Britain, technology agreements have been negotiated and sign-

ed by several union organizations: e.g. one agreement signed by TASS, ASTMS and ACTSS, another one by APEX, AUEW and TASS. In most countries agreements between newspapers' owners and unions involve several fede- rations: in Germany for example, IG-DruPa and DJV, representing the journalists, have reached a common agreement. More recently in Denmark, the concerned unions (journalists, typographs, printworkers and sala- ried employees) only accepted to negotiate with the employers a tech- nology agreement after having agreed among themselves.

On the basis of a closer comparative approach, one could reasonably forecast that the higher the degree of multi-unionism - whether based on craft traditions (GB) or on political/ideological divergences (France) - the greater the likelihood of conflicts to occur and even to be exacerbated as a result of new technology. However, in countries where the principle of "one plant, one union" is implemented (Germany, Sweden), conflicts about contradictory interests between occupational groups are not absent, but they come to the fore within the union or- ganization itself.

Moreover, the introduction of new technology may provoke the setting up of original union relationships. A complete reorganization of union structures may in certain cases appear, as for instance with the crea- tion of "media-federations": following the example of Italy - certain countries have been envisaging such a change (IG-DruPa (1980)).

The search for a "balance" between occupational groups' self-interests and the need for co-ordinated union actions will have to be found; failing this unionism could seriously be weakened.

Union relationships to research and researchers

Unions are more and more involved in research activities. Several confederations have created their own research and investigation cen- ters such as the WSI center (Germany) and the forthcoming Institut for Work and Technics, the new research center connected to the Nor- vegian LO, the Center for Working Life in Sweden (set up in co-opera- tion with the State, managers and unions) and the various independent research institutions working for the French unions (e.g. ARETE, BREAC and IRES). Owing to the new requirements of collective bargai- ning, the unions' need for scientific investigations and knowledge becomes more and more evident. Indeed, new technology, in the same way as health and safety issues, request a high level of information and knowledge on behalf of union representatives - a knowledge which to a great extent becomes only accessible to them through a union - re- searcher co-operation.

German unions have gained an extensive experience of "working with" researchers through the various humanization-projects. The problem of researchers being often nearer to management than to workers' con- cerns, has been stressed, but also the fact that these projects are co-operation projects, that their results constitute thus common knowledge and that they do not therefore strengthen unions' positions in particular, has been put forward (IG-Metall (1980);Hingel (1981)).

The Scandinavian experiences of so called "one-party research" and of "action research" should not suffer from such deficiencies - resear- chers working solely with unions and on the basis of union defined interests; further, the projects are often carried out in close co- operation with union members in specific firms and regions. But even in these cases does a certain malaise often characterize the relationship between researchers and unions (Sandberg(1981),Stange(1982)).

If research and scientific knowledge becomes an inherent part of union
activities, there exists a danger of weakening decentralized levels of
the union and rendering the union's central structures more intellectual and more technocratic. On the other hand could the observed tendency, in Scandinavian countries, of intensifying research activities
on the local level - without direct contact to higher federation
levels - lead to an increased unequality between groups of employees
- those strenghtened by scientific knowledge in situations of bargaining, and those without such support. The so-called "corrective co-
determination right" in the German Betriebsverfassungsgesetz (sec.91)
which provides the works councils with a co-determination right in cases where changes in the workplace are contradictory to "reliable
scientific knowledge" on humanized working conditions, constitutes an
example of how the intellectualization of the relationship between
employers and employees has been formalized.

Seen from the point of view of union membership, the above mentioned
need for a union involvement in research appears to lead towards an
integration of new occupational groups in the labour movement. We refer here to the growing unionization of engineers, technicians and
researchers. Especially in France, the fact that these occupational
groups are getting organized, is marking to a large extent union discussions and union view-points vis-à-vis new technology (Valerenberghe
(1981);Mentré (1981)).

Union - employer relationships

The consequences of the technological issue for the union - employer
relationship will only briefly be evoked. The subsequent expansion
of the scope of negotiation has lead employer organizations to express
more clearly their standpoints, preferences and strategies in the
field of technology. We would like to refer here to the prominent
place that technological change occupies in the so-called Taboo-cata-
logue from the German employer organization, BDA, - it includes the
total refusal of technology agreements on a decentralized level and
accepts only agreements on "major" technological changes; another illustration of the above mentioned obligation of clarification on behalf
of employers, can be seen in the mutual recognition of the employers'
right to "direct and distribute work", which has been reconfirmed in
the Danish central technology agreement (unions consider as a victory
the fact that this right has not been expanded, employers as a victory that it has been maintained),(Dansk Metalarbejderforbund (1981);
Aktuelt, 16 March (1982)).

The technological issue can be looked at as serving as a scapegoat
for a number of other conflictual items between employers and unions.
The general awareness of the problem, its distinctive nature and the
employers' clearly defined technical, social and not least economic
interests in the field makes out of technology an ideal domain for
employers' mobilization.

Co-operation between unions at cross-national level

The understanding of technological development as a social process
that crosses national frontiers appears obvious to most union organizations. Alarmingly few cross-national union activities do although
take place. International secretariats such as FIET and FIOM, regio-

nal organizations like ETUC and NFS are in varying degrees active in the diffusion of information related to experiences and policies in the field of new technology, but they are not policy-making bodies. The TUAC "advises" OECD about union standpoints, but it does not initiate policies.

International union co-operation as a strategy directed against the activities of multi-national firms which emerged at the end of the sixties seems to have withered away together with the deepening of the economic crisis in the seventies. A certain co-ordination of industrial policies has been envisaged between European unions within the EEC and between Scandinavian Unions vis-à-vis the Nordic Council (ETUI (1982);NFS (1982)), but until now no co-ordinated cross-national union policy has been realized.

A cross-national co-operation is required if the intention is to contribute to increase unions' influence on technological development within each national context. Exchange of information across national borders,information on industrial development within various branches (data on the future state of international competition and on the development of production systems and information systems in a given industry as well as across industries) and information on unions' experiences in the field of technology regulations and of social consequences of technology, incarnates a preliminary step in the building up of such a co-operation. This development will challenge without any doubt the autonomy of national unions and will demand their acceptance of a union policy-making and union actions on an international level.

Union - State relationships

In most European countries, the State has actively supported R&D activities in the field of new technology. The French governments' "mission" for information technology, the British governmental 3-5 years programmes in the field of new technology and the consecutive German data-processing, microelectronic and technical communication R&D programmes have been -and still are - indeed developed, presented and carried out with hardly any union influence. Unions' possibilities of having a say in governmental R&D schemes have thus been remaining extremely scarce, though they have in most countries been claiming such an influence in state bodies and in firms executing public remunerated R&D activities (Vangskjær (1980);SID (1980);LO (1981),Hingel (1981)).

German unions have for instance demanded to exert influence on all the R&D programmes of the Ministry of Research and Technology - in line with the employee influence in the Humanization Programme: the scheme on the development of manufactoring technics has particularly caught unions' attention (DGB (1981);IG-Metall (1980A)).

In the programme for the humanization of working conditions do employee representatives formally exercise a major influence upon the programme definition, its execution and its evolution. The works council disposes even of a <u>veto right</u> as to the State financing of such programmes. Nevertheless, the majority of these R&D programmes are deemed to be merely rationalization schemes with virtually no improvement of working conditions involved (IG-Metall (1980);Kissler (1982);Naschold (1979)). One even talks about a "disemployment" by the means of humanization programmes.

The representation of union interests in governmental and ministeri-
al boards and working groups as we see numerous examples of in Sweden, Germany and France, appears equally to be evaluated in fairly
negative terms. Limited concrete results have been obtained,but the
question is if such a representation does not provide unions with a
precious opportunity to formulate and to present global and specific
demands regarding technological development, and if it does not offer
at the same time a major source for collecting information ? A deep
involvement of employees and unions in such activities at firm as well
as at State level presents obviously also the danger of "recuparation"
as numerous examples of employee representation in company boards have already shown.

Also in other spheres of State regulations related to technological
development does one notice unions' involvement: in all Scandinavian
countries, the unions' viewpoints were to a large extent embodied in the
three respective work environment Acts. In fact, State regulations
and directives on the work environment in relation to new technology
(e.g.VDU's, robots), are demanded to be enforced by most European
unions.

In the present economic crisis where the bargaining power of unions
in front of employers is enfeebled at all levels, a certain tendency
of resorting to the State is developing. Given the low level of influence unions presently exert in State bodies, the question whether increasing union involvement in State activities will in the long run
contribute to weaken or enhance unions' power remains open (Crouch
(1979)).

Further, in order to equal out welfare between those employed and
those ostracized from social life, the need of a higher integration
of technology policies, employment and income policies, shows rather
urgent (Leontief (1982)). New technology could thus induce a complete
redefinition of industrial relations and union functions in society.*
*Written in the frame of a project financed by the Danish Council for
Scientific Policy and Planning (PRF) 1981-84.

FOOTNOTES

(1) Not only in a geographical sense (national, regional, company and
    plant agreements) can one observe a hierarchy of technology agree-
    ments in Germany, but also in a technical sense. Their exist thus
    agreements regulating "technological development", specific "tech-
    nologies"(e.g. information technology), specific "technics" (e.g.
    VDU's, NC machine tools, computers) and specific "ways of use of
    technics" (e.g. personnel data registers) (Hingel (1981)).
(2) An instructive introduction to German industrial relations can be
    found in Breum (1981). As to German unions' technology policy ex-
    tensive analyses have been published in Briefs (1980) and Hingel
    (1981). Descriptions and studies on current events in the field of
    information technology regarding the countries in the EEC can be
    found in European Pool of Studies: Social Change and Technology in
    Europe (1981),(1982))
(3) See: Industrial Relations Review and Report no 227 (1980); Man-
    varing (1981). As to current information see footnote (2).
(4) A presentation of the technology policy of the socialist confede-
    ration, CFDT, is published in CFDT (1977),(1980), and of the com-
    munist orientated confederation, CGT, Mentré (1981). As to current
    information on France see note (2).
(5) See Agrell (1980); Nordisk Råd (1981); Hingel (1982). See also
    note (2) for current information on information technology in
    Scandinavia.

REFERENCES

(1) Agrell, A. (ed.), Det teknologiska uppvaknandet - en antologi om svensk forsknings- og teknologipolitik (Liberförlag, Stockholm, 1980).

(2) Auroux, J., Les droits des travailleurs (Documentation Française, Paris, 1982).

(3) Breum, W., Die Gewerkschaften der BRD: Mitglieder, Theorie, Politik (VSA-Verlag, Hamburg, 1981).

(4) Briefs, U., Arbeiten ohne Sinn und Perspektive ? - Gewerkschaften und "Neue Technologien" (Pahl-Rugenstein, Köln, 1980).

(5) Caire, G., Confluences(Note introductive aux textes de M.J.Piore et B.Coriat, Consommation-Revue de Socio-Economie 3 (1982) 3-12.

(6) CFDT (Confédération Française Démocratique du Travail) Les Dégâts du progrès: les travailleurs face au changement technique (Ed. du Seuil, Paris, 1977).

(7) --- Le tertiaire éclaté: le travail sans modèle (Ed. du Seuil, Paris, 1980).

(8) Dansk Metalarbejderforbund, Debatoplæg: Denteknologiske udvikling - teknologien i menneskets tjeneste (Dansk Metalarbejderforbund, Copenhagen, 1981).

(9) DGB (Deutscher Gewerkschaftbund) Bericht: 4. Ausserordentlicher Kongress den DGB - Neues Grundsatzprogram 1981, Gewerkschaftliche Monatshefte, 4 (1981) 292-296.

(10)ETUI (European Trade Union Institute) La politique industrielle en Europe occidentale (ETUI, Bruxelles, 1981).

(11)European Pool of Studies (EPOS), Social Change and Technology in Europe - Information Bulletin no 1, 4, 6, 8, 10 (Commission of the European Communities (DG V/A/2), Bruxelles, 1981, 1982).

(12)Goetschy, J., A new future for industrial democracy in France, Economic and Industrial Democracy: an international Journal, 1 (1983).

(13)Goodrich, C.L., The Frontier of Control (G.Bell and Sons Limited, London, 1920).

(14)Hingel, A.J. Den Europæiske Fagbevægelse over for ny teknologi: Tysk fagbevægelse i spændingsfeltet mellem statslig teknologipolitik og faglige aktioner i virksomhederne (Institut for Organisation og Arbejdssociologi, Handelshøjskolen i København, Copenhagen, 1981).

(15)--- Ny Teknologis Sociale Funktion og Konsekvenser: En analyse af den teknologiske udvikling på grundlag af Karl Marx' og Max Webers videnskabelige traditioner, Ph.D. Thesis, Institut for Organisation og Arbejdssociologi, Handelshøjskolen i København, Copenhagen, 1982.

(16)--- Social Change and Technology in Europe: Information Technology in Scandinavia (European Pool of Studies, Information Bulletin no 9, Bruxelles, 1982)

(17)IG DruPa (Industriegewerkschaft Druck und Papier) Rationalisierung und Humanisierung - unauflösbarer Wiederspruch oder gewerkschaftliche Aufgabe ?, Gewerkschaftliche Monatshefte, 4 (1980) 268-270.

(18)IG Metall (Industriegewerkschaft Metall) Beteiligungen der Betriebsrats bei betrieblichen Humanisierungsvorhaben: Eine Handlungsanleitung für Betriebsräte der IG Metall bei öffentliche geförderten Betriebsprojekten, Schriftenreihe der IG Metall nr. 84 (1980).

(19)--- Entschliessungen des 13. ordentlichen Gewerkschaftstages der IG Metall, Berlin (1980).

(20)Janzen, K-H., Technologiepolitik und Gewerkschaften, Gewerkschaftliche Monatshefte, 4 (1980) 256-262.

(21)Kerr, C. et all. (eds.) Industrialism and Industrial Man (Harvard University Press, Cambridge, Mass., 1960).

(22)Kissler, L. and Sattel, U., Humanization of Work and Social inte-
     rests: Description and Critical Assessment of the State-sponsored
     program of humanization in the Federal Republic of Germany, Eco-
     nomic and Industrial Democracy: an international journal 3 (1982)
     221-261.
(23)Leontief, W., What hope for the economy ?, The New York Review of
     Books,12 August (1981) 31-34.
(24)LO (Landsorganisationen i Sverige) Fackföreningsrörelsen och
     forskningen: Rapport till LO-kongressen 1981 (LO, Stockholm, 1981).
(25)Lyon-Caen, G., Une législation à adapter à la lutte contre le
     chômage, Le Monde, 5 November (1981).
(26)Manvaring, T., The trade union response to new technology, Indu-
     strial Relations Journal 4 (1981) 7-26.
(27)Mentré, J., L'Informatique: Les technologies nouvelles, des ques-
     tions, des éléments de réponse, Options 5 (1981) annex.
(28)Moore, R. and Levie, H., Social Change and Technology in Europe:
     the impact of new technology on trade union organization (Euro-
     pean Pool of Studies, Information Bulletin no 8, Bruxelles, 1982).
(29)Naschold, F., Probleme einer "sozialorientierten Forschungs- und
     Entwicklungspolitik" - das Program "Humanisierung des Arbeitsle-
     bens" am Scheideweg (Wissenschaftzentrum Berlin, Berlin, 1979).
(3o)NFS (Nordens Fackliga Samorganisation) Industripolitiskt samarbe-
     te i Norden - politisk vilja och handlingskraft eller... ? (For-
     laget SOC, Copenhagen, 1981).
(31)Nordisk Råd, Datateknologi i Norden (Nordic Council of Ministers,
     NU 1982:7, Stockholm, 1982).
(32)Roth, K-H., Die "andere Arbeiterbewegung und die Entwicklung der
     kapitalistischen Repression von 188o bis zur Gegenwart (Trikont
     verlag, München, 1974).
(33)Sandberg, A. (ed.) Forskning for förändring - om metoder och för-
     utsättningar för handlingsriktat forskning i arbetslivet (Arbets-
     livscentrum, Stockholm, 1981).
(34)SID (Specialarbejderforbundet i Danmark) Teknologiens udfordrin-
     ger til fagbevægelsen (Specialarbejderforbundet, Copenhagen,
     198o).
(35)Stange, J. and Ivarson, O., Forskning för Demokrati (ASF, Stock-
     holm, 1982).
(36)Streeck, W., Qualitative demands and the neo-corporatist managea-
     bility of industrial relations, British Journal of Industrial
     Relations, 2 (1981) 149-169.
(37)Vanlerenberghe, P., Le syndicalisme face aux changement technolo-
     giques, Cadres CFDT, 297 (1981) 4-7.
(38)Vangskjær, K., Industriudvikling og industripolitik - analyse og
     perspektiver (Arbejderbevægelsens Erhvervsråd, Copenhagen, 198o).
(39)Vester, M., Die Entstehung des Proletariats als Lernprozess, die
     Entstehung antikapitalistischer Theorie und Praxis in England
     1792-1848 (Europäische Verlagsanstalt, Frankfurt a.M., 197o).

TRADE UNION PLANNING AND CONTROL
OF NEW TECHNOLOGY

Experiences from research projects with
Norwegian trade unions

Vidar Keul

Norwegian Computing Center
Box 335, Blindern,
Oslo 3, Norway

The first part of the paper presents the institutional
framework regulating the use of new technology in Norway. This structure has laid the ground for the development of a set of action models and organisational
methods for the trade unions. However, experiences
indicate that the unions find it difficult to use such
models and methods. The problem of planning and control
as well as union intervention in system design therefore,
can not be considered "solved".

The problem of planning and control of new technology
from the union point of view is discussed here in light
of the results and experiences from a series of research
projects conducted as cooperative efforts by the Norwegian Computing Center, some nationwide unions, and
their local branches. One of the main objectives of
these projects was to initiate actions that could
increase union influence over the use of new technology.
The various relations between the projects, union work
and the development of union policies towards new technology allow the discussion of different aspects of the
problem of planning and control. Experiences from the
projects will also contribute to a better understanding
of the conditions necessary for the development of
union strategies with regard to technological change.

Finally, suggestions for further discussions and analyses are presented.

INTRODUCTION

In Norway, the question of trade union planning and control in
relation to new technology (edp) has been focussed on the negotiation of formal agreements. Such agreements (called "data
agreements") have been negotiated since the first half of the
1970s. Data agreements are established at both the local and central levels, corresponding to the structure of enterprises as
well as the arrangements of employer-employee relations in various
sectors of the economy. The agreements have introduced measures
and organisational methods for the trade unions to deal with data
questions. These include data shop stewards, data committees,
specific educational programs relating to data questions, etc. As
a result of this process which has spread to most branches of the
Norwegian trade union movement, the unions now have a set of
general action patterns related to the introduction and use of

new technology.

The development of action patterns which could be put into effect
by the individual unions are connected with the general industrial
relations systems in Norway which is based on collective bargaining. In addition, the unions can also use legislation concerning
Industrial Democracy, and the Working Environment Act to influence
new technology. The data agreements and the legislation form an
institutional structure which outlines the procedures to be
followed when unions influence the processes of technological
change at work.

On the other hand, there is growing recognition of the difficulties facing the unions as they try to put into practice the
provisions of the data agreements. In fact, there is not much
activity observed which relates to such agreements. This probably
reflects the failing capacity of local unions when it comes to
participation in system design processes. The unions have their
formalised agreement system regulating goals and procedures of
system design. But these kinds of regulations are not sufficient
for real union influence over the change processes introduced by
new technology.

There is also a certain tendency to leave the problem-solving
tasks accompanying the introduction of new technology to central
bodies of the trade union movement. Assistance from central
officers is often required to settle cases resulting from problems at the local level. This situation which is adding more
tasks to the already strained union apparatus, is also weakening
the possibilities for decentralisation of decision-making. The
general tendency to transfer cases from the local to the central
level, probably results from the fact that unions have rarely
succeeded in bringing themselves into the planning stages of
system design processes. The kind of union participation in these
processes often is reduced to solving problems which occur after
the introduction of new systems.

In this situation one can hardly talk of union planning and
control with regard to system design as an established practice.
A more valid description is the settling of individual cases
following a "case-by-case" approach. This approach also implies
that certain problems are emphasised: usually unions pay attention to problems relating to formal procedures for the introduction of new technology. On the other hand, there is little capacity for discussing problems of work organisation, job design,
structure of enterprises, general aspects of the decision-making
processes etc., which are connected with technological change.

If local unions and clubs are severely limited in their possibilities for real action concerning the introduction of new
technology, the trade union movement faces a serious problem. On
the one hand, the agreements contain a set of rights and opportunities and much effort is invested in the amendment of these
agreements to guarantee even better rights and opportunities. On
the other hand, experiences point to the lack of active use of
such rights and opportunities by unions actually involved in
trying to influence the processes of technological change. The
unions are investing much effort in constructing agreement systems
as well as procedures for codetermination. However, the constraints
imposed upon union actions seem to leave system design to the
management and system specialists.

Of course, there is the possibility that the patterns laid down by the data agreements are affecting decision-making processes indirectly. For instance, management or system departments may seek to carry out system design in accordance with the provisions of the agreements. This is expected to occur, since management and system designers are becoming more and more familiar with both the regulations on technological change specified by data agreements and the work environment legislation.

While this kind of "enlightened system design" could solve the problem of influencing the design processes, it does not solve the problem of how unions control such processes based on their own objectives with regard to democratic decision-making and good working conditions. Obviously, it does not solve the problem of increasing the unions' own resources on the technology field.

THE PROBLEM OF PLANNING AND CONTROL

The Norwegian trade union movement has taken the viewpoint that new technology should be used in accordance with central political objectives like democratic control of the economy, better working environment, desentralisation of problem-solving and conflict-resolution, etc. To attain such goals, the development of control measures and formal regulations like the General Agreements on Computer-based Systems and the Working Environment Act have been regarded as crucial.

However, the experiences so far with the use of such provisions suggest that trade union influence over technological change requires more than a simple regulation. (Obviously, the problem is more complex than one would think given union rhetoric.) The institutionalisation of technological change may lay the ground for direct union influence over the use of technology and for long-term learning within the unions, which in turn may increase their capacities for intervening into system design processes. But, it may also have the effect of legitimating instances of technological change which have unexpected and unwanted impacts on working conditions and on the promotion of union interests.

The problem of planning and control of new technology is related to the institutional "superstructure", the traditional working methods of the unions, organisational models and methods applied in different sections of the union movement, as well as the specific information systems developed and used when the unions are to take part in technological change processes at work. The problem also relates to the question of describing and categorising technological change and to the development of relevant knowledge on various levels of union organisation.

EFFECTS OF THE GENERAL AGREEMENTS ON COMPUTER-BASED SYSTEMS

The difficulties experienced with using formal regulations suggest that more attention be paid to the organisational processes related to applying such regulations to technology questions. For instance, the General Agreements are themselves products of such organisational processes, i.e. negotiations taking place at the central level. But there is the possibility that these processes will have varying or perhaps no influence at all on the behaviour of unions facing technological change.

Studies conducted on the impact of the General Agreements on
trade union activities show substantial differences from one
union to another. In general, a few unions were relatively active
concerning data questions, while the majority of unions reported
a low degree of activity or no activity at all

During the years after the first General Agreement (1975) there
are some examples of the successful use of this instrument by
local unions. Taking notice of these examples, there are still
good reasons for arguing that the main importance of the Agreement for the trade union movement has probably not been the
active intervention in system design processes. The main effects
of the first General Agreement as well as its succeeding ones
within different sectors of the economy, have been the establishment of structures or patterns for the regulation of technological
change. Once established, such structures have the general effect
of shaping these processes. But it cannot be concluded that the
system design process is directly affected. The formal regulations also form the basis for a gradual building up of trade
union positions vis-á-vis new technology. In general, a development of union action resources has taken place, including the
building up of the local data shop steward apparatus, the procedures for planning and control of system design processes contained
by local data agreements, the educational programs, etc.

Experiences with the practical application of the General Agreements reported by local unions and clubs, shed some light on the
extent and complexity of the problem of planning and control of
new technology.[2] The main aspects of the problem could be summarised this way:

-   Knowledge aspects: There is a lack of knowledge about rights
    and opportunities as well as possible action patterns or
    procedures contained by formal regulations. There is also a
    lack of knowledge about new technology or computer-based
    systems, as well as the problems associated with technolo-
    gical change processes at the workplaces.

-   Organisational aspects: Local unions and clubs are experi-
    encing difficulties with the mobilisation of resources which
    could affect the application of relevant procedures to a
    given problem. As a result, the problems experienced often
    remain rather unstructured, i.e. not suited for the organi-
    sational methods available. When unions or clubs try to deal
    with the problems, they have a tendency to limit themselves
    to discussing arrangements for union representatives in
    projects for system development, etc. There is also a
    tendency to bring unions into system design processes
    relatively late. The unions are thereby typically playing
    the role of a responding part.

-   Participation aspects: General lack of involvement from
    union members and difficulties with attempts at engaging
    members affect working methods with regard to the handling
    of data questions. One effect is that representatives in
    system projects are generally people who are already quite
    involved with union affairs.

The various problems listed above do not only pertain to the
handling of data questions, but to some extent point to general
problems facing the trade union organisations. The problem

description is probably also valid in some respects for the
management counterparts. For instance, lack of knowledge about
data agreements and the use of inappropriate procedures for
system design are often reported.

The experiences of local unions and clubs with regard to planning
and control of new technology cover one part of the overall
problem with the use of data agreements as well as the corresponding regulations based on legislation. Another issue is the
kinds of strategies pursued by local unions and clubs who have
actually done some work on this field over the last ten years.
There is no systematically collected information yet published
which could shed light on this particular question in the Norwegian context.[3)]

THE TRADE UNION PROJECTS AT THE NORWEGIAN COMPUTING CENTER

A series of research projects for the trade union movement were
carried out at the NCC during the 1970s. The projects involved
three national unions: Iron and Metalworkers Union, Commercial
and Office Employees Union, Chemical Industry Workers Union. The
projects are reported on by Nygaard and Bergo (1973) (Iron and
Metal), Pape (1979) and Bauck (1979) (Commercial and Office),
Elden et al (1980) (Chemical Industry).[4)] All of the projects
concerned the problem of planning and control of new technology
from a trade union point of view. Experiences from the projects
therefore allow a closer examination of the general character of
the issue.

One purpose of the projects was to provide the unions with
knowledge on how the use of new technology (i.e. computer-based
systems) could affect working conditions. Furthermore, the projects were to cast light on how trade union members' interests
are affected by the introduction of new technology and how the
unions could influence technological change within enterprises.
The projects also had an action objective: union members were to
develop and put into practice technology control activities and
policies on their own.

In line with such objectives, the trade union projects approached
the problem of planning and control of technology from different
perspectives: educational, organisational, and participative.
Hypotheses concerning the main problem, how to initiate actions
that could increase local union influence on the use of technology in enterprises, were tested by means of experiments with
local working groups and by means of various activities directed
from the central level that were to support local activities. The
experiences with such attempts allow discussing the specific
conditions underlying union actions with regard to new technology
and the problems related to the attempts at intervening in these
processes. In addition, a discussion of the "action oriented"
part of the projects could contribute to an understanding of the
relationship between research projects as one kind of union
effort and the development of union strategies towards new
technology.[5)]

The trade union projects focussed on the concept of "action", as
the central element of the strategy for union control of technological change. The model suggested that influence over planning
and control would result from actions initiated by local unions

and clubs (Nygaard 1977. Fjalestad and Pape 1979). According to
this model, actions were to be based on union members' experiences
from their work situation and on more systematically worked out
knowledge about the impacts of new technology at the respective
workplaces. (During the first stage of the work, the local project
groups described and analysed their own work situations. Aspects
related to jobs, work organisation, enterprise situation, local
union work, etc. were discussed.) Actions were also expected to
be based on union members' interpretations of their interests
with regard to the observed technological change processes at the
workplaces. On the other hand, actions could also result in new
insights, re-interpretations regarding goals and interests, and a
broadening of experiences with action patterns, procedures or
organisational methods. Therefore, knowledge, experiences, and
methods were considered as resources created during the process.

GENERAL ASPECTS OF THE PROBLEM OF PLANNING AND CONTROL

The activities of the trade union projects and the processes of
union work which seem to be affected by the projects, suggest the
need for distinguishing between different aspects of the problem
of planning and control. The following list of categories and
propositions could possibly give some indication of the complexity
of the problem. The different levels suggested and the different
types of planning and control-related processes could also serve
as a basis for further, more specific discussions.

-       Knowledge formation: Union policies imply the application of
        certain concepts to support the accumulation and interpre-
        tation of experiences, and thereby the building of knowledge.
        The educational aspects of the development of union strate-
        gies therefore are crucial, both from the union movement
        point of view as well as that of local unions and clubs.
        Educational programs have to be effected at all levels of
        union organisation.

-       Interest orientation: The application of certain concepts
        and approaches to the problems would also imply the inter-
        pretation of interests. Therefore the building of knowledge
        on various aspects of new technology, work organisation, job
        design, decision-making, etc. must be related to the clari-
        fication of union interests with regard to such problems.
        Accordingly, educational programs will have certain politi-
        cal elements which need to be explicitly discussed.

-       Organisational methods: Union policies towards new techno-
        logy imply the development of methods, arrangements, etc.,
        for the handling of problems by the organisations at the
        central and local levels. This will also involve the develop-
        ment of specific strategies and critical discussion about
        experiences with such strategies.

-       Instruments for planning and control: This aspect concerns
        the elaboration of certain provisions with regard to the
        introduction and use of new technology. In principle, the
        unions have two kinds of instruments available to them:
        negotiated agreements and legislation. In Norway, both have
        have been expanded through regular revisions.

-       Institutionalisation: This kind of process which takes place

at a general societal level is contributing to the association of goals and interests with procedures and rules for
the use of technology. The forms of the institutionalisation
process are affected by the kind of instruments developed.
The way in which these problems are handled by the organisations and parties in the labour market and by political
parties is also important.

Aside from the analytical aspects, the five levels or processes
discussed above could also serve some practical purposes. For
instance, they can set targets for activities and measures for
strengthening the union position vis-á-vis system design.

RESULTS OF THE PROJECTS. DEVELOPMENT OF TRADE UNION STRATEGIES

Aside from the relatively short-term activities initiated by the
unions directly involved with project work, it is difficult to
establish any direct relationship between the project work and
actions developed by local unions and clubs. (The meaning of
actions in this respect is "external actions" aimed at influencing technological change within the individual enterprises.)
Therefore, the projects generally could be considered unsuccessful or alternatively, partly successful with regard to particular
local contexts established by the projects. Such contexts have in
some cases proved relatively productive for further work: Some of
the unions and clubs who took part in the projects continued
their work after the projects were completed and have involved
themselves rather deeply with various types of data-related
activities.

Lack of observable "results" and a failure regarding the diffusion of effects of the projects points to the need for a critical
examination of the project model. Differences concerning the
structure of industries, union organisation, consciousness of
union members with regard to goals as well as action patterns,
etc., should be considered. Such factors are apparently affecting
the validity of the hypotheses underlying the model.

Taking notice of this, one question raised by the projects is the
extent to which action-oriented strategies are transferable from
one particular union field to another. Experiences from the
projects indicate that such strategies need to be worked out with
regard to specific union contexts. In other words, the formalised
lines of action contained by data agreements can not be considered
as definite strategies, but rather as guidelines for the development of strategies. The unions to some extent have to find their
own ways and their own solutions to the problem of influencing
system design and they have to consider these problems in a long-
term perspective.

Looking at the question of "results" from another point of view,
the trade union projects seem to be closely related to the general
development of Norwegian trade union policies concerning new
technology during the 1970s. For example, the projects focussed
on concepts and problems which have been affecting trade union
approaches to technological change. By emphasising the need for
planning and control of such processes, the projects contributed
to bringing the problems into political contexts that had broader
implications for the understanding of the issue. Furthermore, the
projects introduced patterns for the organisational handling of

the problems which to some extent have presented "solutions" for
the unions. Ideas concerning the use of data agreements and data
shop stewards were introduced and elaborated by the projects.
Such solutions point to the need for linking data work with the
regular shop steward system as well as ordinary procedures of
union organisation. In light of later experiences, it should be
noted that these types of solutions do not necessarily imply
local actions, member participation or an increasing overall
level of activity with regard to technology questions.

The various kinds of effects or "results" from the projects indicate the need for a broader perspective on the problem of trade
union planning and control of new technology. For instance, to
focus the expressions of local actions initiated in order to
influence some decision concerning system design would probably
imply too much emphasis on the explicit power relations between
the parties. There is also the possibility, this kind of perspective would overestimate the importance of conflictual relations
on the technology field. Within a broader perspective, the
challenge for trade unions facing new technology is to clarify
the conditions which will allow them to openly promote union
interests in conflictual situations. But at the same time, system
design processes should be able to take place in a participative
manner.

In some other respects, working methods introduced and tested by
the projects apparently did not present solutions that the unions
were able to carry out themselves after project work was completed.
This particularly applies to the local working groups. There are
a variety of reasons why unions and clubs have difficulty with
handling such groups. For one thing, to increase participation by
means of locally based working groups does not eliminate the need
for organisational arrangements or methods that could support
group activities. The regular working modes of the union organisations seem to be less favourable to the maintenance of local
group activities than the particular conditions established
during the research projects. Then, there are differences between
unions and groups of union members which inspire various levels
of motivation to participate. Difficulties with clearly identifying the objectives of group activities could also result from
local circumstances. Finally, there are many practical difficulties for union members associated with taking part in extra
activities like the working groups.

PROBLEM AREAS FOR FURTHER DISCUSSION AND RESEARCH

In concluding the discussion on trade union planning and control
of new technology, some suggestions for further discussion and
systematic studies will be presented. The presentation of the
problem areas are influenced by the particular Norwegian context,
i.e. institutions, trade union structure, organisational methods
and models, etc. Nevertheless, these problems are relevant to a
more general discussion of this issue.

PARTICIPATIVE VS. NON-PARTICIPATIVE STRATEGIES

Participation in this context has a double meaning. It means
involvement by ordinary union members in system design activities
or in union activities related to system design (data work within

local unions and clubs). It also means involvement by the union
apparatus during system design processes, as opposed to negotiation of various aspects of the change process on the basis of
rights established by collective bargaining. In many cases, to
base union participation in system design on member involvement
is unreasonably idealistic. If the union apparatus is to successfully influence design processes, shop stewards and union representatives must play a key role. This will require a closer look
at what can actually be obtained by participative strategies in
situations where action possibilities are restricted by lack of
personal resources, lack of time, etc. "Non-participative" strategies in this context imply a way of having union representation
and participation in system design without the involvement of the
larger membership. For instance, shop stewards and union representatives can play an active part in decision-making processes
related to system design without relying on a "grass-roots"
movement. Non-participative strategies seem to stress the political role of representatives of the union apparatus during
different stages of system design.

CENTRALISATION VS. DECENTRALISATION WITHIN UNION ORGANISATIONS

Apparently, there is a bias related to the use of formal regulations and procedures for controlling system design. They may
lead to increased dependency on problem-solving and decision-
making at central levels of the union organisation. There are
probably many reasons for this kind of development. Often, the
set of provisions and procedures are so complex that it is
difficult to know how they are to be interpreted in individual
cases. This will also open up the possibility for management to
oppose union involvement in system design affairs by using
"juristic" arguments. If a "case" is established at the local
level and the local counterparts are unable to settle it, central
parties will be mobilised and, hence the case will be transferred
from the local level to more competent bodies. Another reason for
centralisation of decision-making in such matters is that these
processes may correspond to established, traditional working
modes within the trade unions. (At least at this point there are
probably marked differences between unions as well as between
countries.) Then, there is also the fact that not all systems are
local systems. The design as well as the operation of the system
may imply coordinated activities both between different levels of
the enterprise structure and between union bodies at different
levels. Such structural conditions are influencing system design
especially within public sectors of the economy. Again, this is
likely to produce a bias in decision-making within unions in
favour of centralised processes.

Centralisation, as well as the concentration of expertise and
problem-solving competence at certain levels of the union structure, could weaken local level abilities for dealing with change
processes. This is likely to occur when local actions are restricted because of lack of resources (time, knowledge etc.) and
when system design processes are organised in such a way that
long-term learning within local unions is blocked.

The trade union research projects at the NCC discussed above
focussed on the local-central relationship within unions. The
projects did not solve these kinds of problems. However, an
important contribution from the projects was to bring out the

problems which need further discussion and research, as well as
systematic efforts at bringing about organisational development.
Obviously, the problems are also related to system design because
the qualities of design depend on the abilities and knowledge of
the actors involved with design processes.

CONFLICTUAL VS. NON-CONFLICTUAL RELATIONS

Norwegian experiences with data agreements seem to indicate that
such agreements have rarely been used as power instruments to
promote union interests in conflicts over new technology. If this
is the case, what are data agreements actually used for? What
strategies are pursued by local unions and clubs who are trying
to make use of such arrangements? (Cf. the reference above to the
study by Schneider and Ciborra.)

Various answers to these questions are possible. For instance,
agreements could be used as a means of formalising information
processes related to system design. Thereby, shop stewards and
union leaders could expect to have higher degree of control over
such processes. As a corollary of this strategy, agreements could
be used by unions as a means of "defining" specific counterparts.
There are many examples which show that unions often have difficulties finding a responsible and informed counterpart in system
design affairs (is it the edp department, the management, the
personal department or some other body?). Formalisation of information processes could present itself as a rational and economic way of acting, given the fact that union leaders often lack
vital resources such as knowledge, information, time to take part
in system design groups, etc.

Formalisation of system design processes by means of data agreements could, on the other hand, be described as an explicit way
of building contracts within an organisation. Besides the formal
ones, there probably are informal contracts between different
groups. From the union point of view, interaction with other
groups within the organisation could be based upon and regulated
with formal as well as informal contracts. So, there is a lot of
questions which could be explored along these lines of argument
related to the problem of planning and control of system design.
To what extent do unions use formalised contracts in order to
influence system design? What are the conditions for successful
use of strategies based upon formalisation?

Data agreements traditionally are justified by democratic arguments. That is, they confirm democratic goals and give a broader
range of groups access to the decision-making process related to
technological change. Democratic arguments could be connected
with both kinds of strategies: negotiation as well as participation. However, the actual practice around union involvement in
system design seems to suggest that other types of "rationalities"
are also functioning. For instance, there are the organisational
arguments suggested above: that the content and use of data
agreements have to be examined as a process of organisational
development or as a way of stabilising the organisations faced
with technological change processes (Ciborra 1981).

Another context for analysing the content and use of data agreements is the requirements that system design should produce "good
solutions" for the users. Within that context, data agreements

could be considered both as a framework for design, as well as a means of specifying procedural demands for the design process. The regulations established by the agreements could serve as a basis for increasing user participation and could also function as a set of rules for solving possible conflicts of interests which may arise during the design process. In other words, the use of the data agreements suggests a bridge between the conflictual perspective and the "common interest" perspective.

FOOTNOTES

1) Keul (1979). This study which was conducted for the Norwegian Federation of Trade Unions (LO), took place 3-4 years after the settlement of the first General Agreement.

2) Keul (1980). This study, also conducted for the LO, examines the character of problems concerning the use of the General Agreement and various data related arrangements by a selected group of local unions and clubs.

3) A study by Schneider and Ciborra conducted 1981-82 among a group of Norwegian unions probably will bring this discussion further. See Schneider and Ciborra, in this volume.

4) A short presentation of the projects in English is given by Fjalestad and Pape (1979). For a more extensive presentation of the projects as well as the context within which project experiences could be discussed, see Keul (1982).

5) Both kinds of questions - the character of the problem of influence and control of new technology and, the relationship between the research projects and the development of union strategies - are discussed in greater detail in Keul (1982).

REFERENCES

Bauck, S. (1979) Commercial and Office Employees' Union's research project, Report no. 5 (In Norwegian), Oslo, Handel og Kontor/Norwegian Computing Center.

Ciborra, C. (1981) A contractual view of information systems, Paper presented at the EEC Conference Copenhagen 1981 on Information Technology - Impact on Representation and Sharing of Power.

Elden et al (1980) The trade union movement and EDP in the process industries, Concluding report (In Norwegian), Trondheim/Oslo, Institute for Social Research in Industry/ Norwegian Computing Center.

Fjalestad, J., and Pape, A. (1979) Research on social aspects of computerization and democratization of working life, in Samet (ed.), Papers from Euro IFIP 1979, Amsterdam, North-Holland/IFIP.

Keul, V. (1979) Data work in trade unions (In Norwegian), Oslo
    Norwegian Productivity Institute.

Keul, V. (1980) Handbook of data shop stewards' work (In Norwe-
    gian), Oslo, Norwegian Productivity Institute/Norwegian
    Federation of Trade Unions.

Keul, V. (1982) The trade union movement, research and data
    technology (to be published in English, chapter of book
    presenting the "EDP and Society" field at the NCC), Oslo,
    Norwegian Computing Center.

Nygaard, K. (1977) The Iron and Metal Project. Trade union
    participation, Proceedings of CREST Conference on Management
    Information Systems 1977, London, Cambridge University
    Press.

Nygaard, K., and Bergo, O.T. (1973) Planning, control and data
    processing (In Norwegian), Oslo, Tiden/Norwegian Computing
    Center.

Pape, A. (1979) Commercial and Office Employees' Union's research
    project, Report no. 4 (In Norwegian), Oslo, Handel og Kontor/
    Norwegian Computing Center.

Schneider, L., and Ciborra, C. (1982) Technology bargaining in
    Norway, Paper presented at IFIP WG 9.1 Conference 1982 on
    System Design: For the Users, with the Users, by the Users.

SYSTEMS DESIGN FOR, WITH, AND BY THE USERS
U. Briefs, C. Ciborra and L. Schneider (editors)
North-Holland Publishing Company
© IFIP, 1983

THE TRADE UNIONS' INFLUENCE ON TECHNOLOGICAL CHANGE

Finn Kensing

Computer Science Department
Aarhus University
Denmark

1. INTRODUCTION

This article presents some of the results from a project about trade unions and technological change and the research method used.

In chapter 2 we shall describe some problems of the application of edp-technology until now. Chapter 3 deals with the research method used, and the main activities of the project will be described. In chapter 4 we shall present our proposals for control mechanisms for the unions against the employers use of technology.

The DDE (Development, Democracy and Edp) project was a research project carried out in co-operation with the Danish trade unions. The main purpose of the project was to increase the possibilities of the trade unions for influencing the application of edp. Another purpose was to develop research and education in the field of system work.

Researchers co-operated with representatives appointed by the local and central organs of the trade unions in the implementation of the project. A considerable part of the project was concentrated on three selected workplaces.

The project was inspired by the Norwegian Iron and Metal Project. The project started in 1971 with participation from the staff of the Norwegian Union of Iron and Metal workers, four local unions and two researchers from the Norwegian Computing Center [13]. The project was on the use of edp and modern methods of planning and control. In 1975 the Swedish Trade Union Council initiated a similar project [14]. The DDE project started in 1977. The projects express the Scandinavian Trade Unions' attempts to democratize the individual workplaces and the society as a whole.

Since then a great number of projects has been carried out in co-operation between trade unionists and researchers in the Scandinavian countries.

As for a further presentation of the DDE project I shall refer to chapter 3 and to [3].

2. THE TRADE UNIONS AND EDP-TECHNOLOGY

This chapter consists of two sections. The first section deals with the edp-based system. The second section deals with the systems development process and systems development methods.

The trade unions are first of all interested in the edp-based systems, as these to a large extent determine the working conditions. But the trade unions must also take an interest in the systems development process, as the elaboration of this determines the possibilities of the trade unions for influencing the edp-based systems.

The chapter is based on experiences from the DDE project. We shall deal with the negative consequences (from a trade union point of view) of the development and application of new technology. Others may mention opposite experiences, but the DDE project and similar projects in Scandinavia support our assumption that the description below expresses a general tendency.

To save space we left out illustrative examples. We shall refer to [2], [3], [6], [7], [8], [9].

2.1. Edp-based Systems and Working Conditions

In this first section we shall consider the consequences of edp-application in five key areas: substance of the work, possibilities for making decisions, professional qualifications, contact between fellow workers and job security.

The substance of the work

When an edp-system is installed at a workplace, the substance of the work is often radically changed. By means of edp-technology it becomes economically possible to automate some of the work functions.

Furthermore, the employers use edp-based planning systems in connection with a changed organization of the work in order to economize on labour, machines and materials.

The employers are in a better position to control the work process when some of the work functions are automated and others are divided between various employees. Increased productivity is another main advantage of the employers with the application of edp-technology. These two consequences are of similar importance in guaranteeing the goal: increased profit.

But for the employees the automation and splitting up of the work functions have resulted in more routine work and reduced possibilities of keeping an overview of the production process as a whole. The coherence of their work has disappeared. Consequently, their possibilities of controlling or even influencing the work situation have also been reduced.

Possibilities for decision-making

In most workplaces the present application of edp reduces the employees' possibilities for making decisions. This goes for their daily work as well as for the development of the workplace as a whole.

Previously, the employees made decisions as far as the daily work
was concerned - now the decisions are automated or made by superior
staff members. Of course, the employees still have a say in relation
to the performance of their jobs. But the trend is clear: still more
decisions have already been made, when the employees start their
part of the work. Consequently, professional discussions, which the
performance of the work demanded previously, have become superfluous. Perhaps your follow workers cannot even help you in cases of
doubt. Their work has also undergone changes so that they are no
longer qualified to help. Previously, the employees could seek assistance from one of their fellow workers, now they have to approach
a superior.

The employees' possibilities for influencing the decisions in connection with the development of the workplace, as e.g. the purchase
of new technical equipment or changes in the organization of the
work, are also reduced. The employers have the power and the right
to direct and distribute the work. The employees' knowledge and
experience used to give them a great deal of influence on some decision. But as a result of the development of edp-based systems,
old structures and processes are broken down and new structures are
created. In cases of major reorganization, the employees might often
attend relevant educational activities. These activities are often
inadequate, though, and the employees' real possibility for influencing the decision-making has been radically reduced. As far as edp
application is concerned many employees have been dismissed with the
reply that they do not know anything about it and that it is the
task of the specialists to make decisions in this field.

Professional qualifications

When edp is introduced the demands on the professional qualifications
of the employees undergo changes. The employers' present use of edp
implies an increased division of labour and a standardization of the
work. Consequently, the employees need less professional qualifications in the performance of their jobs.

The splitting up of the work makes it even more difficult to keep an
overview of the production process as a whole. And due to the incorporation of choices and decisions in the edp system, the splitting
up also implies reduced possibilities of making decisions in relation to the individual jobs, as we have already mentioned above. The
possibilities for variation, insight, creativity and development
have decreased. This is a serious psychical strain on the employees
which often results in errors, irritability, passivity and increased
risk of getting ill.

Contact between fellow workers

When the employers introduce edp, the relations between fellow workers change. Specialization implies less knowledge of and less insight in the work of their fellow workers. Furthermore, the work is
split up into different processes. As a result the various work
functions are evaluated differently and a hierachy is established in
the workplace.

In connection with the reduced knowledge of the work in other groups
this may cause mistrust and lack of understanding of the working conditions and problems of these groups. At the same time the conse-

quences of the organization of the work are that fellow workers cannot help each other any longer. An employee often happens to stand alone, surrounded by technical equipment. When the possibilities for contact - and consequently, the feeling of belonging to a group disappear it gets even more difficult to make a collective stand against the splitting up of the work and the increased exploitation. A joint stand depends on professional and social contact so that collective goals may be attained.

Job security

The employers introduce new technology in order to compete successfully. This implies that in cases of so-called "natural decrease" the vacancies are not usually refilled, and sometimes even dismissals occur. Therefore the employees in the individual workplaces look upon new technology as a menace to employment.

The employers, on the other hand, argue in favour of new technology: if it is not introduced the enterprise will have to close down.

Both viewpoints are correct in a way, but if we look at the application of new technology from a social point of view, the following topics must be discussed: what is produced, which services are performed and under which working conditions shall this take place?

If new technology was used for satisfying some of the needs, which are still not covered [1], it would not imply dismissals or closing down of enterprises. New technology may be used for establishing healthy workplaces in which harmless dyes and binding materials are employed and an effective purifying plant prevents pollution of the factory and its surroundings. New technology may be used for improving the conditions of the sick and handicapped persons, for improving public transport; increased productivity may be turned into better education facilities, nurseries and kindergartens instead of unemployment.

2.2.   Influence on Systems Development

The application of new technology has the above consequences primarily because of the right and resources of the employers to introduce new technology on their own terms. This also holds for the applied systems development methods.

As every other working process, systems development can be carried out in many ways. The employers often choose to form two groups. A project group composed of edp-specialists and some representatives of the so-called "responsible staff" from that part of the compagny which shall have a new edp-system. A steering committee composed of members of the board or heads of departments. The project group carries out the work under control of the steering committee.

The work is divided into phases. In the first phase the purpose of the change is grounded. In the second phase the project group work out a rough draft that fulfils the purpose. If the steering committee accepts the draft, the project group in the third phase writes the programs and perhaps buys new equipment. In the last phase the equipment is installed, the manual procedures are adapted and the employees are trained in the new functions.

Such a project often passes off for 3 - 5 years.

If the employees are to influence such processes in order to influence the resulting products, the edp-based systems, at least three conditions must be changed. The employees must have access to relevant information, they must have the possibility for taking an independent position on the problems and they must in some way participate on the process of decision-making.

Information

Information about the planned alteration - the edp-based system, as well as about the work that is initiated to accomplish the alteration - the systems development process, is difficult to obtain for the employees and the trade unions. Some of the employees get so much information or the information is so impenetrable that they are in the same unfavourable position as the employees who receive no information at all. One does not solve the problem by supplying the management and the employees with identical information. The employees need information worked out on their terms and taking their prerequisites into consideration. The problem is that this information either does not exist or it is not available at the time when the employees need it.

Independent appraisal

The possibilities for taking an independent position on this matter depend on time, money and expert assistance. Today, such resources are reserved for the employers. The time that the user representatives spend on available expert assistance, and the costs of this representation, are not taken into consideration. At present, user representation is part of the management's system development process and serves a dual purpose:

- to obtain access to the professional qualifications of the employees

- to obtain an advance sanction of the planned alteration.

No resources are set aside for the employees' independent appraisal on the problems of systems development in the enterprises.

The process of decision-making

Influence on the systems development also depends on the power to influence the process of decision-making. This power is lawfully in the hands of the employers and is administered by the management.

In the systems development process this is demonstrated in the composition of the competent committees and in the order in which the decisions are made. (Naturally, the power is also used for withholding information and resources from the employees).

If the employees are represented in the control committee of a given project, the lack of information and the lacking possibility for taking an independent position prevent them from exerting real influence. Who represents the employees? That is another matter of importance. Often the management appoints the representatives who therefore feel more responsible to the management than to his or her fellow workers. We only rarely meet representatives in the control committee who are elected by the employees.

The order in which the decisions on the edp-based system are taken interferes with the employees' possibilities of influence. The way of teaching the technical/economic goal of the management is the first matter to be discussed.

How the job design may fit into the technical/economic solution is only discussed afterwards.

The trade unions in Scandinavia have started to make demands on the application of edp, as well as on the systems development processes. The trade unions consider this demand as part of the fight against the managerial right of the employers. In chapter 4 we shall present some control mechanisms for the unions but before that we shall describe the main activities of the DDE-project and the research method used.

3.   THE DDE-PROJECT

This chapter starts with a presentation of and argumentation for the research method used in the DDE-project. Afterwards we will discuss selected activities from the project. They do not pretend to receive an adequate impression of the project, they are here chosen to illustrate how the research method was implemented.

3.1.   The research method

The project was organised with a project group, three workplace groups and a steering committee. The project-group was composed of four researchers (three computer scientists and an engineer, three shop stewards and a secretary). The workplace groups were composed of four to ten members of the local trade union, a researcher and a shop steward from the project group and one or two graduate-students. The steering committee was composed of representatives from the central trade unions and three professors designated by the Trade Union Research Council.

The research methods we were familiar with within computer science were not sufficient because of the character of the project. They had to be supplemented with methods from social science and education/pedagogy. The research method used was inspired by the work of Bergo and Nygaard (1975), the work of Negt (1972) and the work by Freire (1970). Here I will present and discuss the research method in five main points: interest based research, local and central attachment, action orientation, interaction between analyses of working conditions and technology, and research with the trade unions. I find it useful to discuss these five elements separately when analyzing the DDE-project or comparing it with other projects. In the research process, however, they have no meaning until they decide the improvement of the activities we choose to start or participate in.

Interest based research

When the trade unions want to increase their influence on the technological development and when they want to make use of research in these efforts, their possibilities for influence are reduced if the trade unions and the employers' associations should first compromise on the goal, on the details of the research process and on the definition of usable results.

Owing to conflicting interests and the superiority of the employers' resources, the DDE project was carried out as an interest based research project. That means the formulation of problems, the activities and the dissemination of results were governed solely by trade union interests.

Local and Central Attachments

We wanted to support a strategy saying that the local unions at the workplaces are capable of looking after their own interests, and that they to a certain extent may seek assistance from other individuals and organizations. A contradictory strategy is based on consultants from outside the workplace who are summoned when problems arise.

Therefore the local attachment of the project was important. That means we could choose the perception of problems and possibilities for actions in the individual workplace as a starting point. But the joint forces of the unions build upon central activities as well. Consequently, the project's possibility of interacting with the formulation of politics in the central trade union organization was also important.

The roots of the project were local (the project group and the workplace groups) as well as central (the control committee). However, we would carry out the majority of the activities in close co-operation with local union representatives.

The work was to start from the immediate problems of the local union and later on contribute to the long-term process for building up resources within the local union.

Action Orientation

We planned the project to be action oriented. That is, the development of knowledge and actions were to interact.

When one has acquired a certain knowlege of technology, this knowledge may give the basis of an internal clarification and of externally directed actions in relation to the employers. Actions are needed in order to change the present ways of using technology. Furthermore, they may uncover a lack of knowledge and consequently lead to an enlargement of the subject of one's analyses (cp. fig. 1).

Consequently, action orientation in connection with the local attachment means that we (in close co-operation with the local union representatives) were to act in relation to the employees as well as in relation to the employers. By this the project differs from much other research that contents itself with analysing facts and desists from acting in relation to them.

Interaction between Analyses of Working Conditions and Technology

In order to make the comprehension of a given technology operational we wanted to develop it in relation to a well-known work situation. In the workplace groups we wanted to analyse a given use of technology in relation to its interaction with the working conditions.

The reason why we talk about changing the present ways of using

technology is that among other things we want to change the working
conditions. Actions aiming at changing the working conditions must
therefore also include analyses of the working condtitions and the
prerequisites of their alteration.

Consequently, a development of technical knowledge must include:
an interaction between analyses of working conditions and analyses
of technology. On the one hand an analysis of the working conditions
may indicate important alterations in and consequences of a given
use of technology: On the other hand an analysis of a given use of
technology may uncover important alterations in and consequences
for the working conditions (cp. fig. 1).

Research with the Trade Unions

The point of this principle becomes clear by formulating its contradiction: Research for the trades union; the researchers do their
jobs and present the result to the trade unions. It was obvious,
however, that the trade unions would not reach their goal just because of the implementation of the DDE project. Our way of organizing the project had to contribute to the continuation and development of the process in progress. Consequently, the trade unions
need of knowledge had to control the development of the project.

The principle of the active participation of the trade unions in the
research process may be a logical consequence of the principle of
partial research and action orientation. But preferring a democratic
research process, it was only natural that trade unions participation in the control and implementation of the activities was an important element of the organization of the project. This was ensured
by the active participation of the trade unions in the project group,
the workplace groups and the control committee.

The active participation of various trade union organs was to ensure
that the dissemination of the results was an integrated part of the
project work. On the one hand this could guarantee a quick dissemination and on the other hand the experience from using the project
could form part of the continuing project work.

3.2.   The main activities

There were two types of activities. The activities intended for the
unions as a whole shall be described in section 3.2.1, and the
activities intended for the three selected local unions shall be
described in section 3.2.2.

3.2.1.   The activities of the DDE-project

The activities described below are, as already mentioned, selected
to illustrate how the research method was implemented.

A survey of the problems

It was a precondition for the work in the project to get a survey
of the problems for the unions. Problems as to the consequences of
the technology to the working conditions and problems as to possible
actions to influence the use of technology.

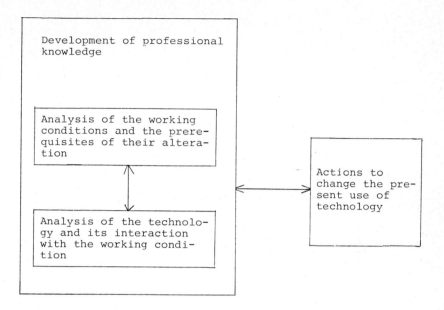

<u>Fig. 1</u>: Action oriented development of knowledge, stating the
substance of the development of knowledge.

<u>The arrows</u>:

→   A certain knowledge of technology and its consequences for the working conditions may give the
basis of internal discussions in the local unions
and of externally directed actions in relation to
the employers.

←   Actions may uncover a lack of knowledge and consequently lead to an enlargement of the subject of
one's analyses.

↓   An analysis of the working conditions may indicate
important alterations in and consequences of a
given use of technology.

↑   An analysis of a given use of technology uncovers
important alterations in and consequences for the
working conditions.

Due to the principle of partial research this survey was not intended
to be all-embracing. We had no intention of assessing all consequences of new technology, but only those of interest to the unions.
Likewise we only looked upon actions which the unions had or might
get possibilities of carrying out. The principles of active participation and of local and central attachments determined how this was
worked out.

Questionaires were sent to the local unions at 165 workplaces
throughout Denmark. The local unions were asked to discuss the use
of edp-technology at their workplaces and answer a number of questions concerning changes in the working conditions and in the local
unions' influence on the applications [5].

The project group visited twelve of these local unions to discuss
their experience with the use of edp. Together with the individual
local unions we worked out a plan for activities that should increase
their influence on the use of edp-technology [6].

The project group wrote a report, thus arranging the experiences
gained through the questionaires and the visits [2]. The report was
spread within the trade unions. It helped many local unions to start
dealing with the problems of edp-technology.

To produce this report all the elements of fig. 1, except "the arrow
to the left", were applied. To apply this we would need more time
and a higher level of activity within the unions.

The workplace groups

Greatest importance were attached to the co-operation with the three
local unions. Some of the activities of this co-operation shall be
described in section 3.2.2. Here I shall concentrate on the methodological reasons for concentrating on these three workplaces.

The main reason was the principle of local attachment within the
unions. The workplace group are the essential organizatorial reflection of this principle. Because of the part that the project group
should play in the action-oriented knowledge production, we had to
concentrate on only three workplaces. Thus we received a reliable
impression of the problems with technology and the working conditions. We closely studied the local unions attempts to increase
their influence and together we elaborated and evaluated their
attempts.

Spreading and debate

It was important for the project to show its solidarity with the
structure and objectives of the trade unions. On the other hand we
also tried to make the unions stick to their objectives. That was
the reason why the principle of research with the trade unions was
put into practice in the way that representatives from all levels
of the unions took part in the control and performance of the different activities. Thus the results from the project could influence
the rest of their union work and thereby a spreading and debate via
the usual channels of the unions have been made possible. Beyond
this the project group took part in and arranged a number of conferences and seminars in which the results from the project were
presented and discussed.

Courses of democracy, development and edp

One of the activities of the project group was to develop a 5-day
course for trade unionists. The researchers of the project group
have written the educational materials and they are teachers on
the courses. A shop steward and a representative from the central
trade union who have shown interest in the problems are also invited as teachers. The aim of the course is to enable the participants to understand how the employers use technology to promote
their interests, and to discuss how the unions can influence the
development in accordance with their interests. Approximately
twenty workers participate in each course, and the number of
courses per year varies from two to eight.

As examples of subjects we shall mention: the use of technology to
control a workplace, possibilities and limitations of electronic
data processing, local unions' influence as to influence on the
use of technology, technology agreements and the work of the central
unions in this field.

The form alternates between lectures and discussions in small groups.
Each day the groups have three-four hours for discussions. Their
task is to write a report to the local unions of one of the group
members. The report shall give proposals for the use of the local
union on how to influence the use of technology at that particular
workplace.

Theorectical studies

A series of theoretically oriented studies within the fields of
management control, organizational development, systems development and research methods were carried out. Part of these studies
were carried out as direct support to the workplace groups [8],
other parts were carried out to develop the theory on the field
[4], [10].

The activities have been carried out by the researchers of the
project group. The socially determined division of labour was
stronger than the principle of research with the unions when these
types of activities took place.

The four other principles were used for the activities that supported the workplace groups. Here I shall emphasize the workplace
group at the shipyard. The local union had tried to influence a
certain use of technology, but had learned that it needed more
knowledge. The workplace group therefore concentrated on producing
that knowledge. This illustrates "the arrow to the left" on fig. 1.

3.2.2. The DDE-project at Danfoss

For two years I was a member of the workplace group at Danfoss. As
in section 3.2.1. I shall here discuss selected activities in order
to show how the research method was implemented. The basis of the
workplace group activities was:

- *Danfoss*, one of the largest, most financially strong and profitable factories in Denmark. It was founded in 1933 in a sparsely
industrialized area. Danfoss is now totally domineering on the
island of Als near the German frontier. In Denmark, Danfoss has
approximately 8000 employees and the enterprise has branches all

over the world. The products include equipment for automatic control
of heating installation, refrigerating plant and airconditioning
plant. More than 90% of the output is exported.

Danfoss energeticly aims at products development and the main part
of the profit is used for the development of new products and for
making the production more effective. The latter is done through an
ongoing development of the production technology, which is often
edp-based. This development is solely controlled by the management.

- *the local union* organizes all the 4500 workers at the workplace.
By tradition very few but the shop stewards are active in union
affairs. There are 52 shop stewards and some of them work full-time
with union affairs. Also by tradition the workers have not questioned
the use of technology. Unsolved problems related to salary and
privacy in regard to two edp-based systems lead to the contact to
the DDE-project.

- *the DDE-project* was interested in establishing three workplace
groups. One of the originally selected local unions did not want to
participate after all, so the local union at Danfoss took over. In
the report from the first phase [2] we had formulated some hypotheses about how the local unions could gain influence on the use
of technology. We would now test these hypotheses and develop them
in the work with the three local unions.

Start and demarcation of activities

It was the local union that contacted the DDE-project to get some
help in their work with some problems concerning numerical control
and registration of personal data. Shortly afterwards the local
union set up an edp-committee consisting of four shop-stewards. They
should work as consultants for the other shop stewards. It was a
permanent committee within the local union. It was not set up to cooperate with the DDE-project, but during nearly two years it chose
to use its main forces in connection with the project.

A workplace group was set up and consisted of the edp-committee, a
researcher and a shop steward from the project group and two graduate
students. The group met twice a month for nearly two years. Then it
was formally dissolved according to plans.

The workplace group was formed in the best conceivable manner: it was
the local union which had some problems and which was interested in
co-operating with the project. Now what did we do?

One of the elements in the research method was to take as a starting
point the perception of problems in the local unions. It was only
natural to start with the problems concerning numerical control and
registration of personal data. The principle of research with the
unions and the principle of action oriented knowledge production
decided how we tackled the problems.

Half of the workplace group devoted its time to numerical control
and the shop steward from the department where they used numerical
control took part in the work. For years the salary of the workers
had been a bargaining counter without an acceptable result. The
preconditions for establishing "the arrow to the left" in fig. 1
were present.

On basis of the discussion about salary we tried to discuss other
questions as well. How is the effect on the structure of qualification and the division of labour between the unskilled workers, the
skilled workers and the engineers? How is numerical control used
in Denmark and abroad and how are the experiences? What can be done
at Danfoss to change the use of technology in accordance with the
interests of the local union?

In preparation for a meeting in the local union we and the shop
steward worked out an introduction to a debate. This is an illustration of "the arrow to the right" in fig. 1. However, the shop steward
assessed the situation so that it would be impossible to discuss it
at the time being. Their argument was that the local bargaining of
salary was transferred to the central level.

The rest of the workplace group devoted its time to the management's
registration of personal data. The edp-committee wanted us to help
in the preparation of a data agreement on this use of data. However,
from the project's point of view it was too narrow a perspective.
We widened the definition of data to include data in connection with
the execution of the job: hours of coming and going, completion of
a job, etc. Thus it became a natural thing to discuss production
control.

We started to analyze some of the edp-systems for production control
in order to explain, how the data registrated by the workers themselves were used for the control of their jobs. But we were on the
wrong track. Even though the shop stewards from the edp-committee
found it interesting to look into production control in this way,
they were sure that the description that we worked out was not fit
for the use of the other members of the local union. That is, the
analyses could not be used as a basis for action (se fig. 1). The
shop stewards explained that the description was insufficient (the
management would not give us any information) and that the subject:
production control was too difficult to start with. Half a year later
we realized that we had done what we thought we should, but nothing
happened. No actions!

Demand for information

During the analysis of the production control the edp-committee
wrote a letter to the management and asked some questions. They
demanded an overview of all the edp-systems of Danfoss. The management refused to answer the letter just as it had earlier refused to
make an arrangement on the working conditions of the DDE-project at
Danfoss, the management had even forbidden us admittance to the
workplace. The refusal to answer the letter started a process of
discussion in the local union. Different possibilities of action
were discussed, the project contributed with our point of view and
we helped to elaborate and to give a more explicit formulation of
the questions. At last the local union decided to discuss the matter
at a meeting of the co-operation committee. Then the management
agreed to take a series of meetings with the edp-committee.

We looked upon this as a victory for the time being. Many people
had been involved in the action: all shop stewares had participated
in the discussions, and the edp-committee wrote about it in the
magazine of the local union. The action had contributed to increase
the understanding of the fact that the management and the local
union did not always have common interests, and of the necessity of

strenghening ones position before bargaining with the management
(about technology). The latter was the argument for the principle
of interest based research. A principle that some of the shop
stewards had questioned from a political point of view.

Furthermore we had co-operated closely with the chairman of the
local union and the edp-committee and in this way contributed
to their actions and activities. The "unsuccessful" activities on
numerical control and registration of personal data had nevertheless led to explicit formulations of aims and demands. This had
been very useful for those who had been bargaining with the management, and for discussions in the local union. Our participation
had thus taken place under the principle of action orientation
(see fig. 1 "the arrow to the right").

Planning the further co-operation

From the struggel to get information the trade unionists learned
that it was necessary to do something to increase the influence.
Likewise a subsequent two-day seminar clarified *what* to be done.

The workplace group, the chairman of the local union and the shop
steward from the department using numerical control took part in
the seminar. We (the DDE-project) had written introductions which
we presented as a basis of discussion. There was a need for:

- knowledge of new technology

- development of aims and possibilities for actions

- an organizing framework in the local union.

We (the DDE-project) wrote a report in order to maintain the common
understanding of what should be the future co-operation. We attached
great importance to start activities that could be carried out by
the local union after the project without our help. We planned to
analyse the use of technology in two departments. We would arrange a
study tour to Norway to compare local experience with those of local
unions in Norway which for years have worked to increase their influence. At last we would arrange a conference for all shop stewards
at Danfoss to discuss aims and possibilities for actions for the
local union. Meanwhile the edp-committee should go on with the
meetings with the management to get useful information. The workplace
group should of course also follow that work.

Analyses of the working conditions and technology

The workplace group saw it as a duty to see to it that everybody
in the local union would know about the changes that take place
when only the employers manage the development and use of technology.
It is a widespread opinion among workers that they themselves know
nothing about technology, and that the necessary information must be
obtained form the management [11]. This paralyses the workers as far
as actions are concerned. We argued that it is at least as important
to collect and prepare the knowledge of the workers, a knowlege
they have obtained through their jobs.

We suggested that the workplace group should act as consultants for

the workers in two of the departments in their attempt to gain influence on the use of technology in the departments.

At the same time we, by an illustrative example, would show the
shop stewards and the workers at Danfoss that it is possible to
start union activities about new technology. We took it for granted
that the work would give a more concrete basis for the discussions
of aims and possibilities for actions in the edp-committee as well
as among the other employees. The co-operation with the workers in
two of the departments was organized as a series of talks. I shall
now describe what happened in one of the departmnets. We (the DDE-
project) had worked out a list of questions as a help for the
workplace group. The edp-committee also used it to inform the other
shop stewards of the initiative and to brief the involved shop
stewards about what the co-operation could led to. Half of the workplace group and four workers (among them the shop steward of their
department) met four times for half a day during two months. We
talked about the production of the department, the content and organization of the work, the control, the development of the department
and aims and possibilities for action of the local union.

After each meeting we (the DDE-project) wrote a report which was
discussed on the following meeting. During the two months "fail-
ures" occured, because things changed. The workers were astonished
that changes took place so quickly. We wrote down, of course, what
we had been talking about at the meetings, but we also added descriptions of new technology that may become important in the department. We described the technology in relation to the functions
which probably would be carried out by the workers, and we described
which functions would be automated. We described the present working
conditions and the preconditions for their change. That is, we
established the interplay shown in fig. 1 as the vertical double
arrow.

In addition we formulated proposals for aims and possibilities for
actions for the workers of the department. This had only been
sporadically touched on before we wrote a draft. Our proposals for
aims were subtracted from the ideas of the workers, but out proposals
for actions were taken from the report of the first phase of the
project [2]. The proposals for actions were very different from what
the workers were used to. Such counter-ideas lead to good discussions
that adjusted their and our understanding of what could be done.
Thus the interplay shown in fig. 1 as the horizontal double arrow
was also established through these talks: It was clear that the
report was a good basis for action, and the report was influenced
by the non-successful attempts that the workers until now have made
to increase their influence.

The report was distributed to all 150 workers of the department and
to all shop stewards at Danfoss. In the department it was used at
two meetings of the workers in which the shop steward and the edp-
committee presented the report for discussion. Together with a similar report from another department this report was used in the
discussions of the consequences which the use of new technology had
led to in the workplace and in the discussions of aims and possibilities for actions.

Thus the principle of taking as a starting point the problems and
possibilities for action of the local union was used in the analyses
of the two departments. At the same time the principles contributed
to increase the understanding of the conflicting interests of workers

and management in relation to the use of technology. This led to an understanding of why it is necessary to use the principle of interest based research also in union work.

Such an understanding is difficult to hold on to in a department with low union activity and poor consciousness. A year after we had finished the analyses, the workers in that department together with the management signed a document saying that they had had influence on the introduction of new technology of the department. From the DDE-project we had no longer a chance to follow the development of the department, but according to the edp-committee there had been no provable changes in the management's way of introducing new technology.

The principle of the union taking an active part in the process of research was observed at several levels. The workers in the department and their shop steward took part in and affected the result of the analyses. Furthermore the report was used in discussion at meetings in the local union. The results from these meetings were used as input to the discussions of the workplace group. The edp-committee took part in the arrangement and accomplishment of the analyses and it was the intermediary to the other shop stewards. At the same time this increases the possibility that such analyses could take place with the help of the edp-committee but without any help from the outside. Finally the shop steward of the project group participated on the preparation as well as in the accomplishment of the analyses.

Other activities

The activities described are representative in the sense that they present how the project employed the methodological principles. To make the presentation complete in relation to an understanding of all the activities of the workplace group, I shall reel off the other activities: the edp-committee participated in the course Democracy, Development and Edp, in a study tour to Norwegian local unions, in a conference with the two other workplace groups and representatives of the central unions. The edp-committee also prepared an aim-action program on technology for the local union, arranged a conference on new technology for all shop stewards on Danfoss, supported the entering into an agreement with the management of one department on the introduction of a special kind of technology in that department.

4. CONTROL MECHANISMS

In the light of the different activities the project has formulated a union strategy for gaining influence on the use of new technology.

Technology agreements are the control mechanism which has been mostly debated in the Scandinavian countries. But technology agreements are not enough. At the concerns that are heavily pressed by competition, it is difficult for the employees to refuse the management's wish to raise productivity by introducing new technology, eventhough they might have a right to do so according to an agreement.

This is a serious dilemma that might be avoided if the employees could point at another technology, which could also raise the productivity but which preserved or even increased the employees' control of the production. Such technology does not exist today. All technology on the market is a result of research and development controlled by the interests of the employers. There is a need for the unions' active support of research and development of new technology so that the employees have the chance to indicate alternatives.

To make the unions able to use those agreements and to develop new technology in accordance with the interests of the unions it is a precondition that there are trade unionists at the workplaces who are able to assess the consequences of the initiatives of the employers, and who are able to act in relation to these initiatives. For every local union it is necessary:

- to analyse and understand the changes and consequences of new technology for the working conditions

- to develop the aims of the local union in relation to future use of technology

- to develop the possibilities for actions to increase the influence.

The work of the local unions, the technology agreements and research and development of technology based on the interests of the unions may together make up a strategy for the unions. However, it is important to stress the connexion between these activities. The one cannot substitute the other.

4.1. Development of new technology based on the interest of the unions

There are very few experiences with development of new technology based on the interests of the unions. Therefore we shall only report from two projects of this kind. The purpose is to present alternatives to the technology introduced by the managements.

The first example shall be the so-called "cabinet-maker project", in which a group of Swedish researchers and cabinet-makers are developing new technology for small cabinet makers' trades. The starting point of the project is to preserve and to improve the strenght of the small cabinet makers' trades by improving the quality of the products and the contents of the work. And also to try to improve the weaknesses: the working environment, the technology and the organization. The project should be looked upon as part of a defense for employment, a raising of the wage level through higher workmanship, the wish of the cabinet-makers to organize the production themselves, and the longterm aim of the unions to take over the means of production. The project which started in 1980 develops new machinery as well as new ways of organizing the work.

In another project the Nordic Federation of Printers together with a group of Swedish and Danish researchers has started to develop new technology and an education-program for text- and picture processing. The project aims at developing technology for the graphic industry, which fulfil the demands of the printers.

Both examples serve the purpose of demonstrating that it is possible to develop new technology in the interest of the unions.

4.2. Technology agreements

A technology agreement must give the unions a possibility to regulate the way in which the management introduce new technology, and it must give a possibility for union activities to increase the influence. To introduce new technology the management need two things from the unions. Firstly they need the knowledge of the employees about how the work is done in details. Secondly, they need the acceptance of the employees. That is why private and public employers in the Scandinavian countries for the last eight years have been entering into agreements with the unions.

It is not possible in this paper to illustrate the great variety of agreements. Instead I shall list what we found should be the main articles of such an agreement.

Information

All the agreements include an article on information, but very few employers inform in such a way that it is possible for the local union to assess the consequences for the working conditions. There is a need for useful information about the changes that the management wants and about the projects which shall lead to the changes.

Local agreements per system

The common interests between employers and employees are not dominating in the field of new technology. New technology is related to employment and the control of the work. That is why new technology is closely related to the right of the employers to control and distribute the work.

Secondly new technology affects areas which are already covered by existing agreements.

That is why for each and every new system there should be an agreement. This is the only way for the unions to increase their influence.

The right of interpretation

Every agreement can be interpreted differently according to what the parties want to achieve. In Sweden there is an agreement saying that it is the interpretation of the employees that is valid, until the employers can prove that they are right.

More resources

Information and agreements are necessary tools, but there is also a need for more resources: time, money and help from advisers. Today the management controls the resources but if the employees are to take part in the development of new technology, the management must set aside resources for the employees, just as they set aside other resources for a project.

4.3. Local union activities

When the activities at Danfoss were described in section 3.2.2 I

already suggested some local union activities. I shall therefore
limit myself to a short presentation of the activities that the
project has given us enough experience to suggest.

Demand for information

Even though the agreements have articles about information it is
necessary for the local unions to fight for useable information on
questions such as:

- what is the aim of the management with new technology?
- which parts of the workplace shall be involved?
- which of the work functions are to be automated?
- how are the consequences?

A responsible management ought to know the answers to these types
of questions, but it is still difficult to get an answer.

Organizing the union work

It is a comprehensive work to increase the influence on new technology. One way of organizing the work could be to set up a technology committee of 3-4 employees. The committee should be responsible
for the union activities on new technology.

Discussions of a certain technology

It might be a good starting point of the union activities if the
shop steward and 2-3 other employees analyse and describe the consequences of the use of technology in a certain department. They might
analyse the following subjects:

- which machinery is used?
- how are the jobs distributed?
- how is the control?
- which changes have been accomplished for the last 3-5 years,
  and how are the consequences in relation to the working
  conditions?

On the basis of such an analysis and description the shop steward
call a meeting in which the employees can discuss which aims they
will work for when new technology is introduced. Which changes in
the working conditions should be avoided? Which changes should be
carried out?

Such discussions are needed among all the employees because they are
the ones, who can suggest alternatives due to their experiences
from the working situation.

How to exert the influence?

The management often wants to involve one or two employees in a
project group to take advantage of their knowledge. If the local
union joins a project group it is important to be sure of the conditions of participation. The management controls the resources and
the experts which means that an employee can easily be forced to

take a joint responsibility for decisions, on which he or she have
had no real influence. It is a good idea for such a representative
to have a group of fellow workers who will be affected by the project
and with whom he can discuss the problems.

The influence can also be exerted through agreements with the management. The agreements could state the function of the technology and
they could state how the technology should be developed. The basis
for these agreements could come from information from the management
and from analyses carried out by the employees themselves.

Demand for resources

Many of the activities that we have suggested demand time, money and
perhaps even help from outside the workplace. Such resources are not
available for the local unions. The management uses large amounts,
a lot of time and many experts to develop new technology. The local
union must try to get money for its own analysis in connection with
a certain project, or it must demand a certain sum per year. It must
demand time for union activities and the right to call in its own
experts.

REFERENCES:

[1]   Cooley, M.: "Architect or Bee?", Langley Technical Services,
            Slough, U.K., 1980.

[2]   DDE 2, Democracy, Development and Edp, DUE-report, no. 2, Compu-
            ter Science Department, Aarhus University, March 1978.

[3]   DDE 4, Edp and the Local Unions, DUE-report, no. 4, Computer
            Science Department, Aarhus University, January 1981.

[4]   DDE 5, Systems Development and Systems Development Methods,
            by Lars Mathiassen, DUE-report, no. 5, Computer Science
            Department, Aarhus University, September 1981.

[5]   DDE 6, A note on the Result of an Investigation by Question-
            naire, DUE-note, no. 6, Computer Science Department,
            Aarhus University, February 1978.

[6]   DDE 7, Edp-Systems and Local Union Work at 12 Workplaces,
            DUE-note, no. 7, Computer Science Department, Aarhus
            University, June 1979.

[7]   DDE 13, Local Union Work and Edp at the Postgiro Office, DUE-
            note, no. 13, Computer Science Department, Aarhus Uni-
            versity, November 1979.

[8]   DDE 14, Local Union Work and Edp at the Aalborg Shipyard, DUE-
            note, no. 14, Computer Science Department, Aarhus Uni-
            versity, May 1980.

[9]   DDE 15, Local Union Work and Edp at Danfoss, DUE-note, no. 15,
            Computer Science Department, Aarhus University, August
            1980.

[10] DDE 17, Actionoriented Interest based Research with the Trade
            Unions, by Finn Kensing, DUE-note no. 17, Computer
            Science Department, Aarhus University, December 1981.

[11]   Freire, P.: "Pedagogy of the Oppressed", Herder and Herder,
          New York, 1970.

[12]   Negt, O.: "Sociological Fantasy and exemplified Learning",
          EVA, Frankfurt/M, 1972.

[13]   Nygaard, K. and Bergo, O. T.: "The trade unions, new users
          of research". Personnel Review, vol. 4, no. 2, 1975.

[14]   Sandberg, Aa. (ed.): "Computers Dividing Man and Work",
          Swedish Center for Working Life, Stockholm 1979.

EVALUATION STUDIES ON TRADE UNIONS EXPERIENCES

SYSTEMS DESIGN FOR, WITH, AND BY THE USERS
U. Briefs, C. Ciborra and L. Schneider (editors)
North-Holland Publishing Company
© IFIP, 1983

TECHNOLOGY BARGAINING IN NORWAY

Leslie Schneider
Harvard University

Claudio Ciborra
Politecnico di Milano

INTRODUCTION

In Norway more than any other country in the world, unions, employers, and the state have tried to shape the direction of technological change at work. Labour-management agreements regulating technological change were first negotiated locally in 1974 and then in certain industries in 1975. Now called "Technology Agreements", they currently cover all sectors of the Norwegian economy. The Agreements guarantee workers and their local unions the right to participate in the development of the new workplace technologies and to negotiate with management about all aspects of workplace technological change. During the past eight years, they have been regularly revised and expanded to include an ever broader range of aspects related to the development and introduction of new technology at work.

To have the right to information, participation, and bargaining in new areas such as technological change is one thing. To effectively exercise these rights, however, is quite another. How have trade unions actually used the Norwegian Technology Agreements? We will try to answer this question by describing the experiences of eight Norwegian organizations and their local unions with the Agreements between the time they were developed and signed in 1975 and today.

The data for this paper were obtained from interviews completed in late 1981 and early 1982 with nearly 100 persons at the eight firms--personnel department and organizational development staff members, systems analysts, and union representatives (in particular data shop stewards). The interviews were semi-structured with an open-ended format to encourage a free exchange of information and ideas and the incorporation of new topics. Interviews lasted anywhere from one to six hours and, in some cases, follow-up interviews were carried out.

The eight organizations we studied--three chemical or paper and pulp manufacturers, three mechanical and electronics companies, one city government and a newspaper--are not a representative sample of Norwegian firms. Rather, they were selected because they have been doing interesting and important work with the Technology Agreements over a period of years. They should give a clearer sense than any random sample of both the development of local union work with the Agreements and the problems associated with their application.

Our research suggests three kinds of findings. First, we discovered two quite different local union approaches to implementing Technology Agreements

which we call the "after the fact" and "before the fact" approaches.
Second, we found numerous examples of less generalizable but equally
important "extra technological" factors (for example, market position,
personal relations in the firm, management philosophy,etc) which both shape
the direction of technological change and affect union influence over it.
Third, we found that, in order to influence the effects of technology,
unions must have a say in the very process of organizational development and
the organization of work itself. In this respect, union attempts to
influence technological change are closely linked to the more general goal
of extending democracy at work

TWO APPROACHES TO LOCAL UNION INFLUENCE OVER THE SYSTEM DEVELOPMENT PROCESS

The Norwegian Technology Agreements define a framework for bringing the
interests of local unions into the practical work of designing and
introducing new workplace technological systems. But the Agreements
themselves do not specify in detail how this is to be accomplished. The
seven-year history of technology bargaining at the eight organizations we
studied suggests that unions have filled this gap in two very different ways.

Local unions who use what we have called the "after the fact" approach try
to influence new workplace technologies proposed and developed by management
primarily by negotiating a special contract for each new system after
management has already decided to buy it. These "system contracts" specify
the conditions for introducing each particular technical system as well as
the training necessary for workers to operate it.

Local unions who use a "before the fact" approach, on the other hand,
actively participate in the development process from the very beginning.
They negotiate the general goals of the system--its main functions,
applications, and consequences--before it is designed or introduced. Unions
who follow this approach become involved in the strategic planning for
computerization and organizational development within the firm, over and
above the development and design of individual technical systems.

It should be kept in mind that the two approaches described above are "ideal
types". In the real world, they are rarely found in their pure form.
Nevertheless, these types are analytically useful for two reasons. First of
all, they provide a means to compare and contrast union experience with
Technology Agreements in a wide variety of settings. What's more, they also
suggest the historical circumstances which shape union work with the
Agreements. We like to think of "after the fact" and "before the fact", not
so much as two separate and opposing approaches to influencing technological
change, but as two moments in a learning process, two points on a continuum
along which unions develop their knowledge and expertise about workplace
technology and strengthen their capacity to shape its impact.

The "After the Fact" Approach

As outlined above, unions pursuing an "after the fact" approach accept the
company's decision to introduce new technology, allow management to develop
new technical systems, but intervene heavily in bargaining over the impact
of technological changes after the system has been developed and
implemented. The advantage of this approach is that it allows union

representatives to study the system and grasp what it does and how it functions, before they intervene. Thus, when they negotiate a specific system contract, they are bargaining about a more or less "known object". Furthermore, this approach requires relatively fewer resources than its "before the fact" counterpart because the union does not have to participate in every single phase of the development process nor respond to every single management proposal for technological change. Instead, the union can marshal its resources and focus them on the last stages of those systems that will actually see the light of day.

Even though the "after the fact" approach is limited to specific systems, such system contracts can nevertheless specify the interaction of that system with the broader organization of work in the firm. Thus, it it clear that Technology Agreements of any kind serve to bring important issues of work organization into the realm of collective bargaining. This strengthens the union's independent decision-making power.

But while some unions using an "after the fact" approach have been able to play a positive role in both the design of new technology and the reorganization of work, this is more the exception than the rule. The "after the fact" approach can open up all kinds of new issues for unions, but it does not necessarily encourage them to develop the tools, resources, or perspective necessary to deal with these issues over the long term. When it comes to moving beyond the incremental amelioration of already existing technical systems, a purely "after the fact" approach can become a barrier to union influence over technological change.

One limitation built in to the very structure of the "after the fact" approach is that the union is rarely able to get information about forthcoming systems early enough to actually suggest alternatives to them. So that new systems can only be modified to a limited degree. "After the fact" also tends to blur the crucial distinction between "union participation" and "user participation" in the development process. The idea of user participation is nothing new. In fact, it is becoming more and more common as systems analysts themselves realize that they can make better systems with the cooperation, information, and knowledge of users than they can alone.

But user participation in the development of particular systems does not necessearily mean union influence over technological change. Often, under the guise of increasing democracy and improving the quality of working life, "participatory" system development projects end up inhibiting the effective participation of unions by involving individual users in solving exclusively technical problems. The actual decision-making power remains with management.

Particular users may get better working systems, but they are unable to influence matters of concern to unions (e.g., working conditions and employment). "We have a one-sided cooperation where the (user) representatives become 'hostages' of the technology," writes Fjalestad (1981). They end up "playing a losing game with democratization."

The "Before the Fact" Approach

Increasingly aware of these and other problems, a small number of unions
have tried to avoid them by developing a different approach: participating
in technological change "before the fact". From the very moment a system is
suggested, the union makes its own proposals about the general goals of the
system--its main functions, its applications in the labour process, the
amount and kind of training necessary for workers to understand and use
it--all before the system is designed. The union also participates in
developing and introducing the new system as well as regulating and
evaluating its implementation and use.

This design-oriented approach--contracting "before the fact"--creates far
more opportunities for influence than its "after the fact" counterpart.
However, it places many more demands on the resources of the local union.
The union must be able to articulate far-reaching demands concerning
technological change for both the short and long term. It must have the
capacity to forecast the implications of particular systems before they
actually exist and suggest alternative design specifications. It must be
able to analyze the way different systems interact with each other.
Finally, the union must be able to evaluate the final system in relation to
the initial blueprint and to identify what went wrong and why.

Unions who use a "before the fact" approach with some degree of success tend
to understand participation in decision-making as both cooperative and
conflictual. After negotiating the general goals and consequences of the
system and the conditions of the system development process in collective
bargaining, union representatives enter a cooperative phase while the system
is being developed. Then, as specific issues arise that cannot be handled
within a cooperative structure--for example, when there is a conflict of
interest between workers and management--the union will enter into a
negotiation phase again. This alternation between moments of negotiation
and moments of cooperation continues throughout the entire development
process.

Where successful, this "before the fact" approach allows unions to move far
beyond narrow particpation in determining the impacts of specific technical
systems. In fact, they have laid the groundwork for the resources,
expertise, and broad-based participation necessary to get not only better
working systems but also to extend democracy at the workplace. They have
developed a comprehensive union policy for technological change and even
participated in the strategic, long-term planning process of the
corporation. What's more, when union education for technological change is
informed by a "before the fact" perspective it becomes far more than just
training for specific systems. Rather, the goals and content of the
programme are comprehensive, including the whole area of design and
development of systems, and the training begins early in the process.

EXTRA TECHNOLOGICAL FACTORS

The choice of union strategy is of course important. But that choice does
not take place in a vacuum. It is shaped, in some cases, even determined by
a wide variety of what might be termed "extra technological" factors. They
can be economic, political, in some cases even personal. Without making any

claims to presenting an exhaustive list of such factors, we will suggest some of those that emerged as the most important.

To take one very basic example: economic crisis and poor market position can make effective union influence over technological change virtually impossible. Despite the early and promising start of one union, the subsequent economic decline and related restructuring of the company forced both managers and union representatives to turn their attention to the more immediate problems of saving jobs. Management was less willing to consider the unions demands about technology, and the union's time and resources were severely constrained. Even this extremely strong local union had little chance of dealing with problems related to technological change in the midst of the company's economic crisis.

But there are other, less obvious, "extra technological" factors. Whether intentional or unintentional, management practices can also be an obstacle to union influence over technological change. In all eight organizations, we observed just how problematic middle managers or systems analysts can be for union work. Middle managers who don't understand or appreciate the importance of worker participation or technology bargaining, try to slow things down or even start reorganization projects of their own. Some try to limit worker participation by using budget constraints to cut time, schedules, and manning for project work. Others formally agree to their employees' participation, but don't find or pay for substitutes for them so those who really want to participate are forced to hold down "two jobs".

Systems analysts who want to maintain hegemony over the area of system development constitute another group who limit union influence over technological change. They often use their power and technical expertise to bypass union participation by preparing the agenda for project work, selecting group members and using unsophisticated and "individualized" techniques for explaining new systems to users.

Cost cutting measures such as buying ready-made systems software packages or hiring external consultants can also be an obstacle to union efforts to influence technological change. To the degree that companies go outside for technical systems or technical expertise, it becomes difficult for unions to shape the process of technological change. The configuration of ready-made systems often reflects a set of choices made in advance about the content and organization of work. At best, unions can specify only minor variations. And consultants because they are chosen and paid for by systems analysts not unions, tend to focus exclusively on designing systems which are technically correct without regard for other factors.

Even when management tries to be progressive by using "modern" approaches to system and organizational development, trade union efforts can be severely limited. New trends in system and organizational development emphasize techniques for the gradual introduction of technological change. Decentralization, system prototyping, and "step by step" development are all said to give unions and users a better understanding of the social consequences of technology. While this may be true in the abstract, in practice those techniques have had exactly the opposite effect. Managements' "slow and careful" development and introduction of new systems for example, can actually prevent users and unions from understanding how individual systems fit together as a whole. They don't know whether a small

project will have big consequences both for themselves or others so it's
difficult for unions to discuss global solutions on their own terms.
Likewise, decentralization of systems and systems development does not
aautomatically mean increased flexibility and local control. It forces
unions to follow up on a larger number of widely scattered system
development projects and makes it more difficult both to keep up with and
control local developments and maintain an overview of technological
developments company-wide.

"Prototyping" is another example. Systems analysts claim that it bridges
the gap between them and the users, thus contributing to the development of
more relevant and "user friendly" systems. But while prototyping can
increase the direct participation of individual users, it often does so at
the expense of totally bypassing the union structure. Prototyping can also
limit user influence to cosmetic input-output features of the system rather
than promoting the kind of broad-based participation that could really have
positive consequences for the quality of the work environment. It focuses
on man-machine interactions rather than the overall system, so the user
participants' attention may be drawn away from how the system will impact
the power structure of the company and ultimately the role of the union. In
order for unions and users to have any real influence over the consequences
of new technology, they must participate in and formulate demands concerning
more than just the format of the information on the VDT screen. They must
work with questions about the planning and control of work, job content and
work organization, and the design of the technology itself.

Another important cluster of "extra technological" factors involves union
organization, resources and practice. Despite the very real gains made in
Technology Agreements, management always has more resources to devote to
these issues than unions (e.g. money, information, technical expertise,
etc), placing the unions at a disadvantage. Developing independent
knowledge and influence in new areas such as computerization places
tremendous demands on union resources. Trade union work has traditionally
been concerned with "today's negotiations", while work with technology
questions requires consideration of both short and long-term consequences.
The precise role of the data shop steward was not clearly defined in the
"General Framework Agreement on Technological Change". Therefore, it had to
be worked out in each case.

COPING WITH LIMITING FACTORS

Unions have been forced to rethink how their organizational structure,
resources, and ways of working can be adapted to meet the challenges and
demands of technology bargaining. Since the Technology Agreements were
signed, they have begun to develop a variety of ways to address these
problems. These range from clarifying the role of the data shop steward, to
developing comprehensive education programmes and union technology policies,
to forming alliances with managers and other unions.

But the ability to form informal and formal alliances with members of
management or with other unions is perhaps the most important step for local
unions to take. We observed four different types of alliances: 1) between
unions and personnel department officials, 2) between unions and systems
analysts, 3) among unions across traditional professional lines, and 4)
between local clubs and their federations.

It is not uncommon, for example, that union representatives and personnel
department officials form an alliance. In many organizations, training and
bargaining about new technology are the responsibility of the Personnel
Department. When an alliance is formed, personnel staff who understand the
important relationship between technology and work organization, support and
encourage the union's involvement in both the strategy and project levels in
the development process. A less common, but even more important alliance is
between union representatives and systems analysts. Both groups seem to
benefit from the informal exchange of information and mutual support on
particular issues or systems.

Another crucial alliance is among different unions at the same workplace,
particularly when it crosses professional boundaries. This type of
cooperation will become increasingly critical as new computer-based
technologies break down the distinction between professional groups. Some
local groups have learned that their best weapon is to form strong alliances
with other unions at the firm and deal with technology questions together.

The last form of alliance we observed is between local unions and their
national trade union federations. With the introduction of standardized
production technologies world-wide, it has become more and more difficult to
control technological change - even for the strongest local unions.
National trade union federations are supporting and coordinating local
efforts through educational programmes, assistance in negotiating conflicts,
and research projects. What began with the pioneering research efforts of
the Norwegian Iron and Metal Workers and Chemical Workers in the 1970's,
has, by 1982, evolved into multi-national trade union oriented strategies
for dealing with technological change. One such project is committed to
concerted action by national trade union federations to influence the range
of production technologies and at the same time to coordinate actions taken
at the local level.

CONCLUSION

How might the concepts outlined in this paper be useful for a local union
trying to deal with technology at work? While it is clear that a "before
the fact" approach has more potential for comprehensive union influence over
workplace technological change, we would not neccessariy recommend it in
all cases. The appropriate strategy for a particular union local depends on
a wide variety of factors--previous experience in dealing with technology
issues, the resources the local can bring to bear, the company's attitude
toward union involvement in technological change, etc.

Our typology is particularly useful in suggesting the necessary conditions
for successful union intervention--whatever the approach. Take the example
of the data shop steward. If a union decides to pursue an "after the fact"
approach, the data shop steward must serve as a "contact person" between the
union and the company. He becomes the conduit of information between the
company and the workers. He represents the "users" in the bargaining
process. The data shop steward in the "before the fact" approach, on the
other hand, plays a significantly expanded role. More than a channel of
information between company and union, he must actually make union policy
concerning technological change for both the short and the long
term. He must set up and manage an on-going process of system development.
Unions must understand these and other requirements before defining their
own strategy for dealing with technological change.

But effectively exercising influence over new workplace technology requires
more than merely choosing an approach. At this point, our concept of "extra
technological" factors becomes especially important. To a large degree,
these factors determine whether any plan will be implemented successfully.
Even the best thought-out union strategy in the world will have little
impact in an "atmosphere" of economic crisis. Likewise, management
intransigeance, whether systematic or not, can limit the possibilities for
union participation in technological change at work. In this regard,
perhaps the most important "extra technological" factor for a local union to
consider is the question of alliances--with personnel managers, systems
analysts, and other unions. It is our belief that the quality of a local
union's alliances is one of the most important factors in determining the
success or failure of its intervention in technology issues.

Finally, our research suggests that union success in technology bargaining
requires what might be described as a far broader "field of intervention".
First, union activity on technology issues must be integrated into the total
work of the local. Instead of becoming an isolated specialty, it has to be
linked to the broader development of the organization and the labour process
itself. In this way, technology bargaining becomes just one part of the
larger effort to extend democracy at work.

Moreover, the struggle for union influence over technological change must go
beyond the particular workplace. With the introduction of standardized
technologies around the world, it is becoming difficult to control
technological change at the local level. Unions must be exploring both
multi-national, national and regional solutions to the problems posed by new
technology at work.

But the scope and complexity of these problems should not obscure one
important fact. The Norwegian Technology Agreements have promoted and
legitimated concern for technology issues at the national, corporate, and
local union levels. They have provided both a form and a context within
which unions can search for their own solutions. They provide a stable
structure that remains and will continue to do so, despite the comings and
goings of particular managers, systems analysts, and union officials.

LITERATURE

Fjalestad, J., Some Factors Affecting Participation in Systems Development,
in: Mambrey, P., Oppermann, R., Partizipation bei der Systementwicklung,
GMD, Birlinghoven (1981)

SYSTEMS DESIGN FOR, WITH, AND BY THE USERS
U. Briefs, C. Ciborra and L. Schneider (editors)
North-Holland Publishing Company
© IFIP, 1983

REGULATING THE USE OF EDP BY LAW AND AGREEMENT

Lars Mathiassen[1]

Birgitte Rolskov[2]

Eline Vedel[3]

The article provides a conceptual framework for characterizing laws and agreements regulating the use of edp. Furthermore it contains a survey and an evaluation of the contents of relevant laws and agreements existing within the Scandinavian labour market. Finally it is discussed how such regulations affect the requirements to the development of edp-based systems.

1. INTRODUCTION

subject This article presents a study of laws and agreements regulating the use of edp within organizations, i.e. the edp-based systems and the system development process. The study is limited to the Scandinavian labour market and it has been carried out as a purely textual investigation[4]. Hence the insight gained is more into the possible consequences than into the actual effects of these regulating mechanisms. Furthermore we focus on the decision and communication processes related to system development, so our study does not cover laws and agreements that directly and merely regulate the design of edp-based systems, for example on matters like personal data and employment. For related studies, see [4] and [5].

concepts Basically we characterize guidelines within laws and agreements as either recommendations or demands, and as regards content we conceptualize the various guidelines using the following categories:

- influence, covering guidelines directly expressing that the employees must or should be given possibilities to influence the use of edp,

- information, covering guidelines on information to the employees about the use of edp,

- education, covering guidelines for the education of employees in relation to the use of edp,

- resources, covering guidelines expressing that the employer must or should provide resources for union activities in relation to the use of edp,

- edp-based systems, covering guidelines on the design of edp-based systems.

overview   In the following five sections, each of these categories is
             discussed in detail. Each section contains: some useful con-
             cepts related to the subject in question, a description of
             the current status of existing laws and agreements, and fi-
             nally some remarkable examples of guidelines. The article is
             concluded by relating the existing laws and agreements to
             the needs of the trade union movement and to the problems of
             developing edp-based systems. All relevant references are
             given at the end of the article.

appli-   It is our hope that the insight provided - both specifically
cations   into Scandinavian laws and agreements and more generally in
             the form of a conceptual framework - can be applied when
             studying or constructing other laws and agreements regulating
             the use of edp and when discussing requirements to system
             development processes.

             Finally, before proceeding with the body of the discussion,
             we want to point out, that this study should be seen as an
             integrated part of interest-based, action-oriented research
             activities carried out in cooperation between trade unionists
             and academics [2]: on the one hand, the insight provided when
             studying isolated aspects of the use of edp, e.g. laws and
             agreements, only becomes relevant when applied in such a
             wider context; on the other hand, we find that the develop-
             ment of strategies for action can benefit, among other things,
             from profound and structured knowledge about various aspects
             of the use of edp within modern societies.

2. INFLUENCE

2.1 Useful concepts
             Guidelines within this category are concerned with: what the
             employees have a right to influence, when the possibilities
             of influencing are given, and finally how the influence should
             be practiced.

what   The employees can be given the right to influence various
             aspects of the use of edp within the actual organization:

             - general guidelines for the use of edp, i.e. guidelines con-
               cerning both the edp-based systems and the system develop-
               ment process;

             - plans for future development;

             - individual projects and systems.

when   If the employees are given the right to influence general
             guidelines and plans, some of the fundamental questions re-
             lated to when the possibilities of influencing are given are
             already determined. However, concerning the individual pro-
             jects and systems it is important whether possibilities to
             influence are given

             - before the project is started;

             - before the final system proposal is chosen;

             - before the system is introduced.

how   The form under which the influence is given has important
consequences for the employees' possibilities to promote
their interests. Various forms are possible:

Negotiations: employees and management exchange viewpoints
with the purpose of reaching an agreement. Violation of an
agreement can result in fines. In some cases the two parts
can be bound to reach an agreement

Discussions: employees and management exchange viewpoints.
The two parts are not committed to pay respect to eventual
agreements.

Hearings: the employees put forward their viewpoints to
management or to some   experts   - often by commenting on
a specific proposal related to the use of edp within the organization. Management is not committed to pay respect to
these viewpoints.

Participation: the employees take active part in the system
development process through representatives in steering
committees, project groups or reference groups.

2.2 Current status
The Swedish as well as the Norwegian laws and agreements give
the employees better possibilities to influence the use of
edp than the Danish, and taken as a whole the Swedish law
and agreements seem to give the best possibilities. However,
the two parts are in very few cases bound to reach an agreement.

Denmark   In nearly all cases the employees are given a right to discuss the design of individual systems. Hence the form is
generally limited to discussions, the exceptions being that
a couple of local agreements allow for both participation
and discussions and that a single local agreement clearly
allows for negotiations. Furthermore these discussions are
primarily to be concerned with the design of individual
systems, whereas the employees only in a few cases are given
a right to influence general guidelines for the use of edp,
plans for future development and individual projects. The
law and most agreements recommend early influence but only
local agreements demand that the employees are given the
possibility to influence the design of a system before the
actual project is started or before the final system proposal
is chosen.

Norway   The Norwegian regulations provide the employees with better
possibilities of influencing the use of edp than the Danish.
The law and all the agreements give the employees a right to
influence the design of individual systems as well as individual projects - in all cases through participation and in
some central and local agreements also through negotiations
and hearings. In addition the central agreements give the
employees a right to negotiate on general guidelines for the
use of edp, with main emphasis on guidelines for the system
development process, and one of the central agreements also
gives the employees the right to hearings and negotiations on
plans for future development. Generally the possibilities of
influencing are only secured before the system is introduced.
However, one central and one local agreement demand that

possibilities of influencing are given before projects are
started.

Sweden   The Swedish law gives the employees a right to negotiate on
almost all issues related to the use of edp. Within the
framework of the law several central and local agreements
make it clear that the right to negotiate covers both general
guidelines for the use of edp, plans for future development,
and individual projects and systems. A number of agreements
also recommend or give the employees a right to participate.
Furthermore, it seems that the employees are given a right
to influence before projects are started.

2.3 Remarkable examples

The Swedish law contains the following sections:

> "Before the employer decides on an important change,
> he must on his own initiative negotiate with the local
> unions ..."
>
> (section 11)

> "On demand of the local union the employer must also
> in other situations negotiate with the union before
> he takes or carries through a decision concerning
> the members of the union ..."
>
> (section 12)

These sections are further clarified in the various central
agreements. As an illustration, the agreement covering the
central authorities contains a chapter on influence issues,
which among other things says:

> "Questions for local negotiations ...
>
> - the aim and forms of rationalization in the
>   individual department,
> - the content, form and amount of information to be
>   given to the employees in relation to rationalization,
> - the involvement of the local union and of affected
>   employees,
> - the education of representatives to enable them to
>   participate in specific forms of investigative ac-
>   tivities,
> - how affected employees should be given possibilities
>   to take care of new or changed tasks."
>
> (section II.1.16)

3. INFORMATION

The employees' influence on the use of edp is of course the
important topic. However, one of the fundamental prerequisites
of influencing is to have access to relevant information.

3.1 Useful concepts

Guidelines within this category are concerned with: what the
employees should be informed about, when the information
should be given and finally how the information should be
provided.

what   The employees can be informed about various aspects of the
            use of edp within the actual organization:

            - plans for future developments;
            - individual projects and systems under development;
            - existing systems.

            Furthermore guidelines can express more detailed requirements
            to the contents of the information.

when   If the employees are informed about plans for future develop-
            ment, it is already to some extent determined when information
            is given. However, concerning the individual projects and
            systems, it is important whether information is given:

            - before the project is started;
            - before the final system proposal is chosen;
            - before the system is introduced.

            We find it useful to distinguish between, on the one hand,
            when management has the obligation (without request) to
            inform about the concerned matters, and on the other hand
            when the employees have the right to get access to existing
            information.

how   Guidelines determining how the information is provided deal
            with several other important questions. In the following
            overview we only cover the question of form of the informa-
            tion, i.e. whether it is written or verbal, in what type of
            language it is formulated etc. Other important questions
            are [1]: firstly, who has the right to receive the informa-
            tion - i.e. whether the information should be given directly
            to all affected employees or only to some of their represen-
            tatives - and, especially in the latter case, whether the
            information is given under promise of secrecy; secondly,
            whether the information is given within working hours.

            3.2 Current status
            Both the Danish and Norwegian laws and agreements contain
            detailed guidelines on information to the employees, but the
            Norwegian generally seem to be more excessive than the
            Danish. Neither the Swedish law nor the central agreements
            are very detailed on this point, instead questions related
            to information are left open for local negotiation.

Denmark   In all cases management have an obligation to inform the
            employees on coming systems, and in several cases it is ex-
            plicitly demanded that this information includes an evalua-
            tion of the possible consequences for the employees. In addi-
            tion all central agreements give the employees the right to
            get further information on coming systems when asking for it.
            The information is, however, generally restricted to deal
            with coming systems; only in a few local cases do the em-
            ployees have a right to be kept informed about plans for
            future projects and about the organization of individual pro-
            jects; furthermore it is only in cases of local agreements
            that the employees clearly have a right to get information on
            existing systems.

Only one local agreement clearly demands that management have
an obligation to inform before a project is started and before a system proposal is chosen. And in all cases it is only
representatives of the employees that are given the right to
be informed within working hours. Finally it is in some cases,
but not all, demanded that the information be written, clear
and understandable.

Norway Like in Denmark management always have an obligation to inform about coming systems; it is also in some cases demanded
that this information includes an evaluation of the possible
consequences for the employees; in addition the employees
often have a right to have further information on coming and
existing systems and on individual projects when asking for
it. Furthermore one of the central agreements give the employees a right to be kept informed on plans for future projects. Hence, in Norway the employees have a right to be informed on more matters of relevance than is the case in
Denmark.

Furthermore, it is stressed that the information must be
given before a project is started or before a system proposal
is chosen. The central agreements even give the right to
other employees than a few representatives to be informed
within working hours, and they demand that the information
given must be understandable, clear and without unnecessary
use of technical terms. It is, however, in no cases demanded
that the information be written.

Sweden The Swedish law and agreements seem to leave the question of
information open for local negotiations. The law does not
explicitly demand that management informs the employees, but
the employees have a general right to get existing information on any relevant issue when asking for it. The central
agreements demand that planning of future projects is well-
documented. One of these agreements gives management an obligation to inform the employees on coming systems and on
individual projects, both in advance and during the project.
The other central agreement does not explicitly give the
employers a right to have this information without asking for
it.

None of the agreements explicitly give the employees a right
to have information on existing systems, and all agreements
leave the question of form open to local agreements.

3.3 Remarkable examples

The Norwegian central agreement covering the private sector
contains general guidelines for how the employees must be
informed about the use of edp. Within the framework of this
agreement the local agreement at Tandberg states:

> "Before a system is developed, a project framework must
> be worked out ... and the local union must have the
> opportunity to put forward their viewpoints on the
> framework before it is finally laid down by management ...
> The framework must include:
>
> - The purpose of the project, which jobs will be affected,
>   and what information needs should be covered.

- What management tries to gain in form of lower
  expenses, higher efficiency or better working conditions ...

- What considerations should be paid to human and
  social aspects and to issues which have to do
  with work organization, job design and working
  environment as a whole ...

- How the project is to be organized and how the
  employees are to be represented.

- A budget and a time plan."

(section 2)

The Swedish agreement covering the central authorities
contains the following:

"The local union has a right to assemble employees
within working hours with the purpose of informing
them ..."

(section 37)

4. EDUCATION

4.1 Useful concepts
Guidelines within this category are concerned with: the <u>type</u>
of education, <u>who</u> is going to participate, the amount of
<u>resources</u> provided for educational purposes, and finally the
employees' possibilities of <u>influencing</u> the form and contents
of educational activities.

type   Two different types of education are relevant. The first is
the <u>job related education</u>. The aim is here to give the participants the necessary insight and skills to carry out the
various functions within a new edp-based system. These educational activities cover a spectrum from, on the one
extreme, simple training in how to operate new equipment to,
on the other extreme, proper education where the participants in addition gain a profound understanding of the
total edp-based system and its relations to the rest of the
organization.

The second type is <u>general education</u>. The aim is here to
give the participants insight and skills to participate in,
or in other ways, to influence the system development
process. These educational activities can be related to a
specific project or they can be even more general.

who   For both types of education we distinguish between whether
all employees or only a few representatives are supposed
to participate.

4.2 Current status
In Sweden this question, like questions related to information, is left open for local negotiation. Danish and Norwegian laws and agreements all contain guidelines on education; but in Denmark educational activities are generally
just recommended, whereas we find several excessive directives on this matter in Norway.

Denmark   Neither the law nor any of the agreements ensure educational activities in relation to the use of edp. In several agreements it is recommended that the affected employees get a job related education, but we find no guidelines suggesting anything but simple training. The law and some local agreements recommend general education, but only for representatives.

However, the central agreement demand that educational activities take place within working hours, and furthermore they provide the representatives with possibilities of influencing the form and contents of job related education.

Norway   According to the law and all central agreements all affected employees have a right, not only to a simple training, but also to a proper job related education; and furthermore representatives have a right to general education in relation to system development and in relation to individual projects.

The central agreements ensure that educational activities take place within working hours and that resources are provided to cover expenses related to educational activities. Finally the central agreements provide the representatives with possibilities of influencing the form and content of all educational activities.

Sweden   The Swedish law contains no guidelines that directly give the employees a right to either job related education or general education. Within the central agreements education is, however, explicitly made a question for local negotiation. In one of the central agreements, representatives are given a right to have a general education, and it is recommended that the employees be given a job related education. Also the question of resources is left for local negotiation, though the central agreements ensure that job related education takes place within working hours.

4.3 Remarkable examples
The most excessive guidelines are found in the Norwegian agreement covering the central authorities.

> "The institution must ensure that representatives and effected employees get the necessary education and introduction to relevant problems. The representatives must always have the necessary introduction to edp-based systems within the institution. The extension and form of educational activities should be laid down by agreement.
>
> Management must in cooperation with representatives ensure that all employees get sufficient information and education on systems under development and in use, so that the employees can understand the significance of the systems and their consequence for both the institution and the employees and their working situation.
>
> Education and information ... is paid by the institution and should be given within working hours."

(section 5.5)

5. RESOURCES

5.1 Useful concepts

Guidelines within this category express that management must or should provide the local unions with resources. Such resources have significant influence on whether the employees can take real advantage of their right to influence the use of edp. We distinguish between three types of resources:

- <u>freedom within working hours</u> for representatives to work on tasks within the local trade union;

- <u>money</u> to be spent on activities within the local trade union. Such money can be used to buy expertise, for educational activities, for visits to other workplaces, etc.;

- <u>special permanent representatives</u> who are protected against arbitrary dismissal.

5.2 Current status

In Norway the employees have a right to elect special permanent representatives, so-called data shop stewards. In Sweden the unions are provided with similar and other resources. Whereas in Denmark the guidelines on this point are few and restricted.

Denmark The law and the central agreements contain no guidelines on resources. Some local agreements allow for data shop stewards, who are protected against arbitrary dismissal. Only a single local agreement provides freedom within working hours for representatives to work on tasks within the local trade union.

Norway In all the central agreements the employees are given a right to elect data shop stewards, who are protected against arbitrary dismissals, and who can work actively for the trade union within working hours.

Sweden Similarly, according to the Swedish central agreements the employees' representatives have a right to work for the trade union within working hours. In addition, the employer is obliged to give the local union money for expert assistance. In one of the central agreements the employer is even obliged to include these expenses in the annual budget. In Sweden there are no special data shop stewards.

5.3 Remarkable examples

The Swedish agreement covering the central authorities contains the following:

"Within the limits of the resources provided by the government, the local trade union can involve own consultants in its activities ...

... in 1978/79 the government provides 4,000,000 Kr. for this purpose."

(section 19)

6. EDP-BASED SYSTEMS

6.1 Useful concepts

The guidelines discussed in the previous sections all deal
with various questions related to the employees' possibilities
of actively influencing the use of edp within an organization. Many laws and agreements also contain guidelines that
directly express requirements to what consequences the use
and development of edp-based systems can have for the employees. In this section we focus on those guidelines that
directly express requirements to the edp-based systems, for
example to the physical working environment and to the contents of the jobs. We have omitted guidelines that deal with
job security and personal data.

6.2 Current status

In all three countries we find a law containing general requirements to the design of edp-bases systems. The detailed
requirements are, however, few and vague.

Denmark   In the law we find a general requirement, that the working
environment should be healthy and safe, and the objective
of most agreements explicitly links together the use of edp
with improved employment, working environment and job satisfaction. A few local agreements contain more detailed guidelines.

Norway   In the law we find similar general requirements to the working
environment and to the contents of the jobs within edp-based
systems. But these general guidelines are not further
elaborated within the agreements.

Sweden   Neither the law nor the central agreements contain requirements to the edp-based system. However, in the central agreements we find recommendations mentioning working environment,
content of jobs and decentralization, and there is another
law in Sweden containing similar general requirements as is
the case in Denmark and Norway.

6.3 Remarkable examples

In the Norwegian law we find the following:

> "Technology and work organization ... should be designed
> so that the employees are not exposed to bad physical
> and psychical strains and so that their possibilities
> of paying respect to safety are not reduced. The design
> should give the employees reasonable possibilities
> for personal and professional development on the job.
>
> When planning and designing jobs one should pay respect
> to the individual employee's possibilities of self-
> control and professional responsibility. One should
> avoid routine work and ... monotonous speed. In
> addition jobs should be designed so that they give
> opportunities for variation, contact with others and
> coherence and so that the employees can keep them-
> selves oriented on production demands and results."

(section 12)

7. DISCUSSION

The previous sections provide insight into existing laws and agreements within the Scandinavian labour market. We close the article by raising two questions: What implications do laws and agreements have on the way edp-based systems should be developed? How could the existing laws and agreements be improved as seen from a trade union point of view?

impli- Looking at the existing laws and agreements as a whole,
cations we find at least the following requirements to the system development process [1]:

1. The system development process must include communication with the employees through negotiations, discussions, hearings and participation.

2. Decisions on the organization of projects and on the design of edp-based systems must be taken in cooperation with the employees.

3. The employees must have information on the organization of projects and on the design of both new and existing systems.

4. The information given to the employees must be easy to understand, clear and without unnecessary use of technical terms. In addition the information must be written.

5. The purposes of a new edp-based system must be explicitly formulated.

6. The consequences of a new edp-based system, as seen from the point of view of the employees, must be analyzed and described.

7. The employees must be given a proper job related education, and at least their representatives must be given a general education.

8. Edp-based systems must be realized to meet the requirements stated within existing laws and agreements.

An analysis of a Scandinavian system development method, RAS [6], clearly shows that this method is far from meeting these requirements [1]. Nevertheless, RAS has been proposed as an international standard for system development methods (ISO-recommendation), and IBM has decided to adhere to RAS within the Scandinavian countries. What about other methods, are they capable of meeting the above mentioned requirements? And what about the existing edp-professional programs, are they capable of producing candidates having the necessary qualifications to meet these requirements?

It is our impression that the edp-profession of today lacks both theoretical and practical knowledge to meet the requirements imposed on the development of edp-based systems by existing laws and agreements.

needs   Even so, the existing guidelines could be more extensive.
Looking at the individual law or agreement, from a trade
union point of view, most guidelines could be improved, often
to a considerable extent, by replacing sections with more
extensive ones from other laws and agreements. This, in
itself, is a very important but difficult task to perform.

Looking at the various regulations as a whole, they only
give the employees limited possibilities to influence the use
of edp:

> "The trade union can, as a minimum, use their right
> to negotiate to delay decisions and tasks for a certain
> period, and the right to receive information can be
> used to get better insight into situations where deci-
> sions are to be taken ... However, the final right to
> take decisions still remains unaffected with the
> employer ..." [3].

As part of a strategy aiming at changing this state of
affairs, more extensive regulations could be made. Such regulations should bind the two parts to reach local agreements
on the organization of projects, and on the design of systems,
and, not less important, they should give the unions the resources necessary to defend their interests in a qualified
and constructive way [2].

Now, we close the discussion by questioning the dominant approach applied in existing laws and agreements. For a long
time, management have tried to control the use of edp by
imposing a rigid structure on the system development process.
We see the new strategies for system development based on
experiments and prototyping [7] as incompatible or even in
conflict with these traditional management strategies: the
experimental strategies are primarily aiming at developing a
high quality product, i.e. an edp-based system, whereas the
traditional management strategies are primarily aiming at
controlling the development process from outside with the
purpose of minimizing costs. We see the dominant approach
built into laws and agreements as one that also primarily aims
at controlling the system development process by predetermin-
ing fixed points for decision and by demanding elaborated
and written specifications of the new edp-based system at an
early stage.

The critique of the sequential phase models is well-known;
and even if written specifications "attempt to bridge the gap
between the user and the designer, they do not serve this
purpose well, because they are incomplete, they take a static
view of requirements, and are often confusing. In addition
it is hard for the end user to visualize the eventual system
from the specifications" [7].

To what extent is the approach built into the existing law
and agreements based on a traditional management view of the
system development process? To what extent do laws and
agreements prevent the use of system development strategies
based on experiments and prototyping? And, if a more experimental type of strategy is in accordance with trade union
interests, what is then the type of guidelines that should
be built into laws and agreements to support such strategies?

FOOTNOTES

1. Computer Science Department, Aarhus University, DK-8000 Aarhus C,
    Denmark.

2. Jutland Telecompany, DK-8310 Tranbjerg J., Denmark.

3. Norwegian Computing Center, Oslo 3, Norway.

4. The study covers three laws (one from each country) and a
    representative selection of relevant agreements (12 central
    agreements and 10 local agreements) made before 1981:

    - Danish law on working environment, 1975.

    - Norwegian law on working environment, 1977.

    - Swedish law on influence by employees, 1977.

    - 6 Danish central, general agreements on cooperation between
      management and employees, 1968-1972.

    - Danish central agreement on technology between TUC and the
      employers' federation, 1981.

    - 7 Danish local agreements on technology, 1976-1981.

    - Norwegian central agreement on technolgoy between TUC and the
      employers' federation, 1978.

    - Norwegian central agreement on technology covering the central
      authorities, 1980.

    - Norwegian central agreement on influence on employees covering
      the central authorities, 1980.

    - 1 Norwegian agreement on technology (Tandberg), 1978-80.

    - 2 Swedish central agreements in continuation of the Swedish law;
      the agreements cover the central authorities, 1978-79.

    - 2 Swedish local agreements in continuation of the law and the
      central agreements, 1979-80.

REFERENCES

Literature

[1]   Scandinavian laws and agreements of importance to system
       development, B. Rolskov and E. Vedel, thesis from Computer
       Science Department, Aarhus University, Denmark, 1981 (in Danish).

[2]   Trade union activity and edp, H. Jacobsen, F. Kensing, M. Kyng
       and L. Mathiassen, Fremad, Copenhagen, Denmark, 1981 (in Danish).

[3]   Management and trade union power, P. Ehn and Å. Sandberg,
       Prisma, Stockholm, Sweden, 1979 (in Swedish).

[4]   Technology agreements in Norway, L. Schneider and C. Ciborra,
       in this volume.

[5]   The trade union response to information technology - Technology
       agreements: consensus, control and technical change in the
       workplace, R. Williams and R. Moseley, in: Information Society
       for richer, for poorer, N. Bjørn-Andersen et al. (ed.),
       North-Holland, 1982.

[6]   Systems development - a constructive model, Swedish Standards
       Institution, Stockholm, SIS Handbook 125, 1975.

[7]   Developing systems by prototyping, B.C. McNurlin, Edp Analyzer,
       vol. 19, no. 9, 1981.

U. Briefs, C. Ciborra and L. Schneider (editors)
North-Holland Publishing Company

USER INVOLVEMENT AND INDUSTRIAL DEMOCRACY:
PROBLEMS AND STRATEGIES IN BRITAIN

Hugo Levie   Robin Williams
Trade Union Research Unit   Technology Policy Unit
Ruskin College   University of Aston
Oxford   Birmingham

The aim of this paper is to further a discussion on
the relationship between user involvement and
industrial democracy.

By industrial democracy we mean a development towards
more control by workers over enterprise and establishment level decisions that determine their own employment, standards of living and the quality of their
working life. Industrial democracy, in our view, can
only be seen as a limited and intermediate goal -
particularly since many people who will be affected
by decisions by major employers are excluded,
especially at a time of high unemployment. Moreover
industrial democracy may be limited to a representation process rather than an ongoing process of
political education involving the whole workforce.
For us, user involvement would mean the involvement of
workers, whose job is based on information technology,
in the design and operation of the system. By this
definition, user involvement is incompatible with an
authoritarian style of management. Moreover, it would
imply, according to us, that the access to knowledge
about the system and training in the operation and
control of the system are no longer management's
prerogative. Finally, we would anticipate user
involvement to reverse certain trends in system design;
it would go against the grain of a high division of
labour, especially the division between creative and
repetitive work.

INTRODUCTION

A discussion of the links between user involvement is not easy,
particularly not in Britain. For one thing industrial democracy
does not exist. For another, in Britain, user involvement is not
at all common practice. Where it occurs it often appears to be
inspired by management - though possibly as a result of concern
about industrial relations problems or uncertainty about systems
design. Such attempts at user involvement may have little in
common with our definition; they tend to be:-

-   a short term response to a specific problem;

-   established outside existing trade union
    consultative procedures;

- limiting the degree of involvement to that
  needed to solve management's immediate
  problems (e.g., winning consent to change,
  tapping the experience of current users to
  improve the design of new systems).

So, in these scarce examples of user involvement, the workers' role
is likely to be passive or constrained.   These constraints do not
lead us to reject user involvement, but to argue that the form and
content of such involvement needs careful consideration.   These
experiments open up important new areas for influence by users and
their unions.   Management attitudes and the goals related to the
experiments may not be monolithic, moreover an important factor in
the outcome of the project is the strategy adapted by users and
their unions.

Our reason for combining these difficult concepts of user involvement and industrial democracy is that unless user involvement is
linked to industrial democracy it may all too easily be degraded
to a fashionable management technique.   On top of that   , user
involvement as part of a strategy to gain more influence over change
within companies   could well be the missing plank in trade union
strategies on the introduction of new technology.   We will draw a
parallel here with the emergence in the 1970's of Health and Safety
as a major new issue for trade union representatives.

This paper is based upon the mechanisms for handling technological
change in industrial relations in Britain; the pattern of bargaining,
developments in management strategy and the problems trade unionists
face in negotiating technological change.   After considering the
successes of union involvement to control work hazards, we discuss
possible strategies by which unions could attempt to influence
technological change and its effects on work.

2.   PATTERNS OF BARGAINING OVER TECHNOLOGICAL CHANGE

(a) The background : industrial relations in Britain

This is not the place to provide a detailed analysis of the structure of British industrial relations, but we can make the following
generalisations.   They provide the background for what follows.

1)   Commitments between employers and unions are
      implemented voluntarily rather than through
      legislation.   In the firm this will be con-
      ducted within broad procedural agreements
      backed up by informal agreements, in particular
      to maintain existing custom and practice.

2)   Bargaining is largely decentralised and is con-
      ducted primarily at plant or company level,
      often within an industry wide framework.   The
      central organisation of trade unions (TUC) and
      especially of employers (CBI) have little or no
      direct involvement in bargaining.

3) The post-war decline in central bargaining has
   been accompanied by the widespread emergence
   of independent shopfloor representatives or shop
   stewards.

4) Although there are craft, industry and general
   unions, most enterprises will be characterised
   by multi-union organisation(1).

(b) Trade union strategies for dealing with change

A possible trade union strategy is one of non-involvement: let management make whatever change they want, we will reduce its effectiveness and clawback most of our gains of the past. Thus, a TGWU
convenor at a British Leyland factory where considerable technical
change was occurring, said, "we will take it in our stride". He
was confident that after the new line was introduced, the unions
could re-establish their labour rights as they had done with
earlier model and tooling changes. Before we talk about trade union
strategies for user involvement and increased workers control, it is
necessaryto indicate that this presumes the confidence, or interest
that workers can influence system design. It also presupposes a
holistic approach to technical and social change, which is not
necessarily compatible with trade union traditions in the UK.

So not all bargaining strategies are aimed at achieving some user
involvement. There are however some problems relating to a fragmented strategy of "clawback" that are pushing trade unions towards
the more holistic, sophisticated strategies:

> a strategy of clawback is not particularly suited
> to coping with the employment effects of new
> technology;

> "clawback" may compound existing divisions bet-
> ween groups of workers and different trade
> unions. This will reduce the unions' under-
> standing of the relationship between different
> changes that are going on and it can further
> marginalise exactly what can be clawed back;

> "clawback" does not take into account that both
> the game and pitch are changing. Components of
> existing trade union power, such as control over
> skills, experience, basic work organisation could
> turn out to be based on quicksand.

(c) Technology Agreements

An ambitious development in union policy for dealing with the
introduction of new technology has been the proposal for Technology
Agreements. The TUC in 1979 published an influential document,
"The Employment and Technology Report". Like earlier TUC policies
it calls for action by government and employers to "smooth the
process of change". However, in addition, it calls for trade union
influence over the process of technological change itself, in order
to minimise possible negative effects on conditions of employment
and union organisation that had been associated with the introduction

of new technology and work systems (e.g., on employment, skills, health and safety). To this end, the report included a 10 point 'Checklist for Negotiators of New Technology Agreements', which covered both procedural aspects on technological change, access to information and substantive issues (e.g., employment levels, hours, and wages, skills, training, machine monitoring etc). Many individual unions produced model agreements to provide more concrete guidance to implement this approach in negotiation.

Union representatives faced substantial problems in achieving these goals in practice. The wave of Technology Agreements which followed, only embodied the TUC and individual union guidelines to a limited degree(2).(See Table 1 overleaf). Below we describe the provisions regarding union involvement in decision making over technological change and work organisation, with illustrations from some of the stronger agreements.

Union involvement in decision making

Overall, few agreements fulfilled the TUC's objective that change must be by mutual agreement. One example was the agreement concluded between the General Accident Fire and Life Assurance Corporation Limited and APEX and ASTMS (general clerical and technical unions) that

> "The corporation agrees not to introduce or
> install any such new equipment without having
> first reached agreement with (the unions) or
> having exhausted (negotiation) procedures in
> this agreement".

To this end the corporation agreed to advise the union of proposals to commence feasibility studies and to provide with details of specifice proposals for the introduction or extension of applications of new technologies which could affect working arrangements, conditions etc.

The notion of prior agreement (mutuality) lacks from most Technology Agreements. Nonetheless, most of the agreements laid down a specific procedure for negotiating change. Change would only take place when agreement had been reached, or the different stages of negotiation had been completed. Frequently, it appears that union involvement would not begin until the later stages of the process of designing new technology systems, even though union policy stressed the need for union involvement from the earliest stages.

Work organisation

The consequences of changed work organisation were typically covered, if at all, to defensive clauses (e.g., dealing with grading or demarcation). Few agreements showed indication of a positive attempt by unions to shape work organisation. For example, in our sample, only four established any sort of procedure or guidelines for dealing with job design. An example of the latter was an agreement between Humber Graving Dock and Engineering Co. and APEX which included a commitment that:

"Full analysis, through joint union/management committees, will take place in respect of the effects of new systems on job content and job satisfaction. Jobs will be carefully designed to ensure that routine and monotony are mini- mised".

Two of the agreements conceded that the job satisfaction of a minority of employees might be impaired by new technology and systems but accepted this in order to maintain the security of employment of the majority.

The failure of Technology Agreements negotiated in practice to achieve the TUC and individual union guidelines must be seen in the light not only of the traditions of reactive bargaining in the UK but more significantly in terms of management strategies on the introduction of new technology and in particular a significant shift in the climate of industrial relations in the UK in recent years. These factors have possibly also slowed down the rate of signing Technology Agreements . At the time of writing, some 300 Technology Agreements have been identified in Britian(3). However, since these typically cover only a part of the workforce, or one plant of a company it is clear that only a very small proportion of the total workforce are covered by Technology Agreements.

Table 1 summarises the distribution and content of 100 Technology Agreements.

Table 1 over........

Table I:

SUMMARY OF 100 AGREEMENTS DEALING WITH TECHNOLOGICAL CHANGE

Number of unions signatory to each Agreement

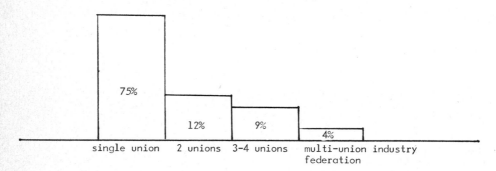

Grade of labour covered

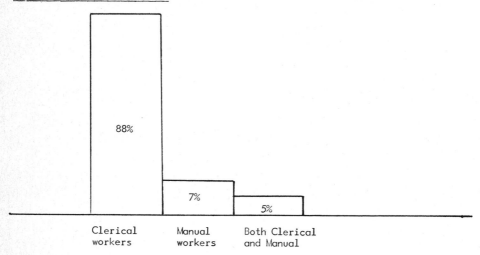

Degree of union involvement

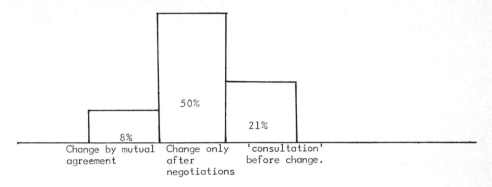

First stage of union involvement

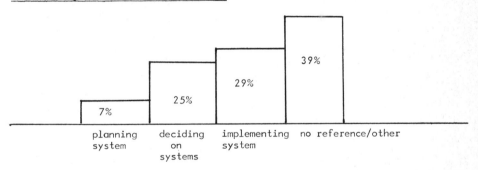

Manning levels

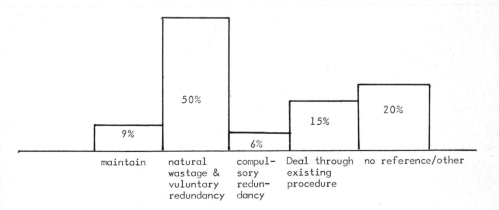

VDU design and installation

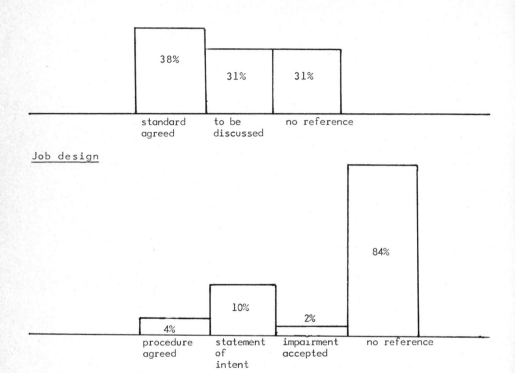

Job design

(Derived from R. Williams and R. Moseley, Technology Agreements, paper presented at EEC/FAST Conference, The Transition to an Information Society, London, 27th January, 1982.)

3.   MANAGEMENT STRATEGIES ON THE INTRODUCTION OF NEW TECHNOLOGY

A central strand in the policy statements of government, academics, and even employers' organisations stresses that the successful management of technological change requires flexibility and the relaxation of demarcation controls amongst the workforce. Despite differences of emphasis these commentators agree on the consequent need to involve workers and their representatives in discussion over change (spanning proposals for Productivity Agreements in the mid-1960's to Technology Agreements in the late 1970's) (4).

This 'social democratic' conception of "a good Industrial Relations Practice" would give unions space to develop involvement in technological change. However, it has increasingly come under attack in management practice. The impact of a world recession which has been particularly deep in Britain, compounded by government monetary policies, has led to record levels of unemployment. This has under-mined the confidence and ability of trade unions to defend trad-itional areas of pay and job security let alone the possibility of achieving a significant extension of their influence. In contrast, an offensive style of management has developed involving the introduction of technological change on a unilateral basis, often linked with imposition of new conditions of labour which formerly were subject to joint regulation.

The premier example of this shift in management practice was the BL Metro line at Longbridge, during the Ryder participation scheme, where a comprehensive joint participation structure had been established that involved unions, amongst other things, in the commissioning of one of the largest single projects of technological investment in the country. This had some limited success (for example, dealing with health and safety problems at Longbridge). Despite this, an offensive was launched by the management against the union organisation which involved the victimisation of the union convenor and the curtailment of shop stewards' activities. Participation collapsed and the final stages of the Metro project were conducted by dictat rather than consultation. Similarly, the introduction of the Triumph Acclaim at BL Body Plant in Cowley 3 years after the Metro was on a unilateral basis. The whole assembly line was bought 'off the shelf' by BL, and while it was being built workers did not know what was going to happen 2 weeks in advance.(5)

This pattern of unilaterally imposed change has been repeated up and down the country. Particular examples of this strategy are "accept change or else" and "greenfield" development.

"Accept change or else" was the choice Reckitt and Colman in Hull gave its workers. Either their workplace, an ultramarine plant, would be totally renovated with the loss of nearly 2/3 of all production jobs; or the plant would be closed altogether. Not surprisingly, the workers and their shop stewards did not feel they had much choice.

The strategy of "greenfield" development has been adopted in different forms. In its purest form a whole new plant is built as an alternative to existing plants. The first sight of the new plant is given to the workers in the old one, when some of them are given the chance to transfer. This strategy is particularly suited to process industry, it appears; new breweries and dairies for example have been opened in this way. However, the same strategy can also be followed where a department, or building on an existing site can be hived off from the production process and equipped with new technology by an outside contractor. This happened for example at British Leyland at Cowley. A building that only was used for storage, was turned into the new paint shop. Access was prohibited to all employees, until some of the workers of the old paint shop were phased in to start production.

Whilst many managers have not wanted, or have not been able to adopt such aggressive styles of 'managing technological change', these experiences, joined with widespread declaration of redundancies in many industries have formed the context of discussion over the introduction of new technologies in workplaces.

In contrast to this rather depressing situation, it is important to note recent proposals for handling change originating from academic technologists and systems designers concerned to utilise the skills and experience of the workforce. In initial experiments, technologists tapped the knowledge of workers to design new systems. It is now suggested that the earlier that users are involved in

systems design, the greater is the opportunity to introduce systems
in a flexibile manner. Ultimately, systems should be designed
with user involvement at every stage, on a continuous and evolutionary basis. This proposal calls for a cyclical systems design
method, open to feedback. This is in direct contrast to the
traditional linear and hierarchical model. The method was held to
offer substantial benefits for organisations implementing change,
in particular in ensuring that new systems were appropriate to the
current needs of the organisation and adaptable to future
requirements. (6)

It remains to be seen whether initiatives by socially concerned
technologists will open up a space for union influence over technological change. In the past, such initiatives have had limited
value for trade unionists because they have been divorced from
union perspectives and concerns. Thus there has been a tendency in
discussion of 'user involvement in system design' to ingore the
relationship between technological change and wider questions of
corporate policy. British trade unions cannot spearate these
concerns, particularly at a time of profound restructuring and
rationalisation in the private sector, and financial constraints and
ideological attacks in the public sector. There are good reasons
why the attention of trade unions has been focussed on to the
immediate threats to jobs and living standards, away from a longer
term strategy. However, exactly because we believe that a trade
union's success in defending employment partly depends on its own
policies on technology, it still is highly relevant and
useful to consider the difficulties unions have experienced
in negotiating technological change.

4.   THE DIFFICULTY OF NEGOTIATING TECHNOLOGICAL CHANGE

In the UK, experience has been that, rather than posing totally
new problems, negotiating technological change accentuates already
existing problems of trade union organisation. One research project based on four case studies gave a detailed account of these
weaknesses of trade union organisation. In "The Impact of New
Technology on Trade Union Organisation" four cases of introduction
of new technology were examined, within British Leyland, Midland
Bank, Tooling Investments (ex-Alfred Herbert) and GEC Telecommunications. In none of these cases was the technological change itself
negotiated. The effects of the changes might be the subject of
collective bargaining, such as redundancies (GEC), changes in job
description (Midland Bank,) changes in working practices (Tooling
Investment), changes in manning levels and grading (British Leyland).
However, bargaining of these issues took place after the investment
in specific equipment had been made (7).

A similar pattern is apparent from the ways in which technology
agreements fell short of union guidelines, where there was a
tendency for union involvement to be provided late in the process
of introducing change or to be limited to some of its consequences,
in particular on employment levels.

Apart from the difficult political and economic context within which
trade unions in the UK have to operate, two major clusters of
problems cause this lack of genuine negotiations: first, the problem
of finding alternatives to the machinery, or software the company is
proposing. Instinctively worker representatives may be convinced
that management are wrong, when they present their own plans as the

inevitable "only way". But without an idea where alternatives can be found, how they can be developed, these worker representatives will have a hard time convincing their own members of the viability of alternatives, let alone management. Second, existing patterns of <u>collective bargaining</u>(i) and <u>trade union organisation</u> (ii)are not exactly conducive to the kind of negotiations we are thinking of.

(i) <u>Collective bargaining</u> is often concentrated in annual wage negotiations and subjects like technological change, work organisation, change in the content of functions do not fit very well into this pattern. Also, the agenda of annual negotiations is often already overloaded. Another problem related to collective bargaining is that it may not take place at the right level to facilitate negotiations on investment plans. Frequently negotiations only occur on one level, whilst investment planning needs to be seen at various levels of concern. Examples of this include a large brewing concern in the UK where all negotiations are done on a regional, or local basis, but where investment is decided by Head Office, and implemented by local management in conjunction with the corporate technology and plant erection subsidiary. In this case there just does not seem to be the platform on which the unions involved could start to negotiate major technological change. At the other extreme, there have been cases where there is some consultation of investment plans at a national level, without any negotiations on detail at a lower level. This happened, for example at British Leyland in the period 1976-1978 and it was not a very useful practice.

(ii) Closely related to these problematic patterns of bargaining are the following weaknesses in <u>trade union organisation</u>:

> There may be a <u>mismatch</u> between the organisation of worker representatives and that of management. (An interesting response to the problem facing clerical workers (APEX members) in the multi-plant firm of Lucas Industries was to seek information on the management structure and to establish a set of union committees in parallel). Particularly where technological change is part of a wider programme or company reorganisation, (which was the situation in the four case studies mentioned above), it may be hard for local worker representatives to grasp the links between different changes that are going on.

> Even without technical change, most worker representatives are already <u>grossly under-informed</u> about managements' plans for the future, and many more mundane aspects relating to the running of the company. This situation can be crudely exposed when they are confronted by major technical change and wonder where these changes come from. What does not help either is that the same worker representatives often have little information about their industry in general. This makes it more difficult to anticipate developments that could take place in their own workplace and to be aware of technological alternatives.

.   New technology can sharpen the <u>divisions between</u>
        <u>different unions</u>. This is of course particularly
        true for the British situation. In engineering,
        the fight between operators (Amalgamated Union of
        Engineering Workers - Engineering Section) and
        programmers (AEUW - Technical, Administrative and
        Supervisory Section) has already become a classic
        linked to the introduction of CNC machine tools.
        In other countries both groups may be contained within
        one and the same trade union; this does not mean that
        the problem does not exist.

.   Technical change can expose major problems relating to
        the role of the <u>trade union representative</u>. If there
        is no active shop stewards' committee, the individual
        representatives may be too isolated to see the links
        between the impact of a new production system on his/
        her section and what is happening to workers in other
        sections. If there is a full-time worker represent-
        ative who does most of the union work, he or she may
        be so isolated from the members and their jobs that
        it becomes difficult to anticipate the effects of
        technological change.

.   Technical change can make it practically <u>impossible to</u>
        <u>continue</u> with an existing trade union organisation .
        For example, because a number of representatives are
        lost through redundancies (accidentally , or as part
        of management's strategy for change), or because
        previously separate departments are merged. We found
        some examples of how trade unions are turning this
        threat into an advantage. Change is bringing different
        white collar unions within GEC Telecommunications
        together.

5.   HEALTH AND SAFETY AT WORK

Controlling the risk to health and safety of work has become a major
area of union influence in recent years, through which unions have
had a significant impact on the technology and organisation of
production. What are the lessons for effective union involvement
in new technology?

Under the 1974 Health and Safety at Work Act, shopfloor union representatives (safety representatives) have had legal rights which
include the right to inspect the workplace, and to receive information and consult about hazards with the employer. This right also
covers proposed changes in production. What is important is not
the legal rights themselves, but the ways that they have been
consolidated as a central part of trade union activity in the workplace.

The effectiveness of shopfloor activity is supported by a substantial information and education programme conducted by the TUC and
individual unions. This developed a critique of existing standards
and approaches to controlling hazards and led to a distinctive trade
union policy embodying a collective approach (e.g., controlling
hazards by re-engineering the process rather than by getting
individual workers to wear protective equipment). In addition, a
variety of sources of information were tapped outside the official

trade union movement, including links with sympathetic academics. As a result, union representatives were often better informed than the managers they were negotiating with.

We can illustrate this by examining the response to the introduction of Visual Display Units (VDUs) which have become the symbol of the introduction of microelectronic-based technologies into the every-day working situation.(8) Union policy documents focussed on the possible health hazards of VDUs (the first TUC education document on VDUs was from a safety representative training course), and in particular: physiological damage (eye strain and damage, radiation hazards, ergonomics of workstation) arising from the construction of the equipment and its installation.

Most of the technology agreements included standards for installation of VDUs or a commitment to discuss them. It has been suggested that trade union pressure has played a major role in stimulating improved design of VDUs.

Trade union standard setting has allowed achievements as part of a programme of union education and organisation. This may offer a way forward for union involvement over technological change and job design. However, the latter areas posed additional problems.

Software and job design received less attention in union policy documents than VDU ergonomics; this difference was even more marked in negotiated technology agreements. A major factor underlying this uneven development is the different nature of knowledge of these matters. Standards can be produced centrally on VDU ergonomics. In contrast systematic knowledge on job design is much less precise and it may only prove possible to define concrete standards in relation to the specific system/jobs involved. Clearly, union involvement on this topic will require much greater development of resources, particularly at local level .

6. A STRATEGY FOR TRADE UNION ACTION

(a) Possible directions for union influence

Trade unions could adopt a range of strategies at company level to influence the nature and impacts of new technology. We would like to pick out three approaches in particular.

(1) Bargaining is limited to major <u>conditions of employment</u> (e.g., wage and employment areas). New technology is discussed only insofar as it cuts across these conditions. This concedes major areas as being management prerogative, and as we have seen, is particularly unsuited for dealing with the impacts of the current wave of new technology.

(2) Bargaining over the full range of <u>effects of new technology</u> and associated working methods including detailed discussion of manning, training, grading/ job evaluation, skill and career development etc. This bargaining constrains, but does not attempt to get involved in management decision making over change - we describe this as EXTERNAL INFLUENCE. Such bargaining may take place a) after the new

system is implemented - "after the fact" b)or
before/during the process of introductory change -
"before the fact". (See for these terms also the
paper by Claudio Ciborra and Leslie Klein).

(3)   Unions may attempt to seek <u>direct involvement in
       management decision making</u> e.g., through joint
       working parties etc., - and in the case of new
       technology they may seek representation in the
       systems design process itself. We describe this
       as INTERNAL INFLUENCE. It is important to stress
       that internal involvement in our view would not
       preclude genuine negotiations, it is certainly not
       identical to collaborative definitions of
       participation.

Real life situations may fall between these three positions. For
example, though the bulk of union activity in Britain formally
corresponds to 1., where union organisation is well established,
informal discussion would take place over a wider range of changes,
e.g., customary methods of working.

(b) <u>External influence, before or after the fact?</u>

Where there is substantial choice about the form of technology and
this is particularly the case with electronic data processing,
"after the fact" bargaining suffers from a major limitation.
By the time the technology is being implemented many characteristics
of the system will have been fixed and the scope for negotiating
over the impacts may be reduced (e.g., manning levels, the way
tasks are organised into jobs - with consequent effects on skill,
grading, training). Whilst earlier agreements or anticipated union/
worker resistance may influence the design of future systems,(9)
the union itself is left with a reactive role. Influence of this
sort is unreliable, especially in the not infrequent situation
where new technology is designed to undermine such job control. (10)

Before the fact bargaining can come into effect <u>before</u> or <u>during</u>
the decision making and design process. Our survey of technology
agreements indicates that discussion at the very earliest stages
of defining the need for new systems, feasibility studies, pilot
schemes, are rare (7%) and mainly occur in the public sector. The
text of a further 25% of agreements made it clear that bargaining
would begin before a decision had been reached, but after the
initial design and selection work had been conducted. Clearly
before the fact bargaining offers the unions a longer time span and
much greater opportunity to seek to shape the impact of new
technology. However, explicit bargaining over change depends on
the ability of the trade unions: i) to assess the whole range of
possible impact of new technology; ii) to assess their own power
and ambitions to modify the technology; and hence iii) to set
their own goals, negotiate them with management and monitor their
introduction. A major problem confronting this strategy is the way
that given policies of new technology and associated systems are
presented as the only possibility - especially given the increasing
tendency to buy 'off-the shelf' packages of equipment and software.
Where a variety of systems are commercially available, they may show
only minor differences, reflecting the factors that have shaped the
 bulk of systems development to date. This tendency both saps the
confidence of the unions to embark on bargaining and obstructs

their ability to propose changes. Internal influence has been
proposed as a means of overcoming these problems.

(c) Internal influence

lt is argued that by seeking direct involvement in decision making
over technological change the unions can actively and explicitly
influence the nature of the system eventually introduced and
consequently the impact it will have on workers. Influencing
system design objectives and methods allows unions to go beyond a
reactive response and generate a positive and progressive model for
change. However, this approach takes unions into technical and
organisational areas that may be far removed from their traditional
skills. Probably many of the existing weaknesses of trade union
organisation (mentioned in section 4) would have to be tackled, if
such a move into new areas were to be successful.

There has been little experience of 'Internal Involvement' in
Britain. The approach derives from experiments in worker participation in the rather different industrial relations systems of
Scandinavia and West Germany (often based on legal participation and
co-determination rights). Experience of such participation in
Britain has been problematic. There have been examples where union
representation on technical committees had negligible influence on
deliberations but enabled management to insist that unions accepted
implementation of a decision to which they were party. Fear of this
so-called 'hostage phenomenon' has led many union members to resist
internal influence. Maintaining an independent union perspective
through such a participatory process would require three forms of
support for trade union representatives:-

 (i) development of an independent trade union pers-
       pective on characteristics required of new
       technology, to help the representatives avoid
       identifying themselves unreservedly with the
       systems being proposed;

 (ii) trade union mobilisation to provide support for
       and maintain the accountability of the union
       representatives;

 (iii) the resources necessary to develop i) and ii).
       For example, time off for joint meetings at work,
       paid educational leave, independent external
       advice, facilities to research the technical
       options.

If this is not done, participation could leave the main body of the
union organisation with only a passive role, whilst the participating representatives would lack power and would have little basis
to make a real input into the development of more user friendly
production and information systems. This strategy raises wider
questions about avenues for industrial democracy and the role of
participatory approaches (issues which divide the trade union movement as well as management). 'Participation' is not a natural
demand for trade unionists, during a period of redundancies and
closures. The combination of technological change and restructuring
and cuts that characterises the current British situation make it
all the more important for unions to integrate their strategy for
technological development with their strategy for the development
of the enterprise. (11)

Some conceptions of internal influence have little relevance for British trade unionists. We would suggest that potential benefits of internal influence can only be realised if it is combined with the bargaining approach of 'external influence'. For example, the deliberations of joint working parties should be open for collective discussion and negotiation (12). This would have to involve changes in the method of introducing microprocessor based production and information systems - with each stage of decision making and design open to amendement.

A convergence of external and internal influence could also be helped along if the evolutionary systems design method already mentioned (6) was adopted more widely. This would certainly create the necessary space for workers to develop their own involvment from their own premises (13).

(d) A way forward for 'external' influence

Certain forms of external involvement could be pursued by trade unions that would help create space for user involvement. Dependent on the political circumstances and trade union traditions, some of the following points would be negotiated with employers, or employers' federations, others might be introduced through state involvement.

The 'shopping list' approach we have adopted indicates the lack of development of union activity in this field, as well as the wide range of opportunities which need to be critically analysed and tested in practice.

   (i)   Consultation and negotiation rights

       The examples of data agreement in Norway, Works Council Law in Germany, Belgium and Holland, and industrial democracy legislation in Sweden, all give a starting point for shop stewards' committees or works councils that want to negotiate new technology. (14) Whether, and how these rights are used is another matter, but their existence could strengthen the hand of trade union representatives that want to develop user involvment - as has happened on the subject of health and safety. One of the things that trade unions will continue to do is to fight for better consultation and negotiation rights. If user involvement was made into a trade union demand, this would have immediate consequences for the kind of extension of consultation and nego-tiation rights that would be sought especially regarding advance planning. (For example, the right to negotiate all feasibility studies that could affect the work organisation).

   (ii)   Information rights

       Certainly in Britain, worker representatives have extremely limited information rights (15). Detailed demands for the right of access to historical and prospective information would certainly help the development of user involvement. Especially if not just the representatives, but also the workers them-selves had the right to know about plans that might affect their job.

(iii) Bargaining levels

It is a common situation in Britain that collective bargaining mainly occurs at one level; plant level, national level, or sometimes regional level. Taking major investment decisions is not a process that happens at one level. If it was established as a basic right, that trade unions can negotiate at all levels of a company, this again would help the development considerably. (The Vredeling proposals of the EEC would certainly help in this respect. However, the recent abortion of these proposals by the European Parliament, after unprecedented lobbying by especially American multi-nationals is just another example of the resistance against any form of democratic involvement of workers) (16)

(iv) Trade union organisation

It was indicated in a previous section that part of the problems trade unions have, facing technical change stem from existing weaknesses of union organisation . Particularly where technical change affects different groups of workers, at different plants, it is hard to imagine more user involvement, without active joint shop stewards' committees at plant level and active combine committees at enterprise level.

(v) Standards of work organisation

As we saw, union standards have been very effective in the field of health and safety or, for that matter, the regulation of the working day. So far the main union standards in this field are those controlling VDU operation times (which enforce a degree of job rotation), but agreements have also been reached on questions of machine monitoring of performance, privacy etc. Commitments regarding job evaluation, career structure etc., may also bring improvements in job design indirectly. Though there has been little development of standards of work organisation, it should be possible to embody the positive achievements of experiments in user involvement within concrete standards that could be adopted in a wide range of similar working situations (e.g., operator programming of CNC machines).

(e) A way forward for 'internal' influence

The previous section was not exhaustive, but it indicated that trade unions could do many things to increase their influence on technical change, via negotiations that are external to the introduction of new technology. This could be complemented with demands of the following more 'internal' nature:

(i) Paid educational leave

The idea of user involvement may be challenging to many workers' conceptions of their own abilities and legitimate roles. Consequently they will need time to gain confidence and to study technological and social possibilities. This will require the right to paid educational leave, in particular for courses run by the trade unions(17).

(ii)   Worker consultants and worker research

Access to outside specialists would greatly facilitate genuine user involvement. Certainly in Britain
the resources for this are unlikely to come from the
unions, who therefore would have to approach the
employers or government to provide them. However,
the relationship between the 'expert' and the workers
involved needs careful consideration. Unless alternative expertise is tied in to union needs, it may
not enable unions to increase the effectiveness of their
influence over change. (It could be argued that the
lack of those links explains the strong dislike in the
British trade union movement for this type of
experiment).

(iii)   The accountability of systems designers

At present systems designers are at the most accountable to management, however, in practice the designers
can have a rather free hand, as long as they generally identify with management's objectives. To some
extent, systems designers may well be able to use this
freedom by becoming more accountable to users. At
present they will involve these users frequently, but
only in a passive role, as sources of information, as
study objects. However, as we have seen, some systems
designers are beginning to seek a more reciprocal
relationship with users. This involvement could be a
basis for the shift in accountability of systems
designers. Another potential avenue might be through
the designers' trade union organisation , though this
channel has been of limited use to date in Britain.
Success on this and the previous matter will be
facilitated greatly by changes in the education and
professional conception of systems designers (18).

(iv)   Experimenting with user involvement

In Britain, there have not been many trade union inspired experiments in user involvement. In fact is is
likely that whatever experiments did take place came
about through management initiative. To ensure that
user involvment in practice gives workers a genuine
influence over new technology, instead of easing its
introduction, unions should not leave the experimenting
to the more enlightened management schools. Moreover,
to help trade unions and workers distinguish between
'real' and 'cosmetic' user involvment, unions need to
conduct their own monitoring of different experiments
in involvement.

(v)   Training on new systems

Maybe one of the best starting points for trade unionists
who want to develop user involvement is the training of
users for new systems. The basic question is whether
the training is limited and narrow, or whether it gives
the user a real understanding of the total system (19).
Does the training pave the way for deskilling and loss
of control over the work process, or does it give the
users a chance to retain or adapt their skills and
control?(20)

vi)   <u>User-friendly systems</u>

In particular, accessibility of the software of a
new system can greatly influence the real chances
to develop user involvement. How easy is it for
users to adapt, or edit programmes? Or, for example, could the worker representatives use the
system to store, or compute some of their own data?

vii) <u>Alternative Models for Technology</u>

An opportunity for unions to shape the technology
(as well as its consequences) through 'external
influence' exists, where micro-processor based
production and/or information systems that fulfil union requirements have been developed in
similar plants. In this situation, unions could
negotiate for this alternative system to be implemented. There are examples of this in health and
safety - e.g., bargaining for safer substitutes
to be adopted for hazardous materials. Unfortunately
there are not that many examples of such alternative technologies, or if they exist, we do not know
about them.

Effective communication systems would be needed to
disseminate the experience of desirable systems to
workplaces facing similar types of automation. This
approach, confers to 'external influence' some of the
benefits of 'internal influence' and would also be a
valuable tool for the latter.

6. CONCLUSIONS

The value of proposals for user-involvement cannot be assessed in
isolation of its industrial relations context. We would argue
that if user involvement is to be more than a short-lived management
technique it must be part of a development in industrial democracy.
However, we are not unreservedly optimistic about such a development taking place. There is little immediate prospect of an
increase in industrial democracy, not withstanding the fact that
with new technology the need for it only grows.

We discussed themeans by which unions could begin to develop
effective influence over the planning, design and introduction of
technological change. Genuine user involvment would only happen
if there was the fullest development of a forward looking union
strategy for new technology. This represents a massive task for
trade union representatives, officials and researchers involving
developments right across the span of trade union activities
including: organisation, (within and beyond the individual workplace), education, research and information services and policy-
making. This expenditure of effort is unlikely unless there are an
increasing number of examples where user involvement has become a
democratic reality and yielded positive results for the users in
terms of relationships in the workplace and the nature of new
systems. Without examples of success many workplace organisations
will lack the confidence and stimulus to embark on such an
ambitious project.

In addition, user involvement will involve not just acceptance of
change, but the active support of many other parties. The experts -
systems designers and analysts, computer scientists - will have
to embrace a change in their role and relationship with users.   A
broader range of groups will be involved in discussion of the
objectives and methods of systems design.   This will be an important
step in shifting technological change away from a mostly uniform
development based on partial definitions of the technical potential
employer's desire to increase their control over "their" workers and
narrow conceptions of economic efficiency.   For user involvement
to be worthwhile the systems design process will need to be more
open.   Its objectives will have to be changed, taking into account
the social preferences of user groups; and its results must be more
diverse - relecting the changed priorities and methods.   These
changes must be taken up, not just by systems designers in industry
and consultants, but must be incorporated in academic training and
research.

Management faces a choice as to whether to accept or resist demands
for greater openness and user-influence in planning technological
change.   If user involvement is to be more than a token gesture,
management must be convinced to provide information to users and
their representatives as well as the resources (e.g., time-off)
needed to utilise this information.   Legislation might play an
important role in this respect.

The important role that government might play in developing the
possibilities for user involvement has received little attention
in this paper - mainly because current government policies in
Britain have operated against such developments.   As well as
legislation, government economic policies and science and technology
policies have an important effect on the rate and context of
technological change.   It is probably no coincidence that many of
the firms signing technology agreements (especially for CAD) were
on Ministry of Defence contracts.   Factors that helped the unions
involved pushing for Technology Agreements were that these contracts with the Ministry of Defence part financed the investment
in new technology, that the contracts gave an outlook on fairly
stable markets and finally that most of these contracts were concluded around 1979 when the trade unions were still in a reasonable
position to negotiate.

The direct predecessor to Technology Agreements was the Planning
Agreement - which involved unions, employers and government.   Whilst
Planning Agreements did not fulfil union hopes (21), it is clear
that state intervention in industry and public sector policy could
provide important opportunities for development of industrial
democracy and user involvement alike (22).

RFERENCES

1.   E. Batstone, I. Benson and S. Frenkel : <u>Shop Stewards in Action</u>, Blackwells, Oxford, 1977

2.   R. Williams and R. Moseley: "Technology Agreements". Paper presented to EEC/FAST Conference: <u>The Transition to an Information</u> Society, London, 27th January, 1982 This paper derives from an investigation at the Technology Policy Unit into trade unions and policies for technological change funded by the UK Social Science Research Council.

3.   The total number of Technology Agreements is not known, but probably exceeds 500. A sample of 225 Agreements is discussed in <u>Survey of New Technology</u>, Labour Research Department, Bargaining Report 22, 1982.

4.   Examples of the discussion on introduction of microelectronics:

       . J. Sleigh <u>et al</u>: <u>The Manpower Implications of Microelectronic Technology</u>, Department of Employment Report, London, HMSO, 1979.

       . Confederation of British Industry : <u>Jobs Facing the Future</u>, Staff Discussion Document, CBI, London, 1980

       . Institute of Personnel Management : <u>Personnel Management and New Technology</u>, IPM, London, 1981.

       . Memorandum by CBI and Secretary of State for Employment to National Economic Development Council, London. Documents NEDC (80)7 and (80)1, dated 19.12.79 and 3.12.79 respectively.

5.   Roy Moore and Hugo Levie: <u>The Impact of New Technology on Trade Union Organisation</u>, report on research sponsored by DG V, Commission of the European Communities, Study 1138-81; Ruskin College, Oxford, 1981.

6.   K.D. Eason: <u>The Process of Introducing New Technology</u>, HUSAT Memo., No. 239, Loughborough University of Technology, Loughborough, August, 1981.

7.   Roy Moore and Hugo Levie, <u>op. cit</u>.

8.   R. Williams and B. Pearce: "Design, New Technology and Trade Unions". Paper presented at <u>Design Policy Conference</u>, Royal College of Art, London, 20th-23rd July, 1982.

9.   For example, a few years ago a British engineering firm bought CNC lathes without tool changers, because they could not then imagine getting agreement to 'one man' (sic) operating more than one machine and they 'had to leave him something to do'.

10.   B. Wilkinson. "The Politics of Innovation in the Workplace", Harper and Row, London, 1983.

11.   This point is brought out most strongly in the policy document on technological change brought out by the biggest general union (mainly for manual workers) - the TGWU - "Microelectronics: Old Problems, New Opportunities", 1980.

12.   This approach is apparent in the proposal by ASTMS for 'Technology
       Conferences' - joint working parties on new technology which are in
       effect sub-committees which refer back to the central negotiating
       committee.   "Technology Agreements", ASTMS Circular GS 245,
       30th August 1979.

13.   Lars Mathiassen and Morten Kyng.   "Systems Development and Trade Union
       Activities". Paper presented to EEC/FAST Conference, The Transition
       to an Information Society, London, 27th January, 1982.

14.   John Evans: The Negotiation of Technological Change, European Trade
       Union Institute, Brussels, March, 1982.

15.   Trade Union Research Unit: Trade Unions, New Technology and Disclosure
       and Use of Company Information, Seminar Report, April 1982. Also.
       "A Sieve with Tiny Holes", TURU Occasional Paper No. 75, May 1982.

16.   Financial Times, 10th and 18th October 1982.

17.   The link between union strategies on new technology and paid educational
       leave is discussed in TURU Discussion Paper No. 28 on Paid Educational
       Leave, November 1982.

18.   For a significant initiative in this field see : Work Research Unit:
       The Design of Manufacturing Systems, Department of Employment, WRU,
       London, May 1982.

19.   Training is often limited in two ways: very little time is allocated to
       it and in that far too short period, the people who are trained for the
       new system only get to know their immediate tasks. Learning how the
       whole system works is not included in the training. At Vauxhall Motors
       in Luton even the vendor of a new office system was unpleasantly
       surprised to find out that the women (TASS-members) who were supposed
       to operate it, had received only 3 days training. This was far less
       than the   vendor of the system had advised.

20.   A lot of insight into the importance of trade union demands on training
       is given in a case study on the change over to photo-composition at
       a Dutch Newspaper concern. FNV Research Department, Amsterdam, June 1982.

21   "State Intervention in Industry : A Workers Inquiry" Coventry, Liverpool,
       Newcastle, North Tyneside Trade Councils. Russell Press, Nottingham,
       1980 and 1982.

22.   A starting point would be provided by "Industrial Democracy and
       Economic Planning" . A framework of discussion accepted by the TUC and
       Labour Party Conference in September, 1982.

TOWARDS TRADE UNION
ACTION AND ALTERNATIVES

SYSTEMS DESIGN FOR, WITH, AND BY THE USERS
U. Briefs, C. Ciborra and L. Schneider (editors)
North-Holland Publishing Company
© IFIP, 1983

PROGRAMME OF DATA POLICY FOR THE CENTRAL ORGANISATION
OF SALARIED EMPLOYEES IN SWEDEN (TCO)

Per Erik Boivie and Olov Östberg

The Central organisation of Salaried Employees in Sweden
P.O. Box 5252, S - 102 45 Stockholm
Sweden

The Swedish workforce is highly unionised, with two million
"blue collar" workers belonging to LO and one million "white
collar" workers (salaried employees) belonging to TCO. At
the 1982 TCO Congress, an action programme was adopted for
the period 1983-1985. Several parts of the programme are of
relevance to "new technology" issues, e.g. the parts dealing
with research policy, industry policy, working environment
policy, general technology policy, and employment policy. Of
paramount importance is the part concerning data policy. The
principles adopted in this sub-programme shall guide the TCO
work on computerization issues for the next three years. One
of the leading principles is that rationalization shall not
be supported unless new work areas and new work tasks are
created to compensate for those disappearing. It is also
stated that TCO shall with all vigour counteract the introduction of work at home akin to remote electronic office
work. The basic principle all through the programme is that
the employees shall be granted a real influence on the form
and content of various phases of a rationalization project.
It can be mentioned that among the research goals set up in
the programme TCO shall initiate general research on office
automation, and that TCO shall escalate the ongoing Swedish
R&D on the next generation of a user-friendly and ergonomic
visual display terminal.

INTRODUCTION

The population of Sweden is just over 8.3 million, and about 72 per cent of the
population between the ages of 16 and 74 is employed or seeking employment. This
gives a labour force of about 4.3 million. Manual and salaried workers in Sweden
have steadily built up two quite paramount union organizations in the Swedish
labour market. LO represents two million manual workers ("blue collar") and TCO
represents one million salaried employees ("white collar"). There are only a few
minor groups which are not affiliated to LO or TCO.

TCO is a central organization representing 20 federations of salaried employees.
The smallest of these affiliated federations has about 1 500 members and the largest
has almost 300 000. The TCO federations represent salaried employees active in all
areas of the labour market, both private employees and employees of national and
local authorities. The growing numbers of salaried employees, changing methods of
production and the process of equalization which has occurred with regard to rates of
pay and conditions of employment have brought salaried and manual workers closer
together in the trade union context. The former cleavage between the two categories
is rapidly being superseded by a common identity.

TCO's standpoints on different issues are based on the activities of its affiliated
federations. The Congress, which is the supreme policymaking body of the TCO, meets
every three years and comprises 200 delegates representing the affiliated federations.

Its task is to establish the principles on which TCO activities in different fields are to be based.

The continuation of the present paper is a close translation of the sub-programme on data policy adopted by the 1982 Congress. The full programme consists of 30 separate sub-programmes. Those dealing with "new technology", other than the programme on data policy, are e.g. the programmes on research policy, industry policy, working environment policy, general technology policy, and labour-market policy.

A TRADE UNION POLICY ON COMPUTER TECHNOLOGY

Continued growth and well-being in a modern industrial nation like Sweden assumes an active utilization of computers and electronics in production and service. Computer technology can contribute to producing new and secure job opportunities, if correctly used. Motivated by industrial and employment policy, this positive attitude towards the use of computers must, however, be combined with fundamental trade union demands about the application of computer technology.

Computer technology will directly affect an increasing number of jobs during the 1980's. Its development is expected to be fast, which will directly affect large groups of salaried employees and change their working conditions.

Computer technology creates opportunities for changing work organization and working environment, and influences the trade unions' possibilities to attain important goals such as work for all, solidarity within the wage policy, equality between the sexes, and a six-hour working-day. Computer technology, in this perspective, becomes an inter-policy area from a union viewpoint, as it can determine overall working conditions.

TCO must make a concerted effort with regard to computer issues since computer technology can create radical changes within working life. Trade union policy must be directed towards the same basic goals as other union work. TCO considers that computer technology, correctly applied, can be a support for this work. But both social measures and trade union influence are required to ensure that computer technology is developed and applied so as to have positive effects. Otherwise development will be determined by employers and multinational companies. In that case, computer technology could be introduced in a way which would force unions to adopt a negative attitude towards new technology, which would not in itself be justified.

TCO believes that it should be possible to employ a "Swedish model" for the utilization of computer technology. Computerization will then be regarded as a support technology and subservient to social decisions in society. Union organizations must have real possibilities to influence the introduction and application of computer technology if this is to be attained. Swedish industry, under such conditions, can develop products and systems which should be attractive on the export market, and this in turn should increase the number of job opportunities in Sweden.

BASIC PRINCIPLES WITH REGARD TO COMPUTER ISSUES

TCO's views about computer issues shall be built upon the following principles:

- A prerequisite for computerization should be that when the number of jobs decreases as a result of computerization, new activities/tasks must be created at the same rate as those lost. Society and employers are responsible for such a development through, among other measures, continued new investments and education programmes. Employees' occupational skills from previous work duties must be put to good use in this situation.

- Computerization yields rationalization profits. These must not lead to a reduction in the number of jobs. Rationalization profits must be made available for effective transfer between different parts within the sphere of production. These profits should also be available for increased purchasing by the public sector or for different forms of support for industry.

- Computer technology can be combined with telecommunication technology. It is TCO's opinion that these possibilities should be put to good use with regard to regional policy and should be used to decentralize different work units. Decentralization should concern complete areas of activity, not just isolated subtasks.

- The development of computer and telecommunication techonolgy makes it possible for computerized office tasks to be carried out in the home. Such home-based office work can create problems with regard to working time, working environment work organization, influence, union work, and also with regard to responsibilities for equipment located in the home. TCO must vigourously counteract the use of comuters for work in the home. In this matter no influential forms should be excluded.

- The employees' right to participate in decisionmaking is of vital importance if the application of computer technology is to lead to positive effects for employees. It is the experience of trade unions that computerization to date has been carried out with the aim of realizing short term economic goals. The justifiable demands by employees for good working environment, meaningful work and a retained or increased level of skill has slipped into the background. Employees will contribute to better functioning computer systems if they are allowed to participate in decisionmaking from the beginning of the system development process.

- Sweden is a welfare state employing advanced technology. Education within the area of computer technology must include an introduction to overall and social perspectives of computer technology. All educational programmes that are required to enable employees to perform new and changed tasks are the responsibility of the employer. These programmes are investment costs and shall be paid for by the employer.

- Trade unions must be allowed to influence computer technology as early as at the research stage, so that it will develop in a favourable direction for the labour force. TCO should encourage inter-disciplinary research projects within the area of computer technology.

Decisions for action

The Congress decision is that TCO shall work to the effect

that retained employment and meaningful work be upheld with the introduction of computer technology

that companies, administrations and organizations provide society with long term investment and employment plans designed to form a basis upon which employment is secured when job opportunities disappear due to computerization or other causes

that employees are guaranteed co-determination concerning the direction and form of rationalization and also during all phases of technology purchasing. Goals and directives shall herewith be defined for the system design process, and the consequences for the employees' working condition shall be analysed

that employees are guaranteed co-determination when planning and development work is carried out by special development companies

that working environment legislation is strengthened so that regulations are introduced about certain minimum demands pertaining to the content of work, possibilities for social contact at work, possibilities to influence one's work situation, and working time for intense computer terminal work. This strengthened legislation should be seen as a complement to regulation by means of co-determination agreements.

that provision be made for employees to be educated during working-hours about the way in which the application of computer technology can change working conditions both in positive and negative respects

that research should be encouraged within, among others, the following areas:

- the development of a user-friendly and ergonomic visual display terminal

- remote electronic office work

- tools and models for system development

- office automation

- procedures for technology pruchasing

- the effects of computerization on work organization

- the effects of computerization on human language and

- the design of selection principles for the collection of information for data bases

that TCO's demands concerning computerization are pursued also on an international basis.

SYSTEMS DESIGN FOR, WITH, AND BY THE USERS
U. Briefs, C. Ciborra and L. Schneider (editors)
North-Holland Publishing Company
© IFIP, 1983

DEVELOPING TRADE UNION INFORMATION
AND INTERVENTION
ON TECHNOLOGICAL CHOICES

Joseph LE DREN
National Secretary of UCC-CFDT
Editor of "Cadres CFDT"

As this conference decided to avoid "the traditional conference rituals", and
be "an opportunity to meet, work, and exchange ideas", this will just be a
short statement on how the union to which I belong, the French CFDT, has recently
been dealing with technological innovation.

Approaching system design as you propose here : "for the users, with the users,
by the users", seems to be perfectly in line with the CFDT tradition of democracy,
which we have called autogestion. It does not mean that everything should be
decided at shopfloor level ; it means that there is no democracy, either industrial, cultural or political, if workers and users at various levels are not
able to have their say on the main choices, to take initiative in the context
of their ordinary work, and make some prevision for their future .

CFDT's activity discussion and research on new technology - tool, process and
design - has already been the subject of studies and publications by our
specialised association, ARETE, or by the various   industrial branches. Two
paperbacks   have given a general survey of our union's position vis à vis
new technology : "Les dégâts du progrès" (Seuil) in 1977, and "Le tertiaire éclaté", in 1980.

Even if some parts of these studies are already outdated, they deal with essential
subjects, such as the evolution of skills, non-manual work, or women's work, all
subjects on which we are having rich discussions here, for instance with Judith
Gregory and Eileen Phillips, or with our Italian friends from the CISL or the
IRES-CGIL.

But I shall insist on the specific action of the so-called "cadres", unionised
at the UCC-CFDT, where we try to bring about confrontation between designers
and users.

There are few unions in Europe, where engineers and members of staff are affiliated at shop-floor and local level, in the same section as the other workers :
this is the case with CFDT. At a confederal level, it also provides a specific
meeting-place where the "cadres" of all branches can have discussions and access
to information.

CFDT also includes teachers and researchers, and the possibility of joint activities between so many various categories makes a potentially good structure for
reflexion on new technologies.

BEGINNINGS

For the last three years, we have organised a large number of meetings, conferences and demonstrations. We have published many pamphlets, posters, notes, studies, and special issues of our periodical "Cadres CFDT", on the organisational, social and political issues of computerisation, office automation, data banks, robots, and other technological issues.

The starting point was the lack of satisfactory information about the impact of computerisation on employment. Like other trade-unionists in Europe, we received an abundance of governmental an managerial talk about computers, innovation, the japanese challenge, and the expectation of "more intelligent" jobs. But :

- unemployment was steadily increasing ;
- no real evaluation was made in the sectors already computerised ;
- we had great difficulties in obtaining adequate information about management's plans : either it came too late, or it was highly technical and hardly understandable.

Only in a few cases (banking, insurance), could we get the information "translated" to the workers'commites. Actually, very few people seemed to be not only willing, but capable of translating the technical data into social information and political suggestions.

As a consequence, our union activity has been aimed, essentially, at obtaining the disclosure of :

- Technical information, at all pertinent levels, in an appropriate language for workers' committees, trade-unionists and workers ;

- economic information about managerial projects and investments, especially those which may be expected to have major effects on employment, organisation and working conditions ;

- scientific information about alternative possibilities, at stages where researchers and engineers can make proposals.

The obvious obstacles were, and still are :

- the multinational structure of these groups, and the inevitable secrecy of their research or market strategies ;

- the limited bargaining power of the trade-unions, perhaps even more so in France for lack of a cultural tradition on technological matters.

Another French tradition being over-centralisation, we insisted on the political dangers of computerisation, and the possibility of control it would give government over the every day life of citizens and communities.

MAY 1981

Since the election of a socialist government (whose election was supported as a major issue by the French trade-unions, expecting a new social policy after 23 years of conservative power), things have partly changes.

An active ministry of Research and Technology, whose responsibility was recently extended to Industry, has introduced a wide-ranging and rather successful strategy of consultation, confrontation and debates. Several missions and commissions have started work. Some of them have already produced their report.

A new law on workers'rights, recently passed in Parliament opens possibilities for workers' expression at shopfloor level.

The public Research center (CNRS) has been reorganised, with an increased budget and new responsibilities, such as to help the private
       sector in developing new competitive industrial options ; or to
       start active social research programs, especially on the connections
       between technology, training and employment.

The nationalisation of the decisive economic sectors and innovation should provide the tool and opportunity for :

- government   control and gearing of technological innovation,

- a place for social experimentation, reflecting the new law on workers'rights :
  in the nationalised firms, the department of industrial relations should become
  a "strategic" department.

All this makes quite a different context for trade-union action, but it is in no way a magic solution :

- the employers remain as they were, most of them nostalgic for the previous
  regime, with many efficient conservative links inside and outside the country;

- the workers are still confronted with unemployment, skill obsolescence, working
  conditions, need of education and training, and for many of them, low wages ;

- the elitist conception of intelligence, hierarchy and advanced technology often
  hinders the social debate : in some technocratic minds, mainly preoccuppied
  with world industrial competition, advanced techniques inevitably contrast
  with social conservatism, and some political officials do not give much thought
  to trade-union participation in democracy.

CONTINUING

Consequently, we continue to develop our specific union activity, aimed at creating a better informed and therefore more efficient union strategy, which means overcoming a certain number of constraints, such as :

- the discrepancy between "traditional" and "new" categories of workers, with the
  cultural obstacles it implies ;

- the survival of some inadequate union structures, with misunderstandings in the
  definition of priorities and strategies ;

- the difficulty in each branch and region, of confronting shopfloor levels and
  top levels of experience and analysis ;

- the difficulty of anticipating the changes, either technological or social ;

- the urgent need for new trends and practice in training, youth and adult education ;

- the probability that in some cases, even a drastic reduction of working time
  will not be an efficient answer to unemployment, and that trade unions will
  have to think of how to share productivity earnings ;

INTERNATIONAL

With regard to international trade-unionism, I would like to underline two points :

1.- French trade-unionism has not been as involved in technology agreements, at
    least until now, as anglo-saxon and scandinavian unions. This might wrongly

give the impression that nothing concrete is being done and decided.

In fact, agreements have been achieved in less formal ways whilst in other neighbouring countries, such as Britain, former agreements have become outdated.

There seems to be a traditional difference between northern and latin countries, in the practice of negotiation and the use of legal procedures ; this should be taken into account in international evaluations, particularly in European discussions and studies.

2.- Technological transfers from North to South will become a question of
   increasing importance for trade-unions and democratic institutions.

We, from his trade-unions are often excluded from information, research and power on new technology. We should therefore be able to understand what it means to be denied it, and the extent to which unemployed capacity of experience and imagination may be left out of the field of innovation in developing countries.

        We cannot share the view of those who tend to consider that technologies may be scattered all over the world as long as they seem intelligent, efficient, or even easy to handle, all this according to the criteria of northern developed societies.

        There must be some explanation of the logic -and not magic- that produces the tool, and some confrontation of those who build the system with those who are expected to adapt themselves to it. (Japan being altogether a special case, a very particular encounter between culture history and technology).

        Our national and nationalised firms being often multinationals, we cannot just be satisfied by increasing our trade with developing countries - particularly for educational systems and information technologies - even if it has positive effects on our level of employment. Constructors' system designs could sometimes be considerably improved if discussed in due time (1).

More and more, we should consider that the tool or system ; however remarkable, results from limited theories and limited cultural backgrounds, either professional or national.

Already, some serious cultural issues have been put to us here in many interventions, particularly Claudio Ciborra, Bryn Jones, Matteo Rollier, Robin Williams and Hugo Levie, or Kristen Nygaard, or the Utopia project, and so many others appreciated in discussion.

Continuing this sort of work may confront the trade-unions themselves with their own limits, in structure and practice. But it should also produce alternative approaches - I dare not say solutions - to such acute problems as skill obsolescence, re-skilling, professional culture and organisational change.

(1) Hereafter are some instances of questionnaires and suggestions we have published, about technological investments, systems or tools. These and some others have been successfully made into posters and sold to local unions all over France.

QUESTIONNAIRES AND SUGGESTIONS ABOUT TECHNOLOGICAL INVESTMENTS, SYSTEMS AND TOOLS

ÉVALUER L'IMPACT D'UN CHANGEMENT TECHNOLOGIQUE

Grille d'analyse de l'UCC-CFDT sur les effets du système d'organisation mis en place lors d'un changement technologique dans une entreprise.

1. EMPLOI
1.1 Comment évolue le nombre d'emplois ? Quel est le bilan ?
    1.1-1 Suppressions
    1.1-2 Créations
    1.1-3 Transferts (avec ou sans changement géographique, ou de secteur)
1.2 Comment évolue la qualité de l'emploi ?
    1.2-1 Hygiène et sécurité
    Conditions de travail physique (bruits, chaleur, posture, etc)
    Conditions de travail psychologique (charges mentales)
    1.2-2 Evolution du temps de travail ?
    1.2-3 Evolution de la qualification ? Evolution des filières de qualification ?
    1.2-4 Evolution de la classification ?
    Comment évoluent les différentes catégories de salariés (ouvriers, cadres, etc) ?
    Comment évolue la répartition homme/femme ? La pyramide des âges ?
1.3 Comment évoluent les statuts (intérimaire, auxiliaire, contrat à durée déterminée, etc) ?
1.4 Comment évolue la politique de sous-traitance (société de services, fournisseurs, etc) ?

2. POLITIQUE INDUSTRIELLE
2.1 Qui développe les recherches sur ce changement technologique ?
2.2 Qui fabrique les matériels et met au point les méthodes nécessaires ?
2.3 Balance commerciale ?
2.4 Rôle de l'Etat dans les incitations au développement ? L'entreprise est-elle subventionnée ou aidée pour ce changement ?

3. FORMATION
3.1 Quelles reconversions sont nécessaires ?
3.2 Quelle formation initiale et permanente ?

4. LIBERTÉ
4.1 Comment évolue le contrôle social sur les travailleurs ?
    ● contrôle des cadences, contrôle des erreurs, contrôle des déplacements,
    ● développement de la notion de « secret », développement des « points stratégiques à surveiller » dus à la centralisation.
4.2 Comment évolue le contrôle sur les citoyens (fichiers, carte d'identité) ?

5. RELATIONS AVEC LES USAGERS ET LES CONSOMMATEURS
5.1 Comment évolue le service aux clients et usagers (relations clients/travailleurs) ?
5.2 Comment sont pris en compte les besoins des consommateurs ?
5.3 Comment évolue la sécurité des populations ?

6. RELATIONS AVEC LE RESTE DU MONDE
6.1 Avec les pays développés : comment évolue l'indépendance de notre pays ? Dans quel sens se font les transferts de technologies ?
6.2 Avec le Tiers-Monde : ce changement technologique favorise-t-il le développement de tous les pays ? Est-il adapté à tous ?
6.3 Quelles sont les conséquences culturelles de ces transferts de technologies ?

7. PRODUCTIVITÉ
7.1 Ce changement produit-il un vrai ou un faux accroissement de productivité ? Quel est le bilan économique et financier de ce changement ?

8. INFORMATIONS ET NÉGOCIATIONS
8.1 Quelles informations sont diffusées aux travailleurs sur les conséquences de ce changement technologique ? A quel moment ? Sous quelles formes ? Quel est le rôle du comité d'entreprise ?
8.2 Quelles négociations direction-salariés ont réellement lieu ? Sur quels thèmes ? A quel moment ? A quel niveau ?
8.3 Est-ce que les salariés peuvent négocier les gains dus à l'accroissement de productivité ?
    ● Hausse des salaires ? Réduction du temps de travail ?
    ● Création de nouveaux emplois ? Augmentation de la qualité de la vie ? etc.

9. CONCLUSIONS
9.1 Quel est le bilan global de ce changement ?
9.2 Quel serait le bilan d'un non-changement ?
9.3 Existe-t-il d'autres solutions ?
    ● utilisation différente de la même technologie,
    ● conception différente du processus de production,
    ● conception différente du produit... etc...,
    ● autre modèle de développement.

CADRES CFDT N° 301, NOV.-DÉC. 1981

LES PROPOSITIONS DE L'UCC-CFDT
SUR LES CHANGEMENTS TECHNOLOGIQUES
1. *Au niveau du système informatique (1)*
NEUF PROPOSITIONS SUR LES INVESTISSEMENTS INFORMATIQUES

1. Le comité d'entreprise doit être régulièrement consulté sur les conséquences de la mise en place des systèmes informatiques, futurs et anciens. Au moins une fois par an, un comité d'entreprise spécial sera consacré aux investissements informatiques.
Dans le secteur public, ce sont les comités techniques paritaires qui doivent être consultés.

2. Pour chaque mise en place de système informatique nouveau le comité d'entreprise et les salariés doivent être consultés dès la conception.

3. Les salariés ne doivent pas être consultés seulement sur les aspects matériels (couleurs, ambiance), mais sur le système d'organisation et de pouvoirs.

4. Pour chaque investissement informatique, la direction doit fournir au comité d'entreprise un bilan prévisionnel faisant apparaître les conséquences du système en ce qui concerne les aspects économiques et financiers, le niveau et la qualité de l'emploi, la modification du système de décision.

5. Pour chaque nouveau système informatique, la direction devra d'abord mettre en place des expériences-pilote d'expérimentation à petite échelle.

6. Le comité d'entreprise doit pouvoir se faire aider par des techniciens extérieurs en informatique de la même façon qu'il fait aujourd'hui appel à des experts comptables.

7. Les salariés et leurs représentants doivent obtenir un minimum de formation sur la technique informatique et ses conséquences sociales.

8. Il est nécessaire de mettre à la disposition des salariés et de leurs délégués un temps d'analyse des dossiers.

9. L'entreprise doit accepter de faire réaliser des études rétrospectives sur l'informatique déjà mise en place.

2. *Au niveau des fichiers (2)*
PROPOSITIONS POUR UN CONTRÔLE DES FICHIERS PAR LES SALARIÉS

Nous proposons que le contrôle des fichiers par les salariés soit effectué à trois niveaux : *conception, réalisation, exploitation.*

1. CONTRÔLE DE LA CONCEPTION

• Les salariés doivent *connaître toutes les informations* qui vont composer une fiche (ceci se trouve en général sur le dossier de la fiche imprimée par l'ordinateur) et exiger qu'elles soient limitées aux informations indispensables.
• Les salariés doivent *connaître la codification* pour enregistrer l'information.
• Les salariés doivent *connaître les modalités de mise à jour* du fichier :
— qui crée l'information ? (en particulier qui crée les appréciations subjectives, s'il en existe, telles que : « assiduité », « qualité du travail », etc.) ;
— qui *modifie* l'information ?
— quel *délai* pour qu'une modification soit effective ? (exemple : il est anormal que le fichier des enseignants soit mis à jour avec trois mois de retard) ; et pendant combien de temps sera gardée l'information ? Ce délai doit être le plus réduit possible, car *chaque personne privée a le droit à l'oubli).*

2. CONTRÔLE DE LA RÉALISATION

C'est un contrôle plus *individuel* : il s'agit pour chacun de vérifier que ce qui est enregistré sur le fichier correspond à la réalité. Les travailleurs devraient aussi avoir un véritable *droit d'accès* à leur fiche personnelle dans le fichier de l'entreprise.

3. CONTRÔLE DE L'EXPLOITATION

Le contrôle passe, à l'intérieur de l'entreprise, par celui des *programmes*. En effet, un fichier peut être dangereux, non par lui-même, mais par l'utilisation que l'on en fait. Les salariés doivent donc essayer de faire la liste de toutes les utilisations d'un fichier, afin, le cas échéant, de pouvoir s'opposer à certaines d'entre elles.

---

(1) *Le terme système informatique recouvre aussi bien l'informatique traditionnelle, que la bureautique, la télématique et la robotique.*
(2) *Propositions présentées au colloque CFDT du 20 mars 1980 : « Identité, informatique, fichiers, libertés » (voir CADRES CFDT n° 293).*

3. *Au niveau des postes de travail*

SEIZE PROPOSITIONS SUR LES ÉCRANS DE VISUALISATION

SE FORMER

1. Les informaticiennes et informaticiens, les ingénieurs, les chefs de projet, les analystes, les organisateurs et tous les cadres qui conçoivent les systèmes informatiques, doivent avoir été formés à l'ergonomie.

2. Les travailleuses et travailleurs sur écrans cathodiques doivent avoir été formés afin de comprendre et maîtriser le système informatique qu'ils utilisent et pouvoir participer à la conception de leur poste de travail : tout utilisateur d'une procédure programmée doit connaître les choix logiques qui déterminent les résultats.

NÉGOCIER L'ORGANISATION

3. *L'organisation du poste de travail* sera négociée avec les salarié(e)s concerné(e)s et tiendra compte de toutes les connaissances de l'ergonomie.

4. *La classification, le mode de rémunération et l'organisation des relations du travail* seront également négociés.

5. Avant de commencer à travailler sur écran, tout employé(e) doit être soumis (e) à *une visite d'aptitude* visant en particulier à déceler les défauts de la vision susceptibles de s'aggraver.

6. Le taux d'utilisation des écrans cathodiques sera limité pour les salarié(e)s de plus de 45 ans.

7. *Le temps de travail* sur écran de visualisation doit être réduit pour tenir compte de la charge mentale et physique qu'exige le poste sur écran en distinguant :
— le travail non permanent d'interrogation intermittente,
— le travail en permanence de saisie « au kilomètre » (peu de lecture de l'écran),
— le travail en permanence de « saisie + contrôle » avec dialogue,
— le travail sur machines à traitement de textes (bureautique),
— le travail sur écrans graphiques (systèmes de Conception Assistée sur Ordinateur – CAO).
Dans ces derniers cas, le temps de travail ne saurait dépasser *deux vacations de deux heures par jour.*

SURVEILLER

8. Dans l'exploitation quotidienne, les salarié(e)s veilleront à ce que le réglage des écrans soit satisfaisant, la qualité des écrans reste constante.

9. *Les pauses obligatoires* doivent être respectées, chaque jour.

10. L'installation systématique de salles de repos appropriées pour l'ensemble du personnel travaillant de façon permanente sur écrans de visualisation est indispensable.

11. Pour le personnel travaillant en permanence sur écran, l'entreprise doit respecter les dispositions de *l'arrêté du 11 juillet 1977*, complété par la circulaire du *29 avril 1980*, qui définit d'une façon précise le rôle du médecin du travail vis-à-vis de l'emploi des terminaux.

12. Pour le personnel ne travaillant pas à temps complet sur écran de visualisation, nous revendiquons un examen ophtalmologique clinique annuel et un examen de dépistage semestriel dans l'entreprise (visiotest) sur le temps de travail.

13. Un renforcement des moyens d'investigation des médecins du travail est nécessaire ainsi qu'une réelle autonomie à l'égard des directions d'entreprises.

GUÉRIR

14. Les troubles visuels et nerveux doivent être reconnus comme maladie professionnelle pour les salariés travaillant sur écran.

15. L'employeur doit assurer le paiement des lunettes rendues nécessaires par le travail sur écran.

16. En cas d'inaptitude reconnue, l'employeur doit affecter le salarié à un autre poste de travail avec accord de l'intéressé(e).

SYSTEMS DESIGN FOR, WITH, AND BY THE USERS
U. Briefs, C. Ciborra and L. Schneider (editors)
North-Holland Publishing Company
© IFIP, 1983

DESIGN OF AN INFORMATION SYSTEM FOR WORKERS

Jürgen Friedrich and Walter Wicke

Abteilung Informatik
Universität Dortmund
Dortmund, Federal Republic of Germany

The contribution reports on the theoretical foundations
and practical experience of a project which tries to
build up a computerized information system supporting
the needs of workers and their representatives in the
various bargaining processes with the employers. This
goal leads to an alternative approach with respect to
the content, the user interface, and the design method
of the system. The software development process realized
in this project can be considered as a special application of "action research",which particularily means to
emphasize the partizipation of the users during the
system design.

1 COMPUTER TECHNOLOGY AND THE WORKER

Traditionally the application of technology seems to be hostile to the interests
of the workers. The increasing productivity of the machinery destroys jobs, the
rising velocity of production processes leads to an intensification of labour,
and the transfer of the main functions of labour to the machine increases the
dependency of the worker and diminishes the value of his qualification. In this
situation computer application works as a "trend amplifier" (Reese et al, 1979)
with regard to the social consequences of technology and furthermore raises some
completely new problems, such as the extraction of cognitive elements (e.g.plan-
ning tasks) from the working process. This also reduces the hitherto outstanding
position of the brain workers, as their knowledge too is simulated more and more
by algorithms.

The cause of the extending negative consequences of computer technology cannot be
found - as we know - in the structure of technology itself, but is the result of
the capital owners' strong influence on both the development process of computer
technology and especially the modes of application and system introduction methods.
This capital interest is mostly formulated in terms of industrial economics
rationality respectively of objective technological needs. According to that
among the management there exists the widespread point of view that there is no
chance for a substantial participation of workers in the computer design process.
Often the workers themselves adopt this managerial position leading to a situation that they only can (or perhaps must) act in a defensive or sometimes obstruct-
ive manner.

As against this mystification of the computer, make-believe to be objectively determined by technological factors, we point out the technological fact that computers
are the most flexible machines ever constructed [1]. Therefore we formulate the hypothesis of the "relative ambiguity" of computer technology: "Ambiguity", because
computer technology is, to a high degree, open to substantially different applications, such as total control of the worker's behaviour in the factory on the one

hand, or supporting the process of self-organizing the labour in working groups
on the other. "Relatively", because in some respects the influence of the capital
interest on the computer development process leads to some pejorative basic
properties, which cannot be compensated by special application programming, but
rather induces an increasing work load in principle (e.g. insufficient error
analysis).

But nevertheless the freedom of action concerning human factors in computer
systems is large enough to demand and realize computer applications which are
directed towards the workers' needs. The one kind of improvement of or by
computers is aimed at the immediate work situation, and will not be regarded here.

The second kind of computer application, orientated towards the workers'
interests, tries to use modern technology to improve workers' position in the
conflict between capital and labour. Computer systems, destined to such a purpose,
have to be alternative: partially with regard to the computer technology itself,
strongly with regard to the methods and modes of computer usage (especially the
handling), and far-ranging with regard to the kind and presentation of computer
content, i.e. information offer.

The project described below tries to realize some aspects of such an alternative,
worker-orientated computer system. The system, called "Workers' information
system environment (WISE)" [2], provides a lot of different Information facilities
to support the position of the workers and their representatives (shop stewards,
trade-unionists etc.) in the several disputes and collective bargaining processes
in the factory as well as in the manufacturing branch as a whole. The design of
the user interface will pay great attention to the usual workers' mode of
communication. The system will be one instrument among others, and therefore a
too strong dependancy of the users will have to be avoided; that also means that
no exaggerated hope should be produced: the systems never will solve the
essential problems (i.e. the political ones) of the workers representatives.
Therefore we stress the "environmental character" of the system.

2 INTERESTS OF THE USER AND THE AIMS OF THE WISE PROJECT

Already by describing the aims of the WISE approach, the complex structure of
the project, including various groups of participants with their respective
interests, becomes visible. First there are three groups of users: Category 1
("passive users") includes those workers, who will use the ready system only
passively, i.e. as a question answering tool; this will probably be the largest
group. Category 2 ("active users") consists of those workers, who will - in
addition to putting questions - actively store some kind of information into
the ready system. Category 3 ("participating users") finally includes those
workers, who immediately participate in the system design process [3]. Secondly
there are two other (non-user) groups involved in the project: The researchers
and the system engineers.

Looking at the whole project there exist two kinds of relevant aims for the
workers: 1) aims with respect to the result of the project and 2) aims with respect
to the process of the system design. The main aim (for the majority of users)
focuses on the material result of the project, that is to say a well working,
powerful, easily accessible, and complete information source. (In this regard the
WISE project realizes a "system design for the user", i.e. the above mentioned
"passive user".) The second group of aims, those concerning the design process,
consists of three "subgoals": a) to gain a strong influence on the conceptualization and realization of the information system, b) to get a manifold qualification by participating in the project, and c) to enlarge and improve the information content of the system by the users.

The first subgoal is realized by an <u>intensive and permanent control</u> of the various steps of the system development process by a special "workers advisory board", and furthermore (though less) by the workers, who take part in the user research activities (cf. chap.4). (As to that goal the project has the character of a "system design <u>with</u> the user", i.e. the above cited "participating user".) The condition for exerting influence on system design is that the participants receive a sufficient <u>qualification</u>, which is therefore defined as a seperate (second) subgoal of the design process. First of all there is the need for "technical and methodical qualifications": The participating workers should get the opportunity to enrich their computer knowledge and to practise system analysis and design methods, which they can use to control and influence computer application in the factory. (In this respect the WISE project serves as a "protected workshop", where workers can become acquainted with computer technology relevant to their task, e.g. as shop-steward, which is not possible under the present conditions in the factory.) The next point relates to "ergonomic qualification", i.e. getting knowledge about social consequences and human factors in computer system design. Furthermore - and this is a very important point - there exists the need for a general "innovative qualification" (Fricke, 1975): The workers should be capable of recognizing the changeability of computer systems according to their own interests, the possibility of having influence, the strategic layer of using the computer for solving the workers' own problems. The third subgoal concerning the design process indicates that the system development is not finished by the release of the system: The goal is directed towards the capability to <u>enlarge and improve</u> the information in the data base, and perhaps furthermore the user interface. (Here the WISE project tries to realize some elements of "system design <u>by</u> the user".)

The <u>aims of the other groups</u> taking part in the project will only be mentioned here: If we stated above some deficiency in the workers' knowledge of computer issues, there exists a reverse deficit in the system engineers knowledge of design methods allowing and supporting worker participation in the design process. (Even the ability to explain computer issues to non-experts is often missing though it is of great importance in every participation project.) Finally the researchers have their aims too: They want to prove participation research methods as well as new ideas in the field of user friendly ("worker friendly") computer applications.

3 THEORETICAL FOUNDATIONS OF THE SYSTEM DEVELOPMENT

3.1 User interest and system content

The results of semiotic not only led to the discrimination between syntax and semantics but also to the severe consideration of the pragmatic aspects of information processes. That means that information is also related to the sense of the action which is addressed by the string of characters under consideration. In so far as the actions of different groups are - caused by different interests - of different kinds too, there is a significant necessity for specific information as to its function in supporting the action process. Therefore an information system which contains at least additional pragmatic information related to the interest conflict in the factory, has to be built up.

3.2 Adapted computer technology

Perhaps the crucial disadvantage of the present type of computer is that it is a "machine" rather than a "tool". This distinction means the following: Machines in general substitute the essential components of the work process leaving out such elements, which are strongly dependent on the functions of the technical system. However there are some computer applications, which seem to be more "tool-like", e.g. interactive programming. In these applications the computer offers the user

various instruments, which the programmer can use or not depending on his own
decision in the different work situations. In this case the computer - functioning
as a brain workers' tool-box - supports the programmer instead of substituting
him [4].

This possible tool character of the computer has to be generalized on all computer-assisted work places, and of course has to be realized especially in the
WISE project. First of all a tool-like computer system must offer simple handling,
must be transparent, and must reduce dependency of the user to a minimum rate.
The WISE computer system should support the tasks of shop-stewards, unionists etc.
in different situations and by manifold tools, and thus realize a high degree of
flexibility and modularity. In addition to this the WISE system will be dynamic,
in offering the above mentioned option of extensibility of the system by the user.
In terms of Illich (1973) a computer system presenting those properties can be
called "convivial".

With regard to the WISE system there exists a second adaptation necessity
concerning the applied dialogue language concept. Socio-linguistic research has
shown that there is a significant difference in diction between workers and the
members of the middle classes. This fact should be illustrated by discussing three
research outcomes being relevant to computer language use (cf. Lau, 1976): 1)
Workers' language is a much more spoken language than that of the middle class,
which is strongly influenced by writing. Therefore orthography is rather unimpor-
tant for the workers' daily problem solving, exactly opposite to the syntactical
requirements of nowadays programming facilities (in which the existence of one
odd "blank" may still cause a major disaster). In the WISE project we have to
avoid such a frustrating system behaviour, in the course of which we hope to learn
from the experiments on fault-tolerant systems. 2) Workers use a language based
on a more totally way of thinking and especially on the application of figurative
terms ("Gestalten"). Contrary to this the problem solving with programming
languages presumes a high level of abstraction and works only with chains of symbols.
To solve this problem we will examine the attempts of leaving the "middle class
approach" of the symbolic programming languages by creating "graphical/visual
languages" (such as VISICALC) or by preparing facilities, which allow the manipulation of whole informational structures on the display (e.g. multiple window systems,
cf. Fischer, Laubsch, 1979). 3) Workers use more than others "reference semantics":
In an actual sentence they often implicitly refer to a former statement. Only
the context of speech opens the full semantics of the sentence. Computers cannot
recognize such reference semantics, all statements have to be formulated explicitly.
Also concerning these problems we will look at the approaches of modern computer
science: facilities to mark former statements with the cursor or to point at a
referred statement on the sreen with a lightpen etc. (instead of totally new
formulation). Summarizing one can say that some effort will be made to take the
workers' common behaviour into consideration by adapting the dialogue language to
their needs instead of pushing the people into an unnatural computer environment.

3.3 From participative to autonomous system design

Methodically the development of the "workers' information system environment" is
based on the concept of action research elaborated in the social sciences [5].
Realizing the action research method, people who are studied in the research
process, leave their usually accepted role of being research object. All participants become acting research subjects whose needs, interests, and actions determine the content and course of the research process. Knowledge gain for the
scientists, practical action facilities for the participants, and valuable
experience on both sides are immediately connected with each other and constitute
aims of the project in the same manner (cf. chap.2).

The participative system design is considered as an application of the action research approach with regard to the chiefly technical and organizational area of arranging work places and of developing computer systems. Carrying out the interests of those being affected by the computer applications more strongly than up to now, is one of the important functions of participation especially in opposition to the system owners, whose economic interests dominate the employees' needs at present [6]. In the WISE project this determining conflict between capital and labour (i.e. system owner and affected user) is missing. Though the workers handling the WISE system are affected users as well (e.g. by its possibly bad hardware and software properties, which require suitable action), they are mainly users, who have the benefit of the system, which they use willingly and according to their own interests. This fact as well as the system engineers' claim with regard to their own work, namely to build up an information system for workers, makes it possible for the workers to not only participate in the design process, but to also decide on important system properties. (Perhaps we can call this a "partially autonomous system design". Partially according to the fact that "only" the decision making is autonomous, but not the implementation as a whole. There remains a considerable dependance on the system engineers' knowhow.) Because of the special character of the system having a widespread and non-uniform user group only a small group of representatives of the subsequent users can participate in the system design, different from how it is in most participative factory projects. A central condition for the success of such a project is the necessity for computer professionals and users to accept that each have equal rights, and that both partners introduce their respective interests and experience into the design process. In the WISE project there exist advantageous circumstances in so far as it is founded on a cooperation between the research group and the German federation of trade-unions lasting several years [7].

4 PARTICIPATIVE SYSTEM DESIGN MODEL

4.1 The need for a cyclical design model

The usually applied software engineering model consists of a number of design steps (product definition, system design, programming, implementation, test, documentation, release etc.) which in principle have to be executed in sequence, each step once in the single software production process. However such a model is rather unsuitable in the case of a participative design process, as all decisions are only taken once at a fixed point. Modifications induced by new user requirements, which result from the progressive learning process of the participating users, break the limited dynamic capability of the linear design process in normal software engineering.

Therefore in the WISE project we follow an alternative software engineering approach, in which most of the above mentioned steps are run through repeatedly (cf. Floyd, 1981), taking advantage of the steadily increasing level of knowledge of the participating workers: This cyclical design model (perhaps better described as being "spirally") enables the participants to enlarge and render precise their former assumptions, demands, and problem solving attemts. The dynamic character of this method essentially improves the chances of participation: As the important decisions do not take place only once in the beginning of the project (in many "participation" projects prior to the beginning), the risk of "prejudiced result" can be avoided. Such a cyclical participative design model requires a fixed group of workers, who are integrated in the system development to a certain degree. In the WISE project there is a so-called workers advisory board, in which the workers act as experts for their own problems (and not as objects for the problems of a professionalized expertocracy). This board has the full range of planning, decision, and control functions during all steps and cycles of the project.

4.2 Modes of participation

Not all of the steps of the WISE system design process have the same weight with
regard to the realization of participation; so we will represent the relationship between design and participation methods only exemplarily in the mostly
affected phases of the project.

It is worth saying, that the most of the project models normally cited ignore
that before the first "official" step of a project, i.e. the product definition,
there is - regarded from the point of view of participation - a very important
"step zero": taking the initiative in the project. In the case of projects led by
workers' interests, research deficits and requirements are developed together by
workers and researchers [8]. The WISE project was developed in this manner deriving
great benefit from an allready existing cooperation between the university carrying out the project and the trade-unions.

Of course the step "system specification", based on a precise analysis of the
present information environment of the affected workers, is an essential topic in
each cycle. Therefore a broad and systematic participation is necessary here.
Although the analysis methods applied in the first cycle of the WISE project
(group discussions; non-standardized interviews with a representative sample of
the potential users; experiments with a "dummy system" by the potential users)
are normal standard in the empirical social sciences, the use of such methods is
rather seldom in computer science projects, even in those which deal with user
interface design. The result of the mentioned first stage of the user research
went into the preliminary version of the system specification. The idea of the
cyclical project model is realized here by the method of dynamic specification:
An actual version of the specification is reviewed by the system engineers and
the workers advisory board after a certain time leading to an updated and more
precise version.

Design and implementation are also organized dynamically in the WISE project: The
method of rapid prototyping (cf. Wasserman , 1982) provides an adequate possibility
to practise user participation in this area. Only partial solutions realizing the
main functions of the respective module are implemented, without regarding
technical aspects like runtime or optimization problems very deeply. The prototypes are tested by the members of the advisory board and in later versions by
a larger group of potential users. This test is the basis for the next stage of
reviewing and updating the specification. In this process the increasing computer
knowledge of the members of the advisory board attains a significant importance,
because it forms the condition for a current improvement of decision and control
concerning the interests of the workers.

The development of the WISE system is going on even after its release for common
use. This necessary advancement is carried out by participation of the active
users (cf. chap. 2). On the one hand they can formulate critique and address
proposals to the data base management concerning both the content of the information system and the user interface; on the other hand the users are allowed
within certain limits to store further information in the data base; such as
reports, case studies, or judgements; or according to their growing system
experience they are perhaps able to generate their own analysis programms.

5 REALIZATION OF THE WISE SYSTEM

5.1 The content of the data base

WISE contains manifold information prepared with respect to the users needs to
all relevant areas of computer application; ranging from computer aided design
to industrial robots, and from computer numerical controlled machine tool to

automatic transport systems in the factory, or from computerized text processing to electronic mail in the office. The pilot version of WISE will contain few documents about most of the mentioned areas only, but will offer detailed information about two issues: personnel management and control systems, and work places with display terminals.

The stored material covers the following <u>aspects</u> of the mentioned issues:
1) Technical information (functioning of various computer applications, product information and comparisions, etc.); 2) economic aspects (affected branches, distribution rate, economy of operation, etc.); 3) information about social consequences (diminishing of work places, increasing work load, health risks, changing qualification requirements, etc.); 4) proposals concerning the work place design (hardware, software design, organizational rules, etc.); 5) information about suitable activities (legal room for action, collective agreements, strategic advance, etc.).

According to the kind and extent of the user's information deficit the system should provide different <u>forms of data</u> ("kinds of documents"): The user is able to demand very short information (up to 15 lines), more extensive information (3 or 4 pages), or annotated bibliographical remarks about the literature on a special issue. Other kinds of stored documents are: Legal texts (including different interpretations), general directions of governmental authorities, and judgments, usefull addresses, notices concerning films, seminar schedules, etc. Finally there will be a glossary too, explaining the computer terminology.

5.2 System properties

On the present (first) stage of the realization only some of the above indicated criteria of a "good" user interface are considered. We will give some examples (in addition to chap. 2): "The system facilities should be easy to learn." The pilot version will operate on the basis of a menu technology as retrieval language. However the more experienced user will be able to leave the menu mode at any position and to ask for certain pages or documents directly by entering respective descriptors. This descriptor mode frees the user from being guided strongly by the system. "The system should be transparent." At any stage of the system the user can go forwards or backwards, or jump to the beginning, or end the dialogue etc. "The system should be extensible." As mentioned above the user gets the opportunity to store new data in a special area of memory (labeled as "unproved"). This area is reviewed periodically by the advisory board adding the valid entries to the data base.

The pilot version of the WISE system will run on a computer system SIEMENS 7.ooo series at the computer science department of the university of Dortmund (FRG). As a basic information retrieval system functions GOLEM, which will be adapted according to the requirements mentioned above by implementing suitable PL/I programm modules.

5.3 Present state of the project

The first stage consists of a one year period (spring 1982 to spring 1983), in which a pilot version has been built up. This version has been worked out by a students project course (i.e. a group of about ten students, accompanied by three scientists, working together to solve a fairly complex problem). The advisory board consists of eight workers and workers' representatives from different industrial branches. After a first theoretical period the project group carried out the user research and translated the results into the systems requirement catalogue. Thereafter various existing data base systems as well as information retrieval systems were compared according to the formulated requirements. First prototypes were constructed, tested, and the results used as feedback for specification review.

5.4 Problems

First of all there is a remarkable point concerning two connected problems, which appeared in the step of product definition: On the one hand the users apparently do not ask for pretentious concepts; they formulate only few claims to user-orientated system properties, and also demand mostly traditional content, such as judgments, collective agreements, etc. On the other hand also the system specialists are strongly fixed upon existing solutions; up to now the specific character of the system as a workers' information system becomes visible only in a few details. Modifying the specification in later cycles opens the opportunity of discussing these problems intensively.

However to some extent these problems are an expression of different interests of the project participants. The participating workers hope for fruitful results from the WISE system as quickly as possible to support their practical problem solving; comfort and userfriendliness of the system seem to be of secondary importance in relation to this goal. For the scientists the participation process as a scientific object is of greater importance than the results. However these differences of interests are not comparable with those fundamental contrasts existing between system owners and affected users in factory participation projects. Therefore the WISE project members still abandoned to establish formalized decision structures becoming effective in the case of conflict. Besides the different interests between the participating groups there are also those (even not essential) within the advisory board itself, caused by different functions, experience, and status.

A third problem results from the so far insufficient qualification. The system specialists as well as the workers entered the project having special qualification deficiencies which was known from the beginning. The above explained aim of qualifying the participants within in the system design process has only been realized a little so far. The reason is that there are severe limitations in the amount of time available on both sides. Under these conditions aims being related to "process components" of the project (as qualification is) are neglected as opposed to those being related to the results.

Finally there are some technical and organizational problems, of which only one should be mentioned here: the uncleared organization of the later access to the system.

5.5 Perspectives

The pilot version of the WISE system described above will serve as the basis for the second design cycle: With regard to the content of the system an extension which encloses the other areas of computer application and its implications for labour can take place. In a later cycle other areas in the field of humanizing the work life could also be included. To facilitate access to the WISE system there are ideas of connecting it to the German videotex system (Bildschirmtext) which will be available for public use in 1983. The question of which institution should take over the system after the end of the research project, will also be examined in cooperation with the trade-unions: Several technology advisory boards exist in the surroundings of the unions, one of which already showed strong interest.

Whether WISE could be used systematically and effectively to support the interests of the workers and their representatives, will finally depend on the kind of participation. We hope that it will be possible to continue the initiated good cooperation between system specialists and users in the long-term project.

FOOTNOTES

1 The reason of course is that computers are consequently divided into the physical machine on the one hand and the task-oriented variable programms on the other.

2 The German nomenclature is "Arbeitnehmer-Informationssystem (ANIS)".

3 The categories passive, active and participating are only able to characterize the users with respect to the development of the WISE system. The "passive user" in this sense can of course take a very active part in the interest conflict in the factory and also in the simple use of the system to support his interests.

4 Nevertheless the working situation of the mentioned programmers is steadily changing too: The programming process is becomming more and more standardized causing a diminishing range of action for the programmers' decisions. Furthermore by the development of computerized "program generators", "constructor systems", "applicative programming languages" etc. even the computer at the work place of the programmer carries out a metamorphosis from tool machine.

5 HAAG et al. (1972) discuss several concepts of action research and present some fields of research and concrete plans.

6 To this point cf. several concepts and experience discussed in MAMBREY, OPPERMANN (1980 and 1981) and especially the theoretical thougts presented by KUBICEK (1979/8o).

7 The practice and some experience with this cooperation and the resulting relations between system specialists and workers are presented in WICKE (1981).

8 To the conception of worker-oriented science cf. KATTERLE, KRAHN (1980) and to the determination of research deficiency especially the essay of BOSCH (1981).

REFERENCES

Bosch, G., Methoden der Defizitanalyse und Prioritätensetzung im Arbeitnehmerinteresse, in: Katterle, Krahn, 1981, 79-1o5

Briefs, U., Zukünftige Anforderungen an die Systemgestaltung aus der Sicht der Gewerkschaften, in: Informationssysteme für die 8oer-Jahre (Linz, 198o) 185-2o5 (Österreichische Gesellschaft für Informatik)

Docherty, P., User participation in and influence on systems design in Norway and Sweden in the light of union involvement, new legislation, and joint agreements, in: Bjoern-Andersen, N. (ed.), The human side of information processing (Amsterdam/New York/Oxford, 198o) 1o9-131

Eason, K., Damodaran, L., Design procedures for user involvement and user support, in: Shackel, B. (ed.), Man/computer communication (Maidenhead, 1979) Vol. 2, 127-139

Fischer, G., Laubsch, J., Object-oriented programming, Notizen zum interaktiven Programmieren (1979), No. 2, 121-14o

Floyd, C., A process-oriented approach to software development, in: Systems
     architecture (Proceedings of the 6th ACM European Regional Conference,
     Westbury House, 1981)

Fricke, W., Arbeitsorganisation und Qualifikation (Bonn, 1975)

Fricke, E., Fricke, W., Schönwälder, M., Stiegler, B., Das "Peiner Modell"
     zur Humanisierung der Arbeit. Qualifikation und Beteiligung (Frankfurt/
     New York, 1981)

Haag, F., Krüger, H., Schwärzel, W., Wildt, J. (eds.), Aktionsforschung
     (München, 1972)

Hedberg, B., Computer systems to support industrial democracy, in: Mumford, E.,
     Sackmann, H. (eds.), Human choice and computers (Amsterdam/Oxford/
     New York, 1975) 211-23o

Illich, I., Tools for conviviality (New York, 1973)

Katterle, S., Krahn, K. (eds.), Wissenschaft und Arbeitnehmerinteresse
     (Köln, 198o)

Kubicek, H., Interessenberücksichtigung beim Technikeinsatz im Büro- und
     Verwaltungsbereich (München/Wien, 1979/8o)

Lau, G., Computersysteme und menschliche Sprechtätigkeit, Das Argument 96,
     18 (1976) 228-235

Mambrey, P., Oppermann, R. (eds.), Partizipation bei der Systementwicklung
     (Internal Report IPES.8o.2o6, Gesellschaft für Mathematik und Datenver-
     arbeitung, St. Augustin, 198o)

Mambrey, P., Oppermann, R. (eds.), Partizipation bei der Systementwicklung,
     Part 2 (Internal Report IPES.81.2o8, Gesellschaft für Mathematik und
     Datenverarbeitung, St. Augustin, 1981)

Murray, G. (eds.), User-friendly systems (Maidenhead, 1981)

Nygaard, K., Worker's participation in system development, in: Mowshowitz, A.
     (ed.), Human choice and computers 2 (Amsterdam/New York/Oxford, 198o)
     71-75

Reese, J., Kubicek, H., Lange, B.-P., Lutterbeck, B., Reese, U., Gefahren der
     informationstechnologischen Entwicklung (Frankfurt/New York, 1979)

Wasserman, A.I., New directions in programming, in: Wallis, P.J.L. (ed.),
     Programming technology (Maidenhead, Devonshire, England, 1982) 367-384

Wicke, W., Arbeitskreis "Computer und Arbeit": Die Beziehungen zwischen Studenten
     und Arbeitnehmern in der praktischen Zusammenarbeit eines unbefristeten
     Kooperationsprojektes, in: Cremer, Ch., Richter, W. (eds.), Beiträge zur
     Öffnung der Hochschulen im Revier (Hamburg, 1981) 77 - 97

SYSTEMS DESIGN FOR, WITH, AND BY THE USERS
U. Briefs, C. Ciborra and L. Schneider (editors)
North-Holland Publishing Company
© IFIP, 1983

PARTICIPATORY SYSTEMS DESIGN AS AN APPROACH
FOR A WORKERS" PRODUCTION POLICY

Ulrich Briefs

Institute for Economic and Social Research
of the German Confederation
of Trade Unions,

WSI/DGB, Düsseldorf
University of Bremen

TOWARDS AN ALTERNATIVE DESIGN PROCESS

There is a growing awareness for the necessity of more user involvement and participation in the design of computerized systems.

No doubt, the really existing design processes are deeply marked by the permanent
need to bridge the gap which exists between the system designers' knowledge and
their mostly formal methods to deploy this knowledge on one hand and the knowledge of "normal" operating staff (workers, clerks, managers, engineers a.s.o.)
and their ways to handle their material jobs and tasks with their intrinsic
logic on the other hand.

In most major edp departments and especially in complex systems design projects
faults, delays, additional costs, dead-end developments a.s.o. are caused by the
propensity of systems designers to impose their solutions or their concepts
regardless of the needs of the workers affected and regardless of the co-operation structures developed and maintained by the workers themselves.(1) Many investment ruins in edp departments are thus due to the ignorance of designers
with regard to the material aspects and structures of the working processes
which are to be "supported" by computer systems or are even due to the arrogance
shown by them towards the "human components" of the "man-machine-systems" they
are conceiving.

The need for users' participation therefore has not only a moral or social
foundation: Users' participation is an indispensable functional requirement for
a rational and sound systems design.

The need for truly participatory approaches in systems design will here be dealt
with under two aspects

1. What are the basic features of systems design
   with regard to a participatory development?

2. How could the systems design process be transformed to become part of a deliberate production
   policy for the workers?

BASIC FEATURES OF THE SYSTEMS DESIGN PROCESS –
CHANCES AND NECESSITIES FOR PARTICIPATION

The design process of computer systems – comprising all the phases from the
triggering off of a system to its implementation (2) is a

- long process
- going mainly on in the departments and hence among the workers
  finally affected by the system
- which necessarily has to resort to the material knowledge of the

                    workers affected
              - in which a permanent production of alternatives is taking place
              - and which finally presupposes conditions of social stability,
                co-operative attitudes, loyalty of workers, disclosure of workers
                information a.s.o.

The design of computer systems - this is often forgotten - is a long and often
extremely difficult process - in most cases longer and more difficult than previously scheduled.

A computerized production control system - in the rather superficial forms
discussed actually - takes five or more years to be completed - even in smaller
plants.

Even in "normal" commercial activity complex systems like order handling or
inventory information systems normally take three years and longer to be made
more or less operative.

Large and complex data base systems require up to eight or nine years at least,
to be fully developed.

All these time brackets hold even more or less when standard systems are implemented: the decisive factor in systems design is the enormous inertia of organizations caused by the necessity to adapt and change often very trivial things
but which in their manifold interconnections add to a very complex "structural
change".

This time dimension of the process of systems design gives necessary but not
sufficient chances for a permanent interference and participation of the workers
affected.

This conclusion from this feature of the design process is paralleled by conclusions from two further characteristics of this process:

Systems design processes have to go on in the departments which afterwards have
to work with the computerized system and the systems designers have substantive-
ly to rely on the material knowledge of the workers affected by the system.

This is one of the main reasons why particularly experienced workers are employed
at the first vdu or at the first CNC-machine tool - a necessity which often
leads to the illusion that computerization is more skill demanding than the use
of former technologies.

The systems design process is characterized by a permanent interaction between
systems designers and "representatives" of the departments.

Under the conditions existing, however, there is one major factor distorting
this process: i.e. the structural power exerted by management. The existing
management system is obviously not only tailored to guarantee the necessary
operative knowledge to be conveyed to the systems designers but it is at a time
endeavouring to increase its control on the work-force. The process of re-structu-
ring conditions in departments is thus controlled by management which often is
more aiming at safeguarding its hierarchical position and privileges than facilitating new productive or rational solutions.

One of the main obstacles for a fully rational systems design is, therefore,
management control of the design process whereas even operative management does
not have the full insight and knowledge of all the processes, information flows
and their interrelationships and ramifications and the manifold forms of the

tacit knowledge of the workers, connected to this information. (3)

Furthermore, one of the main characteristics of the systems design process most prone to participatory approaches is the fact known to every programmer and systems designer: the system design process is a process in which permanently alternatives are produced. Every few weeks or, in some cases, even days the programmers and systems designers are confronted with the necessity to operate a choice which has to be taken out of a certain range of alternative solutions.

Systems design, therefore, is much more an art of "muddling through" than a pre-conceived process entirely controlled by project management or by management in general. (4)

Finally, the systems design process needs conditions of social stability, rest, co-operation, continuity a.s.o.

This basic requirement is linked to the features mentioned before. Both features of the systems design process - the necessity to generate alternatives and to select among them and the necessity to maintain stability - furnish decisive clues with regard to launching a productive policy controlled by the workers. How, then, can such a production policy be put into operation?

STEPS TO PROMOTE A WORKERS' PRODUCTION POLICY BY
PARTICIPATORY APPROACHES TO SYSTEMS DESIGN

First basic requirement is to reverse in a fundamental way the relationship between systems designers and users: it is the users who have entirely to dominate the process of systems design. It is their material knowledge and their ideas and perspectives about products, about services, about production processes which have to govern the systems design process. The systems designers have to adopt a purely servicing mentality and orientation.

If this is achieved it is the workers who have to be permanently made aware and given the chance to control every systems proposal and every subproject and eventually every program and subprogram or even procedure developed within a system according to the following questions

- Is the function (project, subproject, program, subprogram, procedure) something which has to be prevented from being developed (e.g. personnel information systems according to trade union congress resolutions in West Germany)?

- Is the function something which is sufficiently transparent in its technical structures, its risks, its social implications, its alternatives? If not, the systems design process should be at least temporarily stopped (the so-called moratorium) and all the above mentioned points should be checked, made transparent and extensively discussed by the workers.

- Is it a function or are there other or additional functions which should be demanded or promoted by the workers themselves (e.g. systems ameliorating informations for staff instead of management information, systems making transparent ecological implications of production plans instead of minimising personnel cost a.s.o.)?

These questions and the concrete alternative patterns for systems design have to
be put, answered and developed in a broad permanent discussion of all the workers
affected.

The reduction of socially necessary working time forcibly brought about by computerization might be used to give all workers time to discuss systems development and its alternatives in truly democratic procedures: i.e. not in parlamen-
tarian or other representative structures but by a permanent and egalitarian
discussion of the workers at their work place and in the factory on new ways
to design and produce computer systems which suit their interests.

This "democratization of work" could thus together with other measures like
using more time for a de-intensification of work and for a permanent learning
on the job contribute to keep unemployment down and to create new perspectives
for human work in a more and more and deliberately automatized working environment.

This democratic decision-making of the workers is facilitated by the design
principles which are necessary to be followed in systems design: The principle
of modularity e.g. breaks systems down in manageable packages discussable and
controllable by the groups of workers affected, it even permits to prevent
"total systems" from being developed.

Computer systems can be developed according to a philosophy which deliberately,
e.g. in order to safeguard workers' personality rights, stops at certain points
computer operations and makes them restart at a point and in a form where no
sensible information on workers, on their performance, on their behaviour is
processed a.s.o.

To head for total systems with all their vulnerability, their risks and dangers
is essentially a management idea - whose basic idea is to control everything
from an outside hierarchical position - ; a workers' idea for systems design
would be to develop systems very specifically according to the individual and
collective needs of the human actors involved in production and those who really
create social welfare and this may include to renounce to certain systems -
be it even by sacrificing here and there some productivity gains.

The basic criterion to develop from these perspectives with regard to participatory systems design is essentially to head for a non-paramatric approach in
workers control of systems design.

Some of the very charming approaches of direct democracy developed in the
years after the October revolution in the Soviet Union which surprisingly find
a parallelism in certain ideas about "Basisdemokratie" in the alternative movements in West-Europe   could be applied to systems design: a permanent and
broad discussion of the workers affected by and involved in systems design
and an imperative mandate given by them to workers' representatives to inter-
fere with the overall structures of systems design (master plans, organization's
global edp conception a.s.o.)

It would be very interesting to re-think systems designers' rôles according to
these lines, i.e. imposing upon them a permanent obligation to report to the
workers affected, i.e. obliging them to teach workers affected about the internal structures of computer systems and about alternatives, i.e. forcing them
to use a de-technicalized language, i.e. to familiarize themselves with the
material tasks and procedures in the departments affected a.s.o.

Two final remarks are necessary:

This perspective for participatory steps towards a workers production policy in systems design presupposes for its full implementation two major changes:

- Guaranteeing the right to work for everyone, i.e. the abolishment of mass unemployment e.g. by introducing the 35 hours' week and further reduction of working-time, if necessary

- Changing the internal structures in organizations from the traditional military-like,highly alienating command structures to self-management, autogestion, Selbstverwaltung and similar concepts.

Both are very far-reaching requirements questioning the basic structures of the capitalist society. The most fervent forces, however, driving towards such a development are the increasing economic stagnation and crisis of the capitalist system ... if it is rightly understood especially also by the scientific community dealing with systems design.

Footnotes:

(1) This explains partially at least why most major design projects are not terminated as previously scheduled.

Another indication may be that in standard-software systems development the anticipated costs are normally supplemented by a rather large margin to cover the costs caused by these delays.

(2) In many cases even quite a few of the updating and adaptation processes which take place after the formal implementation of a system may be considered as belonging to a permanent process of systems design. This feature of the design process may even be of particular importance for creating a permanent systems design process largely executed by the workers themselves who are affected by the systems.

Here, for practical reasons, the design process is considered to be terminated with formal implementation. Similar conclusions as in this paper will have to be drawn with regard to the permanent process of further development of a system after implementation.

(3) How important this knowledge is is reveiled e.g. by the work-to-rule practices of workers, which show that work processes stop or even collapse if workers do work according to the rules established by management.

(4) This can in view of the emerging so-called software-crisis apparently no longer be tolerated by management. An official from the West-German Ministry of Research and Technology apparently expressed this, when saying that all promotion measures put forward in the field of software technology aim at introducing "reasonable controls" into the process of software production.

TRADE UNION EXPERIENCES IN EDUCATION FOR PARTICIPATIVE SYSTEM DESIGN

SYSTEMS DESIGN FOR, WITH, AND BY THE USERS
U. Briefs, C. Ciborra and L. Schneider (editors)
North-Holland Publishing Company
© IFIP, 1983

A LARGE EDUCATION ON COMPUTERS AND SYSTEMS ANALYSIS

AS A CONDITION TO MAKE THE NEGOTIATION POSSIBLE

F.De Cindio^ - W.Pieroni° - C.Simone^

^ Istituto di Cibernetica - Univ. di Milano - Via Viotti 5 - Milano
° CEDOS - P.zza Umanitaria 5 - Milano

Educations of workers, shop stewards and Trade Union members is seen as a
condition for making the negotiation of the computer based changes in
organizations more effective. The context, the aims, the contents and the
results of an education experience developed in Italy in the frame of the
"right of education" is deeply discussed.

THE GENERAL FRAME

The more and more advanced computerization of the whole productive
structure and of the society in the western world in '80 becomes a fact rather
than a matter of discussion.

It is no longer possible to spend time discussing about computerization
from 'outside': facing a phenomenon which shows such an high development speed,
all the time spent in such discussion is lost. In fact, whatever the outcomes of
this discussion would be, they will neither stop ·nor influence the
computerization process which, on the contrary, goes on without any control.

A more constructive approach may be undertaken by the subjects directly
affected by the computerization process, as workers, Trade Unions, citizens,
etc., trying to answer questions like: is any form of control on the
computerization process possible for these subjects ? and, secondly, if some
control is possible, how to enlarge the effective opportunity for workers,
citizens and T.U. to play a role in the computerization game, i.e., in the
italian situation, which are the first steps in this direction?

The answer to the first question is quite difficult: we agree with those
authors (/1/ , /2/) who have pointed out that in history, man has always been
faced with phenomena evolving linearly. The human society, more precisely the
reasoning aptitude of the human brain, is thus presently not used to dealing
with phenomena evolving espionentially, as computerization does.

Therefore, probably nobody exists who knows how to exercise an effective
control on it and the process progresses in some way autonomously. A proof of
the correctness of this assertion can be the fact that in these last years
almost all forecasts concerning the computer world development have been largely
overcome by the actual process. An important consequence of this consideration
is that the problem of the control pertains not only to the single workers or
T.U. but also to any level of computer manifactures (even the multinational
ones) who are controlling, in the most favorable case, only some aspects of the
whole process (as shown,for example, by the problems of IBM with
microcomputers).

If this is the general context, how can the second question be answered ?

Bearing in mind always the partiality of any action we may undertake, the
maximum effort has to be done in order to give to all the social parties more
and more opportunities for an effective presence inside the computerization
process. Any kind of refusal, either an 'a posteriori' defensive position with
respect to the phenomenon is equivalent to allow the counter-party (whichever it
may be) to play the game alone, leaving to it the possibility of choosing the
strategies to face the exponentiality of the phenomenon.

Taking into account the delay that, in particular in the italian context, has to be payed by all the social parties for what concerns an adequate awarness and knowledge of the phenomenon, a first step to enlarge the possibilities of an active presence <u>inside</u> the process is exactly to enalrge their 'scientific' knowledge of the phenemenon.

In the italian context, this has to be required not only for workers and T.U. but also for the managerial class, either industrial or political. All these must become better equipped to cope with the impact of computerization on the social organization at any level of italian society. If a more effective awarness is reached in this area, it will be possible that the progress of the process becomes more controllable, since it will be more conditionned by the <u>negotiation</u> among the social parties, each one having its own strategy in mind.

THE LOCAL FRAME

More in detail, from the point of view of the italian T.U. , there seems to be some conditions to enhance their presence in the computerization process, in particular of a single firm and of a wider area of the italian productive structure also.

First of all, it is necessary to define and obtain some general frames in which to exercise the control; that means to transform the present context of industrial relations in such a way to guarantee a negotiation for what concerns the computerization process too. But this alone is not sufficient. The acquisition of some right is not enough to exert it: what is needed also is the acquisition of the knowledge necessary to mantain and improve such new context and to use all the opportunities it provides to play an effective role either on the national level or on the level of a single firm.

The present italian context shows some differences at these two levels. For what concerns the national one, istitutions like the so called 'first part of national contracts' can be fruitfully enlarged to cope with the impact of the computerization by means of supporting laws which state some constraints ad hoc for this kind of transformations (following the example of other european countries).

At the level of a single firm or of a single company (which we will denote as 'local', in some way improperly because many companies are actually spread on the whole country) the industrial relations system already allows 'de facto' some information rights about the changes occurring locally. Furthermore, the local bargaining of the work organization is the carrying structure of the italian T.U. .

The industrial context at the local level could be therefore already able to negotiate the use of the computer based technologies; but at this point, the lack of knowledge comes out.

That is why we have concentrated our effort just in giving more opportunities for such a local negotiation about the changes induced by the computerization.

The analysis of the main phases of this process gives some hints how to improve this negotiation.

When a problem arises requiring for a modification of some functionalities of an organizational system and, by consequence, of the work organization of the involved subsystems, eventually of the computer based information system also, a process begins which involves a lot of subjects inside the target organization.

Obviously there are different classes of users, from the top management to the most executory workers, who have a different visibility of their work context and different interests in it; as well as there are different kinds of experts, from those skilled in organization analysis up to computer programmers and operators.

It is well known /3/ that in the development of a (computer based) information system, problems arise among the different experts and that such

forecast mistakes and to understand the possible impacts of a new technology inside an organization.
The set of experiences the authors have done, in their different roles of researchers and responsible for T.U. education, started from the above discussed belief that a large education on computers and system analysis is needed.

THE CONTENTS OF THE COURSE

In these last years the automation of clerical work has begun to produce explosive effects in a relevant set of firms in the area of Milan; therefore this problem has become crucial for the local T.U. . CEDOS (which is responsible for the United Federation CGIL-CISL-UIL of Milan of the so called '150 hours courses', obtained in several national contracts to favour workers education) took the decision to give a particular attention to this area and programmed a first monographic course for spring '80, in the aim to answer to more and more pressing questions coming out from workers and shop stewards: why the strenght of T.U., which in the past allowed to control the changes induced by other phenomena, becomes inable to influence the computerization by means of the usual bargaining ? Does this depend on the fact that computers are a new kind of technology, entirely different from the old ones and which therefore requires a totally new conceptual frame to analyse it ?
The request we have been called to answer to was therefore very precise: it wasn't matter of a basic education to satisfy curiosity on computers. Our job was to give to the course participants tools (i.e. some elements of scientific knowledge) to be immediately used in the negotiation about the already present or immediately future introduction of this new technology.
Before to present its contents, some information about the course and its participants can help to better understand and evaluate our experience. The participants who guaranteed a constant presence were about 60 (80 at the beginning). The course was scheduled in weekly meetings of about 3 hours each, for an amount of 60/65 hours. Almost the participants were or would become end-users of management information systems: this concrete situation influenced the educational experiment in that only the problems related to the construction of an information system supporting clerical work have been considered, neglecting all the problems specific e.g. to the automation of productive processes.
Let us go back to the course contents.
Following the main ideas exposed in the previous sections, the whole question of an effective presence in the computerization process has been decomposed into four more specific ones:
a)   in what frame of crisis/development of the firms the computerization occurs ?
b)   which are the main phases of the computerization process ? who are the subjects involved in these phases ? how and where it is possible for users to have an active presence inside the process ?
c)   which conceptual tools are needed to deal with computerization ?
d)   which are the opportunities offered by the technology ?
These four questions have defined four corresponding main sections of the course.
The first one concerns the firm context where the computerization occurs in order to point out how strictly computerization and organization are linked together, so that any computerization process induces a change in work organization and skills,etc.
The second section makes a detailed analysis of the phases in which computerization goes on. In each one of them a specific emphasis is given to the different subjects involved and to their specific role. The aim was to focalize when and how a control inside the process is possible also discussing the experiences of some european T.U.

problems can become less crucial via a wider use of the methodologies which in particular try to formalize and to support the documentation of the different technical steps. Even if this trend is not marginal with respect to our discussion, we concentrate ourselves on the problems arising between experts and users.

The question is: how to bridge the gap between the roles of experts and users in such a way to make the different classes of users able to better understand and analyze the experts proposals and, what is fundamental also, to discuss the possible choices on the basis of their different, may be conflictual, interests ?

Since the necessity of the presence of some experts in the different phases of the process presently cannot be discussed, it is widely realized the relevance of enlarging the culture of these experts (at present prevalently technical) to the social and organizational aspects of the computerization (see for example /4/).

Although we agree with this claim we think that just this is not enough and it could enforce an approach leading the expert to play as a middleman who solves the conflicts among the users, using the technical considerations as a screen. But which middleman can guarantee his neutrality with respect to a management which is quite often the actual customer ? Even 'double commitment experiences' (in the sense used in /5/) show a positive result only when the experts offer to the conflictual parties a communication frame; otherwise they are useful, always and only, to the strongest part.

Our opinion is that the experts only have to create a common frame (e.g. documents) among the different classes of users, in which their points of view and opinions can compare with, since the communication is in some sense codified.

Therefore there are two main issues where the attention has to be focused, in order to characterize this common frame:
1) some constraints have to be imposed to the project documentation (for those phases where users are involved) so that it is complete, not ambigous and readable by not skilled people too;
2) a programm for a large education on computers and system analysis devoted both
    to workers and T.U. members has to be developed.
Our work followed both these directions.

For what concerns point 1) the relevance to impose some constraints to the project documentation was already pointed out in /6/ and was the motivation for a system description language based on Petri nets whose outlines are given in /7/. What we want only to point out here is that whatever the chosen language to model systems and the constraints to be imposed to the other parts of the technical documentation may be,it is an object of negotiation for T.U. to obtain that these constraints are satisfied.

The attention of this paper is on point 2).
An istitutional education on informatics is totally absent in the italian context. Thus the problem to give a basic education to people, irrespective to the role they play in the society (i.e. students, workers, politicians,...) overlaps the problem of providing a specific education, oriented to solve particular needs. We didn't wont to propose a general program of education which copes with both the requirements. Our claim was that, both the basic and a more specific education have to cover, among the others, at least two different areas:
-   system analysis: if computers are viewed as a 'generalized communication medium' /8/, then, in order to capture the relevance of the introduction of computers inside the organizations, the familiarity with notions like system, model, communication,etc. is required;
-   computer science: knowing the evolution of the foundations of computer science and of the main technology trends is necessary to avoid terrible

The fourth section consists of a set of schemes showing the main present technological trends in order to give a language and some guidelines to be equipped to 'float' in the computer technology sea.

The answer given to the third question needs to be a little bit more discussed because of its 'atypicality'.

In section 2. the massive role played by the experts in the development process of a computer based system has been already pointed out. They ask questions and propose solutions to users in order to model the new system. It doesn't matter if the model is more or less rigorously defined in the project documentation: at the end it will be implemented in a new organization and usually in a new set of computer based procedures. Then, modelling (in the broad sense of building, designing and implementing the model) is the basic activity constituting the system development process: to be able to understand and build models is an essential precondition to play an effective role in this process.

But what kind of models have to be considered ? The traditional organizational theories lead to functional and highly hyerarchical models, which do not support the discussion about parameters as autonomy or mutual interactions: these latter seem, on the contrary, to better cope with the organization of the clerical work, expecially when computer are introduced.

Furthermore the above sketched considerations lead to see the modelling process as the field in which different classes of users and experts communicate each other during the system design /7/: the only way to avoid misunderstandings in their mutual negotiation about the system is to have unambigous models in which it is put in evidence what is modelled, and how, and what is left out. Ambiguity, in fact, is a powerful tool in the hand of the strongest part in any negotiation and workers and T.U. are not in general the strongest one.

As a consequence of these considerations, the third section of the course presents a formal (not ambigous) language for system modelling, which maximally emphasize the communication among subsystems and their autonomy. In /7/ the motivations of this approach are discussed and the language with some hints on the related modelling method are presented and exemplified.

During the course some didactical notes have been produced: a book covering the course contents /9/ and the text of a seminar /2/ which has been organized at the end of the course with the aim of exploring the reasons of the inadequacy of the classical organization theories in the analysis of the computerization phenomenon. In this seminar M.Grandi sketched some outlines of a new organization theory, mainly based on the speech acts approach due to J.Searle and used by F.Flores in the organization frame /11/.

The two notes (in italian) are available at CEDOS.

THE CONCRETE EXPERIENCE

The four sections of the course show an aggregation of educational contents quite new in the italian panorama, in particular with respect to the previous experiences of 150 hours courses about computers and working organization /12/.

In fact a one-day workshop by the section 'Social impacts of computers' of AICA in september 1979 pointed out that the courses given until then might be partitionned in two main classes: a set of courses which focused their attention on the technical aspects (computer hardware and software), an other one which analysed the modifications of the organizations due to the introduction of the computers. The first ones almost completely left out the organizational problems and, viceversa, the second ones neglected the technical aspects.

Our challenge was that it is possible in a single course to give a first knowledge of both technical and organizational aspects; moreover , what is crucial, to make clear that these aspects are so strictly related one to the other that the knowledge of the ones without the others is unuseful to play an active role inside the computerization process: perhaphs it may be also misleading.

It was obvious that the solution might not be the simple merge of the two areas.

Some choices where necessary in order to find the correct amount of information to be given to the participants. The basic principle which supported these choices was that, as outcome of this course, the participants had to acquire the capacity of an autonomous reasoning about the computerization phenomenon in their firm or company for what concerns either the socio-organizational or technological aspects.

A too wide range of topics didn't match this requirement: by consequence some tipical topics of an introductory course have been neglected or briefly mentioned (as, for example, programming techniques, the history of computers evolution or generic computer applications) in favour of those arguments which are strictly related to the experience of the clerical workers having to deal with the computerization of their work.

Our hypothesis was that the first step to understand the process and to become autonomous inside it consists in the awareness of a language (as a tool) to rigorously speak about the various aspects of the computerization: from the organizational models to the computerization phases, from the technological problems and applications to the description of the procedures and processes constituting the skeleton of each organization. In this frame basic and very ambitious was the choice of presenting a formal language for modelling organizational systems.

The success of this course had its basis exactly in the fact that the participants understood and agreed with this point of view. So the fear of a formal language to describe e.g. their every-day work was largely overcome by the most of the participants since they realized that this was the only way either to communicate each other without ambiguities in order to incrementally enrich their own knowledge about the work environment in which a new technology had been or could be introduced, or to rigorously define the procedural part of the agreement during the negotiation (in the sense used in /7/).

It wasn't in the aim of the course to cover all the aspects and problems induced by the computerization, not even in the subarea of clerical work. However the possibility of disposing of some conceptual tools to face someone of them gave rise to two main requests by the participants: the first one was to improve the system modelling method with more analytical tools in order to better discuss, on the system model, the relations among different organizational solutions (eventually based on different technological choices) in particular w.r.t. the work organization and the workers professional profiles; the second one was to improve the views on the present technology and its trends taking into account that the end-users are not interested in too many details, but they need an idea of the opportunities open by the different applications, of the amount of work they embed and so on.

A last point emphasized by the participants was the request of a deeper involvement of the T.U. structure, which actually suffers from the consequence of paying too little attention to the computerization process of all the national industry.

The good results of the experience and the above mentionned requests concurred to define a second-year experience which consists of:

a)   a repetition of the course adressed to workers and shop stewards. This new istance has been committed to a different teaching team to evaluate the possibility of transferring it to people who didn't participate to the definition of the contents and to cover, using different competences, some lacks present in the didactical notes;

b)   the creation of two teams consisting of some students and of the teachers of the first-year course, with the aim of analyzing some particular situations and of verifying how the conceptual tools and the formal language can be used to study in detail computer based changes in work organization;

c) a four days stage adressed to trade-unionists to enlarge the knowledge and
    to stimulate a bigger attention on the computerization process.
The outcomes of these second-year experiences have preserved a positive trend,
but have also shown that much more work is needed in order to overcome the above
mentionned problems.
    More in details, for each one of the three activities:
a) After two years the course is largely consolidated for what concerns the
    areas 2) and 3) and the use of the didactical notes has shown their
    adequacy.
    The area 4) has been decidedly improoved assuming that, even in speaking
    about the technology, the user point of view as to be taken primarily into
    account. By consequence, starting from the description of the applications
    related to the present technology and to the technology of tomorrow, the
    presentation of some technical details is possible in a more natural way
    and can be tailored to the expectations of the participants and to their
    actual skills.
    For what concerns the area 1), the difficulties of improoving the present
    didactical notes have been confirmed. The collection of papers which give
    some stimulating but fragmentary view of the problem, has not been
    substituted due to the lack of a suitable and more omogeneous approach, the
    basic reason being the crisis of the classical organization theories in
    dealing with the computerization phenomenon. Some hints on the new trends
    in organizational analysis which seem to outline an adequate frame to
    discuss the impacts of the computerization on the clerical work are given
    in /7/. Anyhow, much more strudies and concrete experience seem to be still
    needed in this area.
b) The two teams were deeply different.
    The first one mainly consisted of a little group of workers and T.U.
    members employed in a multinational company of industrial engineering in
    which CAD technology is going to be introduced.
    In the second one the presence of a local trade-unionist of the insurance
    companies led to face the computerization of the clerical work in this
    environment.
    The outcomes of both teams have been satisfactory, even quite different.
    In the first case the analysis was carried out at the firm level, the
    result being a deeper and careful knowledge of the process in progress.
    Some concrete themes on which the local T.U. could call the company
    management at a bargaining have been identified: for example, to obtain a
    distributed architecture for the CAD system to be introduced, instead of a
    centralized CAD service department as proposed by the management. The lack
    of lawd to contrain the management at this bargaining has been
    drammatically realized too.
    More details about this experience can be found in /7/.
    In the second case, although the analysis work was always referred to a
    particular insurance company, neverthless the aim was to identify the more
    critical points of the present working organization with respect to the
    continously developing computerization in whatever insurance company, in
    order to identify some guidelines for the national bargaining in this area.
    Some useful suggestions have been recognized here also, but the
    difficulties arise again when one try to apply the outcome of this work in
    the concrete T.U. praxis.
    As conclusion, we claim that the test of the conceptual and formal
    tools for the analysis of two concrete, quite different situations has been
    largely satisfactory; what is needed is to make possible the effective use
    of this work in the different levels of the negotiation.
c) Infortunalely, at this level we have to admit the actual failure. It has
    been neither in the presence of T.U. members at the workshop, nor in their
    active participation. The problem was that once more the most of the

participants was shop stewards and only few were trade-unionists, i.e. the structure of T.U. has been affected by the workshop only marginally.
How to overcome this difficulty, which has not negligible sources either in the italian T.U. culture or in the present context of the italian industrial relations is still a subject of reflection, als in relation with an analogous phenomenon present in other european contexts, where the historical and political situations are quite different.

REFERENCES

/1/ Servan-Schreiber, J.J., Le defi mondiale (Fayard 1980)

/2/ Grandi, M., Problematiche dell'organizzazione e delle professionalità nell'automazione dell'ufficio (CEDOS, Milano, 1981)

/3/ Infotech, State of the Art Report on Software Engineering (1977)

/4/ Nygaard, K., Tasks, roles and interest of information specialists in the 1980, lecture given at the CREST Course on 'Information Systems, Organizational Choices, Social Values', Pisa (1979)

/5/ Basevi, E., (ed.), Esperienze di doppia committenza, Uomini e Computer Come 10 (1980)

/6/ Handlykken, P. and Nygaard, K., The DELTA system description language: motivations, main concepts and experience from use, in: Hunke, H. (ed.), Software Engineering Environments, (North-Holland, Amsterdam, 1981)

/7/ De Cindio, F. and De Michelis, G. and Pomello, L. and Simone, C., Conditions and tools for an effective negotiation during the organization/information system design process, (in this volume)

/8/ Petri, C.A., Modelling as a communication discipline, in: Beilner, H. and Gelembe, E. (eds.), Measuring Modelling and Evaluating Computer Systems (North-Holland, Amsterdam, 1977)

/9/ De Cindio, F. and De Michelis, G. and Pomello, L. and Simone, C., Real System Modelling: a formal but realistic approach to organization design, to appear in Proc. International Working Conference on Model Realism, Bad Honnef (Bonn) (Pergamon, 1982)

/10/ De Cindio, F. and Franchina, G. and Mastrapasqua, F. and Simone, C., Material per una prima formazione sui processi di informatizzazione del lavoro impiegatizio (CITE, Milano, 1982)

/11/ Flores, F. and Ludlow, J.J., Doing and Speaking in the Office, in: Fisk, G. and Sprague, R. (eds.), 'DSS: Issues and Challenge' (Pergamon 1981)

/12/ Ciborra, C. and Maggiolini, P., User-oriented education in informatics: the experiences of some european Trade Unions, in : Lewis, R and Tagg, D. (eds), Computer in Education , (North-Holland,Amsterdam,1981)

THE DEVELOPMENT OF KNOWLEDGE AS A PROCESS OF COLLECTIVE LEARNING AND ACTION

Helga Genrich

Gesellschaft für Mathematik und Datenverarbeitung
Institut für Informationssystemforschung
D-5205 St. Augustin 1, Schloß Birlinghoven

Knowledge about the new technology, how it is developed, installed and used, and knowledge about the possibilities and rights the users have to intervene in this process, are preconditions to design systems *with*, *by* and *for* the users. A case study on how organized employees and civil servants are developing knowledge and action strategies is described.

1. INTRODUCTION

This paper reflects an attempt to combine scientific work and experience in an institute for theoretical computer science and the work of an active member of the ÖTV (union of civil servants).
The notion of user is ambiguous. There is a difference in designing systems *for* the user, whether the user will be the owner of the system or not. Being the owner, the user has the right to decide which system should be used for what purpose and how it should be designed; being only the user but not the owner there is no such right. In our context three kinds of systems are relevant:
1. systems owned by the employers and used by the employees in their every day working context;
2. sytems owned by the public authorities and used by ordinary citizens, e.g. systems for computerized employment exchange. (Even if those do-it-yourself systems will be designed *with* the users, it is hard to imagine that they can ever be systems *for* the users);
3. systems owned by the unions, designed to support the working people in their fight for better working and living conditions.
The last system category seems to be little utopian. Although some initial steps have been made (1), the question, how technical systems should be designed and used in that context, is not yet answered. Systems of the first category will now be discussed.

2. PROBLEM

People who attempt to design systems *for* the users, *with* the users, *by* the users, have to face the prevailing character of scientific work. Production of knowledge is separated from the social uses to which it is put. By this separation scientists seem to be freed from social responsibility. The problem that science is extremely divided from labor but often ruled by the interests of the capital is mystified.
There are computer scientists who consider their work as a symbolic production which must respond to social needs and must take into account the articulation of those needs (2).
However, most of the members of the scientific community insist on a concept which is misusing the notion of scientific *objectivity*: It separates the production of scientific knowledge from its social uses, thinking from feeling, subjects from objects and experts from non-experts (3). Consequently 'hard' science is separated from 'soft' science. "By claiming that they can contribute to software engineering the soft scientists make themselves even more ridiculous. (Not less dangerous, alas!) In spite of its name, software engineering requires (cruelly) hard science for its support." (4)

Perhaps that's why in the FRG more soft than hard scientists try to respond to social needs and not only cooperate with the management but also with unions.
There is some contractual guaranteed cooperation between universities and unions[1]. This cooperation is burdened by numerous conflicts. There is the resistance of the institutionalized science that claims to loose scientific freedom and neutrality. On the other hand, unions have a historically grown mistrust in scientists who claim to know better than workers what the interest of the workers should be (5).
Some of the work done in context with the so called "Humanisierung der Arbeit" turned out to help fasten the process of rationalization (6). Even if people try to re-admit the human subject into the production of scientific knowledge, the problem of transfering that knowledge to the users is not easily solved (7).

Labor needs its own experts to get systems designed *for* the users. Unions have to formulate their own position rather than be reduced to accomplished facts presented by the employers.

Unions in the FRG have possibilities to develop strategies for action: they have legal tools with which to intervene; they have a lot of experience concerning the process of rationalization in the different branches; there are quite a number of organized researchers. Nevertheless, there is no organized communication and knowledge transfer to develop action strategies concerning the different branches and the union movement as a whole.

In the following we want to describe one effort to develop knowledge and action strategies *with, by* and *for* the users which is still in progress.

3. CASE STUDY

Our local union district has to deal with the problems of the workers, employees and civil servants in about 10 small and medium sized communes and in about 150 institutions e.g. hospitals, courts, research institutes.
Until recently the new technology seemed to be one problem among others. EDP, textprocessors and reorganization of work seemed to affect only some sectors of civil service, e.g. revenue administration, and only some professions, e.g. the female ghetto of secretaries.
Very few secretaries have been unionized and if unionized they did not belong to boards or committees. That's why their problems have not been discussed in a realistic way. Problems realized by the union until now are centralized typing pools and the ergonomical insufficency of systems, although most secretaries do not work in typing pools, and the ergonomical question is only one among others and about being solved by the learning process of manufacturers of EDP equipment.

3.1. LACK OF ORGANIZED COMMUNICATION AND KNOWLEDGE TRANSFER

There had been series of seminars and workshops on rationalisation and automation organized by the federal ÖTV, but attending those seminars was seen by most colleagues as a mere hobby. Before finding themselves as user of a video-display-terminal, very few of them realized that the new technology will affect their working and living conditions. Reorganization of work was not recognized as a step to automation.

In our district most of the EDP installations are centralized. There is the ideology that all administrations of the same branches and of comparable size are working alike. The consequence is, that the working process will be analysed only in one administration and then work will be reorganized and techology will be introduced also in all the other administrations of the same type. Thus, the preparations done by the management in order to introduce techniques are not visible in most of the offices. It happened that employees found themselves in front of video-display-terminals without being informed or prepared in advance.
Because of the centralized EDP organization it is possible to keep secret all plans of

reorganization and automation and to exclude the employees and their representatives from the decision process.

Very few colleagues did understand the aim of the employers, and those who did, had no possibility to communicate their experiences and conjectures. The employees' councils could not transfer their experiences and develop action strategies together because there was no organized communication between the representatives of different admini-strations.

The shop stewards of our research institution, due to their work in different projects on office automation, knew about the lack of information and communication among the users. They proposed that the local union should give priority to the problems of new technology.

3.2. EFFORT TO ORGANIZE COMMUNICATION AND TO DEVELOP AND TO TRANSFER KNOWLEDGE

Two years ago, our local union board decided to install a committee, a kind of task force. This task force consists of colleagues from different branches of administration and from our research institute.
We wanted to learn about the actual situation in the different parts of the civil service, about the degree of reorganization and automation in our district, about the working conditions and working products and about legal possibilities and action strategies to prevent installations which offend the interests of the users.
We wanted to learn how workers in other regions and branches succeeded to fight against undesirable systems.
Last not least we wanted to learn as much as possible about the new technology and the process of system design and development.

This knowledge is a necessary precondition to enable the users and their representatives to think about and to fight for systems *for* the users.

To transform our ideas into action, we proceeded in the following way:
Before getting into contact with the shop stewards, with the employees' council and with *real users,* the committee prepared catalogues of relevant problems and questions. To get criterions, we evaluated reports on research projects (8), publications of the unions[2], including the resolutions of the ÖTV concerning new technology (9), the knowledge some of us had got in seminars and workshops organized by the federal ÖTV and our own experiences. These catalogues which differed relevant to the different branches of public administration, turned out to be very useful.

To learn about the actual working conditions in our district, we asked the employees' council for an official invitation to take part in the meetings of the employees[3], we visited meetings of organized colleagues of the revenue administration, the administration of justice and the public savings-banks, we had meetings and two-days workshops together with shop stewards.
It is quite a different experience to read about rationalization measures or to talk to people who have to work under those conditions.

After having got a first overview concerning the situation in our district, we developed, together with colleagues from other union districts a questionnaire. This questionnaire was answered by the shop stewards and organized members of the employees' councils in 30 different administrations of our district.
We got much more information than we had expected and learnt that in some offices the employees succeeded in getting better conditions, than those which had been planned by the employers, by using all legal and other possibilities.

3.3. FIRST RESULTS

3.3.1. GAINED KNOWLEDGE

We learnt about the implemented or planned applications of new technology in municipal administration, administration of justice, labor exchange, hospitals, revenue administration, public savings-banks and public health insurance in our district.
We learnt that many colleagues complain about their working conditions but much more they complain about the insufficiency of the outcome of their work. We will give two examples:

1. Because of the centralized organisation of EDP the administration's notion of 'time' is much different from the citizen's notion of 'time' who needs help. The civil servant who is aware of that fact has no means to change the situation but is made responsible.

2. In the offices of labour administration the work has increased tremendously, due to the increase of unemployment. Instead of engaging more employees, vocational guidance and employment exchange will be computerized. The colleagues are very much afraid that the service for the citizens will be very insufficient and the civil servants trained for doing that job will loose their qualification.

3.3.2. GAINED POSSIBILITY OF ACTING

During the last two years the degree of organization in our district did increase considerably. All our activities led to a lot of discussions in the different offices and many colleagues, including real users of the systems, became aware of their situation and now begin to think about how to fight for better conditions.
The representatives of the employees from different administrations now meet in regular sessions to communicate their experience and knowledge. Because some of them are members of our committee, they are able to inform their colleagues about the measures planned by the employers and to motivate them, to apply legal and other regulations, to prevent undesirable effects for the users.
There are already a few results: In the municipal administration the employees' council succeeded to get an agreement about passwords. They got a written declaration that besides the control of authenticity, no other controll routine will be implemented.
In one administration the employees' council and the employers signed so called guidelines for the installation of VDTs. These guidelines are the best known in public administration. One administration director now is discussing together with the employees' representatives the possibilities of installing decentralized EDP facilities.

3.3.3. FURTHER ACTIVITIES

We presented the results of our work to our local board in a two-day workshop, where we also began to discuss the economical and political conditions which leads to the development and implementation of systems as we find them today. The local board decided to continue that discussion and to prepare a paper on that topic.
We also decided to have regular meetings of the shop stewards and representatives and to support their work by giving them the opportunity to read the relevant publications which will be made available in a systematic way in the union office[4]. We decided to visit exhibitions as the Hannover Fare or the Orgatechnik together and to engage ourselves as unionists in the committees for standardization.
Last not least, we started a series of publications in the local newspapers, to show that fighting for better working conditions for the civil servants meens also a fight for better service for ordinary citizens, i.e. for better living conditions for the working people in general.

3.4. NEXT STEPS

We know that our work did not lead to desirable systems for the users, neither for the employees nor for the citizens. Our first goal was to develop knowledge and action strategies to be able to prevent worse conditions.

We are aware that there are groups of employees – e.g. women – who could not participate in our work to an acceptable extent. We hope this will be changed soon.

We are just preparing a series of seminars for the users which will be hold by the users and will start in November 82.

The shop stewards in our research institution proposed to develop a special training-course on text processing. The aim is to enable the secretaries who are used to typewriters to know as much about the construction of the new systems as possible. A first version of such a course has been developed by two of our colleagues – both women. The secretaries, who had the opportunity to attend that course, are quite glad to know why does happen what happens. We plan to revise the course material for using it in the union context.

There is a special experts' ideology that users want to stay naive users. But we think that this notion of 'naive user' is not at all helpful for the users.

4. CONCLUSION

Our goal is to develop organizational concepts and technologies which really could improve the working conditions, and thus lead to systems *for* the users.

From our experience we know that systems *for* the users cannot be achieved by mere participation. This can only be done by cooperation between the system designers and the working people who will be the users. This has to be a cooperation of partners, who have equal rights, and where information and knowledge flow in both directions (10).

To design systems *for* the users and to implement them is not only a problem of developing technical and organizational concepts or methods of communication and design. It is also a problem of economical and political interests and thus of the relation of power in the particular organization as well as in the society.

Nevertheless, systems *for* the users can only be achieved via a laborious process of collective learning and action by the working people in the factories and offices. They have to find an answer to the question: Which systems should be built for what purpose and how those systems should be designed.

Since many modern management-techniques are attempts to deal with the 'man-problem', it follows that well organized workers with clear goals might well put a brake on management's 'human engineering' designs (11).

FOOTNOTES

1. e.g. the cooperation contracts between the Ruhr-Universität Bochum and IGM (union of metal workers), and between the Universität Oldenburg and DGB Niedersachsen

2. Besides the papers mentioned in the WSI bibliography, the ÖTV had published a lot of Material concerning the rationalization process in the different branches of public service.

3. It is prescribed (by law) that the employees' council convokes at least one meeting of all employees per year.

4. Until now you can find in the union office very few publications and only those by the ÖTV.

REFERENCES

(1) Briefs, U.: The Role of Information Processing Systems in Employee Participation in
     Managerial Decision-Making, in: Mumford E., Sackman, H.(eds.), Human Choice and
     Computers, Amsterdam, New York, Oxford 1975 (IFIP-Publication); Friedrich, J. and
     Wicke, W.: Design of an Information System for Workers, in these proceedings

(2) Petri, C.A.: Modelling as a Communication Discipline, in: Measuring, Modelling and
     Evaluating Computer Systems, Beilner, H. and Gelenbe, E. (eds), North Holland
     Publishing Company 1977

(3) Fee, E.: A Feminist Critique of Scientific Activity, in: Science for the People,
     July/August 1982, Vol.4, No 4

(4) Dijkstra, E.W.: How do we tell truths that might hurt? in: SIGPLAN Notices, May
     1982

(5) Vetter, H.O.: Was erwarten die Gewerkschaften von den Hochschulen? in: Blätter für
     deutsche und internationale Politik, Heft 8/1977, Pahl Rugenstein Verlag Köln.

(6) Naschold, F.: Die Humanisierung entpuppt sich zu oft als Rationalisierung, in:
     Frankfurter Rundschau vom 13.3.80

(7) Pöhler, W.: Mit bescheidenen Mitteln weitreichende Wirkung erzielt, in: Frank-
     furter Rundschau vom 1.9.80; Pöhler, W.: Günstigstenfalls ein Nebenziel der
     Unternehmerstrategie, in: Frankfurter Rundschau vom 2.9.80

(8) WSI-DGB Projektgruppe HdA, Informationspakete: Humanisierung der Bildschirm-
     arbeit, Humanisierung der Textverarbeitung, and Neue Formen der Arbeitsorga-
     nisation, Düsseldorf 1981/82

(9) Anträge 881 bis 904, Protokoll 9. Gewerkschaftstag Berlin 1980, edited by Gewerk-
     schaft Öffentliche Dienste, Transport und Verkehr, Hauptvorstand

(10) Fricke, E., Fricke, W., Stiegler, B.: Arbeiter gestalten ihre Maschinen. Das Peiner
     Modell zur Humanisierung der Arbeit, in: Stimme der Arbeit, 1980 p. 48 ff

(11) Weltz, F., Lullius, V.: Fortschritt in die Sackgasse?, BMFT-Forschungsbericht
     Humanisierung des Arbeitslebens, Dez. 1981

SYSTEMS DESIGN FOR, WITH, AND BY THE USERS
U. Briefs, C. Ciborra and L. Schneider (editors)
North-Holland Publishing Company
© IFIP, 1983

RESEARCH ABOUT RESEARCH-INFORMATION
ON TECHNICS.

Ingela Josefson

Arbetslivscentrum
Box 5606
S- 114 86   STOCKHOLM
SWEDEN

Methods of conveying the results of worklife research are discussed
in a special research project at the ARBETSLIVSCENTRUM (the Swedish
Center for Working Life). The aims of this project, called the
FORM-project, are both theoretical and practical. Different methods
used to convey the results of worklife research to working men and
women and their unions serve as a basis for a theoretical discussion
of the conditions for understanding research. The point of departure
is the fact that the obstacles to understanding can not be removed
by simplifying and trivializing the language of the research reports.
Rather, it is differential experiences and conceptualization of
various problem areas of the researchers and the people whose work
life they study, wich are the most serious obstacles to communication
and understanding.

Two case studies in the project deal with study materials relating to
computerisation: (1) The education and information material DATORN
(the Computer) prepared by and for members of the Insurance Employees´
Union (LO) and (2) The Computer is Coming, TCO/TBV.

The evaluation of DATORN covers a completed education campaign. One
half of the union´s 20.000 members participated in an education
program primarily in the form of study circles concerning the
computerization of jobs at the health insurance offices. Part of the
work of the sutdy circles consisted of preparing written answers to
questions relating to the experiences of the participants regarding
the introduction of new technology.

On the basis of these answers, the insurance workers´ union formulated
and adopted actionprogram on technology at its convention in 1980.

(For a more through description of this project see the action program
"EDP in the social insurance offices" and "Job design and automation
in Sweden").

DATORN is based on research concerning the effects of computerization
wich was carried out by a team of researchers at Arbetslivscentrum.
The content and design of the education material, however, is the
result of a close cooperation between the union and the researchers.

Various drafts of the education manual were submitted to different
groups of members for criticism. One such session was a week-long
meeting of all local union education stewards. Their criticism
concerned not so much the language as the content of the texts.
This was especially true of the technical descriptions of different
computer systems and of the examples of the impact of computerization
experiences. The researchers thought would be of interest to the
insurance workers´ union then involved in a national commission
investigating the need for more advanced computer technology than
that introduced ten years previously.

The mainthrust of the criticism was that the descriptions and examples
were too foreign to the reality in which the insurance employees
lived. "We don´t recognize ourselves in this description!" they said.

As a result portions of the researchers´ texts were replaced by the
members´ own descriptions and anticipations of how future computer
technology would influence thier work. These texts met with more
favourable reactions from the members and led to lively study circle
discussions.

Consequently, our research project focuses on the question: Which
type of knowledge should a study manual om computerization try to
pass on to active union members? Discussions with the members of
this union clearly show that the employees are more interested in
the software than in the hardware. They are also more interested
in the applications of technology which might reasonably be
considered for introduction into their workplaces, than in the
historical developments of the technology. For research to be well
received and understood, it must be structured in such a way as
to relate to the members´ own experiences.

The question is how to organize such research. Which methods should
be used? Which theories should be employed? Which forms of union
participation in the research are best? As a basis for reflection,
there is need for both a more thorough theoretical discussion of
these problems and a consideration of numerous successful practical
examples.

The second case study in our research project deals with the TCO/TBV
education material DATORN KOMMER (The Computer is Coming). The same
team of researchers also participated in the development of this
material. Experiences from the previous project provided both a
basis and a qualification for participating in the new project.

From October 1981 to May 1982, about 5 000 union members participated
in study circles using the study material "The Computer is Coming".
And in the computer courses there were about 14 000 union members
in study circles during 1981-82.

The main problem with this new material was that the manual attempts
to satisfy the different needs of numerous TCO-unions - each
organizing different professional groups. This difficulty was
overcome throyght the development of separate pictoral desceptions.
The name of this complimentary book is "Job Skills and Computerization".

The book uses pictures both of a photographic and litterary character
of such an "open" nature that the "fit" the different unions´
various professional situations.

The pictures do not present research results in the way a written text would. However through the choice of "pictures" the researchers perspectives on the subject would be conveyed.

In the ideal case, the pictures can inspire discussions on the basis of the individual experience of the study circle participants. This is not sufficient however. The first part of the study material, the basic manual, is a more traditional teaching manual. Used together the manual and the picture book are complimentary.

Our project will examine more closely the extent to which the pictures can contribute to the students´ own experiences and thereby positively influence the development of new knowledge.

DIFFERENT ACTORS' ROLES IN PARTICIPATIVE SYSTEM DESIGN

SYSTEMS DESIGN FOR, WITH, AND BY THE USERS
U. Briefs, C. Ciborra and L. Schneider (editors)
North-Holland Publishing Company
© IFIP, 1983

Problems and Promise of Participative
Information System Design

Harold Sackman

Department of Information Systems
School of Business and Economics
California State University, Los Angeles

A comparative overview of contrasting cultural
approaches to participative information system design
provides the initial framework. The common elements of
the participative approach are delineated and
critically evaluated for social and technical
consequences. The promise of participative system
design for social excellence in the public interest is
the keynote of final conclusions and recommendations.

1. INTRODUCTION

Over the last decade, information system design and development
has undergone a major change in the roles of key actors and
stakeholders throughout most of industrialized world--except for
the United States. The traditional approach to information
system design, particularly as practiced in the U.S.A., is
controlled by management, and is technically designed and
implemented by systems analysts, engineers and programmers, with
users and clients playing a largely unsystematic, passive,
reactive role in supplying background "end-user" information, and
then only when asked by the "professionals." Result:
computer-professional oriented systems, not user-oriented
systems, in spite of all the protestations to the contrary made
by information system vendors and by computer professionals.

West Churchman warned us in 1972 that politics and power are more
important than information systems, and that systems analysts
should avoid projecting their values and their world-view on
others. This egocentric "sin" was known to the ancient Greeks as
"hubris", marked by arrogance, excessive pride and overweening
self-confidence. The question arises, should users play a
co-equal role with managers and computer professionals in
information system design?

This question is not as simple as it seems. It runs deep into
the culture and philosophical value-system of labor/management
relations of each country. A global continuum may be invoked to
illustrate the point. At one extreme of the continuum is the
U.S.A., which probably has the lowest level of participative
management, and participative information system design, marked
by traditional adversary relations between management and labor.
Next is Great Britain, with similar adversary relations, but a
more powerful labor union movement including over half of the
working population. British trade unions tend to be "reactive
and defensive" in information system design.

About mid-way on this continuum is Japan, with its cultural
tradition of management paternalism and job protection, consensus
decision making, and strong governmental cooperation and support
(JIPDEC, 1981). Also mid-way are the Central European Economic

Community countries, such as Holland and Germany, and more
recently France (with the election of Socialist Mitterrand), and
Austria. These countries have established national
co-determination policies where management and labor are required
to work together by law. These countries are also characterized
by organizational paternalism and job protection. Unions
constitute almost half of the Board of Directors of large
organizations, also by law. See Briefs (1975) for developments
in West Germany.

Toward the "left" end of the spectrum are the Scandinavian
countries, with a longstanding tradition of industrial democracy,
where industrial co-determination and participative design for
information systems have long been enacted into law (e.g., see
Nygaard, 1980). Goranzon et al (1981) report a "growing wave of
computer awareness in Sweden "for society generally and in
particular concerning the development and democratization of
working life." (P. 56). Schneider and Ciborra (1982) report
Norwegian trade union participation in information system design
and development involving pre-project management/labor contracts,
union monitoring and testing of developing information systems,
and joint ongoing management of operational systems,
characterized by cycles of "cooperation and confrontation."

At the extreme left, we can take the case of Yugoslavia, the
maverick Communist state, where "workers' councils" exercise top
management controls and essentially run the industrial
enterprise. According to their account, their system is working
very well for a relatively backward country under great political
and economic stress (Mestrovic, 1978).

The above is only a suggestive spectrum running from management
dominated, to joint management/labor "co-determination", to
labor-dominated cultural working styles. There are numerous
exceptions and great variations in all the countries cited. In
the U.S.A., in particular, there is much eclecticism and
experimentation. The major point is that there is a vast ferment
of experimentation in participative information system design
going on around the world.

2. CHARACTERISTICS OF PARTICIPATIVE DESIGN

Enid Mumford, Professor at the Manchester Graduate School of
Business, has written extensively on participative information
system design based on her work on English firms (1979). She
found, almost by accident, that substantive user participation
led to marked improvement in information system design. She
systematized a participative system design technique over the
course of almost a decade for large organizations, including
chemical, engineering, insurance, banking, and construction
firms. Mumford's approach illustrates the main elements of the
participative process which involves four broad stages, highly
summarized, as shown in Figure 1. Several aspects of Figure 1
are notable. Note in Stage 1 that users are integrated into the
design team as co-equals at the outset, and are indoctrinated
into the approach with a two-day course. The initial setup is
kicked off by getting consensus from all participants to move
ahead with a new information system. In Stage 2, the main
emphasis is on balancing job productivity objectives with job
satisfaction goals, again emphasizing user requirements. Stage 3

FIGURE 1

FOUR STAGES OF PARTICIPATIVE DESIGN

STAGE 1: GETTING STARTED

- Get Agreement of all Staff

- Form Design Group

- Form Steering Committee

- Teach Users the Principles of Approach--Two-day Course

STAGE 2: STRUCTURING SYSTEM INFORMATION

- Design Group Gathers Information

1. Concerning work problems

2. Concerning job satisfaction needs

3. Concerning potential of computer to assist with these

STAGE 3: NEGOTIATION AND CONFLICT RESOLUTION

- Design Alternative Systems--Sociotechnical

- Discuss with User Staff

- Prepare Detailed Design

- Present to Steering Committee

- Present to all User Staff

STAGE 4: DETAILED DESIGN

- Prepare Hardware/Software Specifications

- Prepare Job Specifications

- Training Program

- Physical Layout of Department

essentially represents a comprehensive consensus process between management, labor, and computer professionals in determining concurred system design. Stage 4 is detailed design follow-on based on prior agreements and monitored by balanced representation on the watchdog Steering Committee. These four stages are fairly typical of minimal requirements for user participation in information system design.

The key advantages and pitfalls associated with participative information system design are shown in Figure 2. The advantages amount to a more fully integrated form of system design that represents all major groups with an informed and vested interest, in a politically acceptable working setting for all parties. The disadvantages essentially amount to the problems of getting consensus among so many different groups, where there may be major conflicting interests that could vitiate or even sabotage the system design effort. Also note that the method of broad consensus is probably more likely to lead to less innovative and more conservative information systems.

The roles of users and computer professionals are significantly changed in participative system design. The user is required to become more computer literate and more aware of the total organizational information flow. Systems analysts and programers lose some of their traditional control over technical design decisions and share technical control with users. They are required to communicate more extensively with all parties, and to act as relatively neutral technical facilitators among conflicting parties. They also have a more pronounced educational role in indoctrinating non-professionals into the arcane mysteries of system hardware, software and communications. In short, computer professionals have an expanded role, including all the technical responsibilities of the traditional approach, plus new psychological, political, educational, and coordination skills.

Computer professional education is inevitably taking a turn toward the broader organizational setting and toward broader social management skills in response to the participative approach to information system design. In the United States, it is my prediction that the participative approach will eventually displace traditional system design by the end of this century, but with features unique to American culture and the American organizational setting.

3. THE SOCIAL CHALLENGE

The discussion up to this point has focused on a limited set of roles and actors in the information system development process, primarily on management and labor and on computer professional. The quest for overall excellence in information system design requires a broader perspective including the roles of vendors, the government, and the public. Looking at all these roles in actual working practice, we find a disconcerting and ominous scene. Below is an admittedly impressionist and oversimplified view, developed at greater length in some of my books (Sackman 1971, 1972, 1981).

Vendors are primarily interested in profits, and the entire computer world is largely driven by short-range market forces

FIG. 2   ADVANTAGES AND PROBLEMS OF PARTICIPATIVE INFORMATION SYSTEM DESIGN

ADVANTAGES

- POSITIVE VALUES
- ORGANIZATIONAL COMMITMENT
- KNOWLEDGE
- JOB SATISFACTION
- EFFICIENCY
- INTEGRATION
- STABILITY
- POLITICALLY RESPONSIVE
- DEMOCRATIC

PROBLEMS

- TRUST
- ELECTION VS. SELECTION
- CONFLICT OF INTEREST
- STRESS
- COMMUNICATION
- ROLE OF COMPUTER PROFESSIONALS
- ROLE OF LINE MANAGER
- RAPIDLY CHANGING TECHNOLOGY
- LONGER TIME TO DESIGN SYSTEM
- MORE MAN-HOURS, HIGHER INITIAL COST
- CONSERVATIVE SOLUTIONS

rather than long-range objectives in the public interest
(Dordick, Bradley and Nanus, 1981). Technological innovation
consistently outraces social verification. Governments at
national and international levels may have sporadic short-range
programs, but do not have long-range plans for the
computerization of society in the public interest. Advances in
information systems are driven by the vagaries of competitive
computer technology and not by social needs.

Management has consistently been well ahead of trade unions in
exploiting computer systems. However, most managers still tend
to be ignorant of computer systems and have characteristically
abdicated responsibilities for system design to computer
professionals. Trade union leaders show a similar syndrome. In
contrast, both labor and management have recognized that
information is power, and political control over this power has
become a growing and disruptive source of organizational
conflict. System quality takes a back seat while managers fight
among themselves and with unions over organizational information
control.

Computer professionals often subvert the system development
process with their narrow sectarian concerns--system analysts,
engineers, and programmers too frequently opt for systems
responsive to their own needs and aspirations rather than systems
responsive to user needs, as mentioned in the earlier reference
to Churchman. The majority of such professionals receive
virtually no training in human communication skills,
organizational and group process, and in team skills, nor in
experimental test and evaluation of the user/system interface
requiring human factors and ergonomics. Such humanistic gaps
lead to unusable, ineffective and counterproductive information
systems.

The user, the rank and file union member, and the general public
are also not blameless in this sorry situation. All of these
groups share an abysmal and deplorable level of computer
illiteracy. Only very recently have governments taken active
initial steps to raise the level of computer literacy in the
general population with significant educational measures. Most
of the general population in the industrialized world, in my
opinion, is dangerously ignorant of computer-based information
systems, from technical, economic, political and social
viewpoints. Further, the general public and the public interest
seem to be last on the agenda for serious planning of social use
of computers.

These problems are not new, nor suprising, they are insidiously
chronic, like a kind of social arteriosclerosis of our computer
systems. For example, Nanus (1975) proposed a balanced initial
set of social objectives for computer-based information services
shown in Figure 3 which are even more relevant today for mass
information utilities.

Participative information system design provides a powerful new
gateway for continually defining and sharpening democratic
excellence in planning and using information systems. Five
recommendations are made to seize this new opportunity.

FIGURE 3

SOCIAL OBJECTIVES FOR COMPUTER NETWORK SERVICES

Public Objectives

1. Protection of privacy and dignity of individuals, and prevention of harmful use of information.
2. Contribution to individuality and self-fulfillment, consistent with the general welfare.
3. Higher priority on public than private services, particularly for education, health, safety and democratic process.
4. Computer services should be self-supporting over the long run.
5. Mass computer services should be carefully planned, guided by continuing research, and managed as a public trust.
6. Equitable distribution of information in the public domain for all classes of society.

User Objectives

1. Fair and equitable service at nondiscriminatory rates for all users.
2. High-quality standards for service with adequate backup facilities for overloads and relatively error-free service.
3. Non-interference of public and regulated services with private and proprietary computer services.
4. Protection of privacy of each individual's personal data by law and by system design features.
5. Maximum flexibility of computer services to facilitate open-end growth and improvement of services.
6. Participation of users in determining standards and types of information services, with continuing user feedback on quality of service received.

Supplier Objectives

1. The right to receive fair profits in return for computer service investments.
2. Contribution to standards and regulatory constraints for products and services.
3. Protection by law against unfair competition, fraud, conflict of interest, etc.
4. Reward incentives for technical and service excellence.

1. Excellence: We should focus on ways to continually improve
    information systems toward increasing user participation and
    aiming at social excellence, rather than regard such systems
    as battlegrounds for personal or organizational power.

2. Total Social System: We need to look at the total social
    system involved in computer-aided information services rather
    than the view of narrow sectarianism. This is more likely to
    lead to authentic cooperation and more effective democratic
    system development.

3. Priority of the Public Interest: At the national level, the
    public interest should have the highest priority in
    information system development, not the lowest priority. The
    public stakes are the biggest and most important of all from
    the point of view of the economy, quality of working life,
    the individual and organizational effectiveness. We are
    headed toward unversal computer terminals in industrialized
    societies by the turn of this century.

4. Computer Literacy: An illiterate population can neither use
    nor appreciate computer-based information systems. Lifelong
    computer literacy is needed throughout school and working
    years to meet this objective, not just a token introductory
    course to salve the social conscience of educators. For
    example, Carnegie Mellon University has just announced a
    policy for all students to have their own personal computer
    terminals for all of their undergraduate and graduate
    courses.

5. Long-Range Planning: Democratically concurred long-range
    plans for the social use of computer services need to
    supersede the vagaries of the commercial marketplace.
    Otherwise the information rich will become richer and the
    information poor will become poorer, further polarizing
    social inequities in a world already stretched taut near the
    breaking point.

As in the current dilemma of nuclear disarmament, we need new
cooperative 21st Century models to succeed in participative
information system design, models aimed at cooperative social
excellence, rather than the self-seeking, confrontational methods
of the 19th Century.

BIBLIOGRAPHY

1. Briefs, Ulrich "The Role of Information Processing Systems in Employee Participation in Management Decision Making," in Human Choice and Computers, (Eds.) E. Mumford and H. Sackman, North Holland Press, Amsterdam, 1975.

2. Churchman, C. A., "Management and Planning Problems," in Computers and the Problems of Society, (Eds.) Harold Sackman and Harold Borko, AFIPS Press, Montavle, N.J., 1972.

3. Dordick, Herbert S., Helen G. Bradley, Burt Nanus, The Emerging Network Marketplace, Ablex Publishing Corp., Norwood, New Jersey, 1981.

4. Goranzon, Bo et. al. Job Design and Automation in Sweden, Center for Working Life, Stockholm, Sweden, 1982.

5. Japan Information Processing Development Center, The Office of Today and Tomorrow, JIPDEC Report, No. 47, 1981.

6. Mestrovic, Matko (Ed.), Socialty of Communication, Zagreb, Yugoslavia, 1978.

7. Mumford, E., and H. Sackman (Eds.) Human Choice and Computers, North Holland Press, Amsmterdam, 1975.

8. Nanus, B. "Multinational Computers and Social Choice," in E. Mumford, and H. Sackman, Human Choice and Computers, op. cit.

9. Nygaard, Kristen "Workers Participation in System Development," Proceedings of Human Choice and Computers, 2., (Ed.) A. Mowshowitz, North Holland Press, Amsterdam, 1980, pp. 71-77.

10. Sackman, H., B. Boehm (Eds.) Planning Community Information Utilities, AFIPS Press, Montvale, N.J., 1972.

11. Sackman, H., Man-Computer Problem Solving, Mason and Lipscomb, N.Y., 1970.

12. Sackman, H., Mass Information Utilities and Social Excellence, Mason and Lipscomb, New York, 1971.

13. Sackman, H., Social Management of Future Computer Network Information Services, Trident Press, California State University, Los Angeles, 1981.

14. Sackman, H., "The Information Rich Versus the Information Poor," Proceedings of the International Seminar on Computers in Developing Nations, 1980 Congress of the International Federation of Information Processing, J. M. Bennett and R. E. Kalman, (Eds.), North Holland Press, Amsterdam, 1981.

15. Schneider, Leslie and Claudio Ciborra, Technology Bargaining in Norway Preprint, Proceedings of the IFIP WG 9.1 Conference on Information System Design, U. Briefs, C. Ciborra, and L. Schneider, Editors, North Holland Press, Amsterdam, 1983.

SYSTEMS DESIGN FOR, WITH, AND BY THE USERS
U. Briefs, C. Ciborra and L. Schneider (editors)
North-Holland Publishing Company
© IFIP, 1983

THE USER AS A REPRESENTATION ISSUE IN THE U.S.

Eleanor H. Wynn
Bell Northern Research
Mountain View, California
U.S.A.

Problems surrounding the impact of new technology on the office worker are representation problems in two senses of the word representation. The political sense of representation is perhaps the first that comes to mind in the context of "System Design: for the users, with the users, by the users." However, the more cognitive sense of "representation", how something is represented in language or in the understanding, applies with equal force to this area of concern. As long as the user can be represented two-dimensionally, stereotypically, adversarially, it is very difficult to conceive of an application of user-driven design that has any depth to it or that has a practical outcome for the organization that accepts such a principle.

This paper will address primarily this more subtle issue of representation, as well as larger scale technical-political issues within an organization that affect the end user's freedom and quality of work. We will also suggest some simple methods, which user groups might use, to turn available information into data that can support their own claims about the nature of their work and the impact of technology, i.e. to "represent" themselves.

Whereas in Europe office workers, professionals and other white collar employees are members of active unions, in the United States, labor is as yet not organized on a large scale in the white collar workplace. The focus of many papers heard at the Riva del Sole Conference was on demands that unions and their constituents would place on employers for a user-oriented introduction and use of computer-based technology. At this time, most office employees in the US don't even contemplate such a stance toward technology. The main hope is just to keep up and acquire the skills needed to adjust to the employment situation.

There exist at present certain advocacy groups, such as Nine to Five. Additionally, a report issued by International Data Corporation, a consulting firm, cites a study done by Kilgour at California State University, Hayward, to the effect that the Teamsters Union participated in 51 elections involving white collar workers in the Spring of 1980, and that two traditional though small white collar organizations, the Office and Professional Employees, and the Federation of State, County and Municipal Workers, have been increasingly active. Also cited was a figure of 600,000 white collar workers represented in ten of the largest unions in the US and Canada. The report estimates that five to ten percent of clerical workers belong to unions. Automation related issues of health and safety, job security, job reclassification, and retraining were reported to arise in about 70% of labor-management interactions involving these workers.

However, organized labor is not at present enough of a force in the
US bureacracy for either vendors or the management of implementing
organizations to express a major preoccupation with it when considering user-related issues. The IDC report was in fact the only
reference to such activity I have seen outside of reports by the
advocacy groups themselves (Gregory).

In the U.S., the wide variety of user-oriented issues are viewed
mainly as marketing questions. In fact, the era of user-oriented
market research has perhaps only just begun with the prospect of
multiplying the population of terminal and microcomputer users
several times over in the next five years. In the last five years
or so we have seen the advent of the computer user as consumer; and
it is at this level that the interest in user-oriented systems, or
user-driven design, exists.

The consumer focus is further enhanced by the probability that a
significant portion of these new users will use computer-based
office systems on a discretionary basis. This is especially likely
to be the case for management and professional workers, and especially in the next several years of this innovation. If the systems
offered are not attractive to these discretionary users, then they
will be used less or not at all, and the "cost-benefits" that would
have justified the purchase of the equipment are not realized.

Workers using systems on a non-discretionary basis, i.e. as the
major means of carrying out their basic work functions, are also
seen as capable of rejecting systems by underutilization, minor acts
of sabotage, and outright leaving the job. Since it can be expensive to train people to use new equipment, when large numbers leave
it becomes noticeably costly to the organization. This was reported
to have happened in the early days of converting secretarial workers
into word processing operators. The turn-over in the first several
years was often quoted as being 100% per year. This failure in personnel terms caused concern among both vendors and buyers of word
processing equipment. One solution devised as a result (which also
solved other problems with word processing) was to distribute word
processing out into the departments served, so that operators would
be closer physically, socially, and cognitively to the departments
and their work objectives. Eventually the turn-over problems
declined as workers especially trained and electing to do word processing became available. At any rate, the capability users exercised to "vote with their feet" created a sensitivity on
management's part to some of the issues of job design and equipment
usability.

The point to be made is that the marketing perspective, which is the
primary force operating in the end user's behalf, can be fairly
powerful. Or perhaps it would be more accurate to say that it could
be a powerful force for good equipment design and job design if it
were carried out with effective research tools. The problems of
effective design for technology, assuming the marketing perspective
to be the vehicle, have to do with two kinds of perceptions or
stereotypes that are both pervasive and generally unquestioned.

So, even if we were to assume the very noblest of motives on the
part of system vendors and decision-mkaing bodies responsible for
system purchases, we encounter a problem of implementing those
motives that is in part epistemologically based.

TWO OBSTACLES TO EFFECTIVE USER-ORIENTED RESEARCH

First, a qualification--one area in which effective research is done is in the straight human factors area. On occasion, this straight human factors research expands out into the subject of job design and workers's skills, but mostly it is rather narrow in scope, confined to the details of the workstation construction and display characteristics, and generally not extending, or not effectively extending, into more cognitive issues like the organization and manipulability of the screen, the cognitive aspects of ordinary procedural tasks, etc.

Another common research tool, traditional systems analysis, can also yield good results if done by someone sensitive to the full range of issues. However, it is heavily subject to rationalistic biases of data processing and management's model of how the organization's work is accomplished. And the individuals trained in this mode of study are quite unlikely to have the sensitivity to make this a user-oriented approach, except in the sense of user that applies to large organizational entities.

Other than these two approaches, which do not cover the full range of issues, user-oriented research is subject to two major apperceptive obstacles to good understanding. These blocks are pervasive, and the biases can extend to user representatives themselves, who may especially be subject to the second obstacle, not understanding the alternative. Incidentally, this is where competent social science research can make a large impact. The problems embedded in the obstacles have to do with shallow reflections on social issues and social groups, and especially with legitimation of the "member's point of view" or "member's analysis" as a major source of valid information.

The two obstacles are, then:

o 1) social stereotypes about users held by technical development groups and the buying organization's management

o 2) the mystification of "science", which is understood as limited to certain narrow methodologies and means of validation--in fact the truly scientific methodology may be one that is very simple to implement and requires neither experts nor complex statistical manipulations

STEREOTYPING THE USER

First of all, who are we talking about as the "user"? The conventional data processing understanding of the user has some ambiguity in it. However, it tends toward an implicit definition of the user as the using department, the person responsible for buying services and equipment, the manager of a function which is automated or uses data processing services. This is a valid definition of the user, though it is not exactly what is meant in this context here. Attention to the user by this definition has merit, and is often discussed in the popular technical journals, such as Datamation, Computerworld, and MIS Week. The issue is a step removed from our present concern for the user, but is a version of the same thing. The difference is that the user-as-department represents directly the goals and understanding of the larger organization's management. It is considered as an entity with valid power, since it controls a

budget. The issue then becomes one of data processing being responsive to the real requirements of this group and not being so technocratic as to ignore the political and operational realities of the
organization.

Also, political philosophies are embodied in a corporation's or
their technical management's choice to centrally control the technical resources or to facilitate the applications-based equipment
choices of the departmental or divisional managers. This is the
sense in which the data processing and communications directors
employ the term "user-driven". In fact, these choices are very
important to the concerns of the Working Group, because the closer
the choice is to the department, the more visible the concerns of
the lowest level end-users become to the decision-makers. It also
implies that there will be a multiplicity rather than a monopoly of
vendors. The consequence of this will be a tendency for more in-
house technical expertise, equipment maintenance, and future planning. If the user-as-department has more control, there is a better
chance that the end-user will have more control, and that the system
will be flexible. There is a less massive, because less centralized, capital investment, and hence more chance to change what
doesn't work.

The user we have referred to in the 9.1 Working Group is, I believe,
the end-user, and specifically the worker at the lower levels.
Managers will also be end-users, but they have a good capability for
self-representation and for having their demands met. Their use
will be highly discretionary at the outset; it is more likely that
their equipment will be of good quality; and the device of choice
for managers is, at present, the personal computer. In fact, only
recently has the manager been revealed as a voluntary user rather
than an enlistment problem. Concerns of two years ago, that
managers wouldn't deign to use keyboards or learn to type, have been
pretty much blown away by their discretionary purchase of personal
computers on an individual basis. These devices are often within an
individual manager's signing authority (they don't need high-level
approval to spend the money), and it is reported by a marketing
manager from a personal computer company that the purchase orders
for the devices may describe them as "office furniture" to avoid the
requirement of capital equipment purchase approval. So much for
managers' resistance to computers.

Finally, we proceed to the end-user that meets with significant
potential problems from the introduction of technology. This is the
person whose job is believed to be well-understood enough to rationalize, re-design, automate, and possibly segment, reduce or de-
skill. The class consciousness of management, in justifying the
roles they occupy and seeing them as qualitatively different, more
cognitive, more skilled, and less automatable than the lower-paid
jobs is quite predictable. It is also the core of the problem.
Research I have participated in (Wynn, 1979; Suchman & Wynn, 1979),
has shown that the cognitive boundary imagined between
professional/managerial and clerical work is artificial. The scope
of the decisions clerical workers make may be narrower, the level of
detail in the problems they solve may be finer and have more constraints, the formal training required may be less, but the nature
of the mental process is not necessarily less complex.

Clerical work that involves handling organizational procedures, such
as order entry and accounting, as well as jobs that involve dealing
with either the public or other companies over procedure-based

issues, all require certain contextual capabilities. They also require a sense of the combined social and procedural constraints, which may operate at cross-purposes to each other. These capabilities include a historical embeddedness in the organization, the ability to categorize people and events, the ability to search for and solve problems and generally to use heuristics and negotiate. Additionally, the capability includes the understanding of basic, perhaps unstated, purposes of the activity, along with its formal requirements. An example is that a person who performs a service, such as a consultant, has a right to collect reimbursement in a timely fashion. This is a social principle too general to be stated in the procedure. When the procedure can't be met because of lack of documentation or authorization at the time when payment, buy social standards, ought to be delivered, competent clerks may find ways to satisfy the social requirement by manipulating the procedural requirement. Many occasions arise where clerks attend conscientiously to the social practicalities of relations with service providers or customers, by going around the dictates of the procedure in some way, while still managing to create a justifiable account of the events. (Suchman, unpublished manuscript, Xerox Corp.)

These capabilities are highly dependent upon a cohesive social organization in the workplace that maintains the body of implicit knowledge (as distinct from explicit procedural knowledge) required to carry out these tasks in optimum fashion. Some automation experiments inadvertently revealed these facts by failing in just those areas where members' knowledge was carrying the spirit of the task, while only the formal procedure was automated. The solution was then to back off to a more moderate level of automation. These adapatations are most likely to be made where customers complain about the lowered level of service and withdraw from the business relationship on that account.

In places where the clerical problem-solving skill is contained within the organization itself, the failings of automation are less likely to be documented, noticed, or corrected.

Studies which reveal such issues are not likely to occur in the normal course of doing market research or systems analysis. Research which is done is likely only to perpetuate, or at least will fail to challenge, the myth that clerical work does not require intelligence, decision-making, and problem-solving. On the contrary, in the common experience what is noticed is the failure of particular individuals to exhibit these characteristics. Like housework, clerical work is noticeable mainly in the breach. When it works properly, it seems to be a natural situation, a background. It is transparent in the Heideggerian sense.

Automation efforts can, in fact, make it "present-at-hand", something one looks at for the first time in a reflective rather than presumptive way. But only if they fail badly enough. The trouble with changing undocumented things is that the points of comparison are lost after the change, and people may or may not realize what it was they had before. They have only their myth of what had been. Without documentation all is surmise, personal perspective, subjective, pure interpretation, anecdote, etc.

Assumptions about the simple-mindedness of clerical work, in the absence of direct observation, become embodied in the equipment designed to serve that task and that user. These assumptions can be self-fulfilling. Just as television programming that assumes an idiot mentality of viewers actually adds to the stupefaction of its consumers and creates a market for more stupefying programs, equipment that assumes a non-problematic task and a dull user contributes to the fulfillment of this assumption. Even intelligent people can become habituated in processes far below their potential. The same is true in the other direction. Users of very powerful intelligent workstations gain scope, challenge, and technical understanding by having an interesting device to interact with and carry out tasks on.

Instead of deep investigation, many of the individuals responsible for technology planning may think they "know" things about the user that involve false or superficial interpretations. This "knowledge" may go unquestioned, being taken as a given or a preestablished "fact." Often such assumptions come from pieces of social theory that trickle into the popular understanding as if they were fact, not theory. The theories themselves may be under debate, or out of date. Assumptions derived from Freudian theory, for instance, about the "neutrality" required of an interviewer (translated from psychoanalyst), or from experimental psychology about the "experimental design" of research, or from functionalism about the separability of social and task or cognitive activities, all impede intelligent research when taken as fact rather than theory. From such sources absurd notions such as "human resistance to change" are glibly cited as the reason workers don't embrace technology. Thinking this to be understood already, the "researcher" does not bother to investigate the practical and legitimate political reasons why technology might be questioned by workers. A related assumption is that "fear" and other childish emotions cause workers to "resist" the progress of technology. Meanwhile the real causes of aversion are not addressed. People rush out to buy microwave ovens, new cars, videocassette recorders, video games, etc. Where is their resistance to innovation in these products? Personal computers were orginally not marketed to the office. Managers in organizations proved to be a spontaneous market for personal computers, completely surprising such vendors as Apple. People buy these innovations because they see a benefit. They resist others because they see a possible disadvantage. A complicated psychology is not required to understand these phenomena.

In my own research, done with interviews of office workers in workstation "pilots", I found the following reasons given by people for being concerned about technology. I prefer the word "concerned" to "afraid" or "resistant", both of which can imply irrationality. The concerns should be obvious to members of the 9.1 Working Group.

o   concern the technology will be hard to learn

o   concern that the person's status will drop relative to others because others might learn more easily

o   concern that the performance criteria will change to the individual's disadvantage

o   concern that work life will be more regimented, that workers won't be able to move around as much, that their work will be paced for them

o   concern that management will make as bad choices about technology in the present and future as they have in the past

o   concern that the equipment will therefore be wrong for the job
      but will soak up funds while pay increases are kept low

o   concern that there will be fewer jobs and their own job secu-
      rity will be threatened

When research is done on such concerns, it is in the form of an
"attitude" survey. Again, the term "attitude" implies an irrational
rather than a rational stance. The way to correct attitudes is
through some kind of psychological massage, advertising, or packaging, not by addressing the underlying issues. I don't mean to be
unfair to those who do in fact carry on serious research, but rather
to reveal what I consider pervasive assumptions that color much of
the research that does get funded. In fact, very large sums of
research money are spent both by organizations planning to buy
equipment and by those planning to sell equipment. The care to make
sure the money is well spent is undoubtedly there, but the theoretical approach that would enable this is often missing.

STEREOTYPES OF SCIENCE

Why isn't the type of research that will reveal both the underlying
capabilities of clerical workers, described in the previous paragraphs, and the legitimate concerns that workers have, carried out
very often? One reason is that designers, implementors and managers
are ignorant of their ignorance. They only see a grey world, not
the grey glasses they view through. Moreover, there is a blind
faith in something called "science" and "scientific method".   In
most cases this means nothing more than loosely throwing around
terms like "validity", "sample", "significance", "cluster analysis",
and displaying results of calculations in graphs, charts, and statistical "maps". The disregard for either the hypotheses used to
collect information or the actual quality of the data itself can be
truly astounding.

We are not referring here to the actual scientific work that takes
place in organizations relating to technology development, where the
proof is in the operation of the device, and where the operatives
are in fact scientists. Rather we mean the presumed social science
work taking place in an environment where the standards of the disciplines are not enforced, and where there is a strong constraint to
look good without any immediate test of validity.

This is a very serious problem because it is a reality-defining
situation using inappropriate tools. The survey questionnaire, for
instance is the research tool of choice because the results can be
made to look "hard." In a technical environment this is especially a
problem because the researcher has to deliver the results to technical people who have a certain epistemology, which they tend to
extend outside their discipline. Analysis based on detailed observation, following from leading edge social science theories, for
instance, doesn't always look "hard" even though it may be far more
sophisticated and truly scientific than the survey result. This is
considered "subjective" because the background of social theory and
its history are not apparent to the technical or business person.

At the same time, paradoxically, one encounters very many intelligent, observant, socially sensitive individuals in management and
technical positions, as well as of course in the line operations--
the workers carrying out tasks. The observations of these individu-

als, while possibly lacking a larger framework of interpretation, nevertheless have the benefit of immediacy and detailed acquaintance with the subject of observation. But observations per se may not count in the epistemology of decision-making, unless they come from the very top management. The legitimation of training and theoretical argument are lacking from these otherwise valid and useful accounts, and so they are neglected and discounted, even by the individuals who make them.

In this way much valuable insight from members of organizations is lost. People do not believe their own valid analyses because they think the truth must come in a graph. All else is "subjective". This is antithetical to the notion of "member's knowledge" presented in ethnomethodology and in the traditional method of anthropology, participant observation. It also masks the large interpretive component in the formal studies, both in the selection of research topic and the hypothesis for investigating, as well as in deciding how to present the results.

Also contained in the superficial model of science is a loathing for complexity. Too many variables, situations that are embedded in a large historical or organizational context, elaborate analyses of individuals about their work situation, are all hard to codify and compute. They are hard to present in the format of "science". They are hard to compare with other situations and quantify, and they require actual thought to figure out. A computational device cannot take over the responsibility for the analysis and results.

SIMPLE RESEARCH TOOLS AVAILABLE

However, the situation, being partly one of awareness, is dynamic. A difference can be made by serious studies and arguments. A serious study does not have to be complicated, just as honest as it can be. Unions and advocacy groups must be prepared to do their own research on themselves. Allegations of bias that might be made will apply with equal force to studies done by management, consultants and vendors. Unions can also hire their own researchers or research advisors. But it is up to the worker advocates to define the issues that will be researched. Most of the expertise that is required already exists in the body of the working group, because that is where the knowledge of the workplace under investigation, and the knowledge of the problems and concerns, exists in the greatest concentration. The problem is in packaging this essentially latent knowledge into a format of "data." There are two basic simple modes for making this transformation:

o   detailed descriptive accounts with an interpretive analysis

o   records of various kinds

Many times the issues worker advocates are trying to get at are contained in the detailed knowledge of how tasks are done, and how aspects of the task affect the worker. Descriptive accounts by the task operative or a co-worker can bring out otherwise unnoticed (to management) features of the task and its problems. Discussion groups can be a vehicle for activating awareness and for creating enough accounts to provide "data." I use the word data carefully because it is such a religious term. Basically it is information that is formalized, or collected in sufficient quantities to be formalized. Events recorded in the memory, generalized upon and illustrated with an example are called "anecdotes". Anecdotes are often based upon basically inert information that has not been systematically recorded. Recording events turns them into data once the record is of a certain size. This points us to the other simple method for doing studies, keeping records.

Records can be created in a variety of forms once it has been decided what the points to be made are. Again the worker representatives are the best people to decide what these are, since they know what their objectives are. Records can be created by having all or a sample of individuals record their observations at the end of a day every day or at intervals of a few days. Or the records can be made whenever a "critical incident" occurs. This is an incident that illustrates the point to be made, or that comprises a randomly recurring situation of some kind essential to the point being made. These can often be compared to organizational records of operations. These records can then be compiled after a period of time and subjected to simple computations.

Short questionnaires can also be distributed. For instance, if there is a lot of diffuse grumbling about a situation that impacts the quality of work, the productivity of a group, or health, etc. the problem may be ignored as long as it is not quantified. A short questionnaire form asking if people have experienced the problem, how they feel about it, and how it affects their work, can give the true dimensions of this issue. It happens, but it cannot be expected, that management would study the problem if it primarily impacts workers. Not all aspects of work productivity are measured. If the problem affects a part of production that isn't measured, there is no particular incentive for management to study or change it. However, they can be made to see it in their interest by an informal worker study.

OTHER ISSUES

Finally, I would like to say what issues I am concerned about from my perspective as a professional working in a large organization that makes and uses technology. I use computer-based systems every day, and would find it cumbersome to do my work without them. In fact, there are more features I would like to have. I wish my organization were on a nation-wide electronic mail network, like my last workplace was, so I could communicate easily with colleagues across the country, or in Europe, as I was able to before. I wish my company would provide access to outside on-line databases so I could locate information to support my work.

I would expect anyone working with terminals or minicomputers to demand a high-quality, high resolution display. In procedural jobs workers should make sure their equipment does not dictate an inexorable sequence but allows them to stop processes, intervene, make decisions outside the options presented by the computer program, and reorder the sequence of tasks where needed. People should attend to the kinds of measurements being applied to performance, as well as to who can access their work files and what another person can do to information one has stored.

The user interface of a system should be flexible, should preferably allow concurrent windows, so that information and processes from different files can be displayed concurrently. The user interface should avoid frustration and confusion, such as obscure command

names. It should not allow irrecoverable errors, like devouring a
whole file by mistake with the user unable to stop or reverse the
process.

The system itself should be open-ended in capacity, so that a user
can become ever more expert, and perform ever more sophisticated
tasks. It should be as self-teaching as possible, and of course,
obvious to operate for a beginner.

As stated in the opening section, there is a difference between a
centralized versus distributed system. It is preferrable, though
perhaps harder for the organization to manage, to allow departmental
or divisional purchase of equipment. Many US organizations, as well
as vendors, are already committed to the "multi-vendor environment".
The single vendor environment favors mainly the very largest vendors
and fosters a long-term commitment to that vendor, as well as dependence upon that vendor both for service and for planning future
technology. It simplifies life but does not necessarily have an
all-around benefit. Moreover, a very large vendor is likely to have
a highly formalized internal organization which may also be
reflected in the types of products they develop.

As much as possible the maintenance capability should be developed
within the organization, or at least control of the maintenance
diagnostics. Certainly other training programs should be demanded
so that incumbents of positions will be able to occupy the new version of the job. Right now in the US, the economics of the labor
market favor this, as there is still a large labor shortage in
computer-related jobs, and especially programmers and maintenance.

I realize that none of the above addresses macro-level issues such
as large-scale displacement of labor, and basically assumes employment stability with the introduction of technology.   This enormous
problem I must leave to others.

In the interest of delivering the paper on time, I must stop at this
point, perhaps abruptly, hoping that these remarks will be of some
use.

SYSTEMS DESIGN FOR, WITH, AND BY THE USERS
U. Briefs, C. Ciborra and L. Schneider (editors)
North-Holland Publishing Company

USER PARTICIPATION AND INTEGRATION IN SYSTEM DEVELOPMENT -
- EXPERIENCES, PROBLEMS AND MEANS OF SOLVING AS SEEN BY
DP-MANAGEMENT

Dr. M. Schroeder

Manager Production Information Systems
Data Processing Division
Voest-Alpine AG
Linz, Austria

An introductory survey is given over the functional
and hierarchical integration of the Software-
Department in the company and of the way cooperation
with user-departments took place in the past.

Illustrated by a large-scale project - the
development of an Integrated Production Planning and
Control System for a Metallurgical Plant - various
problems are shown which can arise during development
and use of such systems.

The preventive organizing tools to solve such
conflict-situations are explained and reported.

1. Introduction

In the following, experiences made during system development in a
Primary Industry Enterprise are discussed. In the foreground is the
steelworks automation with 12,000 employees and a production of
2,910.000 tons per year (1981).

In the beginning of 1970, a far reaching automations wave for important production planning functions in the form of Batch Processing
Systems and also Conversational Systems were realized. Most of these
systems are still in use today.

Since 1973 the originally divided commercial and technical
Development Departments have been centralized and now offer their
services not only within the combine but also externally.
Approximately 300 people are employed in the area of system
development.

The System Development Departments are divided functionally into:

- Business Administration System Development
- Industrial Automation and Electronics
- Development of Technical/Scientific Application Systems

Regional criteria are considered in the sub-divisions.

The Department for Industrial Automation and Electronics is
divided according to the automation object as follows:

- Production Planning and Scheduling Systems
- Process Automation Systems and Process Model development
- Microprocessing techniques

The author of this report is in charge of the sub-division for
Production Planning and Scheduling Systems, which has a staff of
approximately 50 people.

This sub-division was charged by the company's top management to
develop and realize an Integrated Production Planning and Control
System for the Metallurgical Division within 5 years.

The following statements on "user participation" are based on the
experiences gained in the realization of that large-scale project.

Thus "user" are all employess of the company, wich are concerned
with the planned sytem in any way.

From the author's point of view "user participation" means to give
all future users of the planned systems the possibility, to
formulate requirement specifications appropriate to their
individual needs and to develope the final functional spezification
in a way, that realizes companies goals to the highest possible
degree.

In this paper the debatable alternative of deceleration of development and application of the information technology will not be
analysed, since this paper favours technological progress.

2.   Shape of the Cooperation in the 1970's

Since the middle of the 1960's, extensive automation projects, not
only for Commercial application but also for Production Planning and
Control Functions have been developed and used in the steel industry.

In accordance with the available system technology, these systems
were either batch processing systems or partly interactive systems
since manual keyboard input and typewriter output was the only
available method of communication with the user.

At this time automation was the task of a few highly qualified
experts who had the necessary know-how as far as computers and
system development was concerned.

Within a relatively short period, a large EDP-department was established. This department mainly tried to computerise manual procedures without causing any unnecessary delays and to achieve
additional useful effects.

The user was not prepared for this development. After many years of
hard work in order to change to EDP procedures, he was confronted
with the problem of losing flexibility common to manual procedures
without being able to achieve a noticeable ease in work.

A lot of time was required to check computer processed information.
Whenever errors were found it was once again proved that the
automated information processing did not function better than the
procedures used previously.

A stabilization of opinions was seen when it became evident that EDP departments are very expensive. During discussions on the economy of automation which followed, it was asked that the user should reduce his personnel staff and achieve an efficiency which compared favourably with the high EDP costs.

On the one hand the introduction of performance calculation procedures helped to make the discussion about the efficiency of EDP-Applications much more objectiv, on the other hand it misled the ursers to pass over the "expensive EDP-department" and to try to solve system development problems themselves.

This led to negative attidudes beetween user and system designer and reduced the will to co-operate.

In addition to these organizational psychological aspects, a number of technical problems arose that also hampered cooperation between users and designers:

- At this time a generally known and proved systems development technique was slowly being developed and only partially mastered by the designers. These procedures were not available to users.

- The automatic information processing was primarily used for relatively simply and controllable operations, which were also either easy to understand or repeat for the designer. Also for this reason the necessity for cooperative working procedures was limited.

- At the development of more complicated systems the user was involved in defining the scope of functions. However due to this lack of EDP knowledge and high abstractions level, he was not always able to define his requirements. Usually after system implementation the user could define the desirable system attributes - mostly not available - and the undesired properties of the system.

- The new job description of the EDP organizer in many cases led a large number of people from various divisions changing over to system development department. They brought with them necessary knowledge, so that the dependence of the EDP department on the cooperation with other departments was limited.

It must be also stressed that in spite of all these problems a noticeable success has been achieved in the application of information technology.

3. Alteration in the Field of System Development

Due to the revolutionary development of the hard- and software technology at the end of 1970 and the sharp fall in price of the system components the automatic information processing now has numerous economical application fields.

The formerly isolated grouped EDP-systems were quickly expanded and very soon confronted with communication problems. Mostly these problems could not be solved and manual data processing procedures were necessary.

The possibility of realizing an extensive Conversational System with
relatively low hardware costs for practically all operational
functions therefore penetrating into the operational procedure, had a
much stronger impact than the horizontal extension of automation.

It indicates therefore that internal information processing should be
restructured in many areas, if the advantages of the data processing
system are to be effective.

In many cases this has not been taken into consideration.
Sophisticated dialog systems for various internal tasks have been
realized.

High costs for systems development and maintenance and the user's
hesitance to accept proved that the common methods of cooperation
used are no longer effective.

Therefore new cooperation modes are required for every form of system
development, especially for the development of highly interactive and
comprehensive systems.

A project of this type (see Appendix 1 for basic data of the project)
was a reason for us to search for new forms of cooperation. The
results are shown in the following sections.

4. Aims of Cooperation Models for the Development of
    Interactive Systems

In the following we begin with the principle, that - independent of
the previously described problems - in future times information
processing systems will be developed for a wide range of different
problems to an essentially greater extent than up to know.

Therefore in this paper we shall not deal with the conceivable
alternative of retarding the technological development in this
field.

We presume that it will be possible to use computer systems in a
way that avoids their, up to now, realized negative effects and
deals completely with the positive possibilities of use.

It is the author's opinion that this general goal can only be
reached, if there is a division of labour between the user and
designer of a system in a way that proves to be significant from a
socioeconomic point of view.

Therefore

-   systems- and process engineering   as well as
-   organizational psychological goals

are important. These goals will be presented in detail in the
following.

Systems- and process engineering goals:

- In future applications the main problems of automatic information processing will be of a systems engineering kind, and thus
  cannot be solved solely by a systems analyst. The user has to
  recognize his need for automation and in formulating it together with the systems analyst.

- Instead of batch-systems we will develope dialog systems with
  a great number of man-machine interfaces. The ergonomically
  optimal design of this interfaces again can only be done in
  close co-operation between user and system analyst.

  Therefore

  o   physical factors (e.g. stress caused by working at
      terminals)
  o   processing techniques (e.g. screen lay out)
  o   operational techniques

  have to be taken into consideration.

- Future systems will not maintain a stationary but an
  evolutionary attitude. Under this aspect, active participation
  of the user in the development of the system is
  essential.

Organizational psychological goals:

Integrating the user into the process of systems design must be
advantageous for the following reasons:

- The user identifies himself with the system thus essentially
  improving the quality of the system

- The resulting responsibility for "his" system and "his" data
  sets guarantees for the economic operation of the system. This
  aspect is very important in the case of break-down.

- Furthermore according to users and designers joint work helps
  to overcome today's still prevailing polarization.

5.   Problems of User Participation

We now have to put the question why the previously mentioned aims
have not yet - or at least only to a very small extent - been
reached. There are several reasons:

- From a user's point of view computer aided methods critically
  question those manual operations used hitherto thus causing
  negative attitudes.

- The high degree of abstraction and the not user-oriented development procedures lead to an increase of that attitude.

- The profitability of automatic information processing was
  usually based on saving personnel just in the area concerned.
  Surely it is problematic to expect these colleagues to
  cooperate properly.

- It can not be denied that development departments are themselves mystified by the field of automation to a certain
  degree. Furthermore it was advantageous for EDP- departments to
  build up and cultivate some monopolies in knowledge in addition
  to their monopoly in computer resources on an short term basis.

Finally in many cases it was tried to solve the problems of cooperation in a way that the user himself provided with the
resources necessary and developed his systems without the aid of
specialized systems development departments. This alternative also
prevented the introduction of cooperative working methods.

6. Measures for Improvement of Cooperation/Experience Gained:

In the following we show measures taken in order to achieve an optimal cooperation between user and System Development in the
realization of a large project.

In most cases these measures have proved successful.

These comments reflect the experiences gained over many years and
will certainly subject to changes.

In the following areas, measures were undertaken in order to improve
cooperation:

- Overall planning of computer application projects in co-
  operation with user
- Project organization
- User oriented system engineering methods
- User training
- Information and motivation of all participants

6.1 Overall Planning Computer Application

At the start of the project a basic agreement was worked out and
agreed in writing, comprising the following main points:

- Planning of the EDP applications
- Participation of user in system development
- Cooperation in the operation and further development of the
  systems.

This agreement defines responsibilities and tasks of the user and
systems designer and includes all industrial automation projects
(Production Planning- and Control Systems, Processing Functions,
Instrumentation Functions) in all areas of a metallurgical plant.

An EDP Frame Concept which shows the essential information flows
and the automation possibilities has been worked out together with
the user.

Based on this concept a long term EDP Application Plan has been
developed. This plan is continuously updated and renewed for the
whole area due to the development in the automation field and in
the remaining investment activities.

The collaboration of the user in the systems design and the co-operation in the operation and further development of the system was regulated by the goals described in Chapter 4.

Up to now the following experiences have been made:

- The difficulties in jointly formulation of the basic concepts showed that the complex problem of distributing duties can only be solved by thorough discussion based on will to co-operate.

- The second important realization is, that comprehensive basic concepts of system design are absolutely necessary orientation frames for the user as well as for the designer of a system.

- Such orientation frames are not only necessary for technical reasons, but they are an essential prerequisite for the realization of organizing consequences of automation, like structural changes in places of employment, in time in order to set appropriate actions.

6.2. Project Organization

At the start of the project referred to in this paper project organization existed in the company, but it was

- restricted to smaller projects,
- strongly influenced by interdepartmental directives
- by far less known to the user than to the systems designers

The last problem was solved relatively quickly by actions of the departmental management (providing personnel for project work, reevaluation of project work,...)

The following modes of action were set up in the organization of the big project:

- The management of the whole project consists of a represen-tative of both the users and the systems designers. The main task of the user representative is functional specifications, that of the systems designer is managing systems design and implementation.

- The project management reports to a "project-planning-team" that consists of representatives of the divisions concerned.

- The teams for single projects are guided by a project management team consisting of representatives of users and designers.

- The project teams are composed of users and designers corresponding to the needs of the project phases.

This project organization model has shown good results in co-operation till now.

6.3. Systems Engineering

It is the authors opinion that the application of user-oriented
methods of system development is one of the most important prerequisites for the integration of the user into the process of
system design.

In particular, the following process engineering actions are to be
set:

Structuring of the process of development:

The basic structuring of the development process into the main
phases

- functional specification
- systems design and
- implementation

distinctly shows to the user his main role and points of efforts in
this process.

A strictly sequential method of proceeding is impossible in the
development of large systems. Only the conscious use of a phase
concept creates the prerequisite to leave a strictly sequential way
without losing orientation in the development process.

At least it is important to show the user that "his" system has to
be developed, implemented, taken over and operated by him.

Using user-oriented methods and tools

The following methods and tools are necessary to facilitate the
joint functional specifications:

- visualisation of man/machine interfaces (dialogue design at the
  terminal in cooperation with the user)
- performance of application simulations for procedures layout
  and optimization
- prototyping (preliminary development of partial functions)
- use of techniques for visualisation, communication and performance by the project teams
- introduction of "Structured Walkthroughs" for the acceptance of
  phase results

User-oriented guidelines for the systems design

The following guidelines are used to increase the ease of use of
the system:

- dividing the system into small units comprehensible for the
  user
- guaranteeing reconstruction of the algorithms used
- flexible and easily changeable system design

Furthermore all those functions that can be significantly performed by the user in the future, like producing special computations or inquiry- and information-functions, should be reserved for the user.

6.4. Training

Today's users have neither training nor practical experience in systems development and in the operation of the system.

Users now entering the profession certainly know a great deal about programming languages, but they are not prepared for being "active users".

Hence it has to be a principal concern of all parties involved to step into this breach by intensifying education and training in the following fields:

- providing basic knowledge about automatic information processing with special regard to peripheral components of the system ("user-surface")

- training of the user in process engineering with special regard to the use of computers (e.g. computer-assisted planning, process automation)

- training in the basics of systems engineering with special regard to the functional specification phase

- training in organization of and working in projects as well as in teamwork techniques

6.5. Information of Users

A systematic information policy connected with the project can in the author's opinion contribute enormously to the creation of a good working climate within the teams and also within the group of users as a whole. Especially big projects often cause fears, rumours and attitudes that are unrealistic in many cases and can be corrected by a systematic information policy.

Certainly in automation projects of this kind thorough changes in wide ranges are to be expected, so that a fair information policy as concerns the user gains special importance.

It is of crucial importance to involve the members of the works councils shop stewards from the very beginning aiming at gaining them for active cooperation.

In the case discussed in this paper the first concept of the functional specification was already presented to the shop stewards. Furthermore the effects of the planned system on the structure and number of jobs were discussed commonly and a plan for proceeding was agreed upon.

In order to raise the users motivation for cooperation it was tried
deliberately to convince the user, that beside the responsibility
for using up to date production technologies there is - as
justified as this - the responsibility for using up to date
information technology. As soon as these facts are recognized a
further step in efficient cooperation between designer and user is
done.

7.   Summary and Prospects

Hitherto existing practical experiences in trying to find new ways
of cooperation between user and systems designer are throughout
positive.

Essential is the realization that the abandonment of traditional
roles did not at all lead to new problems e.g. caused by
counterrailing tendencies for monopolization.

There resulted efficient and collegial ways of cooperation with
exceedingly positive working climate to a very high degree.

Not all possible solutions were tried up to now in deepth and range
necessary for making generally valid statements. It can uniquely be
deduced from the results existing up to now, that the adapted way
will lead to our aim.

Already now it can be stated that the totality of all modes of
acting presented in chapter 6 will lead to the greatest success
possible and that single approaches are not likely to be
successful.

Our opinion is that today the technological prerequisites for broad
application of computerized information systems are given, but at
the same time there is the danger that human aspects are not enough
taken into account.

User participation is an essential contribution to making use of
the chances provided by a new technology not only without damage,
but even with improving the environment of labour at the same time.

Appendix: Basic Project Data

Project goals:

Development of an Integrated Production planning and Control system
for a metallurgical plant

Main functions of the new system:

-   Order-Entry function and customers dispositions
-   technical order specification (fixing the production steps)
-   capacity planning system (over 100 production steps)

- local disposition-functions for the working areas of
  - o steel factory
  - o hot rolling mill
  - o adjustment factory
  - o cold rolling mills
  - o dispatching departments

  including systems to save actual production dates or dates from checkpoints to the lower process-automation-systems.
- Time Planning and Control System
- Quality Assurance
- Production Information Systems

Expenditure:

- 100 man years system analysts (without users)
- 300 peripheral in- and output devices
- time of realization: 5 years

Expected Advantages:

Cost-Reduction by

- saving energies,
- reducing stocks,
- output improvement
- reduction of operative functions

Effects on Employment

- Operations for
  - o production of documents
  - o transportation of documents and
  - o creating and manipulating of card-indexes

  will be strongly reduced

- Time needed for dispositive functions will remain approximately unchanged because of additional requirements

- Additional working places will be necessary for the operating of the computer systems

FRAMEWORK FOR THE CLASSIFICATION OF FORMS OF PARTICIPATION
IN ORGANIZATIONAL AND TECHNOLOGICAL CHANGE

G. Della Rocca - O. Brivio

Institute for Action Research on Organizational System
Via Leopardi 1
20123 Milano
Italy

0. INTRODUCTION

This paper is an endeavour to construct a framework for the reading
and systematic classification of case studies on work organization
and participation.

A consolidated report will later be prepared on the research which
the European Foundation for the Improvement of Living and Working
Conditions has carried out or has underway for its 1980-81 programs
of research in the area of work organization and participation.

The framework is a useful instrument for evaluating different forms
of participation in organizational and technological change and for
defining what is meant by participation in terms of direct experience
at the workplace in several enterprises.

1. THE STATE OF THE ENTERPRISE AND OF INDUSTRIAL RELATIONS

It is necessary to start by defining "participation" and "company
parties". These two terms have different meanings according to the
context in which they are used. In the first place, "participation"
has been used in relation to the improvement of productivity
conditions and the work of the enterprise concerned. *The enterprise
in this case is the institution which is developing techniques and
methods of participation*. "Role of the parties in a process of change"
means, first and foremost, the participation of *productive roles*,
offices, groups within the company, or even single individuals in
decisions concerning the administration and change of the enterprise.

Secondly, the term "participation" has been used to define *the
participation of other institutional figures in the administration
of the enterprise*, in particular employee representatives. In this
case, "parties" refers to the institution and its guiding bodies:
trade union, workers' representatives at the workplace, company
management, contracting associations, third parties and structures
for mediation and cooperation between the parties. They are *parties*
in the strict sense of the word.

The participation of organizational roles or of parties and the
different persons identified by them are not in conflict with each
other; on the contrary, they tend to intertwine and superimpose upon
one another when there is a change in work organization.

Nevertheless, in analyzing case studies of organizational change the
two forms of participation must be kept distinct, both conceptually
and analytically. In the first place this serves to distinguish the
structural background and constraints underlying organizational
change. The aims and constraints of participation often differ
depending upon whether they stem from the needs of the enterprise
alone or from an industrial relations background as well. The analysis must therefore indicate:

A. The conditions of the enterprise:

   - market characteristics and development

   - characteristics and development of technology

   - work force characteristics and development

B. The conditions of institutional relations

   - the existing system of industrial relations (what points company
     bargaining is focused upon by the existing industrial relations
     system)

   - methods for participation pre-arranged *ad hoc* by the industrial
     relations system, but clearly autonomous from the system of
     negotiations (for example, the structure and effectiveness of
     the rights to disclosure of information in each national con-
     text).

Secondly, it serves to define an evaluation scheme of the types of
participation at the different stages of the process of organizational and technological change. Many ways have been adopted to subdivide
the process, and our task is to classify case studies that are very
different from one another. We propose the following phases of analysis: the setting-up, the process of organizational change, the evalua
tion of the results, the participation in the new forms of work
organization. Each stage would be subdivided into several analytical
levels. We will point out the relevance of the two types of participa
tion concerning the productive role and parties as well. The character
istics of the participation can be explored for each case. The type
of participation (roles or parties) and the interaction between the
two in each phase of the process can help provide a better evaluation
of the process itself.

2. THE SETTING-UP

The role of the various subjects in activating processes of
organizational change, after having established the structural background, is the first aspect required to realize an intervention.

The conditions for setting-up an organizational change with respect to participation are determined by:

- *the problems and the objective underlying the change*, i.e. the problems for which the change has been started and its objective. These factors can determine the area and the roles and parties involved in the change;

- *the initiators of the change*, that is whoever takes on the proposal, responsibility and management of establishing the setting-up conditions;

- *the steering structure*. The structure which will have to control the entire period considered as organizational change;

- *the theory and method of the organizational process*. Theory and methods, whether implicit or explicit, of the change.

3. THE ROLES AND PARTIES IN THE PROCESS OF ORGANIZATIONAL CHANGE

This phase consists of identifying the roles and the parties in the process of change. As seen in section 2, the nature of the problem and the objectives set by the change have already defined the perimeter and the area of participation.

As far as the participation of the various subjects is concerned, an evaluation can be made with regard to their presence in the different phases of the process of change and to the methods adopted by the different subjects in each phase.

The sub-phases of the process taken into consideration are:

A. *Analysis of the problem* (which may in turn imply a restatement of the objectives and can have an influence on the area of participation and involvement).

B. *Planning the organizational design*.

C. *Implementation*.

These three sub-phases are not always necessarily in sequence. For example, analysis of the problem can appear again at the end of phases B and C, or some aspects of the planning can appear along with, or following, phase C.

With regard to the methodological instruments used in the process, three levels of classification have come to light:

A. *The structures* and/or sub-structures used during the process (analysis and research groups, mixed committees for problem solving, committees for administering the formation, etc.).

B. *Techniques for an exchange of information* used during the process (for example, techniques for using and spreading information - or for developing knowledge. These can concern the adoption of

procedural systems, formative processes or problem solving techni
ques).

C. *The decision making systems*, distinct between those inherent in
the administration of the process and those inherent in the
decisions which led to the adoption of the new type of
organization.

The position taken by each role and party must be indicated for both
the sub-phases and methodological instruments.

4. THE ROLES AND PARTIES IN THE EVALUATION OF THE RESULTS OF
ORGANIZATIONAL CHANGE

The fourth analytic phase concerns the classification of the results
and how they have been rated or received by the different subjects.
This level of identification of participation should allow for the
evaluation of the relationship between participation in the process
of change and results of the new organization. In this light, the
results can be analyzed in two ways:

A. *The results compared with the aim of the change*. An evaluation of
the results cannot be made in an abstract or general fashion -
just as with the participation of the various parties - but in
terms of the objectives proposed by the intervention. The results,
in turn, can be subdivided into those of a technical-economic or
social nature.

- *Results of a technical-economic nature* are those aspects which
contribute to defining not only company efficiency (productivity) but also its effectiveness. Besides possible indicators
of productivity, other more specific factors should also be
taken into consideration, such as: the increase in the quantity
and quality of production, defective articles, cost, development of new products, the effective introduction of new technology, the stability of programming, etc.

- *Results of a social nature* are the working conditions
(occupation, mental-physical environment, pay), the employees'
skill attitude and technical/productive knowledge, absenteeism,
turnover, etc.

Quantitative-type parameters should be used as much as possible.

B. *The results according to the evaluation of the various roles and
parties*.
The evaluation concerns both the different organizational roles
(offices-levels of the enterprise) and institutional parties
(managers, trade unions, third parties). The attempt should be
made to understand whether the evaluation constitutes a common
phase of the process which led to the change. In this case, it is
important to know how the evaluation is done. In other words, this
analytical phase examines the kind of role and party participation

in the assessment of the results of the change and how this
assessment is made.

5. PARTICIPATION IN THE ORGANIZATIONAL MODEL

The fifth and final point concerns participation in the new
organization. This last level of analysis must answer the question
of whether and to what extent participation is a qualifying aspect
of the new organization. In this respect, two areas of analysis and
possible classification of the results have been identified: the
dimensions and the type of decision making system in the new
organization.

A. *Dimensions of the new organization*

   A.1) *The environmental and ergonomic dimension* (all aspects
   concerning physical-mental fatigue).

   A.2) *The role dimension* (individual roles, relations with other
   roles in the unit under consideration, relations with other
   company roles and other company units and offices).

   A.3) *The dimension of role development* concerns cognitive and
   skill development.

   A.4) *The development of socio-economic status* is the dimension
   that concerns an individual(s personal career and social
   advancement in the company and in society (qualification
   steps, hierarchical skill position, inclusion in a community,
   etc.). The acquisition of this status presupposes the
   recognition of rights on an institutional basis.

B. *Decision making systems*. The dimensions of the organization alone
   do not define the characteristics of participation. The decision
   making system into which the organizational dimension is inserted
   constitutes the other requisite. Some types of decisions can be
   identified which help to limit participation in the organizational
   design. For example, participation in the definition of the
   objectives of the new organization, participation in decisions
   regarding administrative criteria, participation in decisions on
   selection and on organizational development.

REPORTS FROM THE
WORKING GROUPS

SYSTEMS DESIGN FOR, WITH, AND BY THE USERS
U. Briefs, C. Ciborra and L. Schneider (editors)
North-Holland Publishing Company
© IFIP, 1983

WORKING GROUP REPORT ON <u>THE NATURE OF THE DESIGN PROCESS</u>

Giovan Francesco Lanzara

Università di Bari
Italy

The purpose of this group has been to reflect and debate about the nature

of the design process in order to achieve a better understanding of what

<u>design</u> is both as a cognitive activity and as a social process. We believe

that the attempt to formulate a concept of design might be of great rele=

vance in view of

a. augmenting our understanding of real life system development processes
   and contexts;

b. facilitating communication among different actors involved in a design
   process;

c. developing better design methods than those which characterize present
   practice;

d. developing better skills in those social and organizational actors whose
   influence on system development is weaker at the moment.

The group discussion has been extremely rich,articulated,and controversial,

and the rapporteur's only regret is his own inability to put all that the=

matic richness into few pages. The discussion lead to a preliminary formula=

tion of some questions (which we think relevant),to which we then attempt to

provide tentative answers.

1. How do we study design ?what do we look for ? what do we observe ?
   issue of research method)

2. How can we formulate a concept of design ? (issue of theory)

3. How can we design methods for designing ? (issue of method)

4. To what extent it is possible to make the users being designers ?
   (issue of labor unions practice)

5. To what extent can we change the social and political conditions in
   which design processes are carried out at present ? (issue of politi=
   cal and social practice)

1. The first question concerns the possibility of observing and describing

   a design process. We agreed that it is indeed possible to observe and

   describe a design process,but that it is a contradiction in terms to pro=

   vide a complete formal description or documentation of it. We can study

   design by being part of the design process,by actively intervening into

   the process. We can only provide open descriptions. A possible research

   method to be extensively applied could be to record and analyse the pro=

   tocols of conversations of actors engaged in a design situation. More

   research attention should be put to the phenomenology of real-life episo=

   des and situations. More focus should be dedicated to what a designer

   really does when he designs,and less on abstract models asserting formal

   and normative rules of conduct.

2. The second question has to do with theoretical issues, on which we spent

   some more effort. The discussion lead us to surface a somehow dichotomous

   perspective on how design can be conceptualized, to two different but

   complementary ways of seeing design:

a. Design as an (eminently) cognitive process,i.e. a process of building
   knowledge about phenomena,that can be used for creating new forms of rea=
   lity,for framing and re-framing perspectives on the world,material or
   symbolic artifacts,systems,etc. It seems hard to formulate a concept of
   design without thinking about processes of invention and transformation
   of some artifacts.

b. Design as an (eminently) political process, i.e. <u>a process of strategic</u>
   <u>interaction and exchange</u> among different social and political actors,
   holding different perspectives on what reality is,different interests,
   values and goals,that may be competitive,incompatible,or overtly con=
   flictual,and holding different degrees of power and,consequently, uneven
   abilities to influence the realization of their own and others' interests
   and goals.

The two ways of seeing design certainly lead to very different research
programs and methods. In the course of our group discussion we made a ten=
ative effort to put them together,to treat them as complementary or at least
co-existing,even though we had some problems in spelling out and clarifying
the connections and in finding a group agreement on what kind of connections
and differences there are between the two perspectives.

A possible linking bridge is given by the following argument: it seems
clear to us that what one knows and understands about reality (a real-life
context),the extent to which he is able to conceptualize new forms of thin=
king,or his capacity for inquiry and invention, is not without effect on
his action competence,on his ability to set up goals,to relate goals to
values,and to carry out strategic action. It might be said that when one
generates an idea,he also at the same time <u>takes a stance</u> for that idea.
And "taking a stance", differently put, means "having an interest",or
"playing a game",or "being political".

We made an effort to think about design as a <u>construction process</u>,condi=
tioned by conditioning structures and leading to an understanding of pheno=
mena and to a realization of visions ("structuring the world"). The constru=
ction process takes place in a context in which other processes unfold and
interact with each other. The process can also transform the conditioning
structures (avilable resources,designer's cognitive competence,value sy=
stems,social and interpersonal relationships,political constraints,ideologies,
etc.) The construction processes differ as to the interpersonal dimension

of design: what should be of particular interest in the perspective of this
conference is design as a collective activity taking place among actors in
a group or organization.

Furthermore,several other related theoretical issues were touched and deba=
ted in a rather rapsodic but nonetheless intense way. On these issues it is
impossible to report extensively in this small space,but we recommend fu=
ture focus and attention. Let us briefly list the salient points emerged
in the discussion:

a. every description is a selection of relevant-to-the-descriptor elements,
   then...

b. design is an (eminently) evaluative process...

c.we pretend we know enough about analysis,but how do we evaluate ?...

d. what is the difference between evaluation and judgement ?

e. can we teach fantasy ? how do we facilitate the designer's competence ?

f. how does "tacit knowledge" and "prejudices" influence design processes
   and outcomes ?

A central point that emerged is that design,atleast in its initial stage,
has to do with the setting of problems,or with what we have called the
surfacing of contradictions in a particular design context (technical,
organizational,political) that sbsequently leads to the formulation of
problems and(eventually) solutions. It should be noted that a design
problem is generally conceptualized as a goal to be achieved in a cost-
-effective way by using given means. But most of the times a design pro=
blem surfaces under the more puzzling species of a dilemma. One happens
to want two or more incompatible goals at the same time. Not efficiency
or coordination or quality or equity are to be achieved independently of
each other,but

efficiency	and	equity
coordination	and	flexibility
coordination	and	capacity for innovation

integration	and	autonomy
control	and	generativity
stability	and	development
efficiency of process	and	quality of product
political influence	and	creativity

The competence of a designer has to do precisely with the ability of
bringing these contradictions to light,of generarting technical and
conceptual frameworks within which dilemmas are"solved" or transformed.

3. The third question concerns method: we agreed that formal methods
   such as the stepwise phase-oriented one do not represent what a de=
   signer does in a real life context. These methods suffer from a for=
   malistic bias: they pretend to be complete descriptions that stand as
   procedural prescriptions to be "executed". In our view they are simply
   tools or maps to which a designer refers instrumentally in the course of
   the design process. Every designer,as everey other social actor, knows
   that evaluation does not take place in the last phase of the process
   (the last block of the magic block diagram),but that he is evaluating
   all the time,even when he pretends he's presenting sheer facts.

   We suggest that a design method could be regarded primarily as a method
   of intervention into a reality which can never be completely described
   or controlled. The intervention is articulated in"moments" such as
   asserting,liking/disliking, computing, committing oneself,choosing,
   testing, concerting, coordinating, reconciling, bargaining,etc. We
   hereby recommend further and thorough study on these overlooked me=
   thodological aspects.

4. Emphasis on intervention leads us to the fourth question which di=
   rectly related to labour unions' interests,strategies,and practice.
   In order to augment the design competence of the users,which should
   be more emphatically called <u>actors</u>, it seems to us that the most
   fundamental area requiring some kind of intervention is <u>education</u>.
   Technical education is indeed important: knowing more about products,
   systems,technologies ,and processes. But what seems to be even more
   important is general education. One of the major sources of influence
   and power in any kind of organization is the ability to switch from one
   area to another area of technical knowledge,to be able to draw conne=
   ctions between different fields of knowledge. On the contrary a speciali=
   zed education and skill might turn out to be restrictive. The slogan
   we would like to say is "he who knows more plays a better game". Educatio=
   nal and training efforts should be devoted to develop programs that
   enhance actors' competence rather than,as usual, users' restricted per=
   formance. Competence is the ability to produce different performances
   in a wide range of design situations,and there is not in the world one
   single social actor totally deprived of this competence.

5. Finally, a question related directly to political practice: how can we
   change the social and political conditions in which design processes
   are carried out today ? Current answers to this question emphasize the
   aspect of "getting to control the process from the outside". This is
   a naive but rather common point of view. Obviously a design process is
   not necessarily going to become any better because the control of it
   switches from one interest group to another one. The outcome of such
   a control-oriented strategy might turn out tobe,if successful,that
   users control a bad process without being able to change it. Well,
   what's the point of doing that.

Other groups working on this specific issue from different and more
focused perspectives might come out with different advise,but from
the design perspective of this group we maintain that there is not
such a thing as "changing the political conditions" that is independent
from the issue of "intervening into the design process to make it better"
or of "acquiring better design skills". Only real design quality will help
not to reproduce social inequality.

Actors in the working group

Gro Bjerkhes	Norway
John Kammersgaard	Denmark
Giovan Francesco Lanzara	Italy
Ingela Larsson	Sweden
Lars Mathiassen	Denmark
Andreas Munk-Madsen	Denmark
Hermann Streich	West Germany
Johnny Todenfors	Sweden
Heinz Zullighoven	West Germany

SYSTEMS DESIGN FOR, WITH, AND BY THE USERS   387
U. Briefs, C. Ciborra and L. Schneider (editors)
North-Holland Publishing Company
© IFIP, 1983

REPORT FROM THE WORKING GROUP ON

"INTERNATIONAL COOPERATION, POLICIES, AND STRATEGIES FOR ALTER-
NATIVES IN THE SYSTEM DEVELOPMENT", AT THE IFIP TC 9. 1 CONFERENCE
ON "SYSTEM DESIGN BY THE USERS, FOR THE USERS, WITH THE USERS".

PREFACE

The group consisted of Helga Genrich, W. Germany, Joseph le Dren,
France, Sandra Cook, USA, Anders Joest Hingel, Denmark, Petter
Magnusson, Sweden, Jean Louis Rigal, France, Bertrand Luneau,
France and Kristen Nygaard, Norway (rapporteur).

The group had 6 meetings during the conference. Evidently, the
subject allotted to the group could not be covered in the discussion, and it only served as the general framework within which
the discussions were conducted.

INTRODUCTION

Many papers and discussions at the Conference have related to the
trade union-oriented research which started in Scandinavia around
1970. Three main trends seem to exist:

1. A spreading and further development of projects in the
   research tradition of these "early" Scandinavian projects.
   An associated spreading of activities in the trade unions,
   resulting in data agreements, influence on and participation
   in a large number of specific system development projects.

2. A more recent trend, focussing upon "second generation projects" - aimed at developing new tools for analysis, system
   description, training, information etc. The more ambitious
   of these projects engage in the development of alternative
   technologies in specific areas, based upon trade union related
   values and interests.

3. A spreading sentiment of irrelevance of the old participation
   strategy in the face of current trends in the development of
   the industrialised countries. The rapid structural changes
   in the production system of the world (also called "the
   recession") is strongly related to the use of information
   technology.

Since skills are being built into the production machinery,
employers no longer are dependent upon a highly qualified labour
force. Modern management tools and new world-spanning communication
networks make it possible to coordinate and control production
independent of distances. These factors are being combined and
now result in the exploitation of the unorganised and unqualified
population in the Third World, e.g. in the form of so-called
"Free Trade Zones", by transnational corporations.

In this situation participation projects seem to be of less importance, because often the very existence of the work places are at
stake. It also implies that national trade union strategies no
longer can give solutions to important problems - global strategies
are necessary. This means that the Third World's situation and
interests must be taken into account as an integral part of the
interests of the trade unions in the Industrialised World.

For this last reason the Working Group found that international
cooperation policies and strategies for alternatives in system
development is a key issue to be discussed. Such cooperation may
lead to reevaluation, modification and extension of the values
which the trade unions want to further in participation projects.
It may lead to a different understanding of what the trade unions'
information needs are and in general lead to a new strategy toward
new technology. And in particular, it may create need for information systems which are able to support a more energetic trade
union international strategy and tactics in the information technology area.

THE DISCUSSION

The group felt that many mistakes had been made in the past and
present in the area of transfer of information technology to the
Third World, both by the Third World and the Industrialised World
countries. The transfer is a question of culture, including production culture, and yet, technology must match the culture of
the technology using country.

This match can only be achieved by a close cooperation between
the producers and users of technology. People of the Third World
themselves should have the initiative role. The industrialised
nations must not impose their own view on these Third World nations
through, for example, software and data, also the industrialised
nations should not forget that the Third World may require new
organisational alternatives.

The situation is to some extent similar to the Trade Unions'
situation, when they in the Industrialised World want to control
technology.

It was reported from a recent visit to Africa that some people
felt that their important needs were:

- transportation, and
- training.

To some extent information technology may help satisfying both
these needs (since communication sometimes may substitute transportation).

In the Industrialised World we often argue for the transfer of
simple technologies, whereas Third World people want to be "as
modern as" us. Today this is not necessarily a contradiction.
Technological trends are such that the simplest technologies to
use are in fact the most modern and sophisticated, e.g. soon
electronic data networks will be the cheapest and by far the most
efficient and flexible carriers of information in a very wide
range of formats.

Examples on constructive possible uses, based upon local needs,
of "high technology" in the Third World were mentioned:

- The notion of "community computers" supporting local agriculture, distribution, industrial production etc.

- New approaches to map production, e.g. for resource administration, better suited to local qualification patterns.

The idea that mass distribution of "personal computers" in itself should solve the problems was characterised as naive. However, it is important and difficult to implement strategies which give benefits to the majority of the population of the Third World countries. And benefit should in the information technology area also to an important extent consist of skills, meaningful and useful in the local setting.

The splitting up of work, the shuffling around of production, etc. is becoming more and more prominent in the Industrialised World. Our problems are closely interlinked with those of the Third World, and this calls for a joint, global strategy for the Trade Unions in their policies relating to information technology.

SPECIFIC POINTS

The group during its discussion also raised questions of "what can we do?" There are of course many "we's".

The group felt that researchers and specialists should be much more active in pointing out to trade unions the demand for international cooperation in this field and that they at the same time may be very useful by placing their professional insight at the disposition of the trade unions - locally, nationally and even for work at the international level.

Such cooperation requires, as the Scandinavian experiences show, a discipline and a solidarity with the Trade Unions' objectives and modes of operation. For this reason the large number of voluntary groups, organizations etc. - with idealistic and often very active members - represent a vast potential for assistance to the unions in many countries, but also a problem, since proper cooperation procedures have to be established.

As for the nature of Trade Union strategies, it was felt that it would be more efficient to concentrate upon joint action in special cases rather than an initial emphasis upon achieving agreement on programs which easily become too vague and general. Series of successful cases of action on specific issues will build up a backgound experience in this kind of cooperation.

The establishment of "norms" has been used as means of international Trade Union coordination. An important example is the so-called "Social Clause", setting down demands for acceptable working conditions. It was suggested in the group that a corresponding "qualification clause" also should be considered. Such a clause should set down requirements for the building up of useful and lasting skills in the labour force as an integral part of any production.

It was also suggested that the various international bodies related to the Trade Unions - as e.g. the Trade Secretariats in Geneva - could play a more active role than they do today.

As examples of more ambitious approaches, some of the new "second generation" Trade Union projects in the information technology area were mentioned, these represent attempts at not only influencing the employer-controlled technology development, they actually aim at developing new technology in cooperation with, controlled by the trade unions. The group felt that this strategy holds great promise for the future, if funding may be ,made

available. It was, however, pointed out that technological development should be preceded by active knowledge-building and innovation
processes in which both union members and specialists participate.

The group was informed about the work now starting up, aiming
at establishing in the years to come a "Union Net for Information,
Teamwork and Education" (UNITĖ or UNITE), this being a technologically advanced communications network to serve the Trade Unions
nationally and internationally. It was pointed out that a UNITĖ
may have strong impacts upon Trade Union social structures, and
that, for this reason, the proper development and use of UNITĖ
and associated creation of cooperation procedures and resource-
building also should be considered. A UNITĖ network ought to have
"built-in solidarity".

RECOMMENDATIONS TO IFIP

The group asks IFIP to give the tasks outlined in this report
attention and support as as far as it falls within the objectives
of IFIP. The group feels that IFIP may play an important role in
providing opportunities for people interested to meet. A conference on the issues discussed in the report should be held as
soon as it could be properly prepared, perhaps in 1984. At such a
conference a wide range of backgrounds should be represented -
geographically as well as professionally.

SYSTEMS DESIGN FOR, WITH, AND BY THE USERS
U. Briefs, C. Ciborra and L. Schneider (editors)
North-Holland Publishing Company
© IFIP, 1983

Report from the working group on

DESIGN OF ALTERNATIVES/ALTERNATIVE DESIGN

Morten Kyng

Computer Science Department
Aarhus University
DK-8000 Aarhus, Denmark

Disclaimer   Technology is no panacea, and influencing technology, by participation or by independent design of alternatives, can never substitute more direct political action. "Design of alternatives" is only one element of a union strategy for better working conditions and, on a long view, democratically controlled factories, etc. Other elements could concern reforms in legislation, broadly based programs of study, and development of action programs, cf. the description of such possibilities in the paper on the Utopia-project in this volume. The question of acquiring resources was not discussed in the group, although it is crucial to concrete ventures of developing alternatives.

Why alternatives?   Having the disclaimer in mind, there was a strong belief in the group that alternative systems can play an important role. First it is important to break the technological determinism to demonstrate that changes unfavourable to union members, e.g. deskilling and increased managerial control, are not an inevitable consequence of technological development per se. It is an important task to investigate under what conditions and to what extent new machine tools, new planning systems etc. can be used in a process of reskilling and increasing workers' control over the factory. At present such systems are not developed, let alone put in use.

Secondly, improved tools are needed in a large number of areas where they can support union members, instead of improving the position of management, e.g. information systems, cf. WISE, the project described by J. Friedrich in this volume.

Why alternative design?   Many existing design processes and methods are preoccupied with the question of external (managerial) control. And those involving participation only offer a possibility to influence in a very restricted way; they are not tools offering new groups genuine opportunities to develop their own alternatives; on the contrary, they are tools aimed at improving the situation from a management point of view.

To increase managerial control it is often suggested to

- split the deisgn process into a number of phases, separated in time, and with control points in between, where an external evaluation is made.

- isolate the system development from the rest of the organization, and thus control communication.

- use a specialized, hierarchical work organization.

Furthermore the tools and techniques traditionally used focus on the information processing aspects, ignoring other factors, which are important to the workers in judging the new conditions after the introduction of the proposed edp-system.

Finally, in traditional system development, the goals of management are not questioned; on the contrary: they are considered as the goals of the organization, i.e., harmony is presupposed and conflicts are usually treated as a result of insufficient information from management etc. Consequently, objectives such as "increasing workers' control" are impossible to include in these development processes and methods.

When workers participate under these circumstances, they find it nearly impossible to develop and pursue goals of their own. Their contribution is restricted to minor changes, which are consistent with the goals of management.

Which alternatives?   The alternatives we had in mind in our discussions are not primarily ingenious new inventions, totally different from existing use of technology. Our paradigm is based on a group of people deciding that they want something different from what exists and/or from what they believe will be developed (without their interference). The WISE project and the Utopia project are examples of such alternatives.

In the WISE project the alternative is an information system to be used by workers "to support them in the many disputes and collective bargaining processes in the factory as well as in the manufacturing branch as a whole". The Utopia project aims at developing an alternative system to be used by companies in the graphic industry. A system for high quality production, which supports reskilling and increases workers' control over the factory. If such a system or parts thereof is developed, it remains to be seen whether employers can be persuaded and/or forced to buy it. In contrast, the information system of the WISE project is installed and operated outside the factories independent of management.

Which design process?   As already stated, new groups, not preoccupied with questions of control and profits, need new methods of system development. Methods which support a search for new high quality solutions. What are then the elements in such a process? Among the points made in the group are:

   · A close cooperation among those wanting the alternative and computer system developers, and possibly other experts.

   · A double learning process, in which the system developers learn about the work and objectives of the group which wants the alternative and in which this group in turn learns about system development.

   · A joint development of understanding of possibilities within the area of the alternative.

   · Identify pros and cons in already existing and planned solutions.

   · Characterize the problems and wishes before trying to come up with a solution.

There seems however to be a close relation between perceived existing possibilities and the ability to generate thoughts about new solutions. So where does our "technological fantasy"come from? In our group discussions we noted that even those most inclined to analyze problems and wishes without committing themselves to a particular solution made a fairly large number of references to concrete technology. Well, at least you must be very careful; maybe the alternative you are looking for has nothing to do with computers. But

- alternative solutions (parts of) must at times be discussed in concrete terms, e.g. in terms of some kind of "prototype" (or "pilot project").

- Do not stick to the first concrete "solution", but develop several, learning about new problems and possibilities each time.

Part of the comments made above resembles to a large extent discussions of modern management oriented schools of system development. We will not go into detail, but only state that this reflects the managerial dilemma on the conflict between external control and a high quality development process. A dilemma which gives rise to new opportunities of influence to the unions.

The system designer is one last resource, which we did discuss.

New skills and tools are needed to support the cooperation between the system designers and others participating, and to support the cognitive aspects of the development process.

Workers and their unions are making increasing demands on edp-systems and thus on system designers. At the same time new management oriented methods prescribe more user involvement in systems development, to cope with the growing complexity of the role of edp systems in organizations. Thus different groups advocate "user involvement", and for very different reasons.

Under these circumstances it is important that the designer distinguishes between

- alternative, non-managerial projects and
- management controlled projects

and in the last category between

- projects with some management independent activity, e.g. in a local union and
- projects where all activities are controlled by management.

If system designers want to function as professionals, designing high quality systems, it seems crucial that they support the groups involved in acquiring resources of their own. Otherwise the results of our work will be manipulative rather than good system design.

Finally the designers should have in mind that the main drive must come from those wanting the alternative, although his/her improved skills and tools will certainly help.

Participants in (part of) the discussions

Per Erik Boivie
Sweden

Pelle Ehn
Sweden

Jürgen Friedrich
West Germany

Annette Gahn

Anders Joest Hingel
Denmark

Reinhard Keil
West Germany

Morten Kyng
Denmark

Hugo Levie
England

Jean-Louis Rigal
France

Åke Sandberg
Sweden

Christine Scidel

Carol Smolava
West Germany

SYSTEMS DESIGN FOR, WITH, AND BY THE USERS
U. Briefs, C. Ciborra and L. Schneider (editors)
North-Holland Publishing Company
© IFIP, 1983

REPORT OF WORKING PARTY ON SYSTEMS DESIGN, NEGOTIATION
AND COLLECTIVE BARGAINING AND ON PARTICIPATION FROM A
TRADE UNION VIEWPOINT

Rapporteur: Robin Williams

Technology Policy Unit
University of Aston
Birmingham, England

Composition of the Working Party

This working party was formed by a merger of two groups, which had
been interested in "Systems Design, Negotiation and Collective
Bargaining" and in "Participation from a Trade Union Point of View".
The groups comprised trade unionists, trade union researchers,
industrial sociologists and systems designers from Italy, Sweden,
Britain, Norway, France, Austria and Germany.

Terms of Reference

We started from the position that the trade unions have been major
contributors to the debate about the implications of the current
introduction of edp and associated systems, that the unions have
welcomed this technological change but have felt it important to
influence the process of change to minimise its possible harmful
effects on work. However, trade unions have experienced many
problems in influencing systems design.

The group began by reviewing the most significant strategies for
the 'negotiation of change' in the different countries and discussing how these had worked in practice. We focussed on the advantages and disadvantages of these different approaches (which had to
be seen in the light of management strategy and the underlying
economic and social situation). We discussed the ways that unions
could exert more effective influence over systems design by developing earlier and more direct influence over the systems design
process. This posed strategic and organisational problems for
trade unions and suggested certain changes in systems design processes. Finally we discussed whether trade unions needed to promote
alternative models of information technology.

A variety of mechanisms exist in the different countries for users
and their trade unions to influence change. Systems designers
might not be aware of these. Papers presented at the conference
had explored the situation in Britain and Scandinavia. It was
therefore useful in addition to review the experience of the
Italian trade unionists and researchers in the group, to provide a
broader background to the discussion of negotiation etc. of change.

The Italian Experience of Negotiating over Change

1. Compared to Scandinavia, there has been little experience by
   Italian trade unions in negotiating over changes in computer-
   based systems either at national or local (company or firm)
   level. Where such bargaining has taken place, it has been

under more generally established union rights and procedures
requiring provision of information and advance consultation
over planned changes affecting the work organisation.   The
first national agreement explicitly concerning computer-based
systems will shortly be concluded in the printing industry.

2.   Typically bargaining was conducted after change had been
      introduced and sought to protect workers against possible
      negative effects of change (e.g. on employment, wages,
      working conditions, skills).

3.   One reason for the late involvement of unions was the pattern
      of technological change, which often appeared as a gradual
      introduction of minor changes (rather than a radical trans-
      formation which might have stimulated a stronger approach).
      However, the rate of technological change varied between
      different industrial sectors and information technology was
      changing more rapidly than production technology.

4.   Three models of implementation had emerged:

      (a) Rationalisation - this is the most common situation
      (e.g. at Fiat), where change has typically not been
      negotiated, even though the new technology cut across old
      trade union rights.

      (b) Where the technological content of the product was
      increasing (e.g. Olivetti) - this was the situation in
      many small companies, where generalised bargaining in
      technological change was taking place - primarily because
      management needed the co-operation of workers rather than
      because of trade union strength.

      (c) In some cases where the unions had a high degree of
      awareness and organisation, they had pressed for joint
      union/management groups to be set up to deal with change.
      There were firms in the public sector where these groups
      had gained access to outside consultants and expertise.

5.   In the case of computerisation of clerical work, the unions
      had embarked on workplace bargaining over the organisation
      of work - for the first time (although this did not cover
      systems design <u>per se</u>) - and had begun to develop education
      courses for workers, to allow negotiation before the system
      was implemented.

Participation, Negotiation, Collective Bargaining?

Discussion of these issues was complicated by national differences
in industrial relations systems and the different definitions/
connotations these terms had for people with different backgrounds.
For the purpose of this paper, the following definitions are
sufficient:

Collective Bargaining   - the formulation of rights to protect
                                 workers, by agreement between manage-
                                 ment and trade unions.   This is the
                                 basis for negotiation over change in
                                 Britain and Italy.

| Legislated Participatory Rights | – in Scandinavia and Germany, in addition to rights established by bargaining, unions have rights through legislation (e.g. of access to information, "co-determination"). |
| Participation | – this term has been used to describe an approach whereby trade unions attempt to influence the process of decision making (in contrast to those approaches based on demands over the outcome of decision making). |

Where legislated participatory rights existed, they were frequently combined with collective bargaining. These forms of trade union activity involve a process of collective representation, and negotiation with management. In addition there are situations where management had attempted to involve individual users directly in systems design/decision making. Whilst such schemes might enable management to make appropriate decisions, they were no substitute for negotiation with unions. In this situation there was felt to be the danger that individual users might easily be manipulated.

Despite the differences in industrial relations systems, there were common problems. In particular, even where joint participatory rights and procedures existed, unions still needed negotiated agreements to have real influence over change. The Swedish unions cited the example of the proposed computerisation of the Swedish Telephone Directory Enquiries to illustrate this.

Union Influence over Systems Design

Unions sought to go beyond defensive bargaining over the effects of systems that had already been introduced, and had attempted to influence systems design itself. Two strategies for union influence had emerged:

Internal Involvement in Systems Design, whereby unions attempt to directly influence the methods and process of systems design.

External Involvement, whereby unions attempt to influence technological change, without direct intervention in the systems design process, by posing general demands or constraints on the system to be adopted.

INTERNAL INVOLVEMENT

This has typically proceeded by including workers' representatives on joint project teams. While this approach appeared to offer an opportunity to profoundly influence the nature of the system introduced, this had rarely been achieved – for several reasons:

– it divorced the worker representatives from the union, which was left with a largely passive role;

– the unions were unable to suggest a significantly different system because they lacked concrete alternative perspectives on technology and because many of the decisions regarding the goals of the project and the nature of the systems and equipment had

already been made before the unions were involved.   The systems
available were based on previous massive investments in systems
design which had taken place without union influence, and which
acted as a constraint on future systems development (a simple
example of this is IBM equipment which can only be linked to
IBM hardware).   This problem is growing because of the increasing use of 'off-the-shelf' systems - especially where systems
are developed in different countries by Multi-National
Corporations.   Trade unions need to insist that systems are
developed locally to meet local needs.

There were examples where the systems design process had been
amended (from a linear to a cyclical process) to allow the unions
to negotiate the different aspects of the design process.   Formal
participatory rights were not sufficient to make this involvement
effective;   what was needed was a programme of mobilisation and
education within the workforce and union.

EXTERNAL INVOLVEMENT

This had developed by extending the scope of negotiation over the
whole range of possible consequences of new technology by seeking
agreement in advance over the nature and impacts of a proposed
system.   Such involvement included both formal demands and
informally represented demands (e.g. where managers/systems
designers took account of anticipated union/user resistance
in decision making).   A situation was described where
powerful opposition to office automation had been expressed by
users independently of their trade unions.   The unions needed
to examine whether there were aspects of user aspirations not
covered by union bargaining, and to try and integrate this
within union action.

External involvement had some of the same problems as the internal
involvement strategy - e.g. it required improved union mobilisation
and education to generate an adequate policy/set of demands.
It was less easy to propose changes in systems design.   Moreover
there was a problem that the system eventually introduced might
differ from the one originally agreed, since systems tended to
evolve in ways that were not anticipated beforehand.

Problems Facing Unions in Influencing Systems

We have already mentioned the problems of union education, internal
democracy and mobilisation.   A number of additional problems
facing the unions were discussed.

1.   The existing tools used by unions to gain influence may not
     be adequate for dealing with new technology.   Two examples
     are:

     (a) new technology may undermine the basis of established
     job control (e.g. craft skills);

     (b) the methods of resistance to Tayloristic work systems
     such as piecework bargaining or the strike weapon on
     assembly lines) may be ineffective with the different
     organisation of production with edp systems.

2. New technology frequently affected different sections of the
    work-force unevenly.   This could lead to divisions within
    the trade union preventing effective policy and decision
    making.

    Because of these factors a defensive union response would
    not work.   Unions needed to develop a forward looking
    approach to new technology, linked to new methods of union
    organisation and action.

3. The trade unions lacked the information and expertise to
    play an effective independent role in discussions of new
    technology.   Whilst unions had developed expertise and
    information over, for example, financial performance, or
    work environment in an enterprise, these were not yet avail-
    able for new technology.

Though it was agreed that the unions lacked the cognitive tools
needed to deal with the new technology, there was disagreement
about whether it was necessary for the unions to develop alternative technologies and methods for their design and assessment.
Some felt that unions could adapt existing technologies/methods
to their own ends.

The 'Utopia' project, which aimed to produce a system for
computerised typography based on workers' needs, was a very
important demonstration of the social shaping of technology and
the possibilities of changing this.   However, this approach could
not be applied in all situations.   The trade unions could not
become alternative managers/systems vendors.

There was a need to pool information, particularly at an international level, of examples where trade unions had succeeded in
getting changes in systems design.   This could have two benefits:

- it would arm the unions with practical examples of desirable
   systems, and demonstrate the kinds of flexibility in systems
   design that was possible under existing technology.

- it would allow the unions to assess which methods of intervention
   had produced the best results.

Finally, the unions needed to establish their own requirements
for new technology systems and to make these needs known to
systems designers.   However, unions should not restrict their
role to making systems more acceptable -   leaving the overall
direction and spheres of application of new technology to management, vendors and systems designers.   Trade unions needed to
have a selective policy about technological change.   There were
examples where unions had opposed certain trends in technological
development - e.g. the French union UCC-CFDT had opposed home
working with VDU's.   In West Germany the unions had opposed
'Personal Information Systems' that might be used to monitor or
control workers.   The British printing unions had stopped direct
input by journalists into photocomposition in most newspapers.
This approach had also been used in making positive demands for
new technology - e.g. the Swedish Union of Insurance Employers
required that the new computerisation programme gave an improved
service for and better contact with the public.

The Position of Information Scientists/Systems Designers

Information scientists in industry have a complex role as experts within a power/decision making structure.   A range of different perspectives were expressed within the group, which have been summarised below:

1.   It was suggested that information scientists had a degree of power and autonomy from management within the enterprise, that they were a distinct group with their own professional interests.   It was therefore proposed that users and unions should seek to ally themselves with systems designers. However, this strategy was criticised as anti-democratic and legitimising an elitist role for information scientists.

2.   A more fundamental criticism was that the power and autonomy of systems designers was not 'given' but a product of the balance of forces and relationship between different groups in the enterprise.   Unions strategies should be based on an examination of the internal relationships in the enterprise.

3.   A third position saw information scientists as neutral professionals within the enterprise.   By ascribing a partisan role to information scientists, there was the danger of alienating them from the users and their unions.

These different 'sociological models' of the role of the information scientist were not resolved.   It was agreed to include a general statement on this subject in the recommendations to IFIP rather than to make a stronger statement which might close off possibilities for co-operation with information scientists.

RECOMMENDATIONS TO IFIP OF THE WORKING PARTY ON SYSTEMS DESIGN, NEGOTIATION AND COLLECTIVE BARGAINING, AND ON PARTICIPATION FROM A TRADE UNION POINT OF VIEW

Finally the Working Party split into two sub-groups to draw up recommendations for IFIP. These focussed respectively on the problems of INTERNAL INVOLVEMENT AND EXTERNAL INVOLVEMENT by users and their unions in the process of systems design.

Since the design and implementation of new systems at work would involve a process of negotiation, we posed two questions:

1. What do systems designers need to know about industrial relations issues?

2. How should systems design be structured to facilitate its negotiation in an effective and equitable manner?

The recommendations of the two sub-groups were integrated and reported to the final plenary session of the Conference. This report is presented below as RECOMMENDATIONS TO IFIP (with supporting explanation and discussion). Our recommendations cover the following issues:

(a) The role of the information scientist in relation to established user groups;

(b) The form of trade union influence (internal and external involvement);

(c) The characteristics required of the design process for effective internal involvement;

(d) Finally we included a comment about company education.

A. THE ROLE OF THE INFORMATION SCIENTIST

1. THE CULTURE AND TRAINING OF INFORMATION SCIENTISTS TENDS TO BE TOO ISOLATED.

   As a result, there is a danger that they do not understand, or see as legitimate, attempts by users and their unions to influence systems design.

2. THE TRAINING AND EDUCATION OF SYSTEMS DESIGNERS SHOULD INCLUDE 'ORGANISATION PROBLEMS' SUCH AS INDUSTRIAL RELATIONS AND SOCIAL SCIENCE CONSIDERATIONS.

3. SYSTEMS DESIGNERS SHOULD WORK IN CONJUNCTION WITH HUMAN AND SOCIAL SCIENTISTS, TO TAKE INTO ACCOUNT THE ORGANISATION AND SOCIAL CHARACTERISTICS OF THE WORK SITUATION.

4. THE ACTIVITIES OF SYSTEMS DESIGNERS AFFECT THE WORK OF MANY PEOPLE, WHOSE VIEWS MUST BE CONSIDERED.

   Failure to take these issues into account was felt to be a major factor in experiences where computer based systems

had been a failure either because of the inadequacy of the
system to meet the needs of the organisation, or the inflex-
ibility of the system to adapt to changing circumstances or
because of user resistance.   These experiences were of
sufficient generality to allow the strong statement that:

SYSTEMS WILL ONLY WORK EFFECTIVELY IF THEY OPTIMISE THE
NEEDS OF ALL THE USERS.

IT IS THEREFORE VITAL TO NEGOTIATE SYSTEMS INTRODUCTION.

5.   THE SPECIAL POSITION OF INFORMATION SCIENTISTS IN THE DESIGN
        PROCESS GIVES THEM A SPECIAL RESPONSIBILITY TO CONSIDER THEIR
        RELATIONSHIP WITH THE DIFFERENT GROUPS INVOLVED.

A range of different perspectives on the role of the
information scientist were noted in the earlier discussion.

B.   THE FORM OF TRADE UNION INFLUENCE

The bulk of trade union attempts to influence systems design has
been through EXTERNAL INVOLVEMENT - comprising user demands about
the effects of new systems.   INTERNAL INVOLVEMENT - direct
involvement by trade unions in systems design has been little
developed so far.   Our discussion of internal and external
involvement therefore concentrates on the strengths and weaknesses
of external involvement (which suggested possible advantages and
drawbacks of internal involvement).   In Section C we discuss
ways that systems design could be developed to increase the
possibilities for internal involvement.

1.   STRENGTHS OF EXTERNAL INVOLVEMENT

EXTERNAL INVOLVEMENT (ARTICULATED THROUGH FORMAL DEMANDS) CAN
BE INTEGRATED WITH THE WIDER CONCERNS OF THE TRADE UNIONS
REGARDING INDUSTRIAL DEVELOPMENT.   (Conversely there is a
danger that internal influence may fail or be seen as
irrelevant if it divorces questions of systems design from
these wider issues.)

EXTERNAL INVOLVEMENT CAN BE MOST EFFECTIVE WHERE DEMANDS CAN
BE CODIFIED (FOR EXAMPLE WORKPLACE ERGONOMICS, EFFECTS OF
MANNING LEVELS, WAGES, AND FORMAL ASPECTS OF WORK ORGANISATION).
THESE TEND TO BE DEFENSIVE DEMANDS.

2.   WEAKNESSES OF EXTERNAL INVOLVEMENT

THERE MAY BE A GAP BETWEEN THE OBJECTIVES THAT MAY BE AGREED
IN ADVANCE, AND THE SYSTEM ACTUALLY INTRODUCED.

THERE MAY BE PROBLEMS IN INFLUENCING ASPECTS OF SYSTEMS THAT
ARE DIFFICULT TO CODIFY (this issue is specially problematic
where technological change is advancing rapidly - it demon-
strates also the importance of access of information and
education for users and union representatives).

EXTERNAL INFLUENCE TENDS TO DEAL WITH THE EFFECTS/CONSEQUENCES
OF SYSTEMS DESIGN.   BY REMAINING OUTSIDE THE PROCESS OF SYSTEM

DESIGN, THE SCOPE FOR MODIFYING THE SYSTEM MAY BE LIMITED.
(Conversely, internal involvement appears to offer opportunities to influence systems in a more flexible, far-reaching
and continuous manner.)

C.   THE CHARACTERISTICS REQUIRED OF THE SYSTEMS DESIGN PROCESS
     FOR EFFECTIVE INTERNAL INVOLVEMENT

The internal involvement strategy focusses on ways that the process
of design and implementation shapes the characteristics of the
system eventually introduced.

1.   PROJECTS SHOULD BEGIN BY CONSIDERING THE VARIOUS GROUPS THAT
     WILL BE AFFECTED AND SHOULD BE INVOLVED IN THE SYSTEMS DESIGN
     PROCESS.   It is important to avoid making a simple juxta-
     position of managers and unions, since a variety of groups
     (e.g. middle managers) will be involved in the system
     introduced.   Trade unions should not be seen as substituting
     management's role in the design process.

2.   THE CONVENTIONAL HIERARCHICAL MODEL OF SYSTEMS INTRODUCTION,
     WHEREBY SYSTEMS ARE 'DESIGNED' AND THEN RIGIDLY 'IMPLEMENTED',
     SHOULD BE AVOIDED.

     SYSTEMS DESIGN AND IMPLEMENTATION SHOULD BE FLEXIBLE;   EACH
     STAGE SHOULD BE OPEN TO FEEDBACK AND AMENDMENT BY THE VARIOUS
     GROUPS INVOLVED.   Examples where this had been achieved were
     cited from Sweden and West Germany.   Systems design should
     be a process of 'learning-by-doing' for all the participants;
     it must include feedback mechanisms.   Systems design will
     thus become a continuous, cyclical process.   For this to
     happen,

     LANGUAGES AND CODES SHOULD BE ACCESSIBLE TO USERS (INCLUDING
     THOSE WITHOUT SPECIALIST KNOWLEDGE OF COMPUTERS), TO ENABLE
     THEM TO SUGGEST MODIFICATIONS.

3.   REQUIREMENTS FOR SYSTEM DESIGN.   Certain requirements had
     been set by trade unions.   These should be adopted when
     systems are designed in future   (some of these are appropriate
     for external involvement).

     (a) LANGUAGES SHOULD BE EASY TO LEARN (AS WELL AS BEING CAPABLE
         OF FEEDBACK AND MODIFICATION FOR SYSTEMS REDESIGN).

     (b) DISTRIBUTED DATA PROCESSING SYSTEMS, NETWORKS AND LOCAL
         WORKSTATIONS ARE PREFERABLE TO CENTRALISED SYSTEMS.

     (c) SYSTEMS SHOULD BE DESIGNED TO MINIMISE HIERARCHY AND
         SUPERFLUOUS AUTHORITY, AND, CONVERSELY, TO MAXIMISE THE
         AUTONOMY OF INDIVIDUALS AND GROUPS IN ORGANISING THEIR
         WORK.

D.   EDUCATION IN THE COMPANY

School and trade union education (which were discussed by another

working group) cannot, in the immediate period, solve the problem
of workers education.   Moreover, the company possessed concrete
and up to date information about the state of development of
technology and systems in that sector.   The group felt that it
was therefore important to consider the education provided by the
company.

At present company education is largely determined by the vendor
and systems designer.   It tends to be limited to the minimum
training required to operate the system.   Unions should attempt
to influence the education provided by the company.

The company should provide broader education about systems functioning, to include overall changes in the organisation of production.
This broader training of views should be linked to the process
of work enhancement and upgrading of users.

Finally it was suggested that the productivity benefits of
technological change should not just be distributed through
increased leisure time, but should also be used to provide
educational opportunities for the skill and broader human
development of the worker.

SYSTEMS DESIGN FOR, WITH, AND BY THE USERS
U. Briefs, C. Ciborra and L. Schneider (editors)
North-Holland Publishing Company
© IFIP, 1983

EDUCATION FOR THE USERS BY THE USERS WITH THE USERS

Susanne Kandrup Nielsen

Information Systems Research Group
The Copenhagen School of Economics and Business Administration
Copenhagen
Denmark

In our discussions we were aware that there can be many kinds of users: the public, systems analysts, trade unions. In our discussion we focussed on trade unions but our recommendations go for the other groups as well.

Our discussion started out dealing with the difference between <u>technical features</u> of computers and our <u>every-day language</u>, i.e. our social surroundings.

The problem then, when we look at user education, is that the <u>technical issues</u> and the <u>social issues</u> are <u>not linked together</u>.

We found that either you have courses concerned with technical problems not taking into account the social aspects or you have it the other way round. One way of going about this problem would be to focus on the differences below, implying that in order to understand what a computer is/what it means one should not only describe hardware and technical features but try to get hold of the dialectical issues described in figure 1.

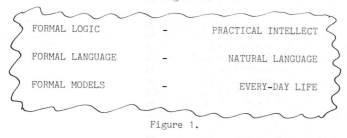

FORMAL LOGIC	-	PRACTICAL INTELLECT
FORMAL LANGUAGE	-	NATURAL LANGUAGE
FORMAL MODELS	-	EVERY-DAY LIFE

Figure 1.

By doing this, you get a realistic picture of what you gain and what you lose by using computers.

For example, in an analytical perspective you can be <u>more precise</u>, <u>more effective</u> in making calculations but this is at the expense of <u>neglecting</u> other aspects and <u>dimensions</u> of every-day life.

Within the group we talked about something which we called the analytical knife. If you want to computerize something you take this knife and start carving slices of reality to fit the computer.

We consider this cutting up of reality one of the main problems in the communication between systems analysts and users in a broad sense.

It is therefore one of the basic issues to overcome the polarization of the discussion for or against computers.

This could be done by focussing on the differences mentioned in figure 1.

This implies a need for more exact criteria when comparing losses and gains related to the introduction of computer systems.

As we see it, we do not at the moment have these criteria, but we recommend that this discussion should be given more attention.

We see this discussion not only as the normal cost/benefit analysis which is part of the normal procedure used when discussing gains and losses in relation to computer systems.

But this must be done by using contrasting education material as exponents for e.g. how to describe a new computer system.

You would for example get two totally different perspectives on what an edp system is if, on one hand, you discussed it on the basis of material as the model presented in figure 2 than you would get if, on the other hand, you used the picture of an edp system operating in the real world like the one presented in figure 3.

The material in figure 2 would make the users concentrate only on the actual functions of the computer system, whereas the picture in figure 3 would form a basis for discussion of themes like "How is this new system going to affect my every-day work situation as a living human being?" This aspect is one of the things very seldom taken into account before the design of a computer system is completed.

Discussing new computer systems from these kinds of different perspectives could contribute to decreasing the gaps between users and systems analysts.

Now, this does not mean that education as a whole should be a passive acceptance of information already formulated as the previous examples but should be organized to fulfill the following purposes:

- create consciousness about consequences and possibilities
- arouse curiosity to learn more
- create activity to find new knowledge in order to change, influence and cooperate during the systems design process

The tool for this could be study circles in the Scandinavian tradition - welcoming every category of user to participate. A study circle is a small group of people getting together to work on a subject which is of specific importance to them. As we, in the working group, did not discuss any specific ways of carrying out study circles, I who present the results of the group will take the liberty of giving an example from a Danish trade union.

In Denmark trade unions encourage their memebers to form such study circles for instance on subjects concerning new technology.

Topics dealt with in these groups could be such as:

- How do we formulate a technology agreement?

- How do we create a debate on new technology within our company?

- Discussions to support our shop steward for her use when attending meetings with the management

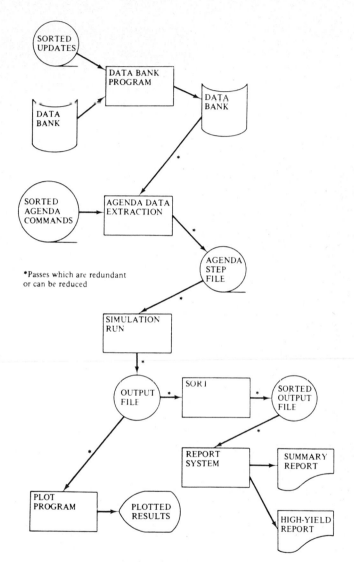

Figure 2. Systems flow or conventional packaging for the MULTISIM system.

This is the formal model most commonly used to describe a computer system.

The meetings of study circles could be organised as follows:

1. Presentation

At the first meeting every member of the group should present herself to the group. It would be a good idea to tell the group briefly about one's family, where one lives, and what education and work one has. It makes the participants feel more like persons belonging to an entity.

Figure 3. This is the real world model of a computer system. This is the way in which most users see a computer system.

2. Rounds

If one after the other in such a study circle talks, it enables persons who are more reticent to have the confidence to talk as much as the more aggressive ones. It also helps one to listen to one another and to break down feelings of competition among the members.

3. Events since the last meeting

It is important to sum up everybody's experience related to the topic discussed since the last meeting because it is on this basis that the group moves on and gains new knowledge.

4. Election of a person responsible for agenda, report, and time schedule of the
    meeting
It is essential to train the participants in expressing themselves verbally as well as in writing, and also to train their capacity of attending and leading meetings. This make the members of the group better prepared in case of confrontations with management. But most of all it is important to document the events in order to gain further knowledge.

5. Self-evaluation

Every meeting should end with an evaluation of the meeting because the only way to improve is to be critical of oneselves. It is not intended as an evaluation of individuals but of the meetings as a whole.

This was just one way of organising a study circle, but a way that most certainly will support the educational purposes mentioned earlier.

On the basis of the things presented here and the further discussions within the group, we have the following recommendations for IFIP:

- that the kind of education mentioned in this summary, e.g. study circles, should be a permanent feature of working life,

- that workers should participate in the design process in order that the gap between the analytical and the social perspective decreases.

Our last effort was to look in the holy books of India where we found the following sentence concerning knowledge:

A little knowledge leads to dogmatism
a little more to questioning
and a little more takes us to praying

Bhagavad Gita (Radhakrishnan)

U. Briefs, C. Ciborra and L. Schneider (editors)
North-Holland Publishing Company
© IFIP, 1983

Participation From The Designers' Point Of View

Peter Mambrey

Gesellschaft für Mathematik und Datenverarbeitung
D-5205 St. Augustin 1
Federal Republic of Germany

This report summarises the overall picture of the
discussions and results of a working group
Participants: Annicchiarico (I);   Kensing   (DK);
Mambrey (FRG); Palmieri (I); Rolskov (DK); Wynn (USA)

The experience we had in our working group was comparable
with   a   system   development   process.   We started very
ambitiously, then became aware of the problems — one was to
find a common language to communicate — and then became
frustrated, because entering into the problems and discussing them led us more and more away from the task of
making recommendations. Before developing solutions we had
to stop, since the available time was over.

At the beginning we started to collect problems by
brainstorming and then achieved a structure as follows:

I Why participation
The role of the designers, the role of the users

II Who should participate, who is the key person for the
designers
The users as individuals; the trade unions; the clients

III How to participate

Focussing on participation from the designers' point of view
requires a common understanding of what designers have to do
and under which conditions they work. There is a big difference, if designers work as employees in an edp-department
of an organisation or if they are employed by a system house
or work as consultants. We decided to confine ourselves to
designers who are not members of the organisation where the
development process takes place. Working outside seems to be
better for organising participation. The designers' involvement in organisational problems is not that great and the
risk of gaining power for the edp-department instead of
advising and supporting users is smaller.

I Why participation?
The reasons can be divided broadly into two main types:
a) Functional reasons

In traditional approaches designers collect information
given by the users. Users are usually treated as information
suppliers. Designers ask them and they give the required
answers. The users are necessary for the design process but
stay passive and are objects not subjects for the designers.
They don't know why and to what reason the information is
needed and if it is used correctly. One can characterise
this type of information flow as a one way street. But this
is not sufficient to design a system which has to fit
organisational and user needs. Not only selective information but the knowledge and experience of the users are
necessary to design a system. The only way to perceive it is
participation. By participation unbalanced information can
be changed into communication, which is a feedback process
with all it implies: learning, understanding, mutual influence and control etc.
There are several assumptions on the effects of
participation. They range from a better recognition of the
users needs through improved acceptance of the system to
"outmanoeuvering" the users, because they could become
hostages of the development.

b) Political reasons

This aspect refers to the picture of man, to the ethical and
anthropological basis of our work. Man should not be the
object in a process but the subject. Democracy requires that
one should be able to control one's own life and this means
working life as well. That is why users have to play an active and dominant role in the design process. They should
have the rights and abilities to manage and to direct the
system design and the product.

What role should the designers play in the development
process?

The designers should be experts in technology, consultants
and facilitators. Their work is a service for those who later have to work with the system. The designer's work is
determined by many different constraints given by time,
budget, management, users, technology etc. But there are
constraints as well which are made by designers themselves.
Designers are not neutral machines who only facilitate, but
are human beings which means that they have their own interests: solving problems and creating systems from their point
of view; being controlled neither by users nor by management; getting on etc.
Like all human beings designers are socialised by their
environment and with respect to their job the professional
education and socialisation is of great importance. Because
of their professional orientation, creating systems for most
of them means solving technical problems and offering technical solutions. The mentality aims at pushing technology
and is technology driven. But system design also includes
social demands. The primacy of technical orientation very
often has limiting effects on participation. The working

group stated that designers suffer from a lack of social
fantasy and competence to communicate.

Above we described where designers should stand but where do
they actually stand? A short explanation:

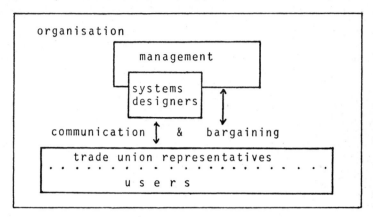

The designers are part of the system development process
which is dominated by management. If they work efficiently,
it means efficient from management's points of view. In the
working group we had a longer discussion if designers can
advise users and management to the same degree or if there
is a need to counterbalance the designers being dependant on
management (by being paid by them). Some members of the
working group stated that if designers worked efficiently
from the employer's point of view, no really good solutions
for the users could be found. By using involvement designers
can possibly take some more aspects of the users into account but this is far from what is meant by satisfying the
users' needs.

An actual alternative could be that designers are employed
by the trade unions and work as their consultants or
publicly paid and work like social workers in social
welfare, e.g. some sort of inspectors etc.

The discussion whether designers can fit both users' and
management's interests led to two different conclusions:
Some members denied that there is a compromise between
capital and labour and so designers can not design this compromise. Some members thougt that there are possible com-
promises which fit both interests so that management and
user interests can be designed as one system.

The role of the user
Dealing with this topic one has to ask who the user is. Is
he the end user or the manager in charge of a department as
well? Which user model have designers in their mind and is
this model correct? We have agreed that there is no ideal

user and that the perfect user the designers whish to have
will never exist.
Two different strategies can be analysed: The one is to
create the ideal user by education etc. But the working
group stated that designers should not "design the users".
So as a second strategy designers have to find and apply
methods which fit the users as they are. An alternative to
these strategies could be an approach in which a direct interaction between users and designers does not exist but instead a third group as a medium, e.g."professional translators". But this will only shift the communication problems
from the designers to the translators. The best solution the
group discussed for optimising the interaction between users
and designers was creating a common language which both
groups could understand. A strong need was expressed for
further development of tools, methods and languages to
assist the interaction.

But the reason why there are communication problems is not
only that there is a lack in methodology or constraints
given by management. There is a strong need for ability to
communicate. This requires personal qualities like social
awareness, social resonsibility etc. A long-range strategy
to improve the situation could be the integration of social
sciences into the education of the designers. A
recommendation of the working group is to improve interdisciplinary education for designers in universities.

II Who should participate?

Very often in participative system development designers
address the users as individuals and try to keep the trade
unions outside. The working group put stress on the point
that both groups, users as individuals and trade unions as
their representatives should .participate. There is - no
doubt - the problem of to which degree the representatives
really represent the users, but nevertheless both groups
have to be involved, especially because their contribution
is different. Users have to participate because their
specific knowledge of their work is necessary for design.
Users themselves know best how the new work place should
look like from their point of view. They have to work with
the system and not the representatives. But they can more
easily be isolated and divided during the bargaining
process. Bargaining power is increased by organising into a
collective. Especially in conflict situations the
participation of trade unions is a necessity. In addition to
their bargaining power trade unions can contribute to more
general aspects concerning the organisation as a whole, concerning ergonomics, assessment and future development.

Other groups who should participate are the clients and the
citizens who are affected by the use of new information

technologies like videotex, cable tv etc. Clients of public services or banking etc. are affected by working hours, location and standard of service by forms designed not for their convenience but for "the computer".

The problems which arise by trying to involve these groups have been postponed by the working group. But we think that in near future the problem area of citizen participation will become more and more relevant.

III How to participate?

Very often users are involved during the analysis stage of system development but not during the design phase, which gives them less chance to participate.

What is the contribution of the users in analysis and design?

How to participate in the analysis?
Nowadays participation very often means involvement of users in a design team. It is a pure formal representation, e.g. in working groups at a low level. The users very often are neither active nor play an important role. We want to talk of participation when the users play an active part during all stages of the development process.

How can the existing situation be changed? We have found that despite all other constraints there is a lack in knowledge and methodology with respect to user-designer-communication. The best way to solve these problems is that designers and users develop a common language for analysis which both are able to understand.

This must be done at the beginning of any process. It implies training of users and designers and the will of both sides to start with a learning process.

How to participate in the design
Of course, the design process also involves analysis, but the main task is to create the system. The users role should be to ask for alternatives, to make demands, and to control the design.

Should the users become designers themselves? The opinions ranged from yes to no. Accordingly the working group stated that users should become designers of their tasks! Only the underlying technical solutions of the tasks should be worked out by the designers.

But the question arose if this would be enough. Is more additional support necessary than merely offering a flexible system? Can even a flexible system be neutral to different interests?

At this point the discussion had to stop because the time was over. Maybe we focussed too much on the individuals and not on groups or collectives. We finished the discussions by raising some more important problems designers have to face

during the design process:
Are the users actually interested in participation?
Users have to anticipate the future system and its impacts,
how can we help them? By painting scenarios? How can we
assess future impacts? Why, as is quite common in system development, do users not participate even if they are invited
and informed? Do they expect that participation will not
change their situation?

SYSTEMS DESIGN FOR, WITH, AND BY THE USERS
U. Briefs, C. Ciborra and L. Schneider (editors)
North-Holland Publishing Company
© IFIP, 1983

SYSTEM CHARACTERISTICS AND USERS NEEDS

John Kjaer

Kgl. Brand Insurance Co.
Copenhagen, Danemark

Five participants from the countries: Austria, Denmark, FRG and USA formed the working group. Systems design, research and systems management were represented. Often implemented systems properties do not meet user needs and as systems design always leads to redesign of jobs and social systems the working group recommends further research on systems development. The working group feels that the different groups of users should be provided with sufficient resources to participate/ conduct research of their own.

CRUDE MODEL

The discussions were based and structured on the following crude model:

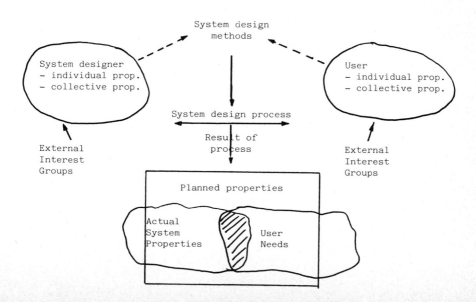

USERS

The concept of user played a considerable role in the discussions. Depending on the level of abstraction the model can lead to different definitions. So, the user is not always the company end user. One way of looking at it is to define user and user needs as social interest. On higher levels the user is a part of the system. Even management can be a user.

The group defined two main types of users or interest groups:

  - users, who can make decisions concerning the system and the system development process. These users are typically managers and some edp-experts having the power to decide on systems properties, resource allocation, time schedule for the development etc.

  - users, who can not make or influence such decisions. Some of these users are working with the system in the organization, others are external to the organization, typically customers, citizens etc.

PROPERTIES AND NEEDS

The working group expressed that system properties should mirror user needs. Therefore the group did not define the two concepts separately, but simply stated the three main areas of properties/ needs. These are the physical interface (work place ergonomy, response time), the interface process (dialogue) and job contents and job satisfaction (autonomy, wholiness, variation, non repetitiveness, control, time pressure, pauses).

METHODS

Basic elements of the system analysis and design methods discussed are:

  - the organization of the work e. g. various strategies for the development and various participants in the process.

  - the analysis and design techniques used, e. g. analytical vs. explorative techniques.

By combining the basic elements different analysis and design methods (models) can be defined.

For description and analysis of a given system design method the group found the following descriptors relevant:

  - the application area

  - the perspective of the system

  - the guidelines for the lapse of the process e. g. the description of how the work process is going to be performed, the tools to be used in the process and the organization of the process.

STATEMENTS

Based on the discussions of the above mentioned concepts the group found that it is social interests which lead the system development process. Because of lack of education and power it is often seen that planned system properties do not correspond to actual implemented properties which again do not meet user needs.

Further the group found that software design is job design and that system design always implicates redesign of social systems.

RECOMMENDATIONS

In the discussions the group felt the lack of a taxonomy/ classification scheme for system characteristics and for user needs. We therefore recommend such a scheme to be developed. Both empirical and theoretical research is wanted.

The group recommends job contents and job satisfaction to be given higher priority in systems development. Normally the development takes place within a given set of constraints such as time, money, knowledge. If possible such constrains should be removed or reconsidered prior to planning of the system. The group also recommends that design/redesign of embedding social systems should take place at the same time as (or prior to) the planning of the system.

One way to control the system development process is to set up contracts between interest-groups. The group therefore recommends such contracts to be made containing definitions of both the out-come characteristics wanted for the resulting system, and the procedural oriented properties. The different users should be provided with resources enabling them to make own education and research. If an agreeable contract can not be reached the system in question is not to be developed.

The overall conclusion is that further research on the systems development process is needed. The research should concentrate on further development of tools and techniques that allows the users to take part in the system development process on their own conditions. Users and researchers from different disciplines should cooperate in the research.

PARTICIPANTS

> Georgine Heindl (Austria)
> Arne Kjaer (Denmark)
> John Kjaer (Denmark)
> Reinhard Oppermann (FRG)
> Harold Sackman (USA)
> Michael Schröder (Austria)

SYSTEMS DESIGN FOR, WITH, AND BY THE USERS
U. Briefs, C. Ciborra and L. Schneider (editors)
North-Holland Publishing Company
© IFIP, 1983

CONCLUSIONS

Claudio Ciborra
Politecnico di Milano
Università della Calabria

"System Design: For, with and by the users" was a working conference.

During the week in Riva Del Sole, conference participants evolved a social and work process which resulted in a serious exchange of experiences and ideas as well as some tentative conclusions and recommendations. This "free-floating" conference organization seemed to enhance the open exchanges which developed between members of this diverse group of experts, practitioners, unionists, and researchers from Europe and America. A Swedish Trade union official had the opportunity to hear "first-hand" about an American anthropologist's field study of office work. An Italian researcher learned about the activities of the "Nine to Five" - Association of Working Women in the United States. And a Norwegian professor of Informatics explained his view of possible union strategies for world-wide computerization to an engineering student from the South of Italy.

A great deal of semi-structured, collective thinking took place during the conference both informally and during "group workshops" which covered a variety of topics. A common regret was that too little time was devoted to these workshops.

Each day, speakers presented formal papers to the entire conference group. Many more papers were prepared than we had planned for. However, because the field of "user-driven system design" is at such an early stage of development, an important goal of the conference was to collect as much original material as possible on the topic. This book is a first step toward disseminating that information to a wider audience of computer professionals and those interested in the impact of computer technology on work and workers.

It is very difficult to draw exhaustive conclusions about the meeting on the basis of such a process. But one obvious outcome is the knowledge that a community of people from a number of different fields and institutions are doing serious work on the issue of user-driven system design from a variety of perspectives. Know - ledge and actions of a local, national, and institutional nature are being developed in many countries throughout Europe, as well as in America and Australia. This conference was probably the first forum where people could exchange experiences. So that, conferences of this sort and other communication structures (data banks, networks, journals, bulletins, etc.) will be even more critical in the future.

The International Federation for Information Processing, IFIP, particulary TC9 and its Working Groups, could provide institutional support for some of these activities. In any case, it represents a communication channel for the computer specialist community on the issue of "user-driven system design".

While the conference in Riva Del Sole did not define precise goals and strategies for the future, it did point out the "state of the knowledge" on the topic. We seem to be in a state of transition from the diffusion of already established experiences and regulatory structures (e.g. technology agreements) to the need for experimenting with new types of interventions and mechanisms to involve users in the design process.

But a few new directions, emerging especially from the workshop activities, can be identified in reviewing the conference discussions. This is what I've learned.

First, there is wide concern, an introspective one, about the system design activity.

When the users really enter into the design process, bringing their values, goals, background, then design itself is no longer an activity which can be functionally planned by the design specialists using some project management techniques. Design becomes a mixed cooperation and conflict game. Roles, competence and choices become fuzzier and highly political. Traditional approaches to design are clearly inadequate if its nature as a multiactor process is fully acknowledged. The proceedings and the discussions during some of the workshops have focused on this problem area and interesting, promising insights have been put forward.

Then, there are a series of themes, some regarding the consolidation and improvement of existing practices, others having more long range implications.

Specifically, the following problem areas for the improvement of existing approaches to participation in systems design have emerged:

- unions need to be more effective in influencing system development. Up to now, involvement has been external to the firm. However, if trade unionists are experienced negotiators and understand this issue, internal participation may provide better insight and knowledge about the systems.

- women represent an important user group, who have special needs and are directly affected by some of the new technologies (office automation, home work, etc.). The main question for them ist one of identity and organization: How can women face the selective impact of new technologies through the existing collective bargaining machinery? And should they form a union, where collective representation at the work place does not exist? Moreover, extensive field research on the impacts at the work place level is badly needed.

- work needs to be studied in alternatives ways, pointing out those aspects neglected by traditional functional analysis: work as a collective problem solving activity; work as a knowledge-creation process; work as a creative activity. An evolutionary conception of the work people perform is critical to finding solid bases for their participation in restructuring work itself using the new tools of automation.

- system design is first of all the design of social and work systems. Appropriate methods and languages must be developed to include social goals in design . Specifically, social clauses have to be included in system design contracts to deal with the social costs resulting from any system development effort.

On a strategic level, the conference papers have contributed to at least three broader issues:

1) Education for the information society. Currently, comprehensive public education concerning impacts of systems, participation in system development and the like is lacking. In some countries, unions and universities are implementing special education programs, but these are very limited compared with the broad social implications of a computerized society. The number of non specialist' users of systems is bound to grow dramatically in the next few years. Accordingly, institutions which traditionally represent the interests of citizens, worker and special users groups should set up large-scale programmes for nontechnical training on the social implications of computers. Teaching materials, videotapes, movies, case studies, concerning "user participation" will need to be circulated intensively among concerned institutions in various countries.

2) Alternative technologies can and must be designed and applied. Participation cannot be limited to the use of existing systems. User needs should shape the technology at the earliest stages, i.e. when design choices regarding hardware and software are made. The task is complex and results can be realized only over the long term. There are no precise theory or approaches available to

guide this work: "learning by-doing" seems the only feasible strategy at present. During the conference, experiences have been presented which seem to bring such a programme from "utopia to reality".

3) A new wave of <u>international union involvement</u> in technological change has been advocated. It is becoming evident that both individual workplace and national strategies lack momentum when confronted with the business policies of the multinationals and with North-South problems, which represent the world context for the introduction of information technologies in the years to come.
What is needed is a parallel, alternative "technology transfer" between industrialized and not so industrialized countries. What is to be transferred are alternative systems, systems introduction policies, findings regarding the implications of computers on work and employment, and so forth. Such a transfer must be supported by special institutions and informational communication structure, such as data banks and networks. The unions, at international level, could play a relevant role in providing institutional support.

ADDENDUM

LOCAL UNION INFLUENCE ON TECHNOLOGY
AND WORK ORGANIZATION

Some results from the DEMOS Project

Pelle Ehn, Åke Sandberg

Arbetslivscentrum
The Swedish Center for Working Life
Box 5606, S-114 86 Stockholm, Sweden

Beginning in 1976, the DEMOS Project worked together with
trade union organizations for three years at four different
work locales. This co-operative effort concerned the unions'
possibilities to influence the planning and use of new technology at the local level in the company. The study also
sought to examine the obstacles and limits confronting this
democratization process. The results of the total project
are illustrated here with experiences from two of the work-
places studied, a daily newspaper and a locomotive repair
shop.

What can the union do to safeguard and promote its members' interests in having
meaningful work when the technology, the work organization, and the supervision of
work is altered? In the two parts of this paper we attempt to illuminate questions
of this type. Initially, we discuss an approach to understanding various technical
changes from the perspective of the rationalization strategies employed by company
management. We then discuss different possible union strategies for developing
knowledge of the issues and formulating appropriate demands.

PART I. TECHNOLOGY AND WORK

1. The newspaper

During the period that the graphic workers' union at a daily newspaper in Stockholm - Svenska Dagbladet - participated in the DEMOS Project, a complete transformation of the production process took place: from lead composing and computer
assisted text processing to complete computer based text processing and photo
setting. The union dealt with this technological change in the following manner.
Independant of the company, they developed plans in three areas. These dealt with
work force placement, work organization, and requisite training for meaningful
work in the new technological setting. Their point of departure was to refuse any
new plant or machinery investments until, at the very least, issues of work organization and employee training were solved. Their demands did not meet with a
great deal of sympathy from the company. Certainly, they succeeded in influencing
the development and structure of the work organization, but only within the framework of a by-and-large given technology. They were unable to influence the choice
of technology and therein one of the fundamental preconditions for work content
and organization. The developments at this daily newspaper must be viewed against
the background of developments in the entire branch.

Graphic production and the manufacture of newspapers and magazines has been
carried out in approximately the same manner for several hundred years. Work in
the composing department of a newspaper has, for example, to a great extent been
a craft.

Now, however, graphic workers find themselves in the centre of a technological
revolution. Within one short decade, they have gone from craft work to automation

to a situation in which computers are central to the entire production process.
Text entry, proof reading, image processing and subsequently page make-up is done
on a computer display terminal from which the finished text is produced on a com-
puter-coupled photo setter. The work process no longer consists of a series of
work stages in which the material is gradually processed by hand with the assistance of machinery. The "raw text" which is initially fed into the computer is
automatically transferred, hyphenated and justified, to a photo setter. The operator oversees the machine, but the processing and transfer of the product (text and
pictures) along with the control of the work process is carried out automatically.

As a result of this new technology, the graphic workers' control over their work
is threatened. An increasing number of decisions are programmed into the machines,
for example, the standardization of advertisement formats. To a great extent production speed is determined by the machinery.

It is also apparent that the graphic workers who operate, oversee and control this
machinery require very little knowledge of their work. It seems that on-the-job
training or perhaps short courses held by the companies selling the new machinery
would be sufficient for learning the new work tasks.

This impoverishment and dequalification of machine operation is but one aspect of
the changes in the work-place. The other is that it creates a need for comprehensive knowledge of programming, control, repair and servicing of the new machinery.
Management's strategy is to provide this training to only a small group of qualified technicians, who can be loyal collaboraters and much easier to control than
the large body of well-organized graphic workers. From a slightly longer range
perspective, it may be expected that not only skilled data programming work, but
also repair and servicing jobs will end up in the domain of machinery suppliers,
external consultants and others, completely outside the scope of graphic workers.

In other words, a polarization of work skills may take place, not only within the
graphic branch but between branches as well. The risk of work disapearing from the
graphic workers' branch effects not only the highly skilled. The most unskilled
tasks (such as simple text entry) can in the future be contracted out to "pirate
companies" which do not use personnel with training in the graphic industry. A new
division of labour follows in the wake of automation.

With the new technology, machine speed reduces production time and so decreases
the work tasks for graphic workers. An example of this is the photo setter which
can replace from 5-10 lino typesetting machines. Now even text entry is done more
rapidly since hyphenation work has been taken over by the computer. Furthermore,
unskilled labour can be employed to carry out a number of the newly simplified
work tasks and thereby reducing work available for graphic workers. With the same
labour effort, more newspapers can be set, printed, etc. The introduction of the
new technology into the graphic branch entails an enormous increase in labour productivity.

In summary, the new technology threatens graphic workers in three areas: control
over the process, dequalification and impoverishment of work tasks, and employment.

2. The locomotive repair work shop

The State Employees Union Local 1050 at the Swedish Railway's locomotive repair
work shop in Örebro, which participated in the DEMOS Project, succeeded in preventing the introduction of a computer-based production planning system. It is
called ISA-KLAR and was developed by the Swedish Rationalization Association.

ISA-KLAR involved interviewing workers on the work shop to determine in detail how
they carried out their jobs. The employees' knowledge of their jobs was collected,
then used by the company management. Work tasks were broken down into small
moments, stored in a computer and coupled with an MTM basis which was compiled

from several big companies.

The following illustrates the work tasks from the locomotive repair shop produced by ISA-KLAR:

1. Get the tools X and Y
2. Go to the under carriage
3. Crawl into position
4. Remove the cotter pin
5. Remove the washer and bolt
6. Repear moments 3-5 for the other bolts
7. Remove.

In addition to the specification of detailed work moments and the time and sequence for them, information is also stored concerning which tools are to be used. Company management wants to use data of this type as a basis for building up the work-place. In this way, possibilities are created for the future control and direction of employees with automatic work orders and instructions. It is important to note that in this instance there is no change in production technology in the work shop. Computers are used solely to increase the intensity of existing work forms.

3. Rationalization strategies

3.1 Work productivity and intensification

One important reason why the union was successful in preventing the introduction of the data system into the locomotive work shop was that it was in no way going to effect or alter the actual instruments of production. Within the graphic branch, however, computers and data systems are themselves production tools. Within the locomotive repair shop, the intention was not to alter the production process. Rather, the direction and control of work and material was to be altered. In all probability it was this factor that made it easier for the union to successfully reject its introduction. Other alternatives existed which were as profitable. In the graphic branch example, however, there were no equally profitable alternatives available on the market. The maximum intensity in the use of labour power (the locomotive repair shop) and the constant introduction of new technology which increases the productivity of the force (as in the newspaper) are two central components in company managements' rationalization efforts.

3.2 Rationalization and work

Rationalization and new technology also change the nature of work, or more correctly stated, the labour process. In all productive activity, people through their labour and with the aid of instruments of labour (tools and machines, for example, a type setting machine) shape a work object (raw material or semi-fabricated goods, for example, a text). As will be illustrated, rationalization can be directed against the worker himself, against his work instruments, or against the work object. What is of importance to our present discussion is that regardless of the focus of rationalization, it has consequences for both the organization and content of work.

Several of the most basic rationalization strategies are summarized in the illustration below. In it we have distinguished between management rationalization strategies for the utilization and for the development of production technology respectively. One reason for this distinction is that the unions' possibilities and strategies for dealing with technological and organizational changes differ completely in the two areas. In the following discussion we will illustrate these strategies with examples drawn primarily from the graphic branch.

However, the specific rationalization strategy chosen by the company management in a given situation is also dependent upon the technological limitations (for example, paste-up and make-up pre-suppose advanced photo setting). Further, the company's economic resources available for investment must also be considered. Finally, as mentioned above, it is also dependent upon union strength and strategy.

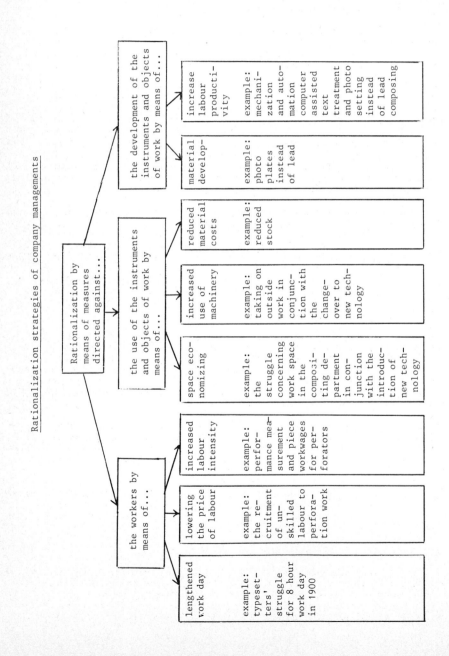

Rationalization strategies of company managements

3.3 Rationalization strategies directed against the work force

The classic strategy employed by management for increasing profits has been to
lengthen the work day without a corresponding increase in wages. In a country like
Sweden this strategy is primarily of historical interest. As early as 1900, for
example, typesetters succeeded in pushing through the eight hour work day even
though other groups still worked 9-10 hours per day.

Nevertheless, rationalization measures aimed at lowering the price of labour and
increasing its intensity to the greatest extent continue to be widely employed.
They are used in both these cases to break down the work process into simple tasks.
In some situations, it has been possible to separate out certain of these tasks
which can be performed by those with less training and education - thereby employing cheaper labour. With the assistance of the computer-based planning system in
the locomotive repair shop in Örebro, the work cycles would have been divided up
so that more skilled labour could have been replaced by unskilled and minutely
directed labour. In such a situation, skills would not be sought nor would training
be provided. Another example of this process is the division of labour between
typesetters and perforators. The degree to which company management succeeds with
this strategy of paying lower wage rates to unskilled labour depends of course on
the union's response. (The union prevented the introduction of the computer-based
planning system in the repair shop. As a result of union demands, perforator's
wages are at the same level as the average male graphic worker.)

Even though company management may not succeed directly in lowering the price of
labour by means of the minute division of work tasks, such an approach often offers
the possibility of increasing work intensity. It is easier for the company to oversee and control workers who only carry out a few simplified work tasks. In the
case of the data system in the repair shop, it would have been possible for the
company to give repair men detailed instructions and closely follow each work moment and then issue new detailed instructions. An example from the composing department is performance measurement and piece work wages for the perforators.

3.4 The use of instruments and objects of labour

Within the framework of the existing technology, it is possible for the company to
reduce its machinery, raw material and general plant costs. One rationalization
strategy in this respect is to economize on the use of plant space. This often
occurs in conjunction with changes in technology. For example, with the introduction of the new technology in the newspaper the company drastically reduced the
space allocated for the composing department. Thus, one of the pre-conditions for
a good work environment and organization were effected.

The increased utilization of machinery is another rationalization strategy. An
example of this is the fact that newspaper composing departments often take on outside work to fill in the idle periods that occur in conjunction with the production
of the newspaper. This effects work organization and control, and perhaps, work
intensity as well.

The reduction of material costs is still another possible area for rationalization.
One example is the introduction of block setting in order to make better use of
expensive photo setting paper. This alters the work organization for paste-up and
make-up.

3.5 The development of the instruments and objects of labour

Competition between companies results in continual developments in the area of work
instruments and objects. The result of this steady technological development is
that fewer workers are required to produce the same product quantity. Labour productivity can be increased by means of the introduction of various forms of mechanization and automation. The limits of the organization, content and direction of

work are also built into the system of machinery.

An historical example of increasing the productivity of labour in this way was the
replacement of the composing stick with the composing machine. A current example
is the introduction of computer-based text and image processing. To a greater extent the work is performed by unskilled graphic workers. Entire departments disap-
per, for example, plate preparation departments when the plates are engraved by
laser beam directed by a composing department computer.

How can the union deal with company managements' strategies for the development
and utilization of technology and work organization? How can the union confine rationalization to socially acceptable and union desired forms? These are the central
issues taken up in the discussion of strategy addressed in the next part of this
paper.

PART II. UNION INFLUENCE

4. Union overview

The technology and work organization in a company often changes gradually - generally at the same pace that new machinery replaces old through normal wear. However, frequently more rapid and thorough changes occur with the development of
new production technology.

Whichever of these situations prevail, it is our view that the union needs to have
a good overview of developments to be able to see the connection between various
changes which may be occuring simultaneously. It is essential that studies carried
out in the face of such changes illuminate the issues of importance to the union
such as emplyment, work organization, work environment so that the consequences
for the entire personnel and all departments are brought to light and eventual conflicts can be solved. The union must aquire a grasp of the ongoing technological-
economic developments and the available negotiating room for union influence and
alternatives that exist.

What can the union do at the local level? How can one best work within the union
in the face of tehcnological and organizational changes? Our discussions here will
be illustrated with examples from the newspaper and the locomotive repair shop referred to above. We shall also discuss three different strategies the union can
use to deal with these issues.

5. Union work in the repair work shop

In 1974, the State Employees' Union was informed by the State Railway's central
administration that a computer-based planning system, ISA-KLAR, would be introduced at its work shops - among other places in Örebro. It represented the management's alternative to piece work wages which the union had gotten rid of after a
long struggle.

5.1 Joint project work

The union was interested in the promised improvements in work methods and material
supply - indicated in the original description fo the ISA-KLAR project. They
agreed to participate in the project groups. However, it became increasingly clear
to the union that their chances for influencing the development of the ISA-KLAR
system through their participation in project groups was minimal. Under the guise
of technological discussions, the State Railway management and its consultant continued the development without the promised improvements. There was never any substantial discussion of the central issue - the future planning in the repair work
shop.

5.2 Independent union investigations

In March 1976, the union established an investigative group with 14 participants. With the support of researchers from the DEMOS Project, it was to investigate ISA-KLAR and work planning in the locomotive shop. It was also supposed to provide information and support to the union representatives sitting in the project groups.

As the investigative work continued, the union concluded that the ISA-KLAR project must be stopped until a co-determination agreement existed to regulate the use of such types of systems. The union also worked out counter proposals for planning and work organization in two work-places. They wanted to demonstrate that it was possible to have a well-functioning work-place without ISA-KLAR. These experiences were also developed to be used as a basis for the coming local co-determination agreement on rationalization. Among the demands can be noted:

- Long range planning of, among other things, technological development, training, and personnel.

- Rationalization must not result in the performance measurements of individuals or groups, nor piece work wages of any type.

6. Union work at the newspaper

6.1 Joint project work

In January 1976, a study of new technology was begun at the newspaper - Svenska Dagbladet. At that time there had already been in operation for many years photo setting parallel to lead composing. However, the major change, the scrapping of lead, still lay ahead of the graphic workers' union at Svenska Dagbladet.

The union was well represented in the project group formed to carry out the study. However, this group only met three times and the actual investigation was carried out entirely by experts from a consulting firm. At its best, union participation in the project group resulted in only marginal adjustments. For example, in the final proposal management had eliminated statements such as "the editorial text is entered by journalists". The technological solution, however, was not altered. The largest number of display terminals were in the editorial departments as had been suggested in the original system proposal.

At the outset, both management and the union employed new strategies. The consultant's studies provided an overall proposal for the introduction of new technology to the composing department.

6.2 Union investigative work

In this situation, and with the support of the DEMOS researchers, the union wrote a letter to the company management. The letter demanded time to work out their own proposal. It also pointed out in which areas the investigation must be supplemented with studies of the consequences of the new system for the personnel. Upon receipt of the letter, the management retreated from their initial proposal. They no longer made reference to a total solution but instead returned to the approach of presenting one machine at a time.

Intially, the union attempted to stand fast with the demand put forward in the letter, but gradually they returned to dealing with various issues after they had arisen. One half year after sending the letter, the union altered its demand for an overall solution to a demand for negotiations prior to the introduction of any new equipment.

Until the installation of the new technology in the spring of 1979, the union participated in a traditional manner in a number of joint labour management project.

For example, one such group was established to look into the new printing method.
On the other hand, the union became involved in a new way in the joint groups which
studied plant and work organization. For the first time, union representatives in
the group worked full time with the study. But what happens to such union issues
as work organization and training when union spokesmen "take over"? The union
spokesmen can become too sympathetic to the technological and economic perspective
they are compelled to work with. This can result from the close co-operation with
management, from the fascination with technology, or the absence of a clear union
position worked out by union leadership and the members.

7. Three strategies

In this seciton, we will discuss union strategies for co-determination in the
larger technological changes within the company.

On the basis of experiences from the DEMOS Project we shall discuss three strategies which the union can apply in this area: Union participation in the companies'
project groups, a model for independent union investigative work in connection with
the companies' studies (the negotiation model) and as a third alternative, perhaps
the union should not become engaged in the company management's planning, but instead focus its efforts primarily at the mobilization and ideological education of
its members.

7.1 Project participation

Today, investigative work in companies is often carried out by a project group with
the assistance of experts. The group is established by the company's management. It
is increasingly common to include representatives from the departments concerned.
Not infrequently, the union is offered a position in the project groups. This participation can provide the opportunity of becoming involved even at the idea stage
of the project. However, the union's chances of exertin significant influence
through such traditional project work is very limited. The problem is that the
union has no real means of exerting power coupled to its project group participation. It is based upon the good will of the employer so there is the risk that the
union will become integrated in the generally unaltered employer's decision-making
process.

7.2 Union investigations and negotiation

Against such a background, is there any reason why the union should participate at
all in the company's project groups? Yes, given certain pre-conditions. To remain
completely outside such groups would close the door on a vital source of information. In our view, the most important pre-condition for such participation is that
parallel to the company's project group, an independent union effort takes place
to build up knowledge and information or for mobilization around union demands.

This involves a clear distinction of the relationship between the parties in the
investigative work, but it does not conflict with demands for democratization of
decision-making in the day-to-day work in the organization. On the contrary, it is
our view that a demarcation of the relationship between the parties in the investigation work (in the planning work) is a pre-condition for the democratization of
co-operation and decision-making in the work organization.

7.2-1 The model

One model for the development of union resources and negotiation has developed in
the DEMOS Project. Exclusively union investigative groups work parallel to the
company management's project groups and provide a basis for discussions at membership meetings and union study circles, for union spokesmen in the management's
project organization, and for local union's position and negotiations with the
management. Particularly in special technical and administrative issues, one can

use external support, from the union, wage earner consultants, or researchers. Study circles concerned with the actual problem area (for example, with planning) can serve as reference groups for union research and consultants.

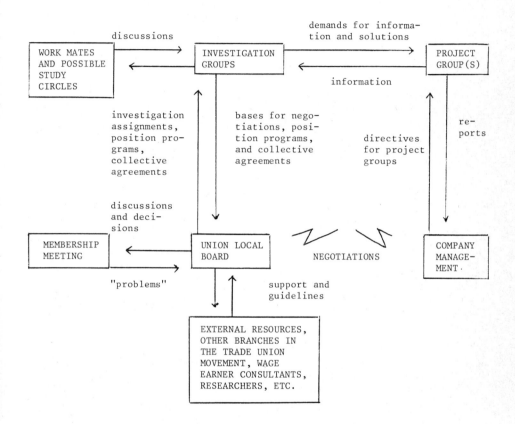

7.2-2 Problems

There is a risk that what we have described can become an investigation based on the employer's terms with union representatives as hostages. One reason that union representatives easily can aquire (or appear to aquire) "co-responsability" is that they often have a rather unclear mandate (as opposed to the situation, for example, with wage negotiations). They must operate on the basis of the general trust of the members. A trust which assumes that they will come to grips with a complicated problem area while, at the same time, maintaining an appreciation of the interests and wishes of the members. They are forced to independently evaluate and adopt positions on various issues. Participation and co-responsibility means that it is more difficult for them to stand on the outside, to obstain, to show "a lack of solidarity" with developing decisions, which they themselves participated in.

In order for participation and negotiations to have good chances for success, it is important that they are a part of long range union aspirations – that a <u>union line</u> exists, preferably formulated in the union position program concerning the actual issue. If a union line is not worked out in advance: can the union manage to do it at the same time it is involved with large and current changes?

7.3 Mobilization around union demands

Independent union investigative work in a new area, for example, new technology, can result in a rapid concentration of tasks and know-how on already burdened union representatives. How does one find forms of working within the union that contribute to activation and mobilization of members?

It is not necessarily true that the union itself needs to develop detailed knowledge concerning future production technology. Rather, the union can emphasize the development of fundamental union principles, for example, the right of existing workers to operate the new machinery regardless of the nature of the new technological solution. Once such basic principles have been established through negotiations, then perhaps the detailed investigative work can be carried out by joint project groups.

One of the most essential pre-conditions is that in long range union activity one succeeds in formulating fundamental principles so that a strong mobilization of the membership can occur around them to push through demands. Another pre-condition is that company management has the resources, competence and will to carry through complementary investigations which arise from union demands that have been agreed to. (On this point, differences may be seen between Svenska Dagbladet where the union's own investigations were important, and for example Dagens Nyheter, the biggest Swedish newspaper, where membership mobilization and demands made upon the company were dominant.)

One risk involved in the union placing major emphasis and effort into working out fundamental principles (rather than developing a detailed knowledge of the relevant technology) is that they may lose the initiative to management and "miss" ongoing and important changes in the company. While the union is involved in working out fundamental principles and negotiating programs, the company can take concrete decisions which make it either difficult or impossible to realize the fundamental principles arrived at.

There would also be the risk that the union lacks the technological expertise and knowledge which would enable them to determine whether or not the company management's proposals for new technology were in agreement with the union's basic principles.

7.4 Selecting a strategy

The union strategy chosen for influencing the introduction of new technology at work should be dependent upon the particular pre-conditions in each case. At this stage, our studies do not enable us to "recommend" one or another strategy. However, the experiences from the use of various strategies indicates certain risks to be aware of: the risk of becoming a "hostage" through participation in a project; The risk that comprehensive union investigation work can hamper other union activities; The risk that mobilization around fundamental principles can cause difficulties when it comes to checking how they are realized in concrete situations.

We have simplified three strategies. In practice these strategies are often combined in different ways depending upon the individual situation. Our most comprehensive views concern independent union investigation and negotiations because that was the union approach tested in the DEMOS Project. We have pointed out many difficulties.

These have to do with the fact that investigation work is very demanding on resources and can thereby threaten other important union activities, for example,
contacts with the membership. There have, however, also been difficult "external"
conditions in a number of the cases. The pre-conditions for independent union investigation work are better, for example, in areas such as personnel policy and
training which lie nearer the employees' own experiences, or if the union can work
in peace and quiet with an investigation (instead of following on the heels of
company management in an acute situation), or if one works with ordinary problems
(and not with revolutionary technological changes) etc.

8. Common solutions

Local union efforts are important and a basis for democratization in working life.
But there are limits to local influence.

There is a need for a co-ordination of local efforts. A long term, comprehensive
and offensive struggle through central organizations – not simply a reaction to
local issues. If this is not done there is the risk that interest will be lost at
the local work-places. The union locals can be overwhelmed and the offensive for
the democratization of working life can appear to be little more than interesting
rhetoric.

There is a need for collective solutions to local problems. E.g. existing technology may hinder realization of local union demands.

Several key words which indicate the direction to be taken are: Union research
policy, union technology policy for product and work quality, "democratically organized demands" by means of purchase policy, and direct contacts between consumers
and producers. What is involved then are fundamental issues of power in the total
economy and society.

(Translation: John Fry)

Sources

The results presented in this article were published in earlier reports from the
DEMOS Project.

The technological alterations at the locomotive repair shop and the newspaper
respectively are described in two reports: Ehn/Erlander/Karlsson and others:
Vi vägrar låta detaljstyra oss, DEMOS report number 10, The Swedish Center for
Working Life 1978, and, Ehn/Perby/Sandberg and others: Brytningstid, report, The
Swedish Center for Working Life (anticipated spring 1983).

The section on strategies for co-determination is based upon our article in Tre
år med MBL, The Swedish Center for Working Life, Liber Förlag, 1980, together
with Brytningstid (above).

A basic book from the DEMOS Project is Företagsstyrning och Löntagarmakt, by
Ehn/Sandberg (Prisma 1982, second edition). There you may also find references
to litterature used within the project.

A discussion of methodological questions in the DEMOS Project is found in Åke
Sandberg: "Trade union-orientated research for democratization of planning in
work life", Journal of Occupational Behaviour, Vol. 4, 59-71, 1983.

The identification of company management rationalization strategies is based on
a dissertation by Torsten Björkman and Karin Lundqvist: Från MAX till PIA, Arkiv
avhandlingsserie No. 12, 1981.

SYSTEMS DESIGN FOR, WITH, AND BY THE USERS
U. Briefs, C. Ciborra and L. Schneider (editors)
North-Holland Publishing Company
© IFIP, 1983

THE UTOPIA PROJECT

On Training, Technology and Products
viewed from the Quality of work
perspective

Pelle Ehn, Morten Kyng, Yngve Sundblad
et al.

UTOPIA is the name of a Nordic research project. It is in the
Scandinavian languages the acronym for Training, Technology
And Product from the Perspective of Skills and Democracy at
Work (Utbildning, Teknik Och Produkt I Arbetskvalitetsperspektiv.) The aim is to develop trade union oriented alternatives
for computerbased text- and image processing in printing
industry. The project work is carried out by printers, computer scientists and social scientists jointly. The UTOPIA
Project was initiated in 1981. The following text contains
background considerations. It is experted from the UTOPIA
Research Program. 2,3

PROBLEM DESCRIPTION

Influencing technology

The experience gained by organized labour and the research conducted by trade unions
during the 1970s concerning the ability to influence new technology and the organization of work at local level suggested a number of problems. One fundamental
experience gained is that the "degrees of freedom" available to design the content
and organization of work which utilizes existing technolgy is often considerably
less than that required to meet trade unions demands. In other words, existing
production technology more and more often constitutes an insurmountable barrier
preventing the realization of trade union demands for the quality of work and a
meaningful job.

Another important experience concerns the trade unions' ability to influence technology at its introduction. This ability is limited in an increasing number of
situations to a choice between saying yes or no to the purchase of "turn-key packages" of technology and organization.

For an increasing number of applications companies purchase "system packages" instead of developing systems themselves. This reduces the influence the trade unions
have at the local level. At best it has been possible to influence the choice of
supplier and the "company adaption" of the system selected. Trade unions lack sufficient power and comprehensive training. So that when new technology is introduced
they can not influence the systems to any great extent.

At the same time, as the area within which trade unions can act is limited, production is increasingly based on scientific and technological expertise. Trades skills
are no longer in demand. These factors have often led to technology being regarded
as adverse or just plain evil --- opinions that are substantiated during the
greater part of existing training when the forces acting on development are not
explained. The resulting animosity towards technology contrasts sharply with the
positive attitude about new technology traditionally held by the trade union movement. When attempting to override this disparity the political character of technology becomes important.

That is, the technology we have today is an expression of a certain historical and social relationship. Technology is an expression of the sort of society we live in.

The same initial position must pervade the discussion of technological alternatives. The relationship between the classes, profits, competition, markets, etc.,
all have a bearing on technology and create different conditions which affect the
quality of work and products.

What can the trade unions do?

The question of what the trade unions can do to influence technology can be partially answered by looking at what is already being done. Attempts are made to reduce the negative effects of technology on employees by demanding reforms in legislation and developing labor management agreements. Efforts are made to mobilize
forces at the local level through the implementation of broad-based programs of
study and the presentation of action programs. Training is demanded in order to
obtain and retain control over new technology and to counteract the degradation of
work. Demands are being made on the actual utilization of technology and the work
rotation associated with it. Demands have also been initiated on suppliers of production technology, primarily concerning the physical working environment. However,
this strategy could best be described as a "defensive" action. This project is
working on a supplementary and as yet untried offensive strategy: The trade union
movement itself draws up the technological and training alternatives and takes
sole responsibility for their implementation and development at local level.

The need to try offensive strategies becomes increasingly pressing due in part to
the above-mentioned tendency to install "turn-key packages" and the short, inadequate training courses provided on the servicing of the new systems. These severely
limit the degrees of freedom within which the trade unions can act at the local
level at individual work-places. But the predominant reason is that it takes a long
time to produce alternatives that meet trade union requirements in terms of the
organization of work and fulfill technical, quality and economic demands, etc.
There is an obvious risk that trade union demands such as economic power and democracy in working life, a meaningful job for everybody, etc., can be obstructed because they are not technologically feasible. A co-ordination of local trade union
efforts is required. What is needed is an offensive, long-term and far-reaching
strategy conducted by central organizations - not simply reactions to local crises.
In the absence of such a central strategy, there is a danger that people at the
local level will lose interest because the demands made on the trade unions at the
local level can be overwhelming. The push for the democratization of working life
can run the risk of being regarded as just a lot of hot air.

Co-ordination and joint solutions can be developed in central trade union and political bodies. Examples include central negotiations, legislation and government
planning.

Another form could be a more "horizontal" co-ordination. Co-ordination channels
would be established directly between workers at work-places and in companies that
encountered the same types of problems. Co-ordination can take the form of a contract between the producers and the consumers, e.g. the local trade union which
orders the development of working clothes from a production co-operative. Such
"democratically organized demands" could be supported by legislation or labor-
management agreements. Orders for more advanced products and entirely new technological solutions could be made centrally. There are several examples of government orders of this type.

On a large scale this type of procurement policy is not without problems. The large
investments can be like the young cuckoo in the nest - difficult to get rid of
should socio-economic, environmental or other considerations make this necessary
at a later date.

Despite this and other risks, this type of centrally-planned procurement can be one approach for a trade union that wants to develop a new organization of work and training. With sufficient resources - a charge levied on production or government subsidies - the trade unions could make their voice heard in important parts of technological development.

It is in this context that the supplementary method proposed by this project should be viewed.

The initial position is to use actions taken centrally by the trade union to influence the actual range or production technology available and the often insufficient training provided in conjunction with its introduction. The trade union at the central level assumes responsibility for working towards collective solutions to the local demands, in addition to supporting actions taken at the local level.

Local trade union demands would be collected and translated into technological and organizational solutions at technological development/training institutes run by the trade unions. In this way, technological/organizational alternatives, based on trade union demands, would be incorporated into the new technology.

What can research achieve?

During the 1970s co-operation developed in the Nordic countries between researchers and trade union organizations on technological development matters, particularly with regard to computer technology. All of these projects include both practical workplace-oriented elements and theoretical and methodological elements.

The workplace-oriented research is aimed at supporting trade union action at the local level and includes the following aims:

- to mobilize people at the local level in respect to new technology

- to evaluate management's utilization of technology in relation to the interests of the trade union movement

- to draw up goals for development and formulate demands for the utilization of technology

- to begin changing conditions at individual work-places

All four goals must also be included in future research work on approaches to the trade union movement's influence over technological development.

But this type of work has a number of limitations. Enormous resources have been invested in the new technology utilized by companies. The technology introduced at any one work-place has, as mentioned earlier, a long history of development, a history of a social, technological and organizational nature. The vertical division of labor has also produced a distribution of costs. Apart from the actual "company assimilation" item, development costs are distributed among many companies interested in similar "standard" equipment. When, on the other hand, a trade union organization presents demands for an alternative utilization of technology, the following two problems result:

- Does it exist at all, or is it feasible that the technology required to meet the demands can be developed?

- If so, is it realistic, in terms of resources, to demand that a single company design and plan such an alternative?

One contribution to resolving these two problems is to perform a trade union tech-

nological development project. Motivation for this work being performed as an independent trade union project includes the facts that management, as opposed to
the trade unions, has:

- relatively unambiguous and well-defined targets for technological
  development (e.g. productivity and efficiency measurements) which
  can conflict with the trade union demands, and

- widespread experience of technological development from the traditional
  company-assimilated viewpoint which gives them an advantage vis-à-vis
  the trade union demands.

Research aimed at developing technology and training based on trade union criteria
can contribute towards changing the criticism levelled at company utilization of
technology. Instead of defending the status quo, an offensive strategy can be developed for another type of technology and improved products. This means a type of
technology that improves the quality of work and the products and that is not in-
flexible but can be dynamically changed at individual work-places as the employees
develop their skills. One important condition enabling this active procedure is
the development of technology and training programs combined with sociological
analyses of the prerequisites of the alternatives. An understanding is developed
of the forces acting on technological development nationally and internationally.

DELIMITATION

Software: Development of systems and training

In general it can be said that the development of production technology is associated with very sizeable investments. The investments are so large that it seems
less than likely that a trade union organization could be made solely responsible
for such development work, at least during the next few years. However, this need
not be the case for parts of modern production technology – software. The development costs or programs are considerably less, generally speaking, than of hardware.
Developing alternative software also enables a dynamic technology to be created, a
technology that can be further developed at local level if alternative training
programs are simultaneously developed.

That the trade unions obtain a degree of control over computer systems in production processes through the establishment of their own development/training institute naturally does not mean that the fundamentals of production technology can be
altered, at least initially. The unaltered machinery, the hardware, will still
constitute a clear limitation to the trade union demands that will be realized.
But in one important respect the development of alternative computer systems and
training based on the trade union criteria would be of great significance – the
opportunity to reunite planning with design in the labor process.

If software can be regarded as a foot in the door for trade union technological
development, then the next question is what type of applications should be covered.

Trade union technological development capabilities are at present restricted in
those cases where new machinery and plant are being developed in parallel with the
automatic information processing for controlling them.

One example is the development of welding robots and automatic handling devices.
These restrictions are in part due to the considerable costs involved, as mentioned
earlier, and the necessity of possessing highly specialized technical knowledge.

Another area is the automation of information processing for the control of machinery and plant already in existence, e.g. software for controlling machine tools
and process equipment. The problem of trade union development of these systems is
that they will be inextricably linked to existing machinery and plant which makes

the possibilities of developing alternatives that meet trade union demands so limitated that it makes this area an unsuitable choice for a first development project.

The automation of work on information

The biggest changes in the labour process in conjunction with data processing occur when the material being processed, the workpiece, is information. There is in the sector at least two applications that particularly lend to themselves to further work:

- systems for text and image processing in the graphic industry

- office automation.

The demarcations of the sectors for both of these applications are, however, complex. What is involved here is a change in the information medium, i.e. in the actual workpiece. When this change occurs a number of new processing possibilities immediately open up. To some extent, however, already existing machinery and plant will also here impose limits on the parameters restricting the development of alternatives.

The fact that only text and image processing in the graphic industry will be dealt with in the remainder of this paper is not due to office automation being regarded as an area of application any less suitable for investigation - quite the contrary, technological development performed by the trade unions would be highly desirable in both these areas. However, this task is far too large a project for a first experiment in trade union technological development. A substantial part of the project work will, however, comprise on-going discussions with representatives of the various trades concerned in the development taking place in the text and image processing sector. The selection of the graphic industry should also be seen against the background of the good contacts that have long existed between the graphic trade union organization in the Nordic countries and the researchers.

Experience gained from the graphic sector can make an important contribution to the trade union movement's discussions on alternative technological development, particularly on the office automation side. This opens the door for widening the scope of the project in the future.

The graphic industry

The graphic industry underwent radical technological restructuring in the 1970s. The industry changed from led composing to data processing and photo-setting. Computers, visual display units, photo-setters, scanners, etc., have been introduced by rationalization over the last ten years. Many of the traditional typographists' skills are not longer in demand. The trade unions have tried to counteract the negative effects of this technology on the number of employees and the content of the work through negotiated agreements. In 1974 a "new technology agreement", the first on the Swedish labor market was concluded.

Among its conditions were certain employment guarantees for graphic workers when changing to new technology. Also included were stipulations on the right to further training and retraining on altered duties and the operation of new equipment. Demands for new technology agreements were presented by the Danish trade union movement in conjunction with agreement negotiations conducted in 1978/9 and 1980/1. This has resulted in a basic agreement between the Danish TUC and the employers. The Danish Typographical Association is pressing a demand for an agreement giving employment guarantees but so far they have not succeeded in achieving results.

In 1980 the Swedish agreement was supplemented by rules covering integrated text processing, i.e. the introduction of technology relating to editorial, advertisement and composing work. Local agreements have also been made in all the Nordic

countries with several newspapers stating in detail the rights of graphic workers
when changing over to new technology. Work at local level, which is often regarded
as a fight for survival, has not infrequently resulted in industrial action. For
graphic workers this has not simply concerned the relationship with management but
also relationships with other trade groups within the company.

ALTERNATIVE TEXT AND IMAGE PROCESSING

The alternative text and image processing systems and training that can be developed within the framework of this project will be based on trade union experience
and graphic trade expertise. They will also be based on the researchers' ability
to outline the technical, economic and social conditions affecting the alternatives and their ability to implement in practice the technical solutions which
fulfill trade union demands.

The concrete utopia will develop as an interaction between hopes and visions on
one side, and a knowledge of the social and technical conditions on the other.
It is naturally impossible to predict the results of this process and present
the form and contents of the alternatives here.

However, the discussions that have so far been conducted between trade union
representatives and researchers indicate some fundamental principles:

- quality of work and product

- utopia and realism

- training for further development

- democracy and equal opportunities at work.

Quality of work and product

"The systems and courses available today invite cheating at work". This statement,
made by a typographist, says a lot about the type of technology which exists today.
Along with the dequalification of trade skills, the quality of graphic products
has also diminished, despite the technological possibilities available. This
relationship between the content of work and quality of the product is attracting
increasing attention in working life research.

The alternative that we develop will emphasize the importance of good quality
products, but this is viewed in relation to the quality of work. High quality
trade skills and trade expertise are regarded as targets in themselves, but also
as important means of achieving the required quality of graphic products.

The attempt to break down the vertical division of labor will be connected to the development of trade skills in new areas of technology which in its turn will form
the basis for high quality graphic production. This means that new forms of utili-

zation of technical-scientific knowledge will have to be tested, putting a new
value on practical experience and giving it a new function in development process.

Co-operation with associated trades, e.g. journalists and office workers, is also
planned. They will be participating in "quality seminars" which will discuss the
new technology and the possibilities different trades have of achieving high
quality work and products.

Utopia and realism

Will the alternative succeed given the conditions of existing market forces and
the organization of work? Should alternatives containing more utopian elements be
formulated? Discussions conducted so far indicate that they should be utopian
insofar as our most optimistic concepts of the quality of work and products should
be realized. They should be realistic insofar as they should be technically possible to achieve. Whether these alternatives will be outside or inside the parameters of what can be assumed to be acceptable to the market cannot be answered
today. Furthermore, the question is not simply economic but is highly dependent on
the control available over the production, trade union, and the company at individual work-places. Analysis of technical/political conditions and an endeavor to
increase awareness of the limits of democratization are an integral part of the
development of alternatives. This is one of the central tasks facing this project
and can be affected by other suppliers' counter-strategies and the success the
trade union has in gaining support for its own alternatives from legislation and
agreements.

A good example of how market conditions can be changed through legislation and
agreements is the environmental laws on car exhaust levels introduced in the USA.
Or nearer home, the West German government's environmental demands on VDTs which
resulted in Datasaab obtaining a large order. This VDT was based on demands made
by the trade unions.

Training for further development

It is the suppliers of new technology who are responsible for providing the majority of the technical training in the graphic industry. This training provides
graphic workers with the ability to manipulate the new technology. As a rule, an
understanding of basic principles is not provided in this training. The vertical
division of labor and the polarization of different trade categories are upheld
and reinforced by existing training.

The training that is to be developed together with our alternative systems will
include the development and maintenance of the technology, the organization of
work and the working environment. It will provide an understanding of the capabilities needed to use and develop graphics skills once the new system is put into
operation. This training will also provide the graphic workers with the knowledge
enabling them to participate in the introduction and adaption of the system at
local level. It should also create a development process where knowledge of and
experience in the use of the system is translated into a further development of
technology and the organization of work at local level. In other words, technological development, training in technology and the organization of work are regarded
as an integral whole. Such training, which aims at providing security of employment
and meaningful work, is fully compatible with the fundamental conditions that the
parties agree should exist when deciding on the introduction of new technology.

Special attention must be paid to two factors concerning central development and
adaption to local conditions and further development. One is to find good <u>methods
of performing development work</u> which do not result in trade union experts taking
over the technological development centrally. Local activities must be encouraged.
"Training for further development" above is one contribution towards achieving
this. The second factor is the <u>relationship between the groups participating in</u>

the central development work: graphic workers and technical and planning experts respectively. Forms of working which prevent a division of labor dominated by the experts must be developed.

Democracy and equal opportunity at work

In addition to developing trade skills, the alternative will naturally have a strong emphasis on elements facilitating a democratic decision-making process in companies. This applies to both the production level (e.g. conditions applying to autonomous work groups and control over production planning) and the management level (e.g. a say in budget and personal planning matters).

The project is unconventional as far as democracy and equal opportunities at work are concerned insofar as the changes are not based on a given technology. Rather, the main thrust will be directed towards developing technology that fulfills particular demands.

Even through the development of the alternative technology is based on technical production, journalists and clerks will also be involved in development work over the long term. They will try to elaborate the different trade categories' demands for the quality of work and product and the development of more democratic forms of working.

THE AIMS OF THE PROJECT

The project is both a development project for technology and a sociological experiment in understanding the conditions relating to that development. It is based on a sociological criticism of technology and attempts to develop from this a new "technician" with practical know-how. The trade union movement has a central role in this experimental work, which encompasses new forms of transfer between technical/scientific knowledge and practical experience. The experiment aims at discovering realistic technological/organizational alternatives, Utopias made real, within a medium-term time perspective (approximately the next ten years). Within this time perspective the project's most general target is to promote the capabilities of trade unions to influence technological development and to defend and develop the status of trade skills in the production process.

In order to create these prerequisities, the project must develop a stystem and a training program that are used at a number of work-places and/or are included in the discussions conducted at a large number of work-places. It should be noted that it is not necessary to introduce the system and conduct training courses at each work-place. But, on the other hand, they must function as a source for the formulation of trade union demands, which presupposes that the systems can be used as points of departure in somewhat similar forms at a number of different work-places. That is to say that "system packages" are developed, though with a high degree of freedom for adaption at local level. These systems have to be developed so that they possess functions that can be used at a large number of work-places, functions that are directly related to many peoples' work. Nordic co-operation established in conjunction with this project provides a good basis for obtaining the power to change words into actions.

The introduction of the trade union alternative systems and the trade union technological training should provide real benefits for graphic workers. First, in relation to other new systems and second to a purely defensive action against the introduction of the new technology offered by the supplier. This demand is the most crucial but at the same time the most difficult to guarantee. One important reason is that strategic and tactical considerations are involved. For example, should alternatives be developed that involve a risk of reduced employment, even though this is substantially less than if available systems on the market were introduced? One important demand to be made of the project is that the differences between the alternative systems and the alternative training and those already available must be made absolutely clear. It can, for example, be a matter of the way in which totality in the work replaces the traditional division of labor.

The project must result in a "technical success". Sufficient resources, both economically and in terms of expertise, must be made available. This is important for the scope the functions of the system will possess, for the technical level of ambition and for the organization of the project. One pivotal condition is the technical competence of the researchers combined with the trade skills and trade union experience of the graphic workers in the project team. The fundamental principle is, as mentioned earlier, to emphasize high quality both in work and product. Behind this is the assumption that these efforts are mutually supporting.

The aims of the project can be summarized in the following points:

- to investigate the conditions required for and to contribute towards the establishment of a Nordic trade union institute for the development of and training in data processing technology and the organization of work in the graphic industry

- to develop, evaluate and study conditions for trade union technological development as a technological/political strategy for the trade union movement

- to develop work procedures for trade union technological development

- to develop trade union alternative systems for text and image processing

- to develop trade union training programs for text and image processing.

ORGANIZATION

The project work is carried out by a Project Group comprising researchers and workers in the filed connected to the Swedish Centre for Working Life (ALC) in Stockholm, the Computer Science Department at Aarhus University (DAIMI) and the Department of Numerical Analysis and Computing Science at the Institute of Technology (NADA) in Stockholm. The graphic workers of the team provide the project with trade union experience and trade know-how. ALC provides primarily competence in social sciences concentrating on the organization of work, working environment, equal opportunities and the strategies and conditions for technological development. DAIMI provides competence for trade union training and methods for the development and description of computerized systems from a trade union perspective. NADA provides competence in computing science such as methodology for program development, user-oriented languages, graphical data processing, text and image processing and training. The different areas of expertise partially overlap. The researchers have long experiences of co-operation with trade union organizations in matters concerning technological development.

In addition to the direct participation of graphic tradesmen in the Project Group, the graphic trade union organizations follow and support the project through a Reference Group. The Nordic Graphic Workers' Union decided at its 1980 Annual Meeting to actively support the project and appointed a Reference Group for this purpose. This Reference Group comprises representatives of Denmark, Finland, Norway and Sweden. The Reference Group and the Project Group hold joint meetings at least twice a year and the Reference Group's chairman participates more actively in the work of the Project Group.

There is a local project group at each participating institution. In principle, each participating institution finances its part of the project work. Each local project group consists of both researchers and graphic workers.

The local project groups maintain continuous contact with the trade union organizations concerned in those countries where they are active.

Footnotes:

1) The UTOPIA Project - Names and addresses:

UTOPIA   UTOPIA
Arbetslivscentrum   NADA
Box 5606   Tekniska Högskolan
S-114 86 Stockholm   S-100 44 Stockholm
Sweden   Swden
Tel: (8) 22 99 80   Tel: (8) 787 70 00

Pelle Ehn   Kerstin Eklund
Bernt Eriksson   Bo Eriksson
Ewa Gunnarsson   Malte Eriksson
Inga Johansson   Kerstin Frenckner
Åke Sandberg   Staffan Romberger
Dan Sjögren   Yngve Sundblad

UTOPIA   UTOPIA
Datalogisk Afdeling   Norsk Grafisk Forbund
Aarhus Universitet   Arbeidersamfunnets Plass 1
Ny Munkegade   Oslo 1
DK-8000 Aarhus C   Norway
Denmark   Tel: (2) 40 13 09
Tel: (6) 12 83 55

Kurt Jensen   Gunnars Kokaas
John Kammersgaard   (Chairman of the Reference Group)
Morten Kyng

2) A full list of references is given in the Scandinavian version of the UTOPIA
Research Program.

3) GRAFFITI is the name of the information paper of the UTOPIA Project.

Numbers of Graffiti published up till now:

1. Facket väljer egen väg mot ny teknik!
   UTOPIA-projektet presenteras (maj 81)
   (The trade union chooses its own way to new technology!
    Presentation of the UTOPIA Project - May 81)

2. Kvalitet i arbete och produkt
   Rapport från UTOPIA/NGU-konfernesen (nov 81)
   (Quality in work and product
    Report from the UTOPIA/NGU conference - November 81)

3. American Graffiti
   Facket
   Arbetsplatserna
   Tekniken (sept 82)
   (The American Graffiti
    The trade union
    The work-places
    The technology - September 82)

4. Lägesrapport
   Ny teknik
   Kvalitet (sept 82)
   (Situation report
   New technology
   Quality - September 82)

The Project also publish more traditional research reports and debate publications.
UTOPIA reports published up till now:

1. Utbildning, teknik och produkt i arbetskvalitetsperspektiv - ett nordiskt
   forskningsprojekt om facklig utveckling av och utbildning i datateknik och
   arbetsorganisation, speciellt text- och bildbehandling i grafiska branschen,
   1981 (Forskningsprogram för UTOPIA). (See under 2.)

2. The UTOPIA Project - On training, technology and products viewed from the
   quality of work perspective, 1981
   (English version of UTOPIA research program.)

3. Arbetspapper från konferensen 26-29 april 1981 i Stockholm.
   (Working paper from the conference in Stockholm 26-29th of April, 1981.)

'THE UNDER-REPRESENTATION OF WOMEN WITHIN WHITE COLLAR TRADE UNION
STRATEGIES IN RESPONSE TO NEW OFFICE TECHNOLOGY'

Eileen Phillips

Sociology Department
City of London Polytechnic
Old Castle Street
London E1 7NT
England

Analysing women's under-representation in trade unions cannot
be understood as solely concerning their lower levels of
participation. Contradictions operating within their relationship both to trade unions and work need to be uncovered if
trade union strategies are potentially to challenge the
organisation of work. In the context of the introduction of
computerised systems, there is a danger that "women's jobs"
are being designed which involve a routine and repetitive
inputting of data. Responses which defend the status quo
only act to reinforce gender divisions in the workforce and
encourage a polarisation of skill levels.

Despite deepening fears in the labour movement about present levels of unemployment, fears which are not eased by the pundit's talk of a leisure society, British
trade unions appear hardly in much state to be developing out of their predominantly defensive role into one of challenging power relations in waged work.
Caught between the need to attempt a salvaging operation on the UK economy (and so
the talk of trade unions welcoming technological innovation) and the likelihood of
ensuing job loss (and so the talk of a shorter working week) it is unsurprising
that the rhetoric often sounds muddled and the action seems minimal. Pessimism
needs to be put to one side if any attempt at analysing how women's relation to
waged work is to raise crucial questions for trade unions. Without this suspen-
sion of defeat, we would be left wringing our hands and no nearer confronting the
near obliviousness the trade union movement exhibits towards sexual divisions, or
at times even the presence of women in its ranks[1] ("the trade unionist and his
wife").

For the clerical unions with a majority of female members, unions which are in the
front line as far as new technology changing and/or erasing jobs, this invisi-
bility may seem unbelievable. Apart from public statements about womens' jobs
being the first to go as they are most routine and therefore most open to automation, little is said or done. To understand this we have to look closer at what
that white collar trade unionism consists of and at the same time try to connect
this to what possibilities are opened up (or closed down) for women with new
systems of working in the office.

Before going on to discuss the place women occupy in trade union organisation it
is important to be clear about the position they occupy in work generally.
Pointing to equal pay legislation, changing attitudes towards roles available to
women these days, the unacceptability of publicly arguing for discrimination
against women, all serve only as a thin smoke screen covering the stark facts
concerning women workers. Women are paid less than men - since 1977 the gap has
increased between male and female earnings in Britain so in 1979 women's pay was
63.6 per cent of men's. Sex segregation in workplaces has increased rather than
decreased this century and means women are concentrated at bottom ends of skill

hierarchies doing different jobs to men - a feature borne out by the comparison
of 13 per cent of women working in skilled manual, professional and managerial
jobs compared to 63 per cent of men.

Changing women's disadvantaged position has proved to be a difficult task but in
the context of new technology radically transforming possibilities in work organisation, it becomes crucial to challenge the ghettoes of women's work - otherwise
change can only mean for those women who remain in paid work a further push into
low-pay low-skill jobs.   The most likely candidates as agents of change which
would improve women's position in the work-force, might appear to be trade unions.
In clerical work where women predominate and where computerisation is taking the
greatest effect, it is particularly important to examine white collar trade union
strategies in the light of their potential for breaking down sexual divisions at
work.

Forms of under-representation of women trade unionists

The under-representation of women in these white collar trade unions which I will
discuss in this paper, does not simply take the form of a low level of female
elected representatives within trade unions, or fewer numbers of women participating in trade union activity.[2] There is an important distinction between attempts
to involve women members by reforming trade unions in a mechanical way and a more
radical re-thinking of the strategies and priorities within workers' organisations.

The former comprises efforts ranging from changing times and places of meetings
to suit women workers, to inserting demands relating to "womens' issues" into the
bargaining package. The problem with this approach is that it can easily be
cosmetic ie. avoids confrontation with the underlying causes which ensure that
women's work continues to be low paid and low skilled and seen by managers, male
trade unionists and to a certain degree women themselves, as "peripheral". This
can be judged by the readiness with which demands relating to maternity and child
care for instance, are dropped once trade union negotiations get under way.

Opposition to ghettoes of "women's work"

Re-thinking trade union strategy if it is to be effective in terms of both involving women and changing their position in the workforce, needs an understanding
of women's relation to waged work. This can provide the framework for a trade
union offensive in terms of challenging managerial prerogatives of control over
the content and division of work tasks. Any attempt to develop trade union
intervention in system design can only succeed in changing the status quo if
there is opposition to the continued existence of ghettoes of unskilled "women's
work". If this remains an invisible problem, then management can utilise women's
labour to de-skill and fragment clerical work further,[3] relying on implicit
assumptions shared by trade unionists and management alike that women are suited
to and prepared to accept routine, repetitive work.

In this paper I will discuss the Civil and Public Services Associations (CPSA)
and the Association of Professional, Executive Clerical and Computer Staff (APEX)
as two unions I have had some contact with in the context of introducing or
expanding computerisation, and hope to raise some productive criticisms. I will
then go on to examine how computerisation can be introduced to increase skill
differentials. I will argue that effective opposition to this cannot be waged by
a defence of craft skills as this ignores the present hierarchy within the workforce in terms of skill and control. A defensive strategy can at best only
prolong the existence of that hierarchy, at worst minimalise the basis for collective action within the workforce.

Forms of trade union bargaining
================================

A starting point is to look at what a trade union can bargain over when management proposes to introduce computerisation into the office: health and safety controls, for example a restriction on the length of time spent at one stretch in front of a terminal; extra payment for using computers either in the form of a once-off payment or an upgrading; productivity bargaining so that any increase in productivity of the workforce is reflected in members' wage packets; status quo agreements so that the new system does not lead to redundancies and at a more sophisticated level, there is no de-skilling of workers using the system. A myriad of difficulties are raised by these negotiating points, not least of which is the fact that any management decision to develop new technology is going to be taken on the basis of its capacity to push up productivity. "Increasing efficiency" can be easily translated into cutting overheads ie. cutting jobs. Union strength can be measured by how far it is capable of at best improving conditions of work for its members, at worst, preventing a deterioration.

If we look at the position women hold both in the hierarchy and in relation to the union organisation, these questions broaden out. For instance, given women occupy the low-skill, low-status jobs, negotiating to preserve the status quo, the existing hierarchies, can be cementing them even more firmly to routine and repetitive work.[4] In the case of the Post Office (now British Telecom) the CPSA was able to negotiate for telephone billing clerks an agreement that the new system would be designed so as to preserve the type of work previously done by clerical assistant and clerical officers grades. This meant constructing a hierarchy of access to the computer program, so that the pass keys issued to CAs allow them to do routine inputting, whereas keys for COs allow them to also access certain kinds of clerical information. Information which includes data on the monitoring of workforce productivity is only available to managerial levels. It could be argued that this rigidification of existing work practices accentuates the barriers to developing knowledge and control over their work for the lower, predominantly female, grades.

Differences in women's relation to work
=======================================

A further complicating factor in this situation is raised by the apparently coincidental introduction of flexi time. Leaving aside the discussion of how far flexi time can operate to develop a highly time-conscious workforce, clocking in and out for perhaps the first time, and vastly increasing productivity in a process invisible to the workers, there remains the potential implications in relation to how future computerisation is designed. Women workers in particular were delighted with flexi time - they felt it was the first time the union had actually done something for them, by steam-rollering management into accepting it. The reasons they gave for enjoying flexible working hours were, somewhat inevitably, the space it allowed them to fit their domestic commitments in with waged work (the men tended to say "oh it's great, you can go out in the week and not have to get up early the next day with your hangover"). This kind of control in their working lives could well precipitate a relinquishing of other types of control in the work situation. One of managements's arguments against flexi time was they needed to know who would be in work and at what time, as a problem may arise which could only be solved by the knowledge in a particular individual's head. The more systems which can be developed pushing in the direction of an interchangeable workforce (anyone can be slotted in at any time) the smoother the overall work flow would be. Obviously this "interchangeability" would diminish the worker's particular relation to their own work and tend to routinise and/or intensify it. This could possibly be something women were willing to "trade-off" in exchange for a greater freedom to control life outside work.

A significant finding of some research done by Juliet Lazenby on the infamous example of word processors in Bradford Metropolitan Council (at the time of introduction they cut the workforce by half) points to another twist in the contradictions embedded in women's relation to waged work. Lazenby found to her surprise when talking to the word processor operators, they really liked the new system. Partly some of the social side of their working environment had been salvaged by grouping the word processors in circles, rather than the rows they had initially been placed in, previous to management being advised that the workforce would be more sympathetic to their introduction if a pleasant working environment was created. Partly the operators expressed enthusiasm for the fact that they were no longer continually bothered by men coming to them and asking for changes in the work they were typing. Having the work fed through the term-inal is often described as one of the alienating aspects of word processing work ie. diminishing the social contact between author and typist.[5] To the women at Bradford, this mechanisation relieved them of a major source of irritation; autonomy from male demands on their attention, even if at the cost of a speed up in work flow (although Lazenby also discovered ways they had created of getting round this) was something they welcomed.

It is interesting that trade unionists often use the example of their female members welcoming "these new toys" as proof of their distance from a basic trade union understanding and their vulnerability to management whitewash. It is important to look below the surface of these expressions of positive attitudes to discover exactly why women might accept certain kinds of new technology, too readily according to their trade union representatives. Without an understanding of contradictions women experience both in terms of home and waged work commit-ments, and in terms of servicing male employees, it is impossible to be other than bewildered by women's responses to new technology. Presenting an alter-native to increases in skill differentials and increases in managerial control, depends on tackling these contradictions.

Male trade unionists

Reflecting on women's dissatisfaction with male demands, either at work or in the home, is not something which comes easily to male trade unionists. Looking back over some notes on an APEX school for new technology representatives, which I attended last year, I came across my rather sympathetic assessment of the problems in the nearly-always-male representatives's kind of trade unionism:

> The question of whether to fight redundancies and how to broaden the struggle around the new technology to include challenging management's right to manage, is closely linked to the question of methods of organ-isation. It seems more than a coincidence that emphasising the necessity for "sharp" negotiators goes together with a lack of optimism about struggle involving the membership. And it's easy to see how a rep could begin to trust his/her assessment of the situation and re-strict the response to winning a better deal for the members. As A. said: "you need good leaders, the membership take from their leaders". I don't doubt A.'s commitment to bettering the conditions of work for the workforce but I do see him both enjoying the control he exercises through the fact that he is a skilled, intelligent fighter, and being blind to what is problematic in his relationship to his members. This relationship revolves round their passivity and this can serve to reinforce an acceptance of power structures operating through the work process. It certainly isn't calculated to precipitate a militance in the face of managerial attack.

A somewhat less sympathetic account would have some strong things to say about the machismo and sexism of trade union representatives, who like another APEX representative say such things as: "People say they're not going to use a system unless there's something in it for me. These are all men, women don't really bother unless you say there's something in it for you. And then they rely on you - they say 'ooh what are you going to get for us?" When I questioned this representative about women workers being in the lower grades, he said: 'they are not ambitious. They're doing it to augment their husband's pay. Once things get better - their husbands pay goes up - they'll leave work, they won't resist. It's not that the company has a policy of oppressing women, it's women not wanting higher grade work'.[6]

What I think is significant about these APEX representatives is that they are working in a manufacturing environment. Despite the work being non-manual, the greatest ethos is attached to those workers who are nearest the shop floor and whose job depends on them engaging in, often aggressive, arguments with manual workers and foremen. Or else status is granted to the usually male workers who deal directly with the customer, and who often have to cope with an irate customer who hasn't received their order on time. When I asked these male workers, in an engineering factory in west London if they considered women could do their jobs, they all pointed to the pressure and agression involved and suggested it would be a rare woman who could cope with it. All the women, working in other jobs, who I asked the same question to, said if a woman wanted to do the job she could.

This links in a very direct way to the trade unionism in the plant. Militancy was seen by both trade union representatives and these male workers as equivalent to fighting for better pay, winning increases off management when new computerisation was brought in. Women were counted, at worst, as pushovers for management, at best, grateful for the man's vanguard activities.

Vanguardist and democratic militancy

An interesting comparison can be made with one of the rare female shop stewards in the Transport and General Workers Union in the same company. She saw it as crucial that her members perceived her as pulling her weight on the line (although the work was individualised, with each operator having their own machine, usually in a group of six operators there would only be four machines working at a time and so the others would be helping out the rest). As opposed to judging the strength of union organisation by how much management had to accept that the working hours of a shop steward would be wholly taken up with union business, she believed that representing members, understanding their views, encouraging their questioning of managerial control, could only be achieved by her being seen as another worker. If members saw her as different ie. not having to do the job, then they would be far less likely to respect her views.

So this shop steward was concerned to develop a democratic militancy rather than a vanguardist one. She justified her position by pointing to examples of union representatives moving ahead of the members and not being able to get their support when needed. The most extreme case of this being a call to strike in opposition to three redundancies at another plant; the members refused to undertake strike action and a number of shop stewards in a dramatic gesture at a meeting tore up their cards and resigned.

Given this scenario it seems important to question how much the failure of trade unions to challenge sexual divisions in the workplace can either be traced to weak trade unionism, or simply an under-representation of women in the trade union structure. Certainly both if women are to keep their jobs, and ghettoes of low-paid, low-skill work are to be dismantled, trade unions need to begin to move away from an arena of struggle solely based on sharp, stroppy negotiators, succeeding in preventing a deterioration of working conditions, or else winning extra payments for the use of new technology.

Job Evaluation - a tool for change?

One possible strategy in relation to bargaining over new technology that has been discussed by APEX representatives, points to the familiar non-recognition of this problem. At a conference to discuss job evaluation schemes (systems of grading jobs)[7] in relation to obtaining upgradings for members using new technology, the idea was voiced that as the categories used in job evaluation did not encompass the new working practices instituted by the technology, people should be graded according to the equipment they use. So for instance, instead of wages clerk or accounts clerk, they would become a Visual Display Operator or RJE Terminal Operator. This strategy is linked to the history of manual shop stewarding in that shop floor workers became defined by the machine they operated. However a major difficulty with this approach is that the title "VDU operator" allows the possibility of jobs being created which ask for simply in-putting of data to terminals. No demands can be made about the contents of tasks, or increasing rather than decreasing the control of the operators.

A recent new technology agreement signed by the National and Local Government Officers Association (NALGO) and a London council, began with the statement: "a repetitive, specialised job done under the strict control of a machine and isolated from other workers meets few of the criteria for a satisfactory job". This agreement show an awareness of how computerisation can be designed in a way that depends on a number of workers feeding data into the system, in a highly routinised and labour intensified way.[8] It is hardly surprising that these sort of jobs are seen as "women's work", not least because management will argue that the main ability needed is dexterity, which in their opinion is an exclusively feminine quality.[9] The other jobs that a computer system can provide, involving accessing information, manipulating it and directing the work flow, are very different. A polarisation of skills in relation to the technology can develop, with the latter group identifying their interests with managerial ones, rather than those of the low paid, low skilled female data operators.

Given this scenario it is clear that women's present position in the workforce is confirmed rather than challenged, the new technology only widening the gap in terms of skill levels, promotion possibilities, pay and conditions between male and female workers. Securing a different outcome involves workers' representatives intervening in the process of design as well as introduction of new computer systems. However there are problems for trade unionists in attempting to step out of their predominantly defensive role; broadly these can be described as revolving round the dilemma of participation or co-option. Any form of participation is open to the description of "helping management do its work", whether in the form of gaining acceptance within the workforce to redundancies or encouraging workers to develop their use of and support of computer systems.

This ambivalence which is prevalent in British trade unionism can be illustrated with the example of job evaluation schemes. It can be argued that introducing job evaluation is an important way that trade unionists put themselves in the position of arguing over job content, skill levels, promotion structures, and that this is crucial given the changes that new technology brings to all these features of the work situation. Yet many trade unionists understand the process of job evaluation which includes detailing the work tasks of their members in order to award points and factors and so evaluate them, as providing management with a means of work measurement and greater control over the workforce. So it is on this basis that trade unions retreat from an engagement with questions of job content, the way work is divided up between workers, and continue to struggle on terrain which they can more clearly see as that of "pay and conditions". Add to this problematic the resistance that male trade unionists exhibit towards criticising the existence of "women's work", the opinions many of them share with managers regarding women's abilities and rights, then it becomes obviously no easy task breaking out of these dilemmas.

The problems involved in securing worker intervention in system design in a way that breaks down the ghettoes of women's work are immense. But unless trade unionism is scrutinised in the light of an understanding of the contradictions in women's relation to waged work and to their trade unions, little advance can be made. It is easy enough for management to capitalise on the divisions that exist within the workforce and a strategy of defence of the status quo can only act to reproduce exactly those divisions.

References

(1) Campbell B., Women, not what they bargained for, Marxism Today, March 1982

(2) Coote A. and Kellner P., Hear this brother: women workers and union power, 1980

(3) West J., New Technology and women's office work, in: West J. (ed.) Work, Women and the Labour Market, 1982

(4) Morgall J., Typing our way to freedom: is it true that new office technology can liberate women?, Feminist Review 9, 1981

(5) Glenn E.N. and Feldburg R., Proletarianising clerical work: technology and organizational control in the office, in: Zimbalist A. (ed.), Case Studies in the Labor Process, 1979

(6) Armstrong P., If it's only women it doesn't matter so much, in: West J. (ed.) op. cit.

(7) Snell M., The Equal Pay and Sex Discrimination Acts: their impact on the workplace, Feminist Review 1, 1979

(8) Special report on women and computing, Computing October 7, 1982

(9) Race against time: new technology and women office workers, National Organisation of Working Women, 1980